SORDID IMAGES

SORDID IMAGES

The poetry of masculine desire

S. H. Clark

London and New York

First published 1994
by Routledge
2 Park Square, Milton Park, Abingdon, Oxfordshire OX14 4RN

Simultaneously published in the USA and Canada
by Routledge
711 Third Avenue, New York, NY 10017

First issued in paperback 2014

Routledge is an imprint of the Taylor and Francis Group, an informa business

Transferred to Digital Printing 2010

© 1994 S.H. Clark

Typeset in Baskerville by
Ponting–Green Publishing Services,
Chesham, Buckinghamshire

All rights reserved. No part of this book may be reprinted or reproduced or utilized in any form or by any electronic, mechanical, or other means, now known or hereafter invented, including photocopying and recording, or in any information storage or retrieval system, without permission in writing from the publishers.

British Library Cataloguing in Publication Data
A catalogue record for this book is available from the British Library

Library of Congress Cataloging in Publication Data
Clark, S. H. (Stephen H.)
Sordid images: the poetry of masculine desires / S.H. Clark.
p.   cm.
Includes bibliographical references and index.
1. English poetry–Men authors–History and criticism.
2. Erotic poetry, English–History and criticism.
3. Masculinity (Psychology) in literature.   4. Man–woman relationships in literature.   5. Misogyny in literature.
6. Desire in literature.   7. Sex in literature   I. Title.
PR120.M45C57   1994
821.009'3538–dc20   93–43826
CIP

ISBN 978-0-415-06801-7 (hbk)
ISBN 978-0-415-75580-1 (pbk)

Publisher's Note
The publisher has gone to great lengths to ensure the quality of this reprint but points out that some imperfections in the original may be apparent.

CONTENTS

	Acknowledgements	vi
	Note on texts	vii
1	INTRODUCTION	1
2	'ALL THIS THE WORLD WELL KNOWS' Lust in Shakespeare's sonnets	35
3	'SOMETHING GENROUS IN MEER LUST'? Rochester as libertine	75
4	'LET BLOOD AND BODY BEAR THE FAULT' Pope's exorcism of desire	108
5	BLAKE AND FEMALE REASON	138
6	'TESTING THE RAZOR' T.S. Eliot's *Poems 1920*	188
7	'GET OUT AS EARLY AS YOU CAN' Larkin's sexual politics	220
	Bibliography	258
	Index	280

ACKNOWLEDGEMENTS

The completion of this book was made possible by the award of a British Academy post-doctoral fellowship, to whose generosity I am deeply indebted. Earlier versions of Chapters 3, 4, 6, and 7 appeared in *Reading Rochester*, edited by Edward Burns (Liverpool: Liverpool University Press, forthcoming); *Pope: new contexts*, edited by David Fairer (Hemel Hempstead: Harvester Wheatsheaf, 1990); *Engendering the Word: feminist essays in psychosexual politics*, edited by Temma Berg, Anna Shannon Elfenbein, Jeanne Larsen and Elisa Kay Sparks (Illinois: Illinois University Press, 1989); and *Philip Larkin: a tribute*, edited by George Hartley (Hull: The Marvell Press, 1987). My gratitude to the editors concerned and also to Chris Bristow, Caroline Gray, Alban Harvey, James Keery, Tim Lustig, Brian Musgrove, Louise Murray, John Phillips, Peter Smith, and John Wood for their criticism and advice. Quotations from *The Collected Poems and Plays of T.S. Eliot* and *Philip Larkin: Collected Poems* are used by permission of Faber, The Marvell Press, Harcourt Brace Jovanovich, Inc., and Farrar Strauss & Giroux. Finally I would like to thank Tricia Dever, Julia Hall, Helena Reckitt, Talia Rogers and others at Routledge for their professionalism and support at all stages of the project.

NOTE ON TEXTS

The text used for Shakespeare is *The Sonnets and A Lover's Complaint*, edited by John Kerrigan (Harmondsworth: Penguin, 1986); for Rochester, *The Poems of John Wilmot, Earl of Rochester*, edited by Keith Walker (Oxford: Basil Blackwell, 1984); for Pope, *The Twickenham Edition of the Poems of Alexander Pope*, edited by John Butt *et al.* (New Haven and London: Yale UP, 1939–69); for Blake, *The Complete Poetry and Prose of William Blake*, edited by David V. Erdman (Berkeley and Los Angeles: University of California Press, 1982); for Eliot, *The Complete Poetry and Plays of T.S. Eliot* (London: Faber, 1969); and for Larkin, *Philip Larkin: collected poems*, edited by Anthony Thwaite (London: Faber, 1988). References to Shakespeare are by poem number and line; to Rochester and Pope, by line number; to Blake, by plate, line and page; to Eliot and Larkin by line number and page.

1
INTRODUCTION

> You tossed a blanket from the bed,
> You lay upon your back, and waited;
> You dozed, and watched the night revealing
> The thousand sordid images
> Of which your soul was constituted;
> (T. S. Eliot, 'Preludes' 25–9)

I have always liked poems that abused women. In simple generational terms, this should not be particularly surprising. Anyone whose early reading habits were influenced by T. S. Eliot would encounter a fearsome array of intensely sexualised verse, Donne, Marvell, Blake, Baudelaire, Swinburne, along with a whole bevy of Jacobean dramatists, whose common feature may in retrospect be seen as a kind of eroticised apprehension. It may seem a straightforward enough decision to reject these early loyalties as a regrettable aberration. Yet responses more complex and persistent than an adolescent craving for shock and arousal must also be involved; this intimacy of sensation is also collective, intelligible, and endorsed.

Men have read misogynist texts meaningfully, attentively, respectfully, and we should at least pause before mocking and decrying that relation. Their force has been registered obliquely, with a variety of stratagems of euphemism and redefinition. But it is rare for an author to be excluded from the canon for this reason. The tradition of overt anti-feminist satire (Marston to Oldham) has perhaps been more occluded than most, but if one considers the other authors who might have merited inclusion in this book – Langland, Wyatt, Spenser, Milton, Swift, Prior, Coleridge, Byron, Keats, Rossetti, Browning, Hardy, Meredith, Lawrence, Yeats, Dylan

Thomas, Hill, and Hughes are only the most obvious – it becomes increasingly plausible to identify the idiom of misogyny with the tradition of English poetry itself. For the male reader, these texts represent, as the epigraph puts it, 'The thousand sordid images/Of which your soul was constituted'.

One must, I believe, accept that these texts have been read not in spite of but for their misogyny. It does not follow, however, that this must be their most banal, predictable and reductive aspect, to be demystified, denounced, and debunked. This book will attempt to raise the question of value in a comparatively uninhibited way, and suggest that this might be their most fascinating and elusive quality. Its initial premises will be:

1 Misogynistic poems, though included among the canonised glories of English verse, have rarely been explicitly acknowledged as such.
2 Criticism has traditionally chosen to distribute them under a variety of different headings – earthy 'Chaucerian' humour, subtly blended tonalities, comprehensive social satire, moods of personal despair, allegories of spiritual quest, and so on.
3 In the wake of feminism, the relation of both male and female readers to these texts must remain at best equivocal: the pertinent question is how we are to value that equivocation.

I shall assume that representation of the sexual is as intimately bound up with negative as well as positive images, with satiric humiliation as well as rhapsodic elevation. It occurs not merely in the overtly amatory genres of love-lyric and sonnet, but also in forms as diverse as the elegy, mock-heroic, verse epistle, dramatic monologue, and epic, all of which will be treated in the course of this book. This more inclusive definition will enable the presence of desire to be acknowledged in a variety of areas customarily segregated from the erotic: belittlement and denigration, bartering and possession, and diagnosis and instruction.

The selection of this particular group of writers – Shakespeare, Rochester, Pope, Blake, Eliot, and Larkin – is intended to provide a representative cross-section of the traditional male canon. I have attempted to counterbalance this personalised emphasis by frequent lateral reference to less illustrious contemporary texts, and by detailed attention to the evolution of their critical reception. Out of respect for historical difference, the chapters on their individual work will be relatively free-standing. No unified narrative will be offered, but I nevertheless hope that my analyses will achieve a cumulative force and consistency.

I have not attempted to provide a single model of misoygny across such a wide spectrum of texts. My indebtedness to recent debates on gender should be evident throughout, but, for the purposes of this study, their insights will only be utilised in so far as they prompt, direct, and inform a more localised process of interpretation. My working assumption is that masculine desire may be understood through the words in which it has been articulated. The texts of the traditional canon, with all due recognition of its partiality of construction, embody this particular kind of language in its most concentrated form. As such, I would contend, they continue to merit sustained and intensive interrogation.

Before embarking on a series of detailed studies in support of this contention, however, I wish to look at the contemporary construction of the apparent opposite of misogyny: love poetry. The introductions to recent anthologies offer a curious network of declared principle and implicit premise. I shall treat this as the descriptive language employed by those who, in the empirical sense of making specific judgements of inclusion and exclusion, may be regarded as the most highly qualified practitioners in this area. Initially, perhaps what is most striking is the absence of dialogue between their criteria and the most influential contemporary analyses of desire as socially constructed, internally dissonant, and interminably unfulfilled.

Yet this apparent antithesis is, I shall argue, chimerical. I will seek to demonstrate that the culturally endorsed form of the 'love poem' contains within itself not merely a capacity for potential emotional reversal but also an implicit reinforcement of a communal masculinity. My subsequent analyses will seek to apply, substantiate, and extend the preoccupations which I shall seek to establish in the course of this introduction.

The anthology of love poetry continues, perhaps surprisingly, to flourish as a contemporary form. This may be attributed to a number of factors. First, the genre, in so far as it displays intensely personal yet universal emotion in the celebration of 'the Beloved' (Stallworthy 1973: 19), conforms to widely held suppositions about the essential nature of poetry itself; second, more mundanely, the predominance of short, self-contained lyrics allows the inclusion of a comparatively large number of pieces of which the vast majority are accessible without prior knowledge; and third, the broad appeal of its subject-matter to a general audience may safely be assumed (as Alan Bold says, 'what could possibly interest the public more than sex' (1978: 15)). And last but not least, they sell well: a perhaps reductive rationale, but not therefore to be disregarded. The chief current collections are:

1 *English Love Poems*, eds John Betjeman and Geoffrey Taylor (1957).
2 *The Faber Book of Love Poetry*, ed. Geoffrey Grigson (1973).
3 *The Penguin Book of Love Verse*, ed. Jon Stallworthy (1973).
4 *The Everyman Book of Love Poetry*, ed. John Hadfield (1980).
5 *The Chatto Book of Love Poetry*, ed. John Fuller (1990).

Each of these collections has its own distinctive strength. Betjeman has a fine melodic ear – if rather a high tolerance of platitude – and a salutary emphasis on middle-aged poignancy over youthful ardour; Grigson is very strong on social poise in flights of passion; Hadfield includes a lot of unfamiliar song-book material from the Elizabethans up to the Romantics; Stallworthy at least tries to provide a fairly comprehensive cross-section; and Fuller is well-disposed towards relatively analytic and astringent pieces. (Of distinctly less merit, but nevertheless of interest in terms of genre, are Charles Osbourne's *Favourite Love Poems* (1988) and Sheila Pickles's *Love: Penhaligon's Scented Treasury of Love and Prose* (1988)). More sexually explicit, but involving a substantial overlap of material are:

1 *Making Love: The Picador Book of Erotic Verse*, ed. Alan Bold (1978).
2 *Bawdy Verse*, ed. E. J. Burford (1982).
3 *A Collection of Erotic Poetry*, ed. Derek Parker (1980).
4 *The Faber Book of Blue Verse*, ed. John Whitworth (1990).
5 *The Literary Companion to Sex*, ed. Fiona Pitt-Kethley (1992).

These compilations feel a greater urge to justify themselves. Burford stresses the sociological interest of popular verse forms in so far as 'they accurately reflect the actual life, manners and morals, speech and thought of their generation' (1982: 35). Pitt-Kethley also resorts to a touchstone of authentic testimony ('has the author ever really had sex?' (1992: xiii)). Bold and Parker prefer to plead the uninhibited celebration of libinal drive and welcome release from the constraints of Victorian prudishness. Whitworth adopts the simple expedient of omitting any introduction, thereby evading the difficulties of establishing the definition and value of 'blue verse'.

INTRODUCTION

In addition to Whitworth, Faber currently have in print not only the collections by Grigson and by Betjeman and Taylor, but also have recently brought out *The Faber Book of Seductions* (ed. Jenny Newman, 1988) and *Deep Down: the new sensual writing by women* (ed. Laura Chester, 1988). Indeed perhaps the most notable recent market trend is for female erotica. *The Virago Book of Women's Love Poetry* (ed. Wendy Mulford, 1990) has rapidly been supplemented by *The Virago Book of Wicked Women* (ed. Jill Dawson, 1992); and the genre extends to such volumes such as *Pleasures: women write erotica* (ed. Lonnie Barbach, 1986, *Herotica I & II* (ed. Susie Bright, 1990, 1992), and *Women on Top* (ed. Nancy Friday, 1991). (Though these collections are by and about women, this does not necessarily imply their audience is exclusively female: Barbach acknowledges that 'while women often find erotica written by men unexciting, the men who read these stories found most of them a turn-on' (1986: xvi–xvii), and this is confirmed by the somewhat *louche* assimilation of Nancy Friday's *My Secret Garden* (1975) in Maurice Charney's *Sexual Fiction* (1981: 15–31).)

It is easy enough to decry these selections as undemandingly middle-brow, including nothing that might jeopardise access to a conservative but lucrative readership. Nevertheless, the significance of the basic form should not be underestimated. It is noteworthy that the anthology has been taken much more seriously in feminist criticism. Rather than being treated as a medium of entertainment for a mythical common reader it is seen as a crucial instrument, not only for giving access to previously neglected writing but also for defining a historical continuity of gender identity. (Hence the intensity and occasional ferocity of debate surrounding the publication of Gilbert and Gubar's *Norton Anthology of Literature by Women: the tradition in English* (1985).) There has been little interest in compilations of male writing since volumes like Susan K. Cornillon's *Images of Women in Fiction* in the early 1970s (see Gallop 1992: 77–100). The general assumption has been very much that such attention merely reveals the interminable repetition of its dominant stereotypes. (This perception underlies the scrapbook format adopted by the most recent publication in this area, Fidel is Morgan's *A Misogynist's Source-Book* (1989); the virtually random collage of quotations decontextualises the material to such an extent that it eventually appears to be the continuous outpouring of a single transhistorical male malevolence.) A far higher priority has been given to establishing outlets for women's writing than compiling instances of sexist writing. Presumably it is felt the existing collections serve this purpose sufficiently well.

'Every anthology', Derek Parker modestly insists, 'aims to please, to entertain, to be enjoyed' (1980: 21), but in the process serves both to define and produce large-scale changes in literary tradition. At the very least, they publicise, provide significant samples to a relatively wide audience, and present an influential version of the contemporary canon. Less conspicuously they both sustain themselves from, and recharge the naturalised vocabulary for, dealing with their respective areas of concern: they both consolidate and contest. Thus, I would argue, the very unguardedness of these more popular collections may perhaps be more illuminating than more recent academic compilations such as John Kerrigan's *Motives of Woe: Shakespeare and 'female complaint'* (1991), and Alcuin Blamires's *Woman Defamed, and Woman Defended* (1992). The professed documentation of specific forms of cultural stereotyping allows the question of value to remain resolutely unaddressed. Put more bluntly, they do not discuss whether there can be a misogynist classic.

As previously noted, love poetry fulfils the most widely held suppositions about the poetic: it idealises, celebrates, deals in elevated but universal human emotions. Yet in terms of simple numerical presence the sprinkling of inclusions from female authors does not alter the fact of the overall massive masculine dominance. In the Penguin collection, for example, only 19 out of 329 poems are by women: the ratio tends to be fairly constant at around 1:15–20. (In recent volumes the ratio is Whitworth, 16 poems and 2 translations by women out of 161 entries; Osbourne 14 out of 186, Fuller 27 out of 374, Grigson 16 out of 401, and even Fiona Pitt-Kethley can only manage a meagre 27 out of 259 selections.)

There is a notable absence of qualms about the gender imbalance of the whole idiom. 'It is true of erotic poetry, as of poetry generally, that most of its practitioners are male' (Bold 1978: 21); 'there is no denying the fact that on the whole it is the male view of women we see in these pages' (Parker 1980: 25); 'so they were male ballads composed by men for men's enjoyment and reflected male standpoints only' (Burford 1982: 22). At no point are these admissions of gender-specificity brought into relation with the language of universal impulse. It is not a question of deriding the

INTRODUCTION

tradition, but of using such acknowledgements as a starting-point for more adequate definition of its peculiarly tenacious attraction. This, I hope, will justify my procedure of treating the introductions to these volumes as a composite argument in order to produce a preliminary mapping of my central concern: the poetry of masculine desire.

Much is made of the democratic intentions of the more explicitly sexual collections, bringing to the common reader what had previously been 'the possession of a tiny minority proud of belonging to an exclusive club' (Bold 1978: 15). The basic point is fair: even the street ballads were only available in exclusive limited editions after 1800. So it becomes possible to argue that these texts 'reflect the standpoint of those ordinary people who were our ancestors, and are in the language used and understood by them' (Burford 1982: 19). There is something suspiciously primeval about these 'ancestors', who subsequently bifurcate into the 'wealthy few' and 'ordinary people'. It is unclear why ballad forms should 'reflect the standpoint' of a specific group in such apparently unmediated fashion. The mere fact of anonymous attribution makes it by no means certain that these are products of the working-class writers rather than, for example, Grub Street hacks. (As Burford himself notes, 'highly respected and respectable versifiers would descend to street level' (1982: 27).)

The 'stark terms' in which the 'principal physical functions' are described are attributed to the 'hard and dirty' life-style 'among the commonality' (Burford 1982: 27). Simple reference to Rochester would be sufficient to refute this as a general proposition, but a broader issue is at stake. Though we may be born *inter urinas et faeces*, this need not entail an automatic equation of the sexual and scatological. All too often 'the satisfactions of the body, from food to sex' are celebrated as representing 'primitive sensuality'. These are deemed good because unitary, unadulterated, uninhibited, then endowed with 'complexity' in so far as admitting 'follies and frailties'. To rhapsodise over man's 'wholesome fulfilment of his natural appetites' is to deny even the possibility of an unwholesome impulse (Untermeyer 1957: xv).

The 'rarefied' emotions of aristocratic love lyric are said to have been 'parodied' in order to make them palatable to the '*hoi polloi*, whose notions – and experience – of sexual behaviour and enjoyment were much coarser and simpler' (Burford 1982: 20). Passing over the enormous cultural condescension, the sexuality expressed in these texts serves as both a downward translation and an intrinsic impulse. The products of popular culture both possess superior vitality to and represent a debased version of elite forms. 'Then as now, sex and crime were the principal interests of the ordinary man and woman; hence these effusions pandered to their prurience' (Burford 1982: 29). A tabloid analogy is lurking behind this, but the charge of 'prurience' contradicts the supposed openness of the proletarian sub-culture. 'In the main little element of love entered into the lives of the poor', but it is still claimed that 'the bawdy street ballads were usually vulgarly romantic to reflect lower-class manners and morals' (Burford 1982: 27). (Though 'vulgarly' could perhaps be construed as 'therefore not romantic at all'.)

'More to proletarian liking', we are assured were 'verses ... which extolled the phallus in its ceaseless quest and conquest of the *cunnus*' (Burford 1982: 29). This is a familiar enough trope (compare Newman on 'the ritualised energy of sexual pursuit' (1988: xi)), but its equivocal status as both testosteronic imperative and literary taste should be stressed. These texts 'reflected the ordinary man's attitude towards his womenfolk – the eternal search by his virile member for entrance into the ostensibly mysterious female pubic triangle' (Burford 1982: 21–2). The 'eternal search' is simultaneously a linguistic inversion of the 'ostensibly mysterious': there is primal libido in these proletarian utterances, but one whose value is inseparable from its demystifying function.

The 'poetic licence in licentious poetry' (Burford 1982: 19) implies imaginative force, technical crudeness, permitted transgression. The 'licentious', in terms of life-style, level of diction, and effect of arousal, is taken as synonymous with 'bawdy ballads, lubricious lyrics and salacious songs', yet on a simple empirical level the Elizabethan epyllion or Restoration libertine lyric were highly crafted aristocratic forms. But if these texts are constituted through burlesque and inverted decorum, then desire itself must be subject to a comparable degree of discontinuity. To be 'composed for bawdry's sake' (Burford 1982: 19) represents a continual interplay of textual variables. 'The perennial chase of the male after the female' (Burford 1982: 19) is contradicted not only by the pursuit of boys in the *Greek Anthology* but also by several poems included in his own collection. And the term 'chase' is particularly inappropriate: given the frequency of defamation, recoil, and avoidance, a more apposite description might be perennial flight.

INTRODUCTION

One might be tempted to set up a sliding scale for love, erotic and bawdy poetry on an axis of spiritual and carnal: love poetry idealises but divorces from bodily pleasure; erotic poetry idealises the pleasures of the body; bawdy poetry insists on those pleasures in contradistinction to spirituality. Another option might be to stress love poetry as proclamatory, persuasive and performative. It is not concerned with communicating a prior state of mind, but itself enacts desire. Bawdy bypasses its immediate protagonists in favour of a communal reception; the erotic presupposes this assimilation while still according priority to an enacted scenario.

None of these terms, however, can subsist in isolation from each other. It is a misguided exercise to attempt to establish different semantic spheres for generic categories. What is significant is the network of exclusions and tensions produced within the working definitions of the field. There is an oppositional relation between love and bawdy, elevation and deflation. Yet the two antithetical principles presuppose each other. There are no expressions of innate impulse, only intertextual couplings, primal parody.

The erotic as a category is a comparatively recent innovation, the sexually explicit redeemed by aesthetic merit. (Though its mediations in high and low culture, folk ballads in connoisseurs editions, should at the very least complicate any premature assumption of immediate accessibility.) In this context it is frequently argued that sexual desire reduces us to a common physicality, provides a welcome relief from cultural pretension, and represents a cathartic outburst of pent-up exasperation. As such, it must rest uneasily with affirmations of romantic love. Indeed, this line of argument seems to lead inexorably to the conclusion that love poetry cannot be erotic. This can be restated: love poetry represents a stage of courtship, of anticipation, a realm of elevated illusion. The erotic represents consummation, the brute act itself: 'Doing a filthy pleasure is, and short' as Jonson puts it ('A Fragment from Petronius', 1. 1). But even this has problems. Is the love poetry so etherealised as to remove all trace of bodily desire; is the sexual expression of love really so inimical to its existence?

One might have expected erotic writing to be hostile to any such intimations of transcendence. Yet it is commonly assumed that they are governed by essentially the same conventions, defined by Derek Parker as 'persuasion, wooing, and triumph' (1980: 27). 'Triumph' implies eventual consummation, but can be read as power of a more general kind. For 'the ceremonies of persuasion' to be 'given full weight' would require an interlocutor rather than an icon. Nevertheless, 'the unveiling leads naturally to a loving conclusion (and reassuringly love, as opposed to or as well as enjoyable sex, is what most poets have in mind . . .)' (Parker 1980: 28). 'Naturally' is an almost fatuous linkage; 'loving conclusion' means presumably 'concluding act of love-making' but also a mental formulation, judgement held 'in mind'. 'Reassuringly', erotic poetry turns out to be concerned with the 'ideal', and in fact to be indistinguishable from the love poetry to which it was initially opposed.

Perhaps the most powerful single assumption in all these collections is that it is not merely love poetry but all expressions of sexual desire that display 'man's changeless responses to the changeless changing seasons of his heart' (Stallworthy 1973: 26). Our common humanity is presumed to be both articulated and reconfirmed through our sexual experience. (Burford has no compunction in claiming that 'the theme is common to all races' (1982: 19), despite offering an English-language anthology of quite a specific and restricted period.)

Stallworthy introduces translations from a wide variety of cultures in order to stress this universality of emotion: 'it is clear that feelings of passionate love common to all mankind have . . . kindled the poets of different periods and places' despite the fact that 'the evidence of the poets is as conflicting as it is voluminous' (1973: 22, 19). Their subject-matter possesses a peculiarly elusive unity in diversity: that which is most original is also most typical. That which is said 'more freshly', 'most personally', is also a kind of enforced utterance ('they say it because they have to'). The power which ultimately scripts the 'actors in the human comedy' (Stallworthy 1973: 19) is nature, biology: 'it is of course, not the Poet but the Organism speaking' (Fuller 1990: 5). Yet its 'statements' are also infinitely 'various'. 'One looks for patterns, common factors, but they are few', but this does not deter Stallworthy from declaring that 'the cycle of the heart's seasons has not changed in 3,000 years' (1973: 26–7). For Fuller also, the vagaries of 'individual taste in the matter of the unique object of desire' must simultaneously acknowledge no 'real uniqueness' because 'the beloved is unique only within that relation' (1990: 1).

'For ever since men and women became what they are', Alan Bold informs us, 'sex has been a central issue between them' (1978: 15); what, one wonders, were they before? The origins of amatory poetry in 'mankind's earliest days' are much speculated on: 'clearly

INTRODUCTION

eroticism predates poetry' (Bold 1978: 20) but the priority that it is granted is purely formal. The genre, we are assured by Burford, has been 'in existence from the earliest time when man first learned to speak' (1978: 20); in a curious cameo of stone-age life, 'as their principal pleasure was copulation, they would undoubtedly have sung its praise in some primitive manner' (Burford 1982: 24). The implication seems to be they would strum while they thrust.

Although C. S. Lewis's argument in *The Allegory of Love*, that romantic love had a specific origin in twelfth-century Provence, is now out of favour, the distinguishing traits of this tradition – idealisation, invocation, a transposed vocabulary of religious experience – are still readily taken as normative. 'Love is the most commanding absolute of our secular age' (Fuller 1990: 4). There remains a powerful residue of the Platonic ladder of the senses in the veneration of the loved one: 'Donne was surely not the first poet to be led to the love of God by way of the love of woman' (Stallworthy 1973: 23). (A strikingly inapposite choice, given that the Jacobean preacher vehemently repudiated the libertine flippancy of his earlier verses.) 'Love is by tradition blind, and, just as the religious mystic is dazzled by the 'darkness visible' of God, so the lover is dazzled by a vision of his goddess, his ideal woman', a convenient explanation of why we look 'in vain for the features, lineaments of a living woman' (Stallworthy 1973: 26). (The ambivalent nature of the compliment is evident in the misattribution of Milton's description of the fallen angels: 'from those flames/No light, but rather darkness visible/Served only to discover sights of woe' (*Paradise Lost* 1: 62–4).)

The normative mode is one of invocation and apostrophe, a convention strong enough for Alan Bold to talk, without apparent qualms, of 'cunt-worship', which is 'evoked in many similes that seek to convey images of infinity' (Bold 1978: 22). And many similes that do not.

If poets 'have transformed the act of love from a rut-and-gut affair to something infinitely precious' (Bold 1978: 18), prior to this rhetorical transmutation the activity still remains merely bodily, even bestial. Wendy Mulford comments caustically on the 'high proportion of the Brag, Boast and Exaltation' in male love-poetry (1990: xiii). The more elaborate the panegyrics, the greater the discrepancy with their object: they serve as 'enduring monuments to a basically spasmodic activity' (Bold 1978: 16). Poems are self-defeating if they proclaim the uniqueness of individual desire: the durability of the text heightens the transience of the impulse. For Fuller, 'this excess of the idea over the reality' serves as 'a beautiful distraction from animal guilt and incompleteness' (1990: 3). But if 'love itself is such a sublimation of instinct that its ready and random visitations can become mythified into something akin to the divine', there remains something chimerical, instantly reversible, in this process: these 'excessive verbal performances' represent 'a conjuror's apparatus with which we consciously agree to be deceived' (Fuller 1990: 3–4). Or more smugly and tersely, in Bold, 'in erotic poetry, as in tennis, the proclamation of love can stand for nothing' (1978: 20). Instead the biological imperative serves as a convenient rationalisation of a libertine ethics of 'natural polygamy' (Parker 1980: 27).

'What is important', Bold tells us, 'is our Platonic vision of the opposite sex' (1978: 28): the Greek philosopher, of course, not only thought visual representation an inferior substitute for the ideal, but also preferred boys. Whether or not 'the centrefold of a girlie magazine' is a fitting location for such 'unearthly perfection', the 'flawless goddess' presents an image which no actual woman can meet and no man possess. Idealisation turns back on itself with a pain of exclusion: to claim to 'measure women by immortal standards' is potentially coercive if not openly condemnatory (Bold 1978: 28).

'Given the relation between sexual and creative energy, the artist is more likely to have more intense moments . . . than most of his fellow men' (Stallworthy 1973: 22); or more explicitly, 'the poets have wielded their pens, like their penises, to give as well as receive pleasure' (Bold 1978: 16). Woman is the necessary condition of this climactic begetting of the writer upon language, but in no way an equal or reciprocal subjectivity. This moves into a kind of Wordsworthian eroticism, celebrating 'moments generating the emotion that, recollected in tranquillity, may crystallise into poems' (Stallworthy 1973: 19). But are these 'moments' a represented scene or a bodily impulse; how much loss is involved in this inevitable retrospect; and, granted the vocabulary is designed for a wholly internalised process, who are these 'moments' with? If 'an artist . . . is a maker', and 'making a poem' produces 'an intensity of awareness and an exaltation comparable' to 'making love' (Stallworthy 1973: 20), the presence of any other party has been wholly elided.

The love poem, whether addressed to paragon of virtue or

sensual temptress, may be seen as exerting a form of control through the projection of 'verbal images of the female anatomy' (Bold 1978: 23). The fetishism involved in such 'unveiling', and the wider implications of the voyeuristic stance are left resolutely unaddressed. Yet whatever the plausibility of scopophilic models with regard to the pornographic image, they cannot be directly transposed on to literary texts. There is no looking in language. The dominance of the gaze brings with it an attendant rigidity that precludes any disaffected male perspective or independent female viewpoint (see Williams 1990: 204–6). Naming the female genital, in Shakespeare's will sonnets, or Rochester's invocation of cunt, is more likely to have an unstable talismanic force. Removing the 'fine words and phrases' that veil the feminine body results not in detailed 'descriptions of female parts', but in 'copulative activities in the living vernacular', identified with an oddly cunnilingual 'vulgar tongue' (Burford 1982: 22).

Sexual representation may be regarded as a secondary mimesis of an event which, though fictive, may still be ethically evaluated in terms of relations between persons. This insistence on an originating 'reality' recurs in many forms, from Bold's 'immortalising precise sexual encounters' (1978: 16) to Barbach's 'real life experience requirement' (1986: xiv). Newman's anthology of seduction scenes is representative of both the strengths and limitations of concern for fairness of portrayal on a Richter scale of 'sexual autonomy' (1988: xiii). A collection obviously marketed in terms of erotic appeal is justified, somewhat dubiously, in terms of documentary validity. 'If there is any relationship at all between literature and life, the history of fictional seduction is bound to throw the nature of our sexual politics into sharp relief' (Newman 1988: ix). There is no consideration of 'seduction' as itself a literary genre, stylised and autonomous: nevertheless the virtually oxymoronic tension between 'fictional' and 'history 'must be broken by 'sharp relief', both a release from and an ecstatic gasp. Even in the act of disavowal, the power of erotic rhetoric may override the narrative frame and transmit itself into the discourse of the interpreter. The most important seduction is that of the reader. Desire in a literary text should be regarded as as much an effect of language activated within the space of the interpretative encounter as the representation of a sexual act.

Furthermore, the erotic can be seen as residing less in the representation of sexual performance than in anticipation, deferral of activity, and, as previously noted, in retrospect. Post-coital poetry is at best nostalgic, a fictive re-enactment of what has been lost by the very virtue of its existence; articulation cannot coincide with the moment of desire. ('Say that you love and you are immediately brought face to face with the likelihood that your love is either completed or incomplete' (Fuller 1990: 1).) At worst, and perhaps more usually, it is the voice of disappointment, betrayal, recrimination: the inability of ecstasy to sustain itself, the moment which cannot be caught as it flies.

The sceptical view taken in the most influential modern analyses of desire is reiterated surprisingly often, though only in passing, in the existing anthologies: for example, Fuller acknowledges that 'the great love poems are usually poems of longing and regret' (1990: 1), and Newman, in somewhat minatory and triumphalist fashion, finds the ultimate moral of seduction that 'that passion and guilt are often inseparable, and that most sexual pleasures are transitory, only to be enjoyed through a knowledge of their absence' (1988: xv).

I now wish to examine attempts to contain this discordance acknowledged at the very heart of desire.

An implicit narrative of sentimental courtship is constructed in which unhappiness, frustration, infidelity, can all be subsumed as transient sub-categories. (The chapter headings to Geoffrey Grigson's *The Faber Book of Love Poetry* are by no means untypical: 'Love expected; Love begun; The Plagues of Loving; Love continued ...'.) Fuller also claims his collection 'underlines its intended dramatic quality by being divided into five acts' (1990: 9), entitled 'Holes in the Heart; Fool – only touch her!; Ask me no more; A durable Fire; Dear Ghost'. Even Laura Chester's *Deep Down* cannot resist claiming that the 'material ... naturally fell into various sections': 'Early On; Looking at Him; To Give and Hazard All; She Fluvial; Dear Enemies; Pure Sex; the Yield'.

Stallworthy offers as an inclusive definition, 'any poem about any aspect of one human being's desire for another' (1973: 19). 'Desire' is treated as synonymous with love, though it surely raises the possibility of frustration and hurt, as well as transience and inherent dissatisfaction. 'Passionate love' is equated with 'a process of internal combustion' (Stallworthy 1973: 22), a metaphor that combines mechanical determinism with auto-destructive conflagration. (It is noteworthy how little reference there is to the predominant modes of classical sexuality: not only passion as a demonic and terrifying form of possession, but also the cultivation of an emotionally disengaged eroticism as a kind of practised skill, and perhaps most crucially the priority of active and passive roles over the gender of partners.)

The model establishes its own internal exclusions: 'there is much else (pure Platonism, misogynist satire, self-congratulation, smut) that I am happy to do without' (Fuller 1990: 8). It will generally shy away from 'impassioned expression of the lusts of the flesh' (Betjeman and Taylor 1957: 7). Appreciation of the 'ribald note' will still 'not be extended to express the sniggering, the merely lewd, lascivious or scatological' (Untermeyer 1957: xvi). Above all, it will offer 'straightforward sexual desire and straightforward carnal copulation' (Burford 1982: 35). Even if 'desire' and 'copulation' could be so readily equated, it remains implausible that either term could be regarded as 'straightforward'. The reduction is necessary, however, if erotic poetry is to serve its paradoxical double function. It must strip away the pretence of what is simultaneously claimed to be a self-evident and unproblematic phenomenon.

What is at stake here in these tendentious distinctions is the preservation of the affirmative nature of the erotic. Anything that disrupts this celebratory ethos is cast out as gross and debasing, or tendentiously recuperated. Even 'the salacious effusions of the Earl of Rochester', it is claimed, 'lose much of their pornographic aspect, since they are out-and-out satires in the main' (Parker 1980: 35–6). To give a single instance of the kind of text that has been routinely excluded as unduly negative: Sidney's famous sonnet on desire, 'Thou blind man's marke', surely by any definition one of the finest erotic poems in the language, does not appear in a single one of the current collections. The criteria of demarcation offered as self-evident result in not merely the omission of cruelty, denigration, repulsion, but also in the implicit disavowal of the very possibility of their existence within the erotic.

Again, what appears most unproblematically stable and unified at the very least possesses the capacity of reversal. In the contemporary tradition of transgressive eroticism, arousal is incited by and inseparable from that which is morally disturbing, even repellant. The introduction to a recent collection of sado-masochistic writings, *High Risk*, claims, for example, to be 'about exposure. The texts here seem naked, they make you feel naked when you read them. They stimulate, they emphasise separately and collectively that desire is as complex as the world in which we live' (Schoelder and Silverberg 1991: xv). This vocabulary of surplus, excess, it may be objected, demands an arguably complacent segregation of the realm of fantasy, and a refusal to accept even the possibility of the site of the object, the victim. Yet it is striking that no attempt has been made to incorporate such an aesthetic of transgression into the selection procedures of more mainstream collections, although such a definition of the erotic is now so widespread as to be commonplace.

An opposition between 'deeply serious' and 'enjoyment' is established that precludes receiving pleasure from solemn, even ascetic, works. The implication is that they remain deservedly unread. 'Erotic poetry is poetry of enjoyment ... though over-serious protagonists of sexual freedom and over-earnest puritans alike seem to overlook the fact' (Parker 1980: 21). The technique of pre-emptive caricature is evident in the redundancy of the epithets, 'over'. As intensifiers, they verge on tautology: are there frivolous puritans or light-hearted protagonists? And what after all is the 'fact' in this case? The physical event of coitus? Vernacular terms pertaining to that occurrence? The central definition is notably unspecific about where the 'enjoyment' is situated: in the author, reader, narrated participants? Motivation, subject-matter, and response are all conflated in a single term. The subsequent justification that 'sex ... is or should be one of the most enjoyable activities known to humankind' (Parker 1980: 21) similarly raises the question of sex for whom and in what circumstances ('should be' at least allows partial exemptions). It is not an activity that a collective and ungendered subject can feasibly participate in.

A linguistic form is habitually presented both as synonymous with and standing in direct causal relation to sex as performed. The proposition, 'erotic poetry celebrates that fact' (Parker 1980: 21), for instance, offers a circular formulation in which desire produces an expression of itself that reproduces desire.

This recessive spiral raises the problem of onanism. Against a tradition of aesthetic repletion, therapeutic discharge of emotion, it is readily acknowledged that erotic representation 'is more often than not ... likely to arouse or titillate the reader', and 'is therefore pornographic' (Parker 1980: 21). There is a conspicuous failure to examine, question, or define this category, and even to acknowledge the possibility that the production, circulation, and consumption of such texts might be in any way problematic. 'There is

INTRODUCTION

pornography and pornography', comments Derek Parker, and this nice distinction allows a 'poetry of enjoyment 'to be separated out from the 'sad stuff' which is 'gloomily repetitive, unimaginative, and often illiterate' (1980: 21). 'Gloomily repetitive' recalls the declaration in Parker's parallel anthology of erotic prose that unadorned representations of the sexual act *per se* must always be tedious (1981: 13); 'unimaginative' brings in an assumption that what is imaginative must always be affirmative; and 'often illiterate' is not merely a class-sneer, but one that undercuts subsequent invocations of the uninhibited vitality of the common people. The 'sad stuff' appears to refer to both the representation and the residue of the physical arousal to which it gives rise. Fuller more tactfully presupposes his reader to be in 'a mood of erotic disarray or erotic speculation' (1990: 1), but the implication is essentially the same. At least Fiona Pitt-Kethley has the merit of outspokenness: 'what I have tried to do is collect together all these orgasms to make one long orgiastic read' (1992: xxi).

'Masturbation as such' it is claimed, 'only rarely makes an appearance' (Parker 1980: 22): 'as such' presumably means dramatically represented, but even this is disingenuous. Rochester's 'Fair Chloris in a pig-sty lay' is dismissed as 'a not very good poem' without further explanation (Parker 1980: 22); whither *The Romance of the Rose*, let alone Keats's *Endymion*? 'Some splendid poems about sexual dreams' (Parker 1980: 28) are exempted from these strictures, but to whose 'desire and fulfillment' do they refer, and how can it be confined within the representation? 'Readers of erotic poetry have been privileged to relive, albeit vicariously, acts that would otherwise have perished' (Bold 1978: 18). The 'acts' surely have 'perished': and it is difficult to see how the reliving can be other than autoerotic.

We are assured that 'of course no one pretends that erotic poems are a substitute for sexual activism' (Bold 1978: 16); but this is precisely what they are, not only in the elementary sense that while reading one is not similarly engaged, but also in their predominantly retrospective stance. (The contradiction of Kerrigan's claim that 'the rhetoric of abandonment seems feminine while wooing belongs to men' is only apparent (1991: 8): lyrics offer a retrospective narration of prospective pleasure.) When 'an ageing poet' recalls the image of 'the Beloved of his youth', 'the one may even become a substitute for the other' (Stallworthy 1973: 20), but this is a benign transformation. 'Occasionally', it is admitted, 'one is rather uneasily aware that the poets are writing to arouse themselves' (Parker 1980: 22), but it is not apparent why this should be culpable. Masturbation cannot be condemned *per se*: at the very least, it seems preferable to acts involving cruelty or exploitation. By certain criteria of sincerity, such writing is the most honest of all, nearest to the coincidence of bodily impulse and verbal expression.

The question remains of why arousal in the reader should be permissible, but not in the author. To find Rochester's verses acceptable if 'written to amuse his hell-raking friends (not the most sensitive or delicate-minded of men)' (Parker 1980: 22), but not if for himself may appear arbitrary if not obtuse. This leads into the more general question of the consequences of making 'a comparative art of love accessible to all' (Bold 1978: 16).

Love poetry might seem to require at least the illusion of a private realm. Yet on basic semantic criteria, an incommunicable desire is a contradiction in terms. Its verbal articulation must necessarily be intelligible.

Desire is essentially self-confirmatory: its pretensions towards motivating a unique intensity of individual emotion requires communal ratification. If, as Bold claims, 'the private sensitivity of poetry' has the capacity of 'effortlessly penetrating the public area of sexuality' (1978: 15), what is striking is that sex is always already visible, on display. Far from erotic writing being 'a comic exposure of what is condemned in public and gleefully practiced in private' (Untermeyer 1957: xv), the illusion of private experience is constituted through its public exposure. Similarly, for Fuller, poetry allows us 'to probe into this locked mystery of the relations of love' (1990: 1). But the 'secrets' to be discovered within the physical entity of the pages of a book, far from being 'exotic and sensational', are discovered to be 'already locked in our own bewildered psyche' (Fuller 1990: 1–2).

The rhetorical proclamation of emotional intensity may not only not preclude further contexts of reception, but presuppose them. Is Donne writing to (the probably illiterate) Ann More or for the Inns of Court gallants whose sophisticated company he so much preferred? 'Ceremonies of persuasion' (Parker 1980: 27) might be thought to demand an interlocutor, but with comparatively rare exceptions (such as the lady in Donne's 'The Flea') this is not forthcoming. Even where a historical recipient may be plausibly adduced – Penelope Rich, Elizabeth Barry, Martha Blount – the genre of love poetry appears virtually completely devoid of the need for biographical corroboration. The point this forcibly brings out is how little the ostensible rationale of seduction is ever functioning. There is a persuading going on, but one preserved, arrested, immobile, unconsummated.

The statement, 'I love you', is opened up to an infinite array of potential addressees. One argument conspicuous by its entire absence is that male heterosexual love poems are primarily for women: a not self-evidently foolish position. On one level, the male reader may be seen as invited to re-enact the passion, participate in the delivery of an outwardly directed discourse: not to feel himself compared to a summer's day, but to imagine himself making the comparison. Yet simultaneously he must also be regarded as at some level the object of this address.

The relation lover–beloved within the poem may be seen as parallel to that of the poet-appreciator outside. Yet there can be no direct mapping of them on to each other: the external frame must also include a public context implicitly male-dominated. The 'one-to-one' relation occurs not with a specific female beloved but with the male reader: 'like sex' but more satisfactory in the relative permanence of its joint surveillance of the 'vivid verbal tableaux' (Bold 1978: 18). Sexual desire is 'public property': the relation between men that it facilitates is what deserves the accolade of a 'dignified privacy' (Bold 1978: 18).

The motivation of the writer is frequently claimed to be 'educational': 'the importance of foreplay ... might well not have occurred to his young male readers' (Parker 1980: 23). 'In case potential lovers are discouraged by the poet's apparent sexual infallibility' (Bold 1978: 16): it is all too seldom discussed why the spectacle of graphically rendered and prolific erotic activity should not deter rather than incite. Nevertheless, from this perspective, Ovid becomes 'the erotic poet *par excellence*': the Roman poet 'speaks as a master of the art of loveseeking to initiate novices into the mysteries of sex' (Bold 1978: 20). 'Mysteries' presupposes a concealment which is subsequently exposed (recalling 'ostensibly mysterious'). The move away from the apostrophic model to the didactic permits an initiation presumably reserved for the male readers (who become 'novices', votaresses if not nuns).

'Once the clothes are off, a few poets retire, carefully closing the bedroom door behind them. Others, however, remain, and for the most part get much closer to describing the mysteries of sexual love than any prose-writer' (Parker 1980: 29). Parker gives a peculiar image of the poets, presumably masculine, going to bed together or simultaneously departing from whatever remains once 'the clothes are off' (nothing seems to be underneath). 'Much closer' suggests an almost physical proximity to the 'mysteries' which, in describing, they, unlike the 'prose-writer', preserve rather than dispel.

'For every poet who takes sex as a simple pleasure', it is admitted, 'there is another who may view it much more equivocally – and indeed while there are Rochesters to show the exquisite contempt of women he demonstrates in 'A whore' who shall blame them?' (Parker 1980: 27). In the phrase 'exquisite contempt', should the emphasis fall on epithet or noun? Certainly, it seems a qualitative improvement on the somewhat vacuous 'simple pleasure'. 'Demonstrates' might be taken as displays, but has the further force of convincingly persuades: 'equivocally' seems to have been transferred back from the object of 'contempt'. The pronoun 'them' seems to refer to 'every poet' and 'another', but these two categories are cited as representing diametrically opposed attitudes. 'Who shall blame them' comes to refer to 'women', and becomes, in the context of 'contempt', a virtual exhortation.

It will now be helpful to examine the issue of satiric representation by considering Stephen Coote's *The Penguin Book of Homosexual Verse* (1983).

Coote's collection is not without problems. It remains unclear, for example, whether homosexuality is to be regarded as culture-specific and historically relative ('largely a matter of personal preference, and, as at all times, convention' (1983: 33)) or the expression of a continuous underlying and permanent impulse ('part of the whole and indivisible body of human love' (1983: 48)). 'The modern "homosexual", when legally defined and clinically separated, is a Victorian bogeyman' (1983: 29); but this does not preclude the use of the term in the title of the anthology because it is 'employed relatively neutrally, analytically, and has survived in acceptable liberal usage' (1983: 49). There is a denial of specificity to the homosexual experience, an authentication through dissolution back into 'courtship's oldest pattern' (1983: 32); and the claim to present 'voices of encouragement' is difficult to reconcile with the admission that 'our history is usually looked on as a history of persecution' (1983: 29). The prescriptive demand for 'an intense and loving relationship' disregards other possible aspects of homosexual experience: brief and vivid encounters; unloving moments+ in a continuous relationship; internalised guilt and self-recrimination; and instances of domination and force.

The inclusion of poems displaying any kind of emotional bond between members of the same sex makes no distinction between homosocial and homosexual relations. 'For all its strength as rhetoric', Juvenal's 'appeal to an old and manly Rome, is horribly in the mode of queer-bashers of all ages' (Coote 1983: 34): the point is surely that the 'appeal to an old and manly Rome' is equally to an all-male and potentially homoerotic bond of citizenship; and the ahistoricism of 'queer-bashers of all ages' needs at the very least further justification.

There is also a regrettable tendency to etherealise the whole tradition. In his sonnets, Shakespeare's 'literary interest was the religion of love rather than the pursuit of sex, contact with the soul rather than the genitals' (Coote 1983: 40). Yet if the tradition of male friendship is taken as broadly Platonic, it is not so much 'relatively indifferent to gender' (1983: 40) as profoundly gynophobic. A striking feature of Coote's collection is how it brings out the lack of any automatic community of interest between male homosexual and lesbian. There is frequently a disparaging comparison between the pleasures on offer from the respective physiques (for example, 'Helen and Ganymede'); love between males can be expounded in terms of eloquent nausea at the female body. 'Too passive a role' is seen as 'womanly and so wrong' (1983: 30); the category of 'pathological' is at one point taken as a synonym for 'effeminate' (1983: 44). Specifically heterosexual fantasies ('fashionable titillation and evident horror') are included to the exclusion, for example, of depictions of female friendship (1983: 42). Lesbian practices are 'luxuriously sinful' and so 'a delight to the voyeur. And the voyeur, of course, was a man' (1983: 43). At this point the gay perspective merges into a common masculinity. Bonding between males, whether genital or not, is frequently articulated in terms of eroticised contempt.

One decision by Coote, in particular, deserves high commendation: the willingness to 'range in tone and content from celebration to satire' (1983: 29), which allows a move away from a celebratory, affirmative ethos, in order to acknowledge the rhetorical force of hostile portrayals. This is justified in terms of documentary interest, but I believe a much stronger case can be made if denunciation is itself regarded as an expression of desire.

Satire may appear inimical to love. It implies condescension, emetic detumescence, physical recoil elevated into communal standards. Yet there is an erotic intensification in the very act of repudiation, which becomes a necromantic invocation and warding off. Even bald didacticism tends to invoke and dramatise its object, and this rhetorical relation is inherently ambiguous. We read not for the moral but to encounter that which is denounced, and so perpetuated and intensified. The voice of condemnation is itself infused with desire: the 'rascal beadle', as Lear points out, 'hotly lusts to use' the whore 'in that kind/For which thou whip'st her' (*Lear* IV.vi. 160–3).

Satirists from Juvenal through Churchill to Campbell have acknowledged inversely the erotic attraction of that which they denounce. With Juvenal, as Coote notes, 'a dream of ancient rectitude forced him to pour scorn on coterie faggots, effeminates and lesbians' (1983: 34), and 'scorn' itself becomes a mode of empathy if not appropriation. 'Charles Churchill's picture of cruising in eighteenth-century London' is described as 'a satire written from the most sexist and reactionary position (as the best satire often is)' (1983: 40–1). There must be a case that the 'best satire' is in fact the worst: defamatory, spiteful, and contributing to more specific forms of cultural persecution. Indeed the ultimate impact of the anthology is that a rhetorically vigorous homophobia overrides a pallidly sentimental if occasionally poignant lyricism.

I would argue that misogynistic verse can similarly be seen as a process of vicarious participation accentuated by explicit recoil. This should not be seen as an alternative to conventions of adoration, but as both situated within and encompassing it. 'Misogynism', it is acknowledged, 'has resulted in a special type of erotic poetry which is sexual in spite of itself' (Bold 1978: 25). A formal definition might be offered in terms of a vicarious participation in a verbal construction that fixes and projects an image. 'The male body is less often rhapsodised', it is acknowledged, but this is somewhat oddly attributed to the fact that 'most of the erotic poets are men' (Parker 1980: 29); yet why should men not celebrate their own bodies, unless, of course, rhapsodising is a more dubious activity than it at first appears? But if 'the male poet's conception of the sexually insatiable woman is invented for his own pleasure' (Parker 1980: 26), this spectacle must represent at least as much a threat as gratification. To be 'insatiable' reduces male arousal itself to a mere deferral of inevitable failure: the representation presupposes this predetermined and solicited trauma.

'The frustration of the over-eager woman is most often a matter for farce; very occasionally, both real lust and real frustration are angrily seen' (Parker 1980: 26). The element of fantasy projection has been elided here: it is a 'woman' with 'real' emotions. 'Frustration' is located both in her, and in the male capacity to check her desires: the term signifies both failure and control. 'Angrily seen' by whom, participants within the poem, author or reader? The projection of 'allegedly predatory attributes' (Bold 1978: 26) on to the female provokes a transference back on to the male spectator, whose arousal is both provoked and disowned by the transaction.

'Salacious poems' are seen as 'portraying women as not only the instigators but the real sexual experts' (Parker 1980: 27); and this characterisation is at least as much a taunting divesting of an attribute as an assumption of power. If 'for a man to succumb to his desire for a woman was somehow shameful', and 'physical contact with women contaminated man's intrinsic spirituality' (Bold 1978: 26), that humiliation itself is actively pursued. It is acknowledged that 'erotic poems written by men' do not necessarily 'enlarge on their sexual prowess', but also include 'lamentations of impotence' and 'mock horror . . . at the rivalry of the dildo' (Bold 1978: 17). The eroticism of failure deserves closer scrutiny than the occasional generic analysis of mock-encomia to wilting organs. The satiric, didactic, and exhortatory modes do not preclude 'lamentation' and 'horror' (why 'mock'?), but contain and accentuate it. Such poetry expresses not merely fear of sexual failure, but desire of it: by no means a predictable gratification of dominance, but often a prostration before a hyperbolically ascribed power.

The 'difference between sexual gossip and erotic poetry' is located in the way that 'the former is frequently unworthy of the sexual act while the latter artistically glorifies it' (Bold 1978: 16). Obviously 'sexual gossip' can be highly arousing, and, in certain circumstances, 'erotic poetry' anything but idealising. Swift and Pope are later dismissed as 'ethical eroticism rather than the real thing' (Bold 1978: 29); and Fuller also finds the eighteenth century 'notoriously short . . . of daring' (whilst somewhat inconsistently praising Browning's 'satisfying objective method' (1990: 7)).

A more important issue is at stake, however. What kind of relation can be posited between a third-person description of sexual desire, and a first-person declaration? Is the analytic always retrospective, estranged, and so devoid of the performative force of personal testimony? Are the two idioms different in kind, rhetorically distinguishable? Or are the two contexts and sets of conventions always implicitly in play in both lyric and satire? It may seem impossible to love in the third person: ethical good perhaps, the virtue that inheres in a body, but not an individual. Yet what the preceding analysis suggests is that apostrophic verse always demands a swerve, deflection of attention, towards the didactic: its relation to the object of desire is at least as much one of appropriation as veneration. The misogynistic is not an epiphanaic medium, or rather the epiphany is defined in terms of the interplay with the deflationary and the demystifying. This cannot be regarded in terms of a communal scepticism puncturing an intensity of personal infatuation: the two presuppose and constitute each other.

After this extended detour through relatively populist accounts, it will now be opportune to consider briefly the new perspectives and definitions that have accrued to misogynistic writing in the brief but prolific history of feminist criticism.

The only hint of unease in the anthologies emerges in the form of laborious jokiness, such as Alan Bold's disquisition on the etymology of 'lib' as to geld ('I wonder how many women would like to march under the banner of Women's Geld?' (1978: 21)), or Derek Parker's retort to the 'determined woman reader in search of antimale propaganda' (1980: 25). She must be 'determined' to keep ploughing through perhaps, but the clear implication is that intelligence itself is an unwelcome intrusion.

'It would hardly be expected that women would find misogynistic poems either erotic or apt', Bold concedes (1978: 27), though on his own admission this would apply equally well to other erotic verse. 'What woman will be entirely happy, for instance, with the preoccupation of so many rampant male poets with extreme youth?' (Parker 1980: 26); but if the issue is child molestation, why should men be entirely happy either? 'Female exasperation' is seen purely in terms of personal sexual behaviour, provoked by correspondingly individualised male vices ('selfishness, boastfulness and vanity' (Parker 1980: 25)). 'Women's fury' is directed not against oppression or brutality but 'at the male predilection for a quick dash to orgasm' (Parker 1980: 24). Even if numerous erotic poets 'recognised, unlike the Victorians, the woman's need for and right to sexual satisfaction' (Parker 1980: 25), the key point is that what is offensive is the endemic definition of women solely in terms of their sexuality as if this subsumed all other forms of political and social 'need' and 'right'.

There is no attempt to engage with the simple and fundamental observation that sexual representation is always bound up with issues of power and domination. For example, Alan Bold observes blithely, and with no apparent qualm, that 'the symbolism is inevitable: seduction becomes a prelude to conquest, and the penis is the ultimate weapon' (1978: 25).

If 'good poets', as Stallworthy claims, 'reflect something of the changing nature of their society', this too can be adduced as evidence: 'a survey of their love poems reveals much that has not changed in three thousand years' (1973: 25). Burford notes 'their women were for copulation and created for that purpose, and bought, sold and married for that purpose'; and it is difficult to miss the intimation that they managed things better in the days when 'King Solomon ruled in concupiscent peace' (1982: 22–3). Where Newman argues that seduction 'can never occur between equals' (1988: ix), an obvious rejoinder is that gender is socially constituted in order to maintain this 'inherent imbalance'. 'To succumb means the downfall of both seducer and seduced, and perhaps the whole of society too' (Newman 1988: ix–x); but seducers have power, prestige, authority, and so are proportionately less likely to be destroyed.

One of the first effective polemic techniques of contemporary feminism was the study of the representation of women in male writers. Once the exposure of stereotype in literary texts had been achieved it was possible to demonstrate how intimately bound up the aesthetic is with the self-perpetuation of patriarchal attitudes across the whole cultural spectrum.

What is really at stake in the exercise is not so much male desire *per se* as its supposed repetition: madonna and whore, whore and madonna. Thus revisionary readings of canonical texts serve as a kind of empirical verification of the global theories of patriarchy enunciated by such writers as Andrea Dworkin and Susan Griffin. According to their eloquent and at times nightmarish analysis, the only legitimate response to these degrading images is one of anger and repudiation: reading 'as a woman' therefore involves a characteristic movement of resistance, outrage, and accusation.

It may be objected that it is tautologous to claim that these texts give insight into men because, as a premise of the argument, patriarchy must already be known for it to be discovered. Elaine Showalter's introduction to *The New Feminist Criticism* states:

> Whereas it had been taken for granted that the representative reader, writer, and critic of Western literature is male, feminist criticism has shown that women readers and critics bring different perceptions and expectations to their literary experience.
>
> (Showalter 1986: 3)

'Women readers' are personalised, 'different', whereas the male is reduced to a composite 'representative reader', whose 'literary experience' can be not unfairly equated with a repository of prejudice, of things 'taken for granted'. Perhaps men deserve no better than to have their own customary move from personal experience to the expression of universals turned against them; but at the very least the supposed essentialism of early feminism is far more blatant and regrettable in this area than on female identity.

To take another example from Showalter, this time from 'Feminist Criticism in the Wilderness', where she adapts Edwin Ardener's anthropological model of dominant and muted groups:

> But if we think of the wild zone (of women's culture) metaphysically, or in terms of consciousness, it has no corresponding male space since all of male consciousness is within the circle of the dominant structure and thus accessible to or structured by language ... Women know what the male crescent is like, even if they have never seen it, because it becomes the subject of legend (like the wilderness). But men do not know what is in the wild.
>
> (Showalter 1986: 262)

There's obviously a slightly ingenuous idealisation of the 'wild' here: our turn on the frontier, boys. What I would take issue with is not the desire to establish an autonomous female realm, but the assumption that male 'consciousness' is well-mapped, without enigma, 'accessible' with relative ease. 'Women know what the male crescent is like, even if they have never seen it': they can peer through us like windows. Showalter should perhaps be more cautious on pronouncing on the transparency of the 'zone' of masculine desire. There are areas of men's physical experience – arousal, penetration, orgasm, detumescence – about which she can only form a derivative judgement, and a patently inadequate one if the sole and all-consuming satisfaction is seen as dominance. There is a very literal and immediate sense in which she simply does not know what she is talking about.

Showalter may be seen as representative of a broader tendency within feminist criticism to reify the determinants of individual male behaviour. Explanatory formulae based on causal relations appropriate to a structural model are frequently transposed on to the motives and behaviour of individual men. This not merely divests them of individual agency, but also precludes the possibility of rational persuasion. Even recent feminist work on moral reasoning, ethically directed responses to the other, tends to disregard the possibility of learned conduct. And this, whatever the limitations of audience and impact, remains one of the great achievements of feminism. Men have learnt something, which, as Shaw says, always feels like losing something.

I have previously suggested that misogynist texts should be valued for the marginalised and customarily repressed elements of male erotic discourse that they express. The tendency within feminist criticism, in contrast, has been to argue for abandoning the male canon. 'Increasingly women feminist readers reach the point where they can no longer read the men. That is, they begin to find the repetition unbearable' (Jardine 1985: 53). The obvious rejoinder is that it is the method of reading that yields such meagre results rather than the texts themselves that should be abandoned. At the very least the model needs to be reformulated to take into account the complexity of interpretation actually achieved in the sphere of oppositional reading. Re-reading the male canon reinforces dependence upon it, but it is by no means clear that feminist criticism should be quite so eager to disavow its own power of renewal. There is still a legitimate impulse of reclamation involved (see Schweickart 1989). The argument has too often been conducted in terms of an *a priori* linguistic exclusion. It is possible to shift it to a hermeneutic level. There is a pleasure of repudiation, a negative movement in relation to the text which is itself a source of ethical value in the form of challenge, difficulty, strenuousness. At the very least, the idea of a necessary development, a move away from an exhausted field of study should be disputed.

I would now like to suggest some point of connection with gynocritics, the study of the distinctive characteristics of women's writing. From the mid-1970s onwards an increasing reaction set in against the continued dependence on male writing of the first wave of feminist criticism. Certain of its basic premises were found increasingly unsatisfactory: in particular the naïve didacticism of its search for role models. Evaluating texts according to how they measured up to a rather nebulous ideal standard had the effect of transforming the literary canon into little more than an interminable litany of defamation.

In many ways the most substantial achievements of this renewed attention to women's writing have been produced by the empirical scholarship of Anglo-American feminism, and its patient recovery of previously obscured historical voices. There are drawbacks to the influx of continental feminism: in particular the lack of an equivalent empiricist emphasis. The priorities of its utopian polemic may well be regarded as different and more significant. But if one wishes to limit oneself to the question of textual interpretation of the male canon, one must recognise severe limitations in work deriving from this tradition. Nevertheless I wish to touch briefly on some implications of *écriture féminine*, the proclamation of an ecstatic language of the female body.

To begin with the somatic theory of writing. Its basic premise is that certain bodily experiences – menstruation, pregnancy, childbirth, lactation, and motherhood – are incomprehensible to men, literally semantically null, with no empirical correlative. A distinctively female writing must aim to bring these experiences to language, to 'write in white ink', as Helene Cixous puts it (1980: 251). (Some of the peevishness of the male response may be attributed to an understandable sense of exclusion: this form of writing refers to states of which he is necessarily ignorant, and for which he has no standard to judge.)

In psychoanalytic theory, to give a brief and highly simplistic summary, the girl is obliged to pursue a far more circuitous and uncertain process of maturation. The absence of a penis means she is unable to undergo the painful initiation of the castration complex: this leaves her with weaker ego-boundaries, endemic passivity and disabling narcissism. This may be accentuated to the point where she is alienated from language itself, permanently 'excluded from the nature of things which is the nature of words' (Lacan 1982: 144). This depletion can be reversed by a revaluation of the pre-oedipal phase. Men are doomed to feel perpetual nostalgia for union with the mother to which there can be no return: they are permanently deformed by bearing the burden of culture. Because women are not compelled to undergo such a

INTRODUCTION

drastic process of socialisation they retain a stronger relationship with the mother, and by extension the generosity of her body, blood, and fertility. They therefore have continued access to the Imaginary, and a truly female language would give expression to the delight or *jouissance* of this unfallen realm.

One counter argument would be that bodily processes at this level are not capable of verbal expression: like describing the workings of the stomach. And the 'woman's sentence' has proved excessively hard to pin down empirically: feminine usages tend to overlap with other disadvantaged social groups, but no linguistic phenomenon can be defined as intrinsically gender-specific. Authority in socio-linguistics resides in the site of utterance – where a message is delivered from – combined with varying degrees of semantic derogation in terms connected with the feminine (Graddol and Swain 1989: 95–134).

In addition, the more general claims made for the female temperament as being more physical, fluid, unbounded, are eminently compatible with traditional forms of gender idealisation. All too often there is simply a direct appropriation of certain theoretical definitions of avant-garde writing produced in the 1960s. It is tempting simply to take *ecriture feminine* as modernism under another name, particularly as James Joyce often appears to be its most significant single proponent. But the oceanic is at best a restricted aspect of the erotic, and arguably a tediously indeterminate one at that. A masculine writing is bound up with questions of power and authority internal to the text: and so engaged in a controlled transgression of limits. In male ventriloquism of female desire, unboundedness is envied but projected, doubly framed by persona and context of reception (see Kerrigan 1991: 12). Such proclamations must be seen at least as much in terms of potential reinforcement, further gratification, as of female autonomy.

Leaving aside these powerful criticisms for a moment, what would a language of male desire look like, a poetry of the male body? Would it be simply one of power, of reiterated control? To return to a psychoanalytic perspective, again abbreviated and in rather rudimentary terms. At the oedipal moment the male child perceives in the female genital the possibility of castration, and suddenly becomes aware that he competes with his father for the attention of his mother. He is forced to forgo this relationship, prized above all others, through fear of the punishment which she is perceived as having undergone. The Phallus, emblem of the Law of the Father (or the threat of castration) comes to symbolise the loss of the maternal body; and it is this primary repression that opens the unconscious. The boy, however, is also rewarded for transferring his emotional demands on to alternative objects of satisfaction. He has now become capable of occupying the coherent subjectivity constructed for him within the realm of language, and the authority attendant thereon. Fear prompts a kind of disengagement necessary to assume the paternal authority: a rite of transition from desire to rationality. The female must be desirable enough to simulate the attraction of the mother while terrifying enough to compel separation. The father is peripheral and may be elided in so far as he is the figure the boy will become. The woman becomes the condition and, paradoxically, agent of initiation into the symbolic order.

This in turn has a dual aspect. On one level, woman is exiled to a public realm of exchange, reduced to a commodity, a unit of value in relations between men. But on another, the male internalises the image of the female, and this reflection or 'specularisation' becomes a crucial element not only in her subordination to his authority but in the very cohesion of his identity. The familiar process of idealisation and degradation does not take place from a position of guaranteed mastery, but may itself be seen as presupposing a fundamental lack or absence.

Such an account is not without problems. The relation of mirror to gaze implied by 'specular' involves a psychic rather than textual economy, and one usually unduly restrictive about what counts as rationality, usually defining it solely in terms of a high philosophical tradition, Plato to Freud (most influentially, Irigaray 1985). Nevertheless, in empirical support, it can be pointed out that while there are plenty of literary representations of female desire – Pope's Eloisa, Blake's Oothon, Tennyson's Marina – there are very few direct depictions of male physiological arousal – what John Oldham describes as 'A squirt of slippery Delight' ('A Fragment of Petronius, Paraphras'd', 1. 5), and Dante Gabriel Rossetti as the moment when 'the last slow sudden drops are shed' ('Nuptial Sleep' 1. 2). On the evidence of the literary canon, men could be said to need something between assertiveness training and consciousness raising about the status of their semen. One can think of isolated exceptions, such as Carew's 'The Rapture', but the vast majority of male erotic poetry requires a reflection back from the female at a preliminary stage even to be set in

INTRODUCTION

motion. The homosexual tradition may appear an obvious exception, but this might be seen as simply involving a surrogate insertion of an alternative image.

A deconstructive model is a helpful way of conceptualising the process: the binary oppositions which structure the text may be read in terms of the systematic privileging of masculine over feminine elements on a dominant axis of gender. But an endless process of deferral is insufficient as a model for this dramatisation of subordination and the production of a composite voice of reason. This involves a structure of prior violence: paradoxically one can only assault that which possesses power. The female term is a point of crisis which may be transposed in the direction of both denial and acceptance, severance and reconnection. There is a continual re-enactment of overcoming, which paradoxically requires an ascription of power to the subordinated term. One should think of this transaction not in terms of depletion or diminishment of the male, but as a kind of enhancement.

There are obviously other psychoanalytic contexts which might be relevantly adduced: Freud's tendency to debasement in love, the idealised mother compelling satisfaction to be sought in an object perceived as already degraded; the Kleinian split between good and bad mothers, an infantile fury at the denial of infinite demand. These share, however, a dependence on archaeology as a mode of explanation: finding something buried within, excavation of a destiny that has already been decided. I would suggest, in contrast, that there is no meaning to be found behind the text. The reader does not get back to authorial neurosis as something to be either re-enacted or diagnosed; but produces his own trauma for his own gratification. In psychoanalysis, the narrative scenario tends to be a one-way transformation: the text allows a circularity, re-enactment, and reiteration that the Freudian paradigm and parable precludes. If there is guilt, it is to be created rather than exposed.

Misogynistic texts are not concerned with expelling the feminine as irrational so much as internalising and preserving it as a continual productive stimulus. Instead of nostalgia for union, they will display desire directed towards a threat that will prompt the necessary transference. But no threat, no desire: it is not an obstacle to satisfaction, but its precondition, occasion and authentication. So it should not be surprising to see misogynistic poetry intimately bound up with a rhetoric of austerity and aloofness. There is no simple antithesis between passion and restraint: the rationality of these texts emerges out of and remains continuously dependent on transformations of images of the female.

These are a speculative set of assertions which will have to stand or fall by the persuasiveness of the following readings. By and large, I will avoid the use of a psychoanalytic vocabulary. Obviously such terms as threat, prohibition, and loss, cannot be wholly detached from a Freudian context. Yet however indeterminate the status of psychoanalysis may be in the relation between analyst and analysand, I feel that in critical discourse it readily becomes a comfortable and even sanctimonious metalanguage. All too often the author is winkled out from behind his text as an object of study to be diagnosed from an implicitly superior vantage. I would set against this Baudelaire's great line from the introduction to 'Les Fleurs du Mal', directly quoted by Eliot in *The Waste Land*: '*Hypocrite lecteur – mon semblable – mon frère*' (76: 64). I believe that the best way of approaching these texts is to respond to their implicit appeal for a masculine solidarity.

There are dangers in this, notably that I fall into the kind of covert endorsement that has been the keynote of their reception. In feminist studies of pornography, the gesture of immersion and re-emergence operates as a generic marker, preventative hygiene (oddly repeated even by Pitt-Kethley (1992: xvii)). For the male critic, this is more difficult to justify. One chooses this area because one likes the texts, and gestures of disavowal can only heighten the suspicion of vicarious gratification.

Must a study of misogyny itself partake of its object? Does one become a misogynist through encountering these texts, and so represent the best testimony to their deleterious impact? (As R. Howard Bloch observes, 'any attempt merely to trace the history of woman-hating is hopelessly doomed, despite all moral imperatives, to naturalise that which it would denounce' (1989: 1).)

First, the encounter is after the event. It has already happened, fear and recoil and repudiation are always already inside us. The key issue is one of complicity in re-enactment and reinforcement. To what extent does the male reader occupy a collective persona? Is this process involuntary and necessary? Are there positive terms for this consolidation, collectivity, or must it be seen as a loss of an essential privacy and freedom? Do we witness, admire, emulate the author as a subjectivity more powerful than our own? Or do we retract, disown, diagnose?

If misogyny categorises, denigrates and is above all obsessed by

INTRODUCTION

the issue of woman, studies of the subject operate at twice removed. In categorising the categoriser and denigrating the denigrator they remain obsessed with the obsessional.

If misogynistic literature is taken as didactic, then what is most striking is its sheer gratuitousness. At every point it purports to record female lust and unruliness and to pontificate upon the necessity of further injunctions and constraint. Yet the indisputable weight of historical evidence is that men have had overwhelming statutory and familial control over the lives of women.

If we are now inclined to refuse the mimetic claim of these texts in any other than a highly qualified sense, they now serve as documentation of the history of male fantasy. But the continued import of this realm should not be underestimated: in so far as representations determine social reality, fantasy constructs truth (see Theweleit 1987, 1989).

Feminism is able to be simultaneously analytic and censorious: both to expose a structure and bear testimony to its injustice. The fictive gap between the feminist reader-construct, stern and unyielding, and the socialised empirical being cannot be repeated by the masculine critic. Instead, adopting this stance produces a voice torn between mimicry and internal differentiation, as both the subject and the object of its own discourse. In statements such as 'the milder varieties of pornography have a comedy (for smugly detached male readers) intrinsic to their derivativeness' (Kerrigan 1991: 64), what can be more 'smugly detached' than the parenthesis itself? The gesture may be regarded as an insidious self-aggrandisement through self-ingratiation: always them, never me.

The corollary of this is that I will confer on my own responses a representative status. This presumptuousness may at times read a little strangely, but I feel that such an avowed gender-specific perspective is a necessary condition of the kind of reading that I shall seek to pursue. What looks tediously predictable to the feminist reader may be profoundly disturbing and self-implicating for the male reader. I hope, however, that this will at least serve to provide some kind of corrective alternative to the common feminist assumption of a generic masculine which may be completely identified with a set of stable and self-interested rhetorics. As Larkin says 'where/Desire takes charge, readings will grow erratic' ('Deceptions' 12–13: 32).

The point is not that there is a healthy libido bubbling under waiting to get out: but that desire itself is experienced in these compromised forms. In my experience, increased self-consciousness through exposure to feminism does not suddenly cancel arousal: it instils a greater furtiveness, self-protectiveness, being too wary to be caught out. The frequent complaints against neglect by male academics have been proved to be simply unfounded. The influence of feminist criticism is prevalent, not merely in the widespread acceptance of gender as a determining factor in textual production and reception but in the imitation of numerous of its generic decorums (with admittedly varying degrees of plausibility). One might argue that as far as male academics are concerned, the encounter with feminist criticism alters one's style rather faster than it changes one's life.

Even this is evidence of a degree of respect, but it does not seem to me to respond to the challenge of feminism with any great conviction or honesty. In Virginia Woolf's famous line from *A Room of One's Own*: 'I thought how unpleasant it was to be locked out; and I thought how it is worse perhaps to be locked in' ([1929] 1992: 31). What is it like to be trapped inside of a set of responses that one can deplore or repudiate but that remain intimately bound up with the experience of sexual desire? In the following chapters I shall explore the difficulties and paradoxes of a poetry that attempts to come to terms with this predicament.

2

'ALL THIS THE WORLD WELL KNOWS'

Lust in Shakespeare's sonnets

It might appear trivial, and even impertinent, to raise the question of misogyny in relation to Shakespeare. Specialist studies of bawdry have confidently embraced this aspect of his work as indicative of its breadth and inclusiveness. Eric Partridge's lexicon celebrates 'the universal-spirited, the catholic-emotioned man' Shakespeare 'so dazzlingly, so movingly, was in life and print' (1947: 4); and this sentiment remains intact forty years later in F. R. Rubenstein's declared intention 'to show that Shakespeare, who we say understood and wrote of the human heart in all its facets, its frailty as well as its nobility, did exactly that' (1989: ix). Similarly, E. A. Colman's concern to demonstrate 'the dramatic or thematic use of indecency' (1974: vi) is repeated in Rubenstein's insistence that despite the seeming 'pointless obscenity' of these 'idle bawdy puns', they perform a structural function as 'signposts' to 'larger metaphors' through which 'meaning is enhanced' (1989: xii, xi, x).

There is a simple historicist rejoinder: what else should be expected from a late-sixteenth-century male, whose routine sentiments on such issues (whether or not attributable to the influx of syphilis) have been memorably described as akin to those of a 'thinking rabbit' on myxomatosis (Rossiter 1961: 138; see also Traub 1992: 71–87)? More interesting, perhaps, is how such a version of heterosexual desire could have been accepted as unequivocally normative for so long. The festive comedies may perhaps be seen as combining respect for the individual with awareness of the broader necessity of social regeneration (see Barber 1959). But this kind of justification, difficult enough to transpose on to the plays of Shakespeare's maturity, is self-evidently inappropriate for the non-dramatic verse, whether the ethereal truisms of *The Phoenix and the Turtle*, the curiously homely eroticised mythology of *Venus and Adonis*, the garrulity of violation in *Lucrece*, or, the texts with which I shall here be primarily concerned, the *Sonnets*.

'With this key/Shakespeare unlocked his heart'. Wordsworth's comment ([1827] 'The Sonnet' (2–3)), presupposes a dichotomy of internal and external, the lyric voice protesting against the 'public means' of the popular theatre 'which public manners breeds' (111.4). This model of concealment and exposure, which treats the self as a 'closet never pierced with crystal eyes' (46: 6), cannot, however, readily be reconciled with the explicit psychology of the 'bosom's shop' (24.7). In the poems themselves, the 'blessed key' that opens the 'sweet up-locked treasure' (52. 1–2) regularly acquires sexual connotations; the term is perhaps more interesting in a musical sense, as arrangement, patterning, than as a kind of linguistic proboscis inserted into an enigmatic interior. The objections against any premature autobiographical reading are almost too familiar to muster: the conventionality of the form; the explicit derivativeness of the motifs; the anachronistic presupposition of originality and expressivity; and the perpetual implicit ingratiation towards any potential patron. The most influential recent criticism has consistently stressed the misguidedness of treating Shakespeare's work as the expression of a unique subjectivity rather than as a cultural practice only intelligible within its context of production and circulation. This emphasis on the collective intentions of Elizabethan theatre may appear less immediately relevant for the sonnets, but they too, I shall argue, authenticate personal desire through a form of communal exchange.

'Did Shakespeare? If so, the less Shakespeare he!'. Browning's rejoinder to Wordsworth, ([1876] 'House', l. 40), brings in an equally anachronistic vocabulary of crafted monologue, psychological naturalism, and analytic detachment. Such a controlled tempo of revelation might apply to Donne's closely knit syllogisms, but there does not seem to be a comparably premeditated deployment in Shakespeare. 'When my love swears' (138) and 'Two loves have I' (144) are probably the closest examples, but the deftness of completion, the witty remodelling of intractable circumstances, brings in an uncharacteristic note of finality.

None of the usual features of the Shakespearean sonnet can be aligned to this sense of termination: the two-way syntactical attachment of individual lines; the extended but somewhat haphazard acting out of underlying conceits (legal, pictorial, financial); the dissolution of arresting interjection into continuous flow; the absence of precise reiteration or development in the third quatrain; and the limply appended final couplets. The general impression is laxly associative, and Ransom's diatribe (1938) against their formal incoherence (albeit against a standard unrealised except in a handful of Spenser's most aridly mathematical compositions) is merely a more aggressive restatement of a widespread unease. So a characteristic critical ambition has been to stiffen up the sequence, so to speak. Reordering has fallen from favour, but can be seen as similarly motivated. The dramatic blank verse, even at its most contorted (*Troilus and Cressida*, or *The Winter's Tale*), can be recuperated by principles of narrative situation, dramatic appositeness, and psychological insight. In the case of the *Sonnets*, if there is no story, invent one. More recent approaches have stressed mythical unity (Wilson Knight 1961), dramatic personae (Hunter 1953), metaphoric linkage (Mahood 1957), linguistic parallelism (Jakobson and Jones 1987), and erotic triangulation (Sedgwick 1985). One might suspect that a concerted effort of repression has taken place to curtail the 'erotic friction' prompted by 'the unmooring of desire, the generalizing of the libidinal' (Greenblatt 1988: 89). There is not merely a shying away, in varying degrees, from the homoerotic elements of the sequence; simpler and more basic questions remain unexamined. Is the presence of desire a form of statement or deviation from meaning? Can it be named or must it exist in a mode of perennial transgression? 'Full of fine things said unintentionally': though Keats's comment made in 1817 (1958: vol. i, 188) begs the question of how these might be distinguished from the fine things said intentionally or whether they are fine only because unintentional, it captures something of the elusive quality of the sonnets' attraction.

The issue is particularly acute in Stephen Booth's copiously annotated edition published in 1977. The effect is one of contagion (or in the *Sonnets*' term, 'base infection' (94.11)); connotations established in the more unequivocally erotic of the sonnets spread by inexorable phonetic logic into previously immune areas. This applies not merely to more obvious examples such as 'use', 'treasure', 'thing', but to the very sounds themselves – 'con', 'awl', 'pr' and 'o'. The Ovidian themes of transformation, mutability and desire appear to be re-enacted on the level of semes and phonemes, which 'present-absent with sweet motion slide' (45.4). Such attentiveness to the 'figures of delight' (98.11), it has frequently been complained, 'too often lapses into perverse intricacy, and, in the discovery of impossible innuendoes, sinks into puerility' (Kerrigan 1986: 65–6). One may become justifiably impatient with the incessant editorial nudges, but the question of demarcation remains. Booth, after all, is positively ascetic in comparison to more recent commentators. Rubenstein's lexicon claims 'to cover *those many* acts usually ignored in textual footnotes – the erotic practices of heterosexuals and homosexuals (including lesbians), perverts, castrates and the impotent' (1989: xii). To this end such uncompromising glosses are offered as 'heart', 'Arse. Bowel: by trans. heart'; 'love', '1. A flatus. . . 2. Nothing'; 'mind', 'Buttocks; physical passion'; and 'soul' also as 'Buttocks' via the play on 'Sole: the bottom of a thing' (1989: 122, 151, 161, 248). Yet even Rubenstein's indefatigable excavations of the anal and scatological fail to stabilise the text. After the initial claim that 'the corpus of Shakespeare's work mirrors life' in presenting 'all kinds of sexuality, both as symbol and as substance', it eventually transpires that 'the amount of actual sodomy in the plays cannot be measured by references to it' (1989: xvii). Rather it is 'a frequent Shakespearean metaphor for betrayal or murder . . . to be buggered means to be figuratively emasculated, unmanned, rendered powerless', anything, it seems, except to perform a sexual act. The same displacement, in a heterosexual idiom, is evident in Partridge, who concludes that the plethora of terms for the female genitals must necessarily imply that 'the pudend has become less a thing desired, however ardently, or a place sought, however eagerly, than a symbol' (1947: 24). The naming of sexual organs, orifices, far from specifying a zone of eroticism, opens up further vistas of linguistic dissemination.

In this chapter I wish to comprehend this rhetorical instability in terms of the intersection of apparently antithetical modes. On the one side, there is second-person address, lyric apostrophe; on the other, didactic statement, collective opinion. To regard the sonnets as a declaration of love is hardly novel, but what has been underestimated is the simultaneous presence of a third-person commentary upon desire. The coherence of the sequence, I shall argue, lies in the tension, what Greenblatt calls 'chafing' (1988: 88), between these two vantages. I will begin by looking at the presentation of the sonnet tradition in Joel Fineman's *Shakespeare's Perjured Eye*, followed by consideration of Eve Sedgwick's analysis of homosocial bonding in *Between Men*, and Joseph Pequigney's treatment of homosexuality in *Such is my Love*. I shall then offer a series of close readings of specific sonnets that will attempt to mediate between the two positions. After brief examination of precedents in Spenser and Sidney, the final section will examine the famous disquisition on lust in Sonnet 129, and attempt to demonstrate the continued presence of an invocation of desire within an apparent renunciation of it.

The extravagance of Fineman's opening claim – 'in his sonnets Shakespeare invents a genuinely new poetic subjectivity' (1986: 1) – provokes admiration and incredulity in approximately equal measure. Can one distinguish between an ordinary subjectivity and a poetic one; what is the preceding normative state; and what kind of causal influence can these little-known and seldom-republished texts have exerted for the first two hundred years of their publishing history? The stress on the 'poetry of praise', the 'epideictic purpose' (1986: 1), certainly connects erotic, political and religious discourses; the poem as dispenser of compliment rather than outlet of vision is undoubtedly central to Renaissance poetics. (Though on a specifically generic argument, one would wish to know what happened to epic, drama and history, the narrative forms, if panegyric is to be the 'master model'.) Something in the *Sonnets* may, however difficult to define, be deemed 'genuinely new': not to be found in classical or medieval verse, nor in the immediate line of descent through Petrarch and Ronsard: the technical demands of the form played off against the supposed intensity of the emotion. The earlier English sonneteers get something of this geometrical aspect, a kind of spacing rather than sequence of desire; but it is extremely rare in Shakespeare, where an initial declaration tends to prompt a pre-emptive narration of envisaged response.

Fineman argues that the exhaustion of the sonnet tradition, now divested of its 'original and traditional force', compelled the development of a 'new first-person posture'. (It is never certain whether there is anything behind the persona, constructed personality.) Shakespeare rewrites praise through the medium of epideictic paradox and in this way 'invents, which is to say comes upon, the only kind of subjectivity that survives in the literature successive to the poetry of praise' (1986: 2). We are offered a before-the-fall kind of argument, in which a hypothetical unity is dispersed into modern complexity (and 'comes upon' is surely an inadequate idiom of the process). What is notable in Fineman's account, however, is the stress on the potential for parody and denigration: the epideictic mode 'controls in advance its own transgression, predetermining and to some extent anticipating the character of its own undoing' (1986: 3). The final renunciation of Petrarch's *Rime Sparse* (366. 111–12, 'Medusa et l'error mio m'an fatto un sasso/ d'umor vano stillante'; Medusa and my error have made me a stone dripping moisture)) or the envoi to Chaucer's *Troilus and Criseyde* ('O yonge, fresshe folkes' (5.1835–69)) become structurally inevitable. A striking contemporary example of this reversal is the open denunciation that concludes Barnes's *Parthenophil and Parthenope* ([1593] sestine 5). Praise always stands in relation of non-coincidence to its object, hinting at a potential satirical contrast. To 'compare thee to a summer's day' (18.1) is also to assert a degree of unlikeness; and one must not forget the element of threat within the *carpe diem* tradition. Marvell reminds the coy mistress, somewhat gloatingly, 'Worms shall try/That long-preserv'd Virginity' (27–8); and Shakespeare himself achieves an almost Popean asperity towards those who 'live unwooed and unrespected fade' (54.10). If love poetry is defined as exhortatory, even coercive, idealisation, the reversal is always latent, perhaps inevitable; in so far as earthly love simulates and rivals divine, it solicits its own eventual abandonment. It necessarily moves from praise of the beloved to reflecting on the adequacy of its 'couplement of proud compare' (21.5) when set against its posited ideal. If the sonnet is 'not only a poem of praise, but characteristically a poem about praise', the same reflexivity can be found in any love lyric. The genre is concerned not with the transmission of a prior emotional state, addressed to a specific lover, but with a linguistic intensification of its own construction; it is language adoring itself. This presentness of self-articulation, the 'egocentric particularity of the here and now of the I', subsumes all temporal and spatial markers (Fineman 1986: 9). Instead of degrees of authenticity of passion, we should look for self-consciousness in the rhetoricity of the medium, the '*merely literary* figure of a self' (Fineman 1986: 10).

In Sidney's 'Astrophil and Stella', the solitary activity of poetic composition presupposes both the scrutiny of a beloved and circulation to a wider courtly audience; the verse is at times pre-emptively defensive, at others soliciting admiration, offering itself simultaneously as an exemplary emotional narrative and an irritatingly ineffectual campaign. Yet the sequence brings out an inherent contradiction in the verse of courtship. It seeks to ingratiate and then persuade, but, if successful, it necessarily alters and (arguably) defiles the status of the very object of its adoration.

This is neatly encapsulated in Shakespeare's Sonnet 142, 'Love is my sin', where the mistress can only retain her 'dear virtue' in so far as she displays 'hate of my sin', desire to seduce, which is necessarily 'grounded on sinful loving' (1–2). (Greville plays with the same paradox in 'My reason is but power to dissemble' and 'Of Mans false lust disguised with devotion' (*Caelica* 10.14; 36.12).) Stella's elegant rejoinder that she 'would not let me, whom she loved, decline/From nobler course, fit for my birth and mind' (62.7–8) remains an insuperable obstacle to effective progress. In stark contrast to the emphatically post-consummation nature of Shakespeare's second sequence, Astrophil's primary delight seems to consist in sophistical rejoinders to reasonable curtailment. The interspersed songs, especially the eighth, hint at bodily consummation, but their overall effect is one of a fervid groping eroticism, faintly clumsy and ill-considered, preoccupied with questions of location and prohibition of physical access. Within the sequence itself, however, utterance is not so much a deferral of as a substitute for 'sweet but unfelt joyes' (24.11; compare Greville, 'the joys of neare enjoying' (*Caelica* 40.6)).

Yet, as previously noted, praise itself always has the potential to become a 'satire to decay' (100.11). Sidney constructs the object of his adoration in order to contrast it with the actual woman; he seeks to persuade her by offering a version of their relation – tyranny, servitude – which must preclude the fulfilment of his suit. The phenomenology of compliment is at best self-reflexive, at worst self-defeating; it demands not recognition of its ideal but deviation from it. As in Yeats, a certain vindictive reification is always a possibility: the true Stella becomes the deracinated and arrested image, not the obstinately uncooperative wife. Both Platonic and Protestant traditions have resources for the renunciation of the empirical, the contingent, as an untrustworthy copy ('Leave sense, and those which sense's objects be' (10.7)), and there is something almost Humeian about the internalisation of Stella's image. It is manifestly inadequate, but not expected to be otherwise: in comparison with Virtue, 'Beauty can be but a shade/Which elements with mortall mixture breed' (5.5–6). Even if Beauty inheres in Virtue, or vice versa, the very presence of the archetype is an implicit condemnation of the human manifestation of these qualities. If Stella 'shrines in flesh so true a Deitie' (4.13), her bodily person can only be a residue, that which is expelled from the very aesthetic brought in to win her: 'Let *Vertue* have that *Stella*'s selfe; yet thus, / That Vertue but that body graunt to us' (52.13–14). Insofar as you are not the perfection that I ascribe to you, you may be mine: Astrophil laments because his adoration is not pure, but if it were pure it would only exist in terms of gravitation towards an ideal which Stella is not and cannot be.

Fineman's somewhat laborious attempts to locate within the sonnets anticipations of 'contemporary speculation . . . in a theoretical mode' does not detract from the strength of his argument in a more limited generic application. Two questions in particular deserve close attention: 'what happens to the sonnet when its poet ceases to admire that which he desires', and why does he 'first praise what is ugly, and then, even after recognising the folly of his praise . . . continue to desire that which he condemns' (Fineman 1986: 55–6)? This, it should be noted, reinstates the problematic of how best to link the two sections of the sonnets, 1–127 and 128–154, addressed to the youth and the dark lady respectively. Fineman treats the division as an allegory of the 'paradoxical relationship between vision and language'. In the second, Shakespeare offers 'a poetics of a double tongue rather than a poetics of a unified and unifying eye, a language of suspicious word rather than a language of true vision' (1986: 15). Instead of offering the unified stasis of the 'ideally specular', these poems 'regularly associate the lady with a disjunction occasioned by verbal duplicity' (1986: 23, 17). The realm of linguistic paradox in which she exists provides the link between formulaic inversion and savage repudiation: she looks like language speaks.

'It is only as a figure of false speech, specifically of a false epideictic speech, that the lady comes to occupy this peculiarly charged erotic place in the sequence as a whole' (Fineman 1986: 17); such an identification arguably reinforces a distrust of independent female expression prevalent throughout the Elizabethan period. This particular strand of deconstructive essentialism is nicely caught in Fineman's phrase, 'the heterogeneity of the lady, her essential duplicity' (1986: 17). Whatever the difficulty in defining the extent and virulence of the contagion ('Suspect I may, yet not directly tell' (144.10)), it permits a deeply consoling certainty of identification. A famous instance occurs in Sonnet 20, where the youth is said to possess 'A woman's gentle heart, but not acquainted/With shifting change, as is false woman's fashion' (20. 3–4; also 89, 118, 121); the same sentiment is expressed more tersely in Donne's 'Women's Constancy', 'you/Can have no way but falsehood to be true' (12–13); and perhaps most poignantly in Greville,

LUST IN SHAKESPEARE'S SONNETS

> Let me no longer follow Womenkinde,
> Where change doth use all shapes of tyranny;
> And I no more will stirre this earthly dust,
> Wherein I lose my name, to take on lust.
> (Greville, *Caelica* 71.15–18).

In the poems of the second sequence, Fineman argues, 'a homosexual, erotics of ideal admiration' is replaced 'by a heterosexual and *therefore misogynous*, desire for what is not admired' (1986: 188; compare 288). The argument has two unexpected consequences. First, as the erotic is the duplicitous is the linguistic, it follows that a poetry of union, idealisation, and visual compliment, must be entirely sexless, devoid of even the possibility of genital consummation. 'The specific virtue of this ideal, homosexual desire is *not* to be erotic': 'love and all love's loving parts' (31.3) must be placed within wholly segregated economies. Second, heterosexual desire is not blemished by but constituted through accusation and recoil: 'strong eroticism . . . can only be constructed in misogynistic terms and achieves closure through its fixed dissatisfaction' (Fineman 1986: 304).

At this point, I wish to defer further discussion of the 'lusty misogyny' (Fineman 1986: 17) of Shakespeare's newly invented 'poetics of heterosexuality', in particular that of Sonnet 129, and to look at recent studies from an explicitly gay perspective by Sedgwick and Pequigney.

Sedgwick describes the *Sonnets* as 'a kind of floating decimal in male homosexual discourse': the absence of 'factual grounding' has resulted in a 'tradition of reading them plucked from history' (1985: 28–9) (obviously an overstatement in the sonneteering context, which has been invoked early and often). This 'decontextualisation' is deemed to 'provide a license for interpreting the sonnets as a relatively continuous erotic narrative played out, economically, by the smallest number of characters – in this case four, the poet, a fair youth, a rival poet, and a dark lady' (1985: 29). At the very least the spareness of this (highly traditional) scenario may be disputed: it is continuously subject to correction by the mocking, hurtful, censorious world, all too frequently 'disposed to set me light/And place my merit in the eye of scorn' (88.1–2).

The symmetry of the sequence shows 'the speaker cares as much about the fair youth as about the dark lady, for whom in the last analysis, they are rivals' (Sedgwick 1985: 29). (This presumes a commensurate notion of 'caring', and also the unstated presence of the lady throughout the first sequence which, as Sedgwick herself observes, is notable for 'the almost complete absence of mention of women' (1985: 33).) Under the 'destabilizing force of gender difference', however, 'the promise of symmetry starts to derail' (1985: 31).

> Two loves I have, of comfort and despair,
> Which like two spirits do suggest me still;
> The better angel is a man right fair,
> The worser spirit a woman coloured ill.
> To win me soon to hell, my female evil
> Tempteth my better angel from my side,
> And would corrupt my saint to be a devil,
> Wooing his purity with her foul pride.
> And whether that my angel be turned fiend
> Suspect I may, yet not directly tell;
> But being both from me, both to each friend,
> I guess one angel in another's hell.
> Yet this shall I ne'er know but live in doubt,
> Till my bad angel fire my good one out.

According to Sedgwick, Sonnet 144 can be broken down into a 'table of pairings': comfort/despair, better/worser, man/woman, right fair/coloured ill, angel/evil, saint/devil, purity/foul pride, angel/fiend. (Certain details of the analysis may still be queried: the bifurcation of 'two spirits' into angel/spirit is ignored in line two, and the final doubling of good and bad angels is also overlooked.) The urbane propositional control is however deceptive: there is no tableauesque balance equivalent to Lodge's 'I wage the combat with two mighty foes' (*Phyllis* 25.1). Here the endeavours are all 'one-way' (Sedgwick 1985: 31). The narrator is active in terms of governing verbs, but these are merely having, guessing, suspecting, not knowing, and living in doubt. The woman preserves a 'monopoly of initiative, desire and power' (1985: 32): 'foul pride', for example, would more usually be associated with the male erection, and 'my saint' with a chaste mistress whose 'purity' might offer 'comfort'. 'My female evil' (an absolute synonymity: a saint may be corrupted to a devil, but no reverse conversion is possible) concentrates her efforts on the 'better angel', who appears to possess no other trait than fairness. Hence the curious passivity of the knock-on effect 'when a woman woos' (41.7). The narrator, despite being apparently ignored by her, regards the seduction of a third party as a strategem 'to win me soon to hell'. The possibility of a counter-balancing 'heaven', as Sedgwick notes, is 'made to evaporate' (1985: 33): all that remains is an envious voyeurism and a malicious anticipation of a final 'firing out'. (The parallel in Lear's 'Die for adultery' speech (*Lear* VI.125–30) is even more explicit in the source in Samuel Harsnett, 'lodging the devil . . . in the inferiour parts' (1604: 63).)

In the first sequence, woman functions as at best an overriden obstacle, something which understandably prompts the attitude of 'indifference, or perhaps active repulsion' in the youth that must be overcome. The second sequence, in contrast, presents a 'heterosexuality that includes women' and therefore 'threat and chaos' (Sedgwick 1985: 34). The initial exhortations to 'breed to brave' time (12.14), with their convenient elision of the maternal body, envisage a progression 'via the heterosexual, the manly, toward the homosocial or men' (1985: 32). The dynastic transmission of 'lines of life' (16.9) threatened by the decision to 'stop posterity' (3.8) is paramount. At this point, there is no opposition between homosexuality and heterosexuality: male–male love is 'set firmly within a structure of institutionalised social relations that are carried out via women' (1985: 32).

In the second sequence, the 'irruption of an actual female', even 'for the most part perceptible only as a pair of eyes and a vagina', terminates all reference to the duty of reproduction; and there are repeated allusions to the lady's 'powerful might' and 'strength and warrantise of skill' (150.1, 7). The key point of Sedgwick's argument is the possible strengthening of homosocial bonds through an apparently disruptive presence: 'Thy might/Is more than my o'er pressed defence can bide' (139.7–8), but this temporary destabilisation permits eventual consolidation.

There are certainly numerous instances to support the claim that 'sharing sexual territory with other men' serves as 'a way of participating in a supraindividual male power over women' (Sedgwick 1985: 36). In the lines, 'Beshrew that heart that makes my heart to groan/For that deep wound it gives my friend and me' (133.1–2), 'gives' implies both hostility and benefaction, a sundering of males and yet a reinforcement of mutuality through sharing the 'deep wound' of the vagina. (Compare Sidney, '*Love* gave the wound which while I breathe will bleed' (2.2).) In Sonnet 134 the permutations of the triangle are further developed:

> So, now I have confessed that he is thine,
> And I myself am mortgaged to thy will,
> Myself I'll forfeit, so that other mine
> Thou wilt restore to be my comfort still.
> But thou wilt not, nor will he not be free,
> For thou art covetous, and he is kind;
> He learned but surety-like to write for me
> Under that bond that him as fast doth bind.
> The statute of thy beauty thou wilt take
> Thou usurer that put'st forth all to use,
> And sue a friend came debtor for my sake;
> So him I lose through my unkind abuse.
>   Him have I lost, thou hast both him and me;
>   He pays the whole, and yet am I not free.

The poem opens with a testimony not of personal emotion but of a reluctantly acknowledged state of affairs (as in 'Let me confess that we two must be twaine' (36.1)). 'Mortgaged to thy will' conflates legalese with expansive receptivity in a declared willingness to 'forfeit' self for 'that other mine'. This will provide 'comfort', as in Sonnet 144, but also implies the 'centric happiness' of those who 'have . . . digg'd love's Mine' (Donne, 'Love's Alchimie', 11.1–2). The restitution of friend and sexual access become synonymous. The antithesis, 'thou art covetous, and he is kind', that attempts to separate the two spheres, is immediately undercut by the equation of writing and coitus: a sexual amanuensis providing 'surety'. The 'bond' of contract rapidly transforms into one of coupling, 'that him as fast doth bind', both securely and rapidly. (There is no hint of literacy in the lady, in marked contrast to Astrophil's wish that 'Pleasure might cause her reade' (1.3).) The third 'thou wilt' reappropriates usury as an image of female sexual initiative, 'all to use', in an obvious innuendo. 'Unkinde abuse' is both an injury given and received; but perhaps the more direct meaning of denunciation should be stressed. 'Abuse' of the lady's 'use' leads to 'him I lose', both in the sense of breaking relations and freeing from obligation. (Other examples of this simultaneous release and deprivation include 'And, losing her, my friend hath found that loss' (42.10), and 'The charter of thy worth gives thee releasing' (87.3).) There is considerable consolation in the indirect physical contact offered by sharing a woman's body: 'Thou dost love her because thou know'st I love her' (42.6). 'Thou hast both him and me' suggests instant reunion of the sundered parties: 'But here's the joy: my friend and I are one./Sweet flatt'ry! Then she loves but me alone!' (42. 13–14). 'He pays the whole' is both bludgeoningly crude and yet also protectively idealising: the friend remains affluent, a patron, a picker up of tabs. 'Yet I am not free': from the debt, from the demands of the lady, with his own favours. (Compare Greville: 'But when I thought my selfe of her selfe free,/All's chang'd: she understands all men but me' (*Caelica* 39.13–14).) The '(w)hole' becomes synonymous with the otherwise elided lady: payment by one male leads to response by another. She herself is both everything and nothing, mere orifice and ultimate enclosure.

This doubleness is most explicit in the famous (or notorious) Will sonnets, 135 and 136:

> Whoever hath her wish, thou hast thy Will,
> And Will to boot, and Will in overplus;
> More than enough am I that vex thee still,
> To thy sweet will making addition thus.
> Wilt thou, whose will is large and spacious,
> Not once vouchsafe to hide my will in thine?
> Shall will in others seem right gracious,
> And in my will no fair acceptance shine?
> The sea, all water, yet receives rain still
> And in abundance addeth to his store;
> So thou being rich in Will add to thy Will,
> One will of mine, to make thy large Will more.
>   Let 'no' unkind, no fair beseechers kill;
>   Think all but one, and me in that one Will.
>
> If thy soul check thee that I come so near,
> Swear to thy blind soul that I was thy Will,
> And will, thy soul knows, is admitted there;
> Thus far for love my love-suit, sweet, fulfil.
> Will will fulfil the treasure of thy love,
> Ay, fill it full with wills, and my will one.
> In things of great receipt with ease we prove
> Among a number one is reckoned none.
> Then in the number let me pass untold,
> Though in thy store's account I one must be;
> Or nothing hold me, so it please thee hold
> That nothing me, a something, sweet, to thee.
>   Make but my name thy love, and love that still,
>   And then thou lov'st me for my name is Will.

The dizzying polysemy of 'will' includes what one wishes (hence the occasional cheery note of unassertive fantasy); second, one's future intention, or faculty of volition; third, specifically carnal desire (merging with the broader theological usage); fourth, penis (compare 'fleshes his will in the spoil of her honour' (*All's Well* IV.iii. 14–15); fifth, vagina ('O indistinguish'd space of woman's will': *Lear* IV.vi.270), linking to the 'defect' (149.11) and 'insufficiency' (150.2) which requires 'addition' (compare 20.11); sixth, William ('Make but my name thy love'). Or any combination thereof. Recent work in the history of medicine provides a context for this apparent interchangeability of male and female genitals (see Greenblatt 1988: 66–93; Laqueur 1990: 114–15). Nevertheless the sense of overload remains. The very term is 'to boot' and 'in overplus', placing identity itself in its very instability and surplus: 'more than enough am I'.

It would seem inevitable that such erotic metamorphoses would lead at least to intimations of alarm. Yet the dominant tone seems to be a kind of quizzical banter and fond respect alongside a courtly and disarming hyperbole ('love-suit sweet' does not jar), which dispels the potentially aggrieved note in 'vex' and 'kill'. The first 'thou hast thy Will' is a pledge of loyalty, a grudging acknowledgement of the lady's right to her own way, and an attempt to procure her 'wish', consent, supported by the later 'fair acceptance'. The obscenity is tender and unrecriminative: 'I was thy Will', for example, situates itself within a bodily interior while offering a poignant reminder of a shared past. 'Things of great receipt' suggests benign amplitude; and 'large and spacious' recalls the generous natural fecundity of 'And being frank she lends to those are free' (4.4). 'Hide' suggests a certain snugness of relinquishment (taken up in 'I come so near', 'please thee hold/That nothing me', a proximity conspicuously absent in the youth sonnets, and reinforced by the nursery rhyme jingle of 'will will fulfil'). The libertine fantasy of an infinite capacity of sexual assimilation ('Good is not good, unless/A thousand it possess/But doth wast with greediness' (Donne, 'Confined Love', ll. 19–21)) still preserves a generous tribute to 'abundance', combined with a lyric evocation of a sparkling sea-surface ('shine'). The masculine gender of 'addeth to his store' remains disconcerting, though compare Sidney, 'What Oceans of delight in me do flow' (69.4). Instead of demanding to be distinguished from the 'number', the narrator is happy to 'pass untold'; unaudited within the 'store's account'. (The lady's 'being rich' is never reducible to the laborious reiterations of 'addition'.) The poem is unusual in acknowledging 'will in others', desiring persons rather than deracinated commentary. 'Whoever' implies open access: the exhortation to remove the restraint of '"no" unkind' (picking up the 'unkind abuse' of the preceding sonnet (134.12)) is not specific to the speaker. There is a communality among the 'beseechers', rather than isolation and exposure to a hostile world. 'Thinke all but one' gets its curious stress-freeness from the identification with the collective masculine, an escape from fractious differentiation.

Sedgwick acknowledges the element of 'playful exhilaration' provoked by the dark lady's 'gargantuan, distracted catholicity', but glosses it somewhat restrictively as 'a desire to consolidate partnership with authoritative males in and through the bodies of females' (1985: 38–9). This contemporary model of circulation and exchange fails to pursue the sequence's own distinctive refusal of erotic privacy by the interpolation of a constitutive public gaze ('the world may see my pleasure' (75.8)). Nevertheless Sedgwick touches on something crucial in her recognition that 'to be fully a man requires' not simply domination of a woman, but also 'having *risked* transformation by her' (1985: 40).

There are numerous advantages to this model. It enables a move away from the moral adjudication of texts with regard to their representation of women on to a more nuanced investigation of masculinity as a phenomenon in its own right. A subtle and flexible interplay is established between infra-textual mechanisms and broader cultural circulations understood in terms of the same semiotic model, uniting anthropological and historicist perspectives with (in Sedgwick's case) a virtuoso practice of reading. Homosexual panic precedes reincorporation within and reinforcement of the homosocial continuum: the text is motivated by the dual imperative both to articulate and to contain this point of rhetorical crisis. (For a more hostile appreciation, see van Leer 1989a; and the subsequent exchange, Sedgwick 1989; van Leer 1989b.)

There seems no obvious reason, however, why such a reading should demand an attenuation of complexity in the first sequence. Nevertheless it is claimed that rivalry for a male is 'less radically threatening' (Sedgwick 1985: 40) despite the ubiquitous jealousy and fear of displacement. Sedgwick superbly catches the 'strong anticipatory self-protectiveness in the speaker's attitude to the youth'; an explicit ascription of motive, predetermination of responses, most frequently 'forestalling of disloyalty or regret' (1985: 43). Richard Barnfield, in the only other Elizabethan sequence addressed to a male, 'The Affectionate Shepherd' (1594), continually emphasises the decorative appeal of 'Cherry-lipt Adonis in his snowie shape' (27.1). Shakespeare, in contrast, repeatedly presents the youth as unadorned and 'single' (e.g. 3.14; 8.8). His image is preserved as 'unified and static' whereas the 'contagious self-division' of the dark lady is displaced on to and internalised by the speaker who thereby becomes 'hystericised, reduced to the voice of his resistance and his hating submission to her' (Sedgwick 1985: 44–5).

The 'genital allegory' expounded by the founding text of gay studies, as with Fineman, has the unexpected effect of massively accentuating the 'impression of sexlessness' of the youth. There is, if not a prudishness, at the very least a circumspection in dismissing the issue of the degree of 'genital sexual relationship between these men' as 'irrecoverable' (Sedgwick 1985: 35); a collective bonding is rather too readily substituted for specific erotic acts, particularly in view of the frequent explicit physicality: 'Sweet love, renew thy force; be it not said/Thy edge should blunter be than appetite' (56. 1–2).

In this context, Joseph Pequigney offers a salutary restatement of what one might have thought obvious: 'the foremost subject of the sequence is a love between men' (1985: 1). Pequigney is undoubtedly correct that the textual history has been one of shying away and scaling down, responding to the 'embarrassment and scandal of homosexuality' with 'various stratagems' of denial of 'perversity'. The friendship, it is insisted, is 'decidedly amorous' – 'passionate to a degree and in ways not dreamed of in the published philology' (1985: 1). This triumphalist note is perhaps a little overstated: it is hardly a 'very well-kept secret' that the sonnets contain such 'unsavory subject-matter' (1985: 17), as the briefest of glances at the commentary on Sonnet 20 will confirm. 'Verbal data are clear and copious in detailing physical intimacies between them' (1985: 1); the language of the sonnets is surely 'copious' in a way that precludes such positivistic certainty. One may readily accept that, given the reception history, it is legitimate for the text to 'be paraphrased', but still have misgivings about some of the subsequent 'raw definitions' (1985: 42, 44): 'treasure [=fecundate] ... some place [=womb]/With beauty's treasure [=sperm] ere it be self-kill'd' (1985: 16). Pequigney himself engages in his own form of 'glossarial censorship' in distinguishing between 'heterosexual bawdy' and 'homoerotic statements' (1985: 51). Even if the love displayed in the sonnets is 'quintessential not because it is not homoerotic but because it is' (1985: 75), it does not follow that this has therefore been purged of all impurities. It is claimed, for example, 'there is no reason to hold that the youth is a nobleman' despite the conventions of patronage, general air of fulsome reticence, and at times explicit master-servant idiom ('Lord of my love, to whom in vassalage' (26.1)). There is a refusal to acknowledge the at times explicitly sado-masochistic dimension of their relationship: 'Being your slave, what should I do but tend/Upon the hours and times of your desire?' (57.1–2). Masculine mutuality is presented as monogamous, equal, and rightly prized above the love of women. Heterosexual feelings are somewhat puritanically denied to the youth (why should he not be bisexual?), with an insistence upon a purely conjectural fidelity apart from a 'simple slip into licentiousness, immediately repented and long past' (allowing 'the basest clouds to ride/With ugly rack on his celestial face' (33.5–6 (1985: 142)). 'What potions have I drunk of siren tears/Distilled from limbecks foul as hell within' (119.1–2) is firmly attached to cunnilingus rather than fellatio (1985: 138); and it is even denied that carnal relations occur with the lady on the grounds that entering 'the fiery and morbid hell of her pudendum' would, on the evidence of Sonnet 144, have resulted in contracting syphilis (1985: 147, 152). Pequigney is eventually faced, however, with an insurmountable difficulty in explaining how such an idyll could end.

It is easy enough to mock some of Pequigney's more visible excesses: the confidence of his at best speculative narrative demarcations; the stridency of his genital literalism; the protective idealisation of the relation with the youth; and in particular the somewhat unnuanced application of the Freudian model of bisexual development. 'The psychological dynamics' of their relation, it is claimed, 'comply in large measure with those expounded in Freud's authoritative discussions of homosexuality' (Pequigney 1985: 1); the nineteenth-century clinician is invoked to predict the course of an Elizabethan sonnet sequence. It should come as no great surprise that 'the persona, like most literary characters, is not given a childhood, and his unconscious is a puzzle' (1985: 96). Even if one accepts that Sonnet 20 may be persuasively read in terms of the creation of the penis, surely this need not entail the resuscitation of Freudian doctrine in its crudest form: 'women for want of this prized organ are less fortunate and complete than men' (1985: 83). For my purposes, the most interesting consequence of Pequigney's argument is the way that the homoerotic love of the first sequence is yet again desexualised and the heterosexual lust of the second taken as synoymous with condemnation. Lust is a 'sheer and remittant carnal passion, devoid of the sustaining effects of respect, admiration, and affection for its object', whose 'hallmark' is a 'combination of desire and disrespect' (1985: 165, 146).

Where Fineman stresses a logic of inversion internal to the epideictic tradition, both Sedgwick and Pequigney emphasise the importance of exchange between men in the sequence. The next section will attempt to unite the two perspectives. First, it will examine the homosocial within the semantic detail of the poems, and then study its interaction with the apostrophic mode of promise and declaration.

Shakespearian desire cannot simply be equated with a mood of *odi et amo*, possession by a desire for an object that simultaneously fascinates and repels. The classical theme is not entirely absent in the first sequence, emerging powerfully in the triangular situation of Sonnets 40–42. Generally, though, it emerges most strongly towards the end of the second cycle: in 150, for example, it is asked 'Who taught thee how to make me love thee more,/The more I hear and see just cause of hate?' (9–10). Paradoxically, one could say that hate does not necessarily involve hostility. The 'civil war' which 'is in my love and hate' (35.12) is more a kind of permutation which does not disrupt the format of apostrophe. When Sidney talks of 'the ground of this fierce *Love* and lovely hate' (60.11), there is a self-cancelling quality to the antithesis; and Drayton pushes this to the brink of self-parody: 'Your love and hate is this, I now do prove you!/Your love in hate, by hate to make me love you' ([1619] 'Idea' 19.13–14). Sonnet 145 initially focuses on the desecration of 'those lips' by 'the sound that said "I hate"' (1–2), yet the final volte-face, '"I hate", from hate away she threw, /And sav'd my life saying "not you"' (13–14), reduces the term to a semantic counter evacuated of all intentional content. The tension and cumulative power of the sequence lies not so much, as Fineman argues, in a systematic inversion of allegiance – 'But, love, hate on for now I know thy minde' (149.13) – as in the degree to which this testimony is assimilated in or resistant to the ubiquitous public scrutiny and the pressure of 'vulgar scandal' (112.2). This, I would suggest, may be illuminated by Sedgwick's concept of the homosocial, which may be used not merely to situate the poems in the context of an implicit cultural exchange, but also to identify the dramatisation of an external perspective within them.

I would like to substantiate this emphasis with a series of close analyses, beginning with Sonnet 127:

> In the old age black was not counted fair,
> Or, if it were, it bore not beauty's name;
> But now is black beauty's successive heir,
> And beauty slandered with a bastard's shame:
> For since each hand hath put on nature's power,
> Fairing the foul with art's false borrowed face,
> Sweet beauty hath no name, no holy bower,
> But is prophaned, if not lives in disgrace. (1–8)

On one level, the opening line offers a truism (black was not white); on another, an explicitly sexual statement (black was not cunted fair), a reading supported by numerous other usages such as 'Which in their wills count bad what I think good?' (121.8) and 'Only my plague thus far I count my gain' (141.13)). This composite of logical contradiction and obscenity is evident throughout the second sequence, for example, in the play noted by Booth in 'That in my mind thy worst all best exceeds' (150.8) on 'worst all' and whore's hole (Booth 1977: 523). The often cited parallel in Sidney, 'That whereas blacke seemes Beautie's contrary/She even in blacke doth make all beauty's flow?' (7.10–11) is notably lacking in any such innuendo.

What may reasonably be called a nominalism of desire permits a transference of 'beauty's name': the resulting 'slander' lies in the insulting duplication of genuine 'beauty'. Promiscuity produces a 'bastard', a fecundity which might appear to confound singleness by producing a 'successive heir'. The homophone on 'bore', 'bower', and the subsequent 'born' reinforces the procreation motif. If 'beauty' had no 'shame', she would acquire offspring of her own soon enough; yet if she was not 'cunted' in the sense of fertile, she would also be subject to denigration of a different kind (in which case 'bastard's shame' could claim a measure of jeering superiority). In the context of time, beauty is necessarily in thrall to 'nature's power', most eloquently in the stress on the 'fading mansion' (146.6); and if the face was initially 'foul', the disembodied and ungendered 'hand' is surely performing a sensible redress. (No such blurring of 'art' and 'nature' occurs in relation to the youth: 'Ah, wherefore with infection should he live/ ... Why should false painting imitate his cheek' (67.1, 5).) Here the nervously reiterative 'false' is attached to 'borrowed': a typical doubling which leaves open the possibility of a true borrowed face. (Similarly, in phrases such as the 'world's false subtleties' (138.4), 'false plague' (137.14), and 'false bonds of love' (142.14), it is falsehood which guarantees durability). It is not a question of true versus false, but of a kind of internal duplicity which lends a paradoxical stability to the lady. There is no positive term for 'beauty', 'no name, no holy bower' with which it may be identified: instead it is 'prophaned' by its very nature, 'lives' (and so thrives) 'in disgrace'.

> Therefore my mistress' brows are raven black,
> Her eyes so suited, and they mourners seem,
> At such who, not born fair no beauty lack,
> Sland'ring creation with a false esteem.
>   Yet so they mourn becoming of their woe,
>   That every tongue says beauty should look so.   (9–14)

'False esteem' demands to be read as parallel to 'bastard's shame', but 'false' can again be taken in an equivocal sense, particularly in the context of the subsequent relativising of beauty to fashionable approbation. ('Creation' is presumably synonymous with 'nature's power' but could also include art and invention.) The mistress mourns the way in which artificial beauty is valued, but is herself praised for the 'becoming' way in which she grieves. (The pun on 'becombing' is supported by 'tong' in the following line (see Prior 1982: 15–16)). This raises the suspicion that she herself is 'becoming' in the different sense of mutable, adapting herself to the demand of 'false esteem' that she should 'look so'. (The same play is evident in 'Whence hast thou this becoming of things ill' (150.5).)

So this sonnet can be seen as establishing the crucial opposition of the whole sequence. On the one hand, there is an assertion of the self-sustaining force of a private interchange of vows, often flaunting their own inversion of reality: 'Then will I swear beauty herself is black' (132.12); 'say this is not,/To put fair truth upon so foul a face' (137.11–12). On the other lies the insidious power of 'false esteem' and what 'every tongue says'. These appear to respond to a given state of affairs, but in fact acquire a determining force: the opinion which ostensibly offers a retrospective evaluation in fact has brought about the initial situation.

In Spenser's *Amoretti*, the sphere of private emotion must at all costs be shielded from the 'venomous tongue, tipt with vile adder's sting' (86.1); and in Greville's *Caelica*, there is a similarly sharp demarcation: 'I feele within, what men without me blame' (60.10), and in consequence, 'The world in two I have divided fit;/My selfe to you, and all the rest to it' (60.17-18). In Shakespeare, this division is maintained in the first sequence to the youth. The narrator himself cannot be 'in disgrace with Fortune' without being similarly exposed to 'men's eyes' (29.1), but the youth, though repeatedly urged to 'live yourself in eyes of men' (16.12), and to prize 'Those parts of thee that the world's eye doth view' (69.1), remains ultimately impervious to 'others' seeing' (121.4 see also 16.9-12). Public condemnation becomes inverted compliment: 'That thou art blamed shall not be thy defect,/For slander's mark was ever yet the fair', and so 'doth but approve/Thy worth the greater' (70.1-2, 4-5). Similarly, 'The tongue that tells the story of thy days,/Making lascivious comments on thy sport,/Cannot dispraise but in a kind of praise' (95.5-7).

In the second sequence, however, what 'the world well knows' (129.13) converges with the interior emotion of the lyric voice to produce a distinctive equation of accusation and eroticism. In Sonnet 131 there is a singularly ungallant refusal to protest against public defamation:

> Yet in good faith some say that thee behold
> Thy face hath not the power to make love groan;
> To say they err I dare not be so bold,
> Although I swear it to myself alone.
> And to be sure that is not false I swear,
> A thousand groans, but thinking on thy face,
> One on another's neck, do witness bear
> Thy black is fairest in my judgement's place.
>   In nothing art thou black save in thy deeds,
>   And thence this slander, as I think, proceeds. (5-14)

The narrator responds to the denigration of 'some say' by uttering an oath 'to myself alone', and therefore is unlikely to influence the detractors. The subsequent testimony offered by his rapidly accumulating 'groans' ('one on another's neck') is equally unpersuasive. 'In my judgement's place' suggests both that which substitutes for the faculty and the location in which it has taken residence (as in 'where is my judgement fled,/That censures falsely' (148.3-4)). The subsequent sexual innuendo of 'in nothing' identifies this with the 'forfended place' (*Lear* V.i.11), and the 'place' where an 'unthrift... doth spend' in the procreation sequence (9.9–10). The 'groans' emitted retrospectively become sexual, an unseemly queue of fellow participants in the 'deeds' (compare 'in the very refuse of thy deeds' (150.6)). The initial 'slander' has been vindicated, prompting not merely the voyeuristic lingering of 'as I think', but a strangely placid acceptance. This may be compared to Othello's fantasy of 'the general camp,/Pioneers and all' having 'tasted' Desdemona's 'sweet body' (*Othello* III.iii.349–50), where panic at infidelity is more than compensated for by a pleasure in the implied collectivity. (Other aspects of the play that might be usefully related to the sonnets are the scripting of Othello's desire by external commentary and his abrupt and startling inversion of idiom during the play: 'She's gone; I am abus'd; and my relief/ Must be to loathe her' (*Othello* III.iii.271–2).)

The self-recrimination with which Sonnet 137 opens seems to be locked within a private disorientation.

> Thou blind fool, Love, what dost thou to mine eyes
> That they behold and see not what they see?
> They know what beauty is, see where it lies,
> Yet what the best is, take the worst to be. (1–4)

The eyes, perhaps subject to syphilis, that which blinds, 'take the worst' for 'the best' despite knowing 'what beauty is'. They see 'where it lies', where it tells untruths and where it commits infidelities, yet it is also possible that beauty is beautiful precisely because it 'lies', and so is contrasted rather than identified with the 'best'.

> If eyes corrupt by over-partial looks
> Be anchored in the bay where all men ride,
> Why of eyes' falsehood hast thou forged hooks,
> Whereto the judgement of my heart is tied?
> Why should my heart think that a several plot,
> Which my heart knows the wide world's common place?
> (5–10)

'Eyes' falsehood' refers both to the deception of the lady's eyes and error of the narrator's own. The 'judgement of the heart' is similarly both a verdict on and by. ('Forged' is both strengthened and deceived; a play revived in Geoffrey Hill's 'The Turtle Dove', 'forged passion upon speech' (l. 23.) The final image is from land enclosure: the 'several plot', *the private piece of ground*, is opposed to the public grazing of the 'wide world's common place'. 'Common place' also suggests both cliche ('All this the world well knows') and promiscuity ('O thou public commoner', *Othello* IV.ii.72; 'common stale', *Much Ado* IV.i.64). The equation of sexual availability with anonymous opinion does not, as one might have expected, lead to a protest against the loss of intimacy in the besmirching of a private relation. 'The bay' suggests bay-mare as well as cove (recalling 'The sea, all water, yet receives rain still' (135.9)), but in retrospect, even 'where all men ride' may be taken positively; at the very least, the narrator's attachment cannot be seen as perverse or exceptional. The rhetorical constitution of his desire renders it both broodingly solipsistic and wilfully externalised: like the mistress herself, it is simultaneously callously self-withholding and infinitely available.

'Wide' has an obvious sexual connotation, but also something of the generous collectivity of 'wide world' and 'wide universe' (19.7; 109.13). There is a similar play in the line, 'And sweets grown common loose their dear delight' (102.12), where 'loose', cease to possess, is also to release, liberate. This paradox is taken up again in Sonnet 140, where 'testy sick men' require 'no news but health' (7–8):

> For if I should despair, I should grow mad,
> And in my madness might speak ill of thee.
> Now this ill-wresting world is grown so bad
> Mad sland'rers by mad ears believed be.
>   That I may not be so, nor thou belied
>   Bear thine eyes straight, though thy proud heart go wide.
>
> (9–14)

'To speak ill of' is both to slander and to be truthful. Its motive seems less that of delirium than of participation: the final innuendo on 'straight' and 'wide' is as much for the 'ill-wresting world' as against the lady. Slander here seems located in the desire of the speaker to utter and the audience to receive it, rather than in some transgression against nature by the lady. The final pledge is not, it should be stressed, that the speaker will not continue to 'speak ill', only that he will not necessarily be believed. Promiscuity is somehow instantaneous with the assimilation of an utterance: 'belied' implies both to be disparaged and to be made love to, so to be heard of is to be whored. There is a characteristic penetration of external opinion to the very core of an emotional bond: feeling is always staged, performed, adjudicated.

Sonnet 152 takes up the theme of the artifice of sincerity:

SORDID IMAGES

> In loving thee thou know'st I am forsworn,
> But thou art twice forsworn, to me love swearing;
> In act thy bed-vow broke, and new faith torn
> In vowing new hate after new love bearing.
> But why of two oaths' breach do I accuse thee,
> When I break twenty? I am perjured most,
> For all my vows are oaths but to misuse thee,
> And all my honest faith in thee is lost;   (1-8)

The relatively straightforward sequence of 'new hate after new love' is mediated though oaths and vows until it becomes a kind of outguessing perjury. The degree of 'breach', physical penetration as well as verbal infidelity, does not result in simple accusation. Instead it becomes grounds for conceited self-proclamation: a kind of perverse competitiveness simultaneously exists alongside self-recrimination. 'To misuse thee' is to use you appropriately after your kind: the absence of 'honest faith' does not disallow the possibility of a dishonest faith more convenient for both parties.

> For I have sworn deep oaths of thy deep kindness,
> Oaths of thy love, thy truth, thy constancy,
> And to enlighten thee gave eyes to blindness,
> Or made them swear against the thing they see;
> For I have sworn thee fair – more perjured I,
> To swear against the truth so foul a lie.   (9-14)

'Blindness' most obviously refers to the mistress but also to the speaker, and the 'blind fool, Love' itself. To 'swear against' is both to accuse and pledge allegiance to 'the thing they see', presumably the female genital, which will be equated with 'truth' itself in the final line. The verbal assertiveness, even abuse, of 'sworn thee fair' is not wholly retracted in 'so foul a lie': the utterance reverberates within an interim exhortatory mode sustained rather than negated by external opinion. This is encapsulated in the phrase, 'more perjured eye', which locates the identity of the speaker in the catachresis between linguistic and visual idioms. The fidelity of his desire is not compromised but produced by his simultaneous consciousness of untruth.

The most sustained example of this mode comes in the famous Sonnet 138:

> When my love swears that she is made of truth
> I do believe her though I know she lies,

> That she might think me some untutored youth,
> Unlearned in the world's false subtleties.
> Thus vainly thinking that she thinks me young,
> Although she knows my days are past the best,
> Simply I credit her false-speaking tongue;
> On both sides thus is simple truth suppressed.
> But wherefore says she not she is unjust?
> And wherefore say not I that I am old?
> O, love's best habit is in seeming trust,
> And age in love loves not to have years told.
> Therefore I lie with her, and she with me,
> And in our faults by lies we flatter'd be.

The movement of the poem is smooth, balanced in its reversal, contained within a tone whose assurance verges on the smug. The speaker is a raconteur of female illogicality, though his eventual attitude appears to be one of grateful collusion. The initial 'when' comes to imply whenever, a cyclic, predictable, inescapable pattern of response and counter-response. Here the woman gets the power to 'swear that she is made of truth': a hyperbole whose duplicity is so apparent that it becomes a bond of trust. She cannot be 'made (maid) of truth' if she sleeps with the speaker, yet cannot be his love if she does not. 'Believing' seems less an internal state than a signal of assent, hinting at without committing itself to the parentheses of 'in so far as this is possible' or 'one must be desperate to accept this'. One can presumably decide to believe something whilst knowing the contrary. 'She lies' is an imperturbable continuous present. The lady does not speak falsely as an event, in response to particular circumstances, but as an almost ontological condition: she is sexual, therefore she not merely tells but is herself falsehood (compare Felperin 1988: 88–90). An almost talismanic force is vouched in the 'mis-thinking' someone; a variant on idealising love as pragmatic, commonplace, and premeditated. There is an extension of the necessity of social deceit, euphemism, into the erotic sphere, but the level of mutual understanding implied in successful deception is far from negligible. 'Love's best habit' might indeed be discardable appearances; similarly 'seeming trust' might not be its semblance but its only available form. What, after all, is wrong with flattery if one takes the whole idiom of compliment itself as one long temptation to bad faith in praise? The apparently lax 'I do believe' in retrospect seems quietly remonstrative – difficult though it might be to accept, 'I really do'. 'Simply I credit' has a similar implication of 'as if naïvely', the most economical course of action. The possibility arises that there might be lovers' genuine caring 'subtleties' opposed to the world's 'false' ones; there is after all something poignantly companionable about 'lying with' someone. If one cannot return to the state of 'untutored youth', this equilibrium of mutual disbelief might be no small consolation.

So it is possible to develop the equation of femininity and rhetoric towards a self-contained and almost idyllic bond founded on duplicity. (Compare Sidney, 'I am resolv'd thy errour to maintaine/Rather than by more truth to get more paine' (67. 13–14).) This, however, must be seen as very much the exception. The oath of affirmation sworn by the individual lover towards a beauty synonymous with erotic deceit remains in continuous conflict with the cumulative pressure of collective experience. This, however, leads not to the puncturing of illusion but to a kind of recurrent relief in capitulation: the reinforcement of a masculine bond after a temporary deviation. Sonnet 148 explicitly contrasts fallible sight with communal assessment:

> If that be fair whereon my false eyes dote,
> What means the world to say it is not so?
> If it be not, then love doth well denote
> Love's eye is not so true as all men's 'no'. (5–8)

'Love's eye', the sight of the individual lover, is bound to be less accurate than that of 'all men's'; its affirmation ('aye') cannot match the force of their collective denial, 'no'; the feelings of the self ('I') will be dissipated when met by a less illusioned knowledge. In Thorpe's 1609 edition, the final line is punctuated as 'all men's: no': if this reading is preferred, the final negation can be taken as a refusal to accept the first, or perhaps all these meanings. Booth also comments on the probable continuous obscenity due to 'the concentration of the phonetically related words – *not*, *note*, *no*, and *O*' (1977: 521); and 'all men's (k)no(w)' is of course a 'common place'. The passage offers a striking example of how the semantic ambiguity of the sonnets is permeated by the continual presence of a collective judgement.

Desire must be seen not as having 'that within which passes show' (*Hamlet* I.ii.85) but as a public linguistic act: a bonding of the self not merely with the object of its desire but also with the audience of that transaction. Thus the internal triangulation of friend/mistress/

poet cannot be isolated as a narrative core of the sequence: equally important is the assimilation of the sexual drama to the 'wide world's common place' (137.10).

So the declaration, I love you, should not be seen as a surging forth of emotion that guarantees the good faith of the statement, an internal impulse seeking an outlet in language – 'Lest sorrow lend me words, and words express/The manner of my pity-wanting paine' (140.3–4). It is better understood in terms of entering into a performance, a public gesture constituted through its literary and generic density. Emotion is not so much expressed as staged: it does not prompt a causal sequence of action/reaction, assertion followed by acquiescence or refusal, but appeals beyond the putative addressee to a wider, anonymous community.

In these analyses, I have taken poems most obviously classifiable as lyric addresses, promises, pledges, declarations, which not merely presuppose but dramatise their own engagement with a masculine collectivity. I wish to look at the reverse process in Sonnet 129, where an apparently generalised utterance can be shown to contain within itself a comparable pattern of apostrophic inversion. First, however, I shall take a detour through two sonnets by Spenser and Sidney, which, I believe, will help to clarify and support the claim that there is a continued invocation of desire at the heart of its apparent repudiation.

> Trust not the treason of those smyling lookes,
> until ye have theyr guylefull traynes well tryde:
> for they are lyke but unto golden hookes,
> that from the foolish fish theyr bayts doe hyde:
> So she with flattring smyles weake harts doth guyde
> unto her love, and tempte to theyr decay,
> whome being caught she kills with cruell pryde,
> and feeds at pleasure on the wretched pray:
> Yet even whylst her bloody hands them slay,
> her eyes looke lovely and upon them smyle:
> that they take pleasure in her cruell play,
> and dying doe them selves of payne beguyle.
> O mighty charm which makes men love theyr bane,
> and thinck they dy with pleasure, live with payne. (47)

A grim exemplum of female erotic power here intrudes upon the previously plaintive tranquillity of Spenser's courtship sequence, the *Amoretti*. Obviously in so far as any mistress withholds the

favours which would instantly de-idealise her, she may be called
'cruel' (somewhat tautologously, 'Fayre cruell, why are ye so fierce
and cruell' (49.1)); but this hardly justifies such a depiction of
premeditated dismemberment. Initially there appears to be an
explicit split between the masculine 'ye', who are implored to 'trust
not', and the victims on whom the destructive force of the anonymous 'she' is exerted. 'Traynes' has the most obvious meaning of
'treachery, guyle, deceit, trickery', but also suggests the 'elongated
part of the robe or skirt', and a snare for an animal, making a scent
by dragging something, usually raw carrion, along the ground
(OED 7). It is syntactically possible to read the 'bayts' as hiding the
'hookes', a more reasonable way for fish to be 'foolish', but why
specify the colour as 'golden' unless the 'hookes' are visible? It is
equally possible to equate them with the 'smilyng lookes', paradoxically hiding the bait of the animal flesh. (Ralegh also uses the
image of the hook as alluring in itself in 'A Farewell to False Love':
'A gilded hook that holds a poison'd bait', 1.12; and other examples
include *Antony and Cleopatra*: 'My bended hook/Shall pierce their
slimy jaws' (II.v.12–13), and Donne's 'The Bait': 'For thee, thou
need'st no such deceit,/For thou thyself art thine owne bait', (ll.
25–6).) Here the very injunction, 'until ye have theyr guyleful
traynes well tryde', seems to urge taking the bait to sample the
'treason': one must 'have tryde'in the sense of 'test the quality of'
in order to 'have experience of' (OED 7, 14).

So 'flattring smyles' lure 'weake harts' to their 'decay', both to
the means of their downfall, destruction but also glancing at the
popular truism of sexual self-expenditure: 'since each act, they say,/
Diminisheth the length of life a day' (Donne, 'Farewell to Love' (ll.
24–5; see also 11.1–4)). It is not perhaps surprising that the lady
'feeds at pleasure', but the satisfaction taken at the feast is curiously
mutual: 'they take pleasures in her cruell play,/and dying doe them
selves of payne beguyle'. The lovers seek to 'beguyle' or 'divert
attention from' what is acknowledged already to be a state of
'payne': it is therefore little surprise that they 'love theyr bane',
poison, when it enables them to 'dy with pleasure'. This is somewhat more complex than the familiar equation of death with sexual
climax. The 'mighty charm' is the illusion that makes the 'payne' of
life tolerable, and enables 'men' to respond to its trials with dignity.
In typical fashion, Spenser accentuates the appeal of that which he
ostensibly denounces: what initially appeared a masochistic frenzy
acquires a peculiar note of stoic consolation. 'Men' gives the

closing aphorism a specifically masculine application; but here no distinction is made between the victims within the frame, and the onlookers whom one would have presumed to learn something from their example. The attempt to define, denounce and expel the 'mighty charm' that appeared to be confined within the exemplum only results in its re-emergence as prior to both speaker and addressee. A comparable process, I shall argue, can be discerned within Shakespeare's Sonnet 129.

In Sidney, one kind of self-constitution is offered through homage, union with the object of praise and aloofness: I praise therefore I am. Yet this is locked into a series of rhetorical and conceptual aporia, notably the self-defeating nature of persuasion in this context, and displacement of Astrophil's 'boiling sprites' on to the compensatory satisfactions of 'wailing eloquence' (16.3; 38.11). Desire, however, proves to be an irreducibly disruptive force, whose specific and declared aims – 'Give me some food' (71.14) – render circuitous self-prostration somewhat redundant. At times it is explicitly equated with sin, involuntary response, the sign of a fallen will: 'Desire/Doth plunge my wel-form'd soul even in the mire/Of sinfull thoughts, which do in ruine end' (14.6–8). So only failure protects Astrophil's virtue: to have no cause for bemoaning would mean having reason for self-loathing. But the sequence as a whole presents 'sharpe desire' (49.11) as indisputably necessary to the libidinal economy as a motivating force, and sole guard against the potential immobilisation of a stance of priapic apostrophe. Sidney envisages a series of stratagems to harness its power, ranging from sublimation ('all selfnesse he forbears/Thence his desires he learnes' (61.7–8)) to innoculation ('Cannot heav'n's food, once felt, keep stomackes free/from base desire on earthly cates to pray?' (88.8–9). None of these, however, prove satisfactory: 'But thou Desire, because thou wouldst have all,/Now banish art, but yet alas how shall?' (72.13–14). Astrophil certainly never makes it to a higher plane, and the drifting off into peevish apathy and undeniably carnal lunges displayed towards the closing stages of the sequence have tempted much recent criticism towards an ironic reading of the persona (see Lanham 1972; Roche 1987; Duncan-Jones 1991). The instinct of the Victorian editors to round off the sequence with an appropriate declaration of 'loathing of all loose unchastitie' (15.13) is thus eminently comprehensible.

> Thou blind man's marke, thou foole's selfe chosen snare,
> Fond fancie's scum, and dregs of scattred thought,

SORDID IMAGES

> Band of all evils, cradle of causelesse care,
> Thou web of will, whose end is never wrought;
>
> Desire, desire, I have too dearely bought,
> With price of mangled mind thy worthlesse ware,
> Too long, too long asleepe thou hast me brought,
> Who should my mind to higher things prepare.
>
> But yet in vaine thou hast my ruine sought,
> In vaine thou madest me to vaine things aspire,
> In vaine thou kindlest all thy smokie fire;
>
> For vertue hath this better lesson taught,
> Within my selfe to seeke my onlie hire:
> Desiring nought but how to kill desire.   (31)

This sonnet, along with 'Leave me, O Love', has traditionally been plucked out of *Certain Sonnets* to conclude 'Astrophil and Stella'. In both poems there is a total removal of any context of address, and the lyric voice finds a satisfactory formal closure in its self-directedness. The apostrophe insists upon a making present of that which is to be repudiated: a simultaneous invocation for 'fond fancies' to ' (s)cum' whilst denouncing them as 'scum'. The 'dregs' imply barrel, sediment: thus the 'fond fancies' and 'scattred thought' of desire are simultaneously heavier and lighter, above and below, surfeit and residue.

The first line refers to agency in a public realm; the second to an unseemly product of internalised mental activity. So desire is simultaneously the prompting towards an external goal and the result of a private process. The 'marke' is both a sexual target ('Let the mark have a prick in't' (*Love's Labour's Lost* IV.i.125); and also a stain reminiscent of the 'stamp of one defect', the 'dram of eale' (*Hamlet* I.iv.23–38). This in turn may be linked to an implicit narrative of conception: 'marke', the stain of original sin; 'snare', vagina; 'scum', female arousal; 'dregs', ejaculation; 'band', cradle, and 'web' (cloth), swaddled child.

Up to this point, these could be a series of riddles awaiting a solution. 'Desire, desire, I have too dearely bought' is a nicely self-contained apostrophe: the play on 'too/two' matches both the doubling of the term and the duplicity of the faculty. The claim, 'Desire, desire I have', is later reversed in 'thou hast me', a declaration of possession that is never subsequently rescinded: 'me brought' becomes a virtual ablative absolute (me having been brought). 'Dearely', costly, retains the possibility of intensely, passionately: 'mangled' has the sense of 'pressed cloth'; and 'ware' is a term for a piece of merchandise, transferred to women ('applied jocularly', as in the contemporary 'bit of stuff'; further applied to 'the privy parts of either sex' (OED 4b, 4c)). But it is also, etymologically, 'be on careful guard', wariness, with subsidiary meanings of war and wear (out). Most obviously what is purchased is not worth what has been paid for it; but there is a running counter-suggestion that it is the war, wariness, and wearing out that mangles the mind and proves too high a 'price'.

Desire is initially known in terms of a kind of future perfect recrimination ('I will have suffered'), which then switches to a more orthodox tense. 'Who should my mind to higher things prepare': for all the powerful resonance of the line it remains uncertain whether it is a rhetorical question or regulative imperative. In 'Leave me, O Love', the 'mind' also 'aspires' to 'higher things', but here it is difficult to shake off the possible innuendo: compare 'I crav'd the thing which ever she denies' (63.6). The antecedent to 'who' is presumably the narrator talking of preparing his own mind, but the force of 'thou' makes it almost reproachful, expecting 'desire' to perform as well as to necessitate the preparation. Similarly, desire seems rebuked for having been too long asleep. Line seven may be read as 'me asleep who should...', but equally as 'thou hast brought me sleep'. 'Brought' seems to demand some locative or at least further detail (to ruin); it is again tempting to read a-sleep as a retrospective object, which would introduce an element of post-coital fulfilment. Desire that brings deep relaxation must be happy, fulfilling, though other possible readings are 'you have brought me to a state in which I long while asleep', or 'to a state in which the longing for higher things is asleep'.

Now there is a shift into a powerfully verbal mode to describe what desire has failed to do – seeking, making, kindling 'in vaine'. 'Vain things', though contrasted with 'higher', become dangerously close to a synonym, particularly when qualified by 'aspire'. The lesson taught by virtue recedes into a far-off past (with a homophone on bitter/better), and the 'onlie hire', reward, commission, within the self is at least as much pathetically solitary as nobly self-sufficient.

'How to kill desire' becomes the prescription and description of the poem, looping back to the beginning. It initially appears that it must be summoned and apostrophised in order to be repudiated. But the stoicism of 'within my selfe', apparently endorsed by 'Desiring nought', is immediately undercut: to 'still' desire might be more appropriate than the exaggerated aggression of 'kill'. 'Desiring nought' asserts a continuous state of attraction towards the 'nothing' which may also be the 'fair thought that lies between maids' legs' (*Hamlet* III.ii.108–16); the only counter-impulse being 'how to kill desire' (the future intent is announced as a self-fulfilling prophecy). The more denunciation, the more satisfaction, hence more invocation of the force to be condemned. (Compare Greville: 'With two extremes so multiply the vice,/As neither partie satisfying other,/ *Repentance still becomes desires mother*' (*Caelica* 11. 12–14).)

Thus repression of desire becomes a form of desiring desire, and I now wish to examine the extent to which this structural principle may help illuminate Shakespeare's Sonnet 129.

> Th' expense of spirit in a waste of shame
> Is lust in action, and, till action, lust
> Is perjured, murd'rous, bloody, full of blame,
> Savage, extreme, rude, cruel, not to trust,
> Enjoyed no sooner but despised straight,
> Past reason hunted, and no sooner had,
> Past reason hated as a swallowed bait,
> On purpose laid to make the taker mad;
> Mad in pursuit, and in possession so,
> Had, having, and in quest to have, extreme,
> A bliss in proof, and proved, a very woe,
> Before a joy proposed, behind a dream.
>   All this the world well knows, yet none knows well
>   To shun the heaven that leads men to this hell.

The sonnet responds to the implicit question: what is lust. This, strikingly, is the sole usage of the term throughout the entire sequence, in the only one of Shakespeare's sonnets containing 'no personal or corresponding possessive pronouns'. (Sonnets 5, 68, and 94 use only third persons (Jakobson and Jones 1987: 202).) It is no one's lust in particular, not my or your or even his or her lust, but lust in general. (The impact of the immediately subsequent line, 'My mistress' eyes are nothing like the sun' (130.1), comes not so much from the bathos of its pert inversion, as from the reintroduction of both a possessor ('my') and an object ('mistress') of desire.) The declarative vehemence appears to be propositional, demonstrative, an 'absolute statement' that lust is 'vorticose, centripetal, obsessive' (Kerrigan 1986: 57).

Interpretation of Sonnet 129 hinges on the authority of its conclusions, whether it has the right to define. Some critics have been led to suspect that it is little more than a set-piece declamation, a bravura rhetorical exercise. Thomas Wilson's *Arte of Rhetorique* (1553) has been cited as a probable source (Peterson 1965), on the somewhat less than conclusive grounds that it outlines 'the main grammatical schemes employed' (antithesis, amplification, synonymia, gradation, regression, homioteoleuton (same endings), traduction (words of the same root but with different endings)); contains comparable exempla (such as 'Lust hath overcome shamefastness, impudence hath overcome feare, and madnesse hath overcome reason'); and offers a free translation of Petronius's *Foeda est in coitu et brevis voluptas* ('If man do any filthy thing and take pleasure therein:/the pleasure goeth away, but the shame tarrieth still').

The most powerful counter-reading, originating in Richard Levin, and powerfully amplified by Helen Vendler, treats the sonnet as a dramatic monologue. According to Levin, the opening quatrain is an 'outburst of disgust', an 'unqualified condemnation of the entire act of lust'. In the second, the speaker is 'reacting to that reaction', leading to a comparative muting as 'inner turmoil has also decreased': in the third, we get a 'definite weakening of the emotional stresses 'and a 'corresponding increase in the intellectual mastery of the experience'. The 'diminuendo' is reflected in the appearance of 'bliss', 'joy' and 'heaven' which counterbalance and eventually exceed 'woe'. The final couplet is not a 'conclusion' but a 'denouement', a 'form of rationalisation both before and after the fact', a means of 'assuaging his guilt' and 'establishing in advance an excuse for surrendering anew to the same temptation' (Levin 1965: 175–81).

For Vendler, 'what masquerades as description of an impersonal essence (lust) is in fact a description of an action by a personal subject' (1973: 184n). 'Wonderment and perplexity . . . supervene over guilt' in a movement 'from violent self-blame, "past reason" to an 'equally violent blame of an unspecified other', and then to eventual arrival at 'an implied ethical norm of temperance' (1973: 191–2). 'Shakespeare is showing us that we over-react with self-disgust after, just as we over-reacted to desire before' (1973: 186): the sonnet's 'progressive evolution of thought' (1973: 182) offers a kind of therapeutic expulsion of hostility preceding mature acceptance. I will return to this reading later, but at this point it is sufficient to note that the apparent ease with which the sonnet becomes 'an easily understood dramatic situation' (Levin 1965: 175) is purchased at the cost of dubiously normative assumptions about human behaviour. Most obviously, it is simply assumed that the speaker is masculine ('how the lustful man *feels*' (Vendler 1973: 184)) while elsewhere according a universal applicability to the experience. Second, if, as we are assured, 'the course of feeling enacted in the sonnet seems common enough: self-loathing, repentance for the self-interest and ruthlessness of desire' (Vendler 1973: 192), the question still remains of the necessity and significance of revulsion. In his review of Jakobson's analysis, I. A. Richards could be seen as calling the poem's bluff simply by raising the question of whether the poem would be simply morbid if 'lust' was replaced by sex (1970: 589).

'Lust' must inhere in a subject, as a faculty or emotion. It retains the characteristics of both a transcendent principle and somatic impulse. The poem exudes an odd sense of transparency, of the collapse of distinction between physiological and mental states. The 'spirit' that claims insight is itself subject to 'lust in action', the continuous process of 'expense' and 'waste': the ostensible subject necessarily infiltrates the mode of its delivery. It would be necessary to speak from not merely a post-coital but a post-mortem perspective (that assumed by Sidney's 'Leave me, O love'), for its prudential maxims, on its own premises, to be effectual. (This stance is frequently adopted towards the youth, for example 'If thou survive my well-contented day' (32.1; see also 71 and 72).) Instead retrospection is flattened out into a continuous plane or tableau. Time-divisions are blurred by the undifferentiated use of the past participle; 'enjoyed' is presumably prior to 'despised', but the terms have an existential concurrence because of their apparent syntactic identity. The conflated participles make all phases of experience seem equally past, producing what Vendler aptly describes as the poem's 'magisterial distance' (1973: 185).

'The poem admits no other finites than the third person singular of the present tense' (Jakobson and Jones 1987: 203), with a resultant pressure on nouns to contain discrepant temporal possibilities. The complexity, or perhaps awkwardness, comes from this interplay between disjunction and synonymity and the condensation of subject–verb–object into a single semantic unit. In the quatrains most of the substantives are related to verbs (Jakobson and Jones 1987: 211); expanse, spirit (lat. *spirare*), waste, action, bait, taker, pursuit, possession, quest, proof. Throughout the poem it is difficult to stabilise the etymological force of nouns which refer to conditions that themselves undergo change. (The static parataxis of the first four lines of Sidney's 'Desire' sonnet has the similar effect of activating the latent verbal force of terms such as 'blind', 'marke', 'fool', and 'snare'.)

The opening phrase combines semen with soul, the emission of the one implying a literal reduction, diminishment of the other. 'The expense of spirit' occurs, therefore, at the expense of spirit, thereby betraying 'My nobler part to my gross body's treason' (151. 6). Soul mutely seeps out of the body whereas seminal fluid controls the faculty of reason. (Compare the famous lines, 'Then were not summer's distillation left/A liquid pris'ner pent in walls of glass' (5. 9–10), where the homophone on still, steel, distil throughout the sonnets simultaneously suggests dissolution and entrapment.)

'In a waste of shame' sets up similar problems of foreshortened causality: 'in' takes on a locative, bodily sense, the actual spirting of 'spirit'. No hint is given of irrigating 'a waste or desert land' (OED 1), only 'a wasting of the body by disease' (OED 9c); 'to flow away as to be useless' (OED 10); and 'refuse; useless byproduct (OED 11). There is a further connotation of being '*unclassed* by lust' (Greene 1982: 148), a more pragmatic homily based on an empty-pockets, morning-after scenario. (Compare *Lear* II.i.100: 'To have th' expense and waste of his revenues'.) The play on waist and vast sets the boundlessness of the one against the mincing, petite quality of the other ('Down from the waist they are centaurs,/Though women all above' (*Lear* IV.vi.124–5)). Ejaculation into the female body opens up a purgatorial expanse of let-down, an afterwards. (The resonance of such phrases as 'among the wastes of time' (12.10), 'my dear time's waste' (30.4), and 'waste blanks' (77.10), is nicely caught in Eliot's lines from 'Burnt Norton': 'Ridiculous the waste sad time/Stretches before and after' (Eliot, 1969).) Like 'expense', 'shame' exists in different temporal dimensions: as a continuous constraint or a specific consequence, a prohibition to preserve chastity or the after-effects of violation. It also acquires a causal status: the shamefulness that prompts desire, and which is perversely sought through it. Thus the opening line can be read in terms of either parallelism or chiasmus: 'expense' becomes 'waste' so 'spirit' becomes 'shame'; 'expense' is a 'shame' so 'spirit' is a 'waste'.

'Lust in action' appears to specify the very instant of enactment: 'till', however, initiates a temporal move to a prior state. The sonnet see-saws between 'before' and 'behind', 'no sooner' and 'straight', with the point of actual coincidence ever more elusive. 'The effacement of the functional limit between adjectives and adverbs' (Jakobson and Jones 1987: 209) has the effect of reducing temporal qualifiers to syntactically aligned states, with the verbal force of nouns.

Even prior to consummation, lust intervenes vigorously in a wide variety of cultural spheres. 'Perjured' (linking with the later 'purpose' and 'proposed') gives a curious sense of already having betrayed an oath before it has been given: 'not to trust' in the widest possible range of human bonds. The fourth line can be read as a possible narrative sequence: broken vows produce violent thoughts leading to a gory outcome demanding inevitable recrimination. Subsequent epithets refer more to states of mind, continuous qualities: 'savage' links to 'waste'; 'extreme' back to 'expense' and also to the use of chiasmus throughout the sonnet. 'Rude' takes us back to 'waste', lack of civility, but also hints at a lack of literary elegance, and perhaps more interestingly lack of sexual experience (inexpert, unskilled). 'Cruel' is appropriated from a Petrarchan idiom (compare Sonnet 131, 'Those whose beauties proudly make them cruel'), and restored to brutality and malice. 'Full of blame' might perhaps be blameworthy, but also suggests the attribution of guilt to justify subsequent abuse. As with the uses of 'extreme', there is a complex self-reflexivity with regard to the poem's own adoption of a stance of 'blame'.

Violence and retaliation may seem primarily male prerogatives; but, as Vendler says, 'they presuppose a victim' (1973: 183). 'Enjoyed', by synesis, introduces the person enjoyed as an extra inferential object, taken up in 'despised' (suggesting that, once lust is satisfied, the person driven by it despises himself, the passion, and the recipient of his desire). Although technically governed by 'is', a verbal force is introduced into the sentence at this point. 'Hunted' breaks the sequence of predicates, applying not to 'lust' itself but to the person lusted after. Again there is an overlay and a duplication: the reasons for pursuit merging with the object of pursuit. The tone has shifted from uncontrolled outburst to a kind of sensualised sophistry.

Jakobson and Jones comments that 'the sonnet has two topics – the lust and the luster': the woman who is the object of lust, it is claimed, 'is neither mentioned nor intimated in the sonnet' (1987: 211, 214). Yet the female body remains a vestigial presence throughout the poem, implicitly called forth by the implacable sequence of coital verbs, 'Had, having, and in quest to have' grimly equated with 'hunted', 'had', and 'hated'. The absent feminine that arouses this response is simultaneously repudiated by it: the incitement, the occasion, and the receptacle of desire. There is a lurking image of the female body as a trap, tempting and then engulfing, 'full of' semen and therefore 'blame' (linked to 'waste of shame' by the only grammatical rhyme in the poem (Jakobson and Jones 1987: 199)). The 'taker' is the first specific agent to emerge out of the succession of epithets, but, as Jakobson and Jones point out, like the 'men' of the final couplet, one who undergoes rather than acts (1987: 206), and who, though implicitly active in the sense of possessing sexually, in swallowing the 'bait' is himself swallowed. A 'swallowed bait' might simply refer to the person who inspires lust: the subsequent 'on purpose', however, implies an anterior intelligence even if the woman is regarded as having 'laid' herself (down, open). There is a problem of displaced agency, a kind of internal disjunction within the sonnet that produces its peculiarly feverish energy.

The idea of centring is crucial to Jakobson and Jones's attempt to assimilate the peculiarly elusive and disconcerting reading experience that the sonnet offers to its 'essentially homogeneous and firm thematic construction' (1987: 202). This is supported not merely by enumerating parallels between various combinations of quatrains and couplet, but also 'the first seven centripetal afferent lines, moving in a direction toward the center of the entire poem, and the further seven, centrifugal efferent lines, proceeding in a direction away from its center' (1987: 199). (Richards goes so far as to mark the point (after 'laid') with a large black dot.) In its own way this apex, pivot, would be 'the inalterable essence of the depicted passion', both comprehending and coinciding with desire, 'certain o'er incertainty,/Crowning the present, doubting of the rest' (115. 11–12). Such a closure is only achieved at the cost of disregarding the failure to encapsulate the moment of desire on a syntactic level. The failure of centring leads, I contend, to the instatement of an always prior motivation from which the text derives its power.

The search for a pivotal moment between 'in pursuit' and 'in possession' recommences. The so/woe rhyme, repeated from 127, attempts to close the semantic space of 'had, having, and in quest to have'. The repetition of 'extreme', however, militates against any identifiable point of repose, and instead separates out into 'joy proposed' and 'dream'. If one is so reckless as to trust Thorpe's 1609 punctuation, 'proud' has the sexual sense of pride, but also the momentary pathos of achievement, pivotally situated between 'in proof' and 'wo' (possibly 'wo(man)). The legalistic, almost forensic, 'a bliss in proof', is immediately reversed in 'proved a very woe'. Throughout the sonnets, the terms proof, prove, approve, reprove, continually straddle the experiential and judicial: 'Suff'ring my friend for my sake to approve her' (42.8); 'desperate now approve' (147.7); and most significantly, 'merits not reproving' (142.4) where denouncing involves retempting, re-experiencing. There is also the strikingly ambiguous temporality of 'in proof', as both anticipation and verification of experience already undergone; though adversarial, part of the suasive exhortatory rhetoric, it relegates its own explanations to compensatory fantasy, 'When love converted from the thing it was,/Shall reasons find of settled gravity' (49.7–8). The insight is 'past reason' both in claiming an insight so fundamental as to surpass it, and involving an excessive, irrational degree of repudiation. 'Reason' has also been 'hunted' in self-justification, and the term retains the predatory sense of that which reason hunts, allying it with the 'murd'rous' qualities of lust.

Lust and reason are not opposites but complementary, prospective and retrospective; reason (tinged by the repetition of 'past') is a summoning and re-enactment, justified as penitence, self-recrimination, but actually serving to intensify the original sensation, a means to 'spend/Revenge upon myself with present moan' (149.7–8). The sonnets to the youth possessed the comparative stability of a displaced visionary presence. Here there is only a kind of self-generating momentum internal to the utterance. It does not stay within a formal system of inversion, but produces a power of accusation which becomes its constitutive feature. Lust fuels itself by a kind of prospective regret, for a future that one has accepted responsibility for and yet sees as wholly predetermined. This produces the animus in excess which is the eroticism of the poem: the very condition of its expression is frenzied capitulation.

As in Spenser's 'Trust not', humanity is specifically gendered as 'men' in the final couplet. It has an obvious air of summation: it has no adjectives (except 'this'), participles, indefinite articles and relational verbs, and contains the only plurals and relative clause of the poem. Its four present tense verbs seem designed to provide a kind of timeless vantage outside of the temporality of 'lust'. 'All this the world well knows', a variant of the 'wide world's common place', must be brought into relation with the subsequent admission 'yet none knows well'. Is the voice of the narrator identified or opposed to that of the 'world': does the sonnet propound proven truth or worthless truism? If 'lust in action' necessitates an experiential deception, but one to which all men are addicted, it seems the poem can do nothing other than reiterate the impossibility of imparting its own conclusions. The very claim to the authority of personal experience, articulation of what has been proved on the pulses, entails not merely the secondariness but the irrelevance of its own message.

Vendler protests that in Jakobson and Jones 'the linearity of the poem is lost sight of and the many small points of suspense and climax ignored' (1973: 198). Yet her own gloss, 'finally that we will do it all over again if the occasion arises, that desire is unteachable' (1973: 193), is remarkably close to his insistence that 'the semantic leitmotif of each strophe is one of tragic predestination' (1987: 204). The first strophe characterises lust; the second gives passive participles and final taker; the third uses active participles to depict the taker's behaviour and brings forward images of lust as the object of his strivings. It is tempting to assimilate the sonnet to a biological determinacy of moral guilt, the belief in 'general evil' enunciated in 'All men are bad and in their badness reign' (121: 14).

It should be noted, however, that despite the final 'hell', there is no direct equation of 'lust' and sin in the poem. Jakobson's claim is based more specifically on the parallelism of 'taker' and 'men' implying a comparable setter of 'bait': 'both personal nouns (taker, men) characterize human beings as passive goals of extrinsic nonhuman and inhuman actions' (1987: 206). Even the 'taker' is a victim, and 'the final centrifugal line brings the exposure of the malevolent culprit, the heaven that leads men to this hell' (1987: 204). So thematically this is possible if questionable: strophic parallelism precludes taking 'heaven' as a direct antithesis to 'hell', pleasure as opposed to suffering. (Levin's reading is particularly strong on the linkage of 'heaven' to the implicitly positive 'blisse in proof', 'ioy proposed' and 'dream', in contrast to Jakobson's reductive gloss of 'dream' as 'phantom' (1987: 202), a physically impossible ambition ('as recalled by an exhausted male'), supported by Lucrece (211-2); 'A dream, a breath, a froth of floating joy'.

The benefits of structural analysis lie not in demonstrated symmetries, whose ultimate significance may be questionable, but in its residue: what remains recalcitrant. Where the verbal proliferation of the Graves–Riding analysis culminates in the somewhat feeble conclusion 'that lust is all things at all times' (1929: 71), Jakobson's analysis precisely delineates how the claim to objective authority is produced and the moments at which a rhetorical excess not so much destabilises as ultimately reinforces it. The very determination to define the centre of the poem exposes its recessive motivation.

'On purpose layd' sets up a similar conundrum to 'bait' in the Spenser sonnet. If women are intrinsically rather than tactically deceitful, who lays the 'poisoned bait' of female sexuality to begin with? The question is whether the teleological vacuum of that which decides that the 'swallowed bait' shall be 'on purpose layd' inheres in the female or stands behind her. The structure of apostrophe, explicit in Spenser, latent in Shakespeare, remains broadly comparable. There is no blame for the sorceress as such, but instead a kind of stoic acquiescence in the cyclic predestination – 'the heaven that leads men to this hell' – that serves as a prior motivating force. Barnfield can offer the eschatologically stable and morally reassuring conclusion that 'Love is a fiend, a fire, a heaven, a hell;/Where pleasure, paine and sad repentance dwell' (33: 13–4). In Shakespeare, as in Sidney, the very terms of indictment are implicated in that which they denounce. Jakobson acutely spots the congruence between 'swallowed' and 'knows well' (Jackson and Jones 1987: 207), and to 'shun' recalls both 'hunted' and 'sooner', with a play on ' (s)hun t(he)' reminiscent of Sidney's 'fond fancies (s)cum'.

In this chapter, I hope to have substantiated a claim made in my introduction: that generically considered, there is much greater cross-over between lyric and satire than usually assumed. Even the most apparently impersonal and didactic of the sonnets contains within itself a structure of apostrophic address: it summons that which it simultaneously denies and repudiates. Shakespeare, or his narrator in the sonnets if one prefers, does not so much condemn what he desires, but desires in the form of condemnation.

In my next chapter, however, I shall examine a different and more contestatory relation between private and public desire in the poetry of Rochester.

3

'SOMETHING GENROUS IN MEER LUST'?

Rochester as Libertine

Given Rochester's undisputed status as 'one of the dirtiest poets in the canon' (Porter 1982: 61), one might have thought any sustained consideration of his work would at some point involve detailed analysis of the issue of misogyny. This has not, however, proved to be the case. It is not that feminist criticism has neglected his writing: in the last twenty years, Fabricant (1974), Wilcoxon (1979), Wintle (1982) and Nussbaum (1984) have all provided illuminating commentaries. Yet compared to the attention devoted to the niceties of satiric form or the problems of textual attribution, this aspect of his work has suffered at least comparative neglect.

The issues involved appear to have been regarded as simultaneously too self-evident and too problematic. The general impression given is that Rochester has been too readily indulged by his proponents and too easily dismissed by his detractors, and that both parties have tended to rest their respective cases upon the more restricted question of obscenity. Yet even the infamous question, 'Whether the *Boy* fuck'd you, or I the Boy', ('The Disabled Debauchee' (40)) looks positively anodyne in comparison to the physiological explicitness of Dorset's 'strange incestuous stories/ Of Harvey and her long clitoris' ('Colon' (44–5)), or claims that Mulgrave's 'feeble tarse' could only be stirred by 'a straight well-sphincter'd arse' ('A Faithful Catalogue of our most Eminent Ninnies' (112–13)). As Dustin Griffin observes, 'his obscenity and misogyny are mild when compared to Oldham or Robert Gould or a number of anonymous Restoration satirists' (1988: 55). Barbara Everett finds the presence of these terms evidence of 'a betrayal of human sense and meaning to mere grunting phatic gesture' (1982: 22); perhaps, but they may equally well be seen as part of the Royal Society ideal of purifying the dialect of the tribe. As Defoe observed, not disapprovingly, 'As they conceiv'd lewdly, so they wrote in plain *English*' ([1722] in Farley-Hills 1972: 192).

Rochester may not be quite as briskly common-sensical as Suckling ('As for her Belly, 'tis no matter, so/There be a Belly, and a Cunt, below' ('The Deformed Mistress' (27–8)), but there is still little sense of uneasy lingering on threatening physicality. A line such as 'A thing whose bliss depends upon thy will' ('The Discovery' (23)) seems almost to disdain innuendo (see Farley-Hills 1978: 45); and even 'Her hand, her foot, her very look's a *Cunt*' ('The Imperfect Enjoyment' (18)) is more concerned with the naming of parts than demonisation of the female body. Rochester, unlike Dryden, shows no inclination to 'cry cunt' in order to 'friske his frollique fancy' ('An Allusion to Horace' (74)). Instead there is a kind of tactile empiricism concerned to define the qualities of the object at hand. Rochester's 'And a Cunt has no sence of conscience or law' ('Against Marriage' (8)) makes the same play as Shakespeare's 'Love is too young to know what conscience is' (151.5); but without an equivalent erotic charge of phonetic decomposition: 'con-science', 'con-sense', 'cunt-sense' (see Booth 1977: 525–6). Rochester is equally disinclined to extend the trope in the manner of Oldham's 'Her conscience stretch'd, and open as the Stews' ('A Satyr upon a Woman' (85)). Elusiveness within a formulaic diction is far more characteristic than lurid or surreal metaphoric extrapolation.

Sexual explicitness must be seen not as a regrettable occasional blemish in Rochester's poetry but as one of its chief attractions. The phenomenon is, however, by no means a simple one. The powerful misogynistic elements would lead one to expect a reinforcement of masculine authority, covert or explicit strategies of dominance: 'And therefore what they fear, at heart they hate' ('A Satyr against Reason' (45)). Yet this is not supported by the history of reception. The '*Lady*' in 'Timon' famously 'Complain'd our love was course, our *Poetry*,/Unfit for modest Eares' (102–3); the 'Prologue' to *Sodom* declares, 'I do presume there are no women here/'tis too debauch'd for their fair sex I fear' (p. 3); and Robert Wolseley felt obliged to insist 'neither did my *Lord Rochester* design those Songs the *Essayer* is so offended with . . . for the Cabinets of Ladies' (1685: 21). Nevertheless, of an admittedly sparse documentary record, female readers from Aphra Behn to Barbara Everett have proved singularly undeterred by this aspect of his work, and willingly heeded the opening address of 'Signior Dildo': 'You Ladyes all of Merry England' (1).

There must, I would argue, be 'something Genrous in meer lust' in Rochester's poetry ('A Ramble in Saint James's Park' (98)) for this response to be possible. In order to locate and define this quality, I wish to look first at his work in the context of anti-feminist satire, and generic inversion of lyric. I will go on to assess the degree of 'progressiveness' in his libertinism, in the context of recent models of homosocial bonding; and then conclude by analysing his distinctive plaintiveness and vulnerability, and exploring some of the paradoxes of the truth of the failure of the body in his verse.

Rochester's most visible satiric antecedents lie in French libertinism, notably Boileau, but a strong case can be made for his work as a key confluence of these predominantly neoclassical models with the native tradition of declamatory abuse stemming from Marston to Oldham. 'The baton', as Porter infelicitously remarks, 'never went through Dryden' (1982: 58), whose work lacks both the finesse and unpredicable intensities of these acts of verbal violence sublimated into conversational facility.

The 'grave discourse/Of who Fucks who and who does worse' ('A Ramble in Saint James's Park' (1–2)) may appear self-cancellingly oxymoronic, but Rochester's satiric voice can rise to an almost Johnsonian force, particularly in its use of prosopopoeia. A line such as 'And Dissobedience ceace to please us' ('A Ramble in Saint James's Park' (150)) combines a suavity of antinomian hedonism with an unillusioned summation of human perversity. 'Youth in her lookes, and pleasure in her bed' ('A Letter from Artemiza' (196)) may be compared to Gray's 'Youth on the prow, and Pleasure at the helm' ('The Bard' (74)): social naturalism and allegorical voyage converge in their *frisson* of transience and premonition of inevitable loss. In 'But we, poor Slaves to hope and fear,/Are never of our Joys secure' ('The Fall' (9–10)), 'Slaves' brings in a note of *précieux* gallantry, 'secure' a typically protective enclave, and the lilt precludes the sobriety of, say, Johnson's 'On the Death of Dr. Robert Levet'. Yet 'hope', 'fear', and 'Joys' offer themselves as, if not inductive generalisations, then still psychological presences of collective intelligibility. For all the deceptive lightness of formulation, there is always an epistemological claim to sentimental lyric in Rochester.

There is no declared or fixed standard of valuation: even if one selects 'generosity' as a key term it is defined customarily in terms of its present absence, that which human beings are unable to fulfil. Artemiza's famous 'Love, the most gen'rous passion of the mynde' (40) is hedged around by ironies of tone and delivery which accentuate the fragility of the satisfaction envisaged. If her discourse exhibits 'some graynes of Sense/Still mixt with Volleys of Impertinence' (256–7), it is this very discrepancy which imparts such a unique value to the 'Cordiall dropp' which must make the otherwise 'nauseous draught of life goe downe' (44).

One does not read Rochester expecting condemnation as a stable and conscious stance: instead there are momentary intensities of denigration. He might be dubbed a writer of philosophical lyric and satiric epiphany. Gilfillan found in Rochester a 'gross anomaly' between 'a severe castigator of public morals and of private character' and 'a naked satyr who gloried in his shame' (1856: 20): but, as his phrasing suggests, an essential continuity exists between the two attitudes. (Significantly, 'satyr' is virtually the only term Vieth chooses not to modernise in his edition of the poems (1968: xlvi).)

It will be helpful to glance at the Elizabethan satirist, John Marston, in order to clarify the relation of the satyr to the satirist who 'Takes pleasure, in displeasing sharp controule' ('In Proemium' (8)). His 'Certain Satyrs' and 'Scourge of Villanie' [both 1598] are delivered by the persona of Kinsayder, the term for a castrated dog. The uncouth vehemence of his fulminations is explicitly compensatory: to 'shake a Satyrs knottie rod' combines masturbatory with aggressive overtones (SV 2.38). 'Who'le coole my rage? who'le stay my itching fist' (SV 2.9), and the outpouring of clotted verbosity itself becomes synonymous with sexual release: 'Yon Pine is fayre, yet fouly doth it ill/To his owne sprouts, marke, his rank drops distill/Foule Naples canker in their tender rinde' (SV 1.20–2). 'When inundation of luxuriousnes,/Fatts all the world with such grosse beastlines', it is demanded, 'Who can abstaine? what modest brain can hold,/But he must make his shamefac'd Muse a scold?' (SV 3.140–3). The act of scourging is also the act of summoning. This tumescence of invective seeks to 'plow/The hidden entrails of ranke villanie' ('In Proemium' (16–17)). When eventually 'rage is spent', the satirist may assume a post-coital lassitude: 'So haue I seen the fuming waue to fret,/And in the end, naught but white foame beget' (CS 4.16–18).

Aspects of this persona are immediately visible in Rochester. 'An

Allusion to Horace' claims that 'A Jeast in Scorne, poynts out, and hits the thing,/More home, than the Morosest Satyrs Sting' (28–9), but both modes are similarly constitutive of and constituted by their object of abuse. Timon, for example, is introduced with an inquiry whether 'thou droop'st after a Nights debauch' (1); and in 'The Disabled Debauchee', the speaker meditates from the vantage of '*Days* of Impotence' (13), though in a tone of generous solidarity rather than flailing castigation. In 'The Epilogue (to Circe)', the 'Malitious Criticks" those 'Who Envy Pleasure, which they cannot taste', are motivated by 'Impotence': but to 'have no Joy but spite' is itself no minor gratification (4, 12–15). (Gilbert Burnett's memoir of Rochester's death-bed conversion records him remarking that 'a man could not write with life, unless he were heated by Revenge' (1680: 26).)

'Fair Chloris in a Piggsty lay' may be seen as continuous with the recurrent injunction in anti-feminist satire to penetrate the boudoir's inner space: in Rochester's poem, however, the reader's voyeuristic intrusion is implicated and undermined. The ambivalence of Felicity Nussbaum's comment is significant: 'the reader may catch himself sharing the antifeminist sentiment, and wishing, perhaps with Chloris, that the rape had taken place' (1984: 62). Whose fantasy is this? The male reader's of assaulting Chloris, the female reader's of being assaulted, or the male reader's fantasy of the female fantasy of being assaulted? Does this express male desire for female submission; male fear of female self-sufficiency; or celebration of natural impulse in whatever form ('Nature thus kindly eas'd' (37)). The final possibility is at least qualified by the presentation of the ejaculating male as a 'bosom Pigg . . . Who now expires hung in the Gate/That leads to Floras Cave' (13–15), a carcass bleeding to death in the female body. (Compare Milton's 'To roll with pleasure in a sensual sty' (*Comus* (77)), and also Blake's narrator in 'I saw a chapel all of gold', who 'turnd into a sty/ And laid me down among the swine' (15–16 E468).) Rochester's poem depicts a world whose deities, 'Not pleas'd by *Good* Deeds; nor provok'd by *Bad*' ('Lucretius' (6)), are singularly unconcerned with Chloris's pleasures or sufferings. Her masturbatory idyll, far from being a retreat from reality, is surely a preferable self-sustaining realm. The question is raised not whether she is better off without a lover, but whether she has no choice but one day to play it all through for real.

None of the generic continuities with anti-feminist satire are altogether straightforward, given Rochester's penchant for self-burlesque and what Hazlitt called 'his extravagant heedless levity' (1930–34: v.83). Perhaps a more profitable avenue to explore is the retention of an eroticised and substitutional relation to the object of abuse, which leaves the reader with the impression of female power enhanced rather than defeated. Nothing in Rochester's tirades is designed to last. One never comes away from his verse, even from the flytings, with a sense of reconfirmed authority. The passion is too contained within the utterance, the termination of voice too abrupt, too total.

John Oldham's 'A Satyr upon a Woman' offers an exemplary instance of forthright and sustained vilification:

> Grant my rank Hate may such strong poison cast,
> That ev'ry Breath may taint and rot and blast,
> Till one large Gangren quite orespread her Fame
> With foul Contagion, till her odious Name,
> Spit at and curst by evry Mouth like mine,
> Be Terror to her self and all her Line.   (46–51)

Here the roles of prosecutor, judge and executioner are all conflated as Oldham invokes the power of 'Contagion' in order to 'rhime her dead' (81). The display of unmotivated hatred is so far in excess of its ostensible target that its very perpetuation becomes the ultimate purpose of the poem. The speaker of Rochester's 'A Ramble in Saint James's Park', provoked by his mistress's infidelities, similarly pledges 'with all my Power/To plague this woman and undoe her' (151–2).

> May stinking vapours Choak your womb
> Such as the Men you doat upon
> . May your depraved Appetite
> That cou'd in whiffling fools delight
> Begett such frenzies in your Mind
> You may go mad for the North wind
> And fixing all your hopes upont
> To have him bluster in your cunt
> Turn up your longing Arse to the Air
> And perrish in a wild dispair   (133–42)

The power of the 'North wind' to 'bluster' is equalled by that of the narrator himself; and the 'frenzies' and the resultant 'wild dispair' are also evidently his own. Denunciation of the female body itself becomes a sexual act performed upon it: 'perrish' may be read in specifically erotic terms (compare 'perrish't in that first surprize' ('T'was a dispute' (9)). Yet the imperative, 'Turn up your longing Arse', possesses a homoerotic dimension; 'the Men you doat upon' applies to the narrator, obsessively ingratiating himself via the medium of his abuse. Corinna is denounced for an 'Appetite' which, though 'depraved', retains the capacity for 'delight' and to 'Begett'. In the later curses, 'I'le make her feel my scorn and hate/Pelt her with scandalls, Truth or lies' (156–7), the interchangeable nature of the terms underscores the indiscriminate and ineffectual nature of the abuse: momentary, impassioned, paradoxically ecstatic.

Rochester's passages of incomparably eloquent sexual antagonism, notably the final sections of 'A Ramble in Saint James's Park' and 'The Imperfect Enjoyment', also retain a close connection with the mode of inversion of 'On Mistress Willis' and 'By all *Loves* soft, yet mighty *Pow'rs*'. To give perhaps the most extreme example, 'Mock Song':

> I swive as well as others do,
> I'm young, yet not deform'd,
> My tender heart, sincere and true,
> Deserves not to be scorn'd.
> Why *Phillis* then, why will you swive,
> With *Forty Lovers* more?
> Can I (said she) with *Nature* strive,
> Alas I am, alas I am a Whore.
>
> Were all my body larded o're,
> With Darts of love, so thick,
> That you might find in ev'ry *Pore*,
> A well stuck standing *Prick*;
> Whilst yet my *Eyes* alone were free,
> *My Heart*, wou'd never doubt,
> In Am'rous Rage, and Exstasie,
> To wish those *Eyes*, to wish those *Eyes* fuckt out.

This might be taken as obscene parody, simple inversion of Scroope's original lyric, but this would be to underestimate the mobility of the poem's ironies. The declaration, 'alas I am a Whore', partakes of the Cretan liar paradox. I am a whore, therefore untrustworthy, therefore not to be believed: an honest proclamation of deceit. The 'Darts of Love' themselves might be emanating from rather than entering into: compare Cowley's 'Anacreontique: Beauty': 'They are *all weapon*, and they dart/Like *Porcupines* from every part' (19–20). The erotic potential of meat lies in the infinite penetrability of a body reduced to mere flesh, 'Larded o're' with semen and cooking fat, 'in ev'ry *Pore*'. (This is memorably exploited in Alina Reyes's *The Butcher* (1992); and also apparent in the term, 'meat-shot', in contemporary pornographic film-making (see Williams 1990).) An 'Am'rous Rage, and Exstasie' of multiple penetration is not necessarily exclusively female: in 'Song', the respective pleasures of speaker and mistress are not so much opposed as conflated: 'While I, my Passion to pursue/Am whole nights takeing in/The lusty Juice of Grapes, take you/The lusty Juice of Men' (20–4).

The most stunning volte-face, however, comes in the final line. The 'Eyes', which initially seem merely another available orifice, become those of the male narrator and audience. A more violent and by extension castratory reversal is difficult to imagine: 'To wish those *Eyes*, to wish those *Eyes* fuckt out'.

Ken Robinson, in 'The Art of Violence in Rochester's Satire', stresses this potency of abuse, but remains equivocal about whether this is a controlled effect or anguished outburst. Two antithetical propositions are delivered in close succession: there is a 'residual violence so strong that it seems to defy efforts to contain it'; and a 'spontaneous violence that tests to breaking point the strategies of containment' (1984: 94–5). The commentary as much as the poetry 'treads a tightrope over the seething torrents of raw vehemence' (1984: 106), in its desire that a primal nausea should be mitigated, shaped, and checked by ironic control. But one must query the either/or of this proposition. Whether regarded as personal or generic, this pattern of inversion, mutual accentuation, is crucial to the impact, and appeal, of the verse. The 'viciousness' is not 'held in check' but accentuated 'by the wit that focuses it' (1984: 105). We do not, I believe, flinch from this aggression, but are attracted towards it. The key question is whether it remains locked within a kind of internal self-abrasion, or whether it can be seen as part of a more intricate and productive set of textual relations.

I now wish to discuss this issue in relation to Rochester's lyric voice.

Rochester has regularly been seen as representing the culmination and expiry of cavalier and metaphysical lyric. But despite the occasional, if explicit, reminiscences and imitations of Cowley and Cleveland, there is no comparable sense of the end of the line: that, as Anne Righter puts it, 'all the words of love have already been used, and its possible attitudes exhausted' ([1967] 1988: 16).

Rochester undoubtedly employs a sentimental rhetoric which in any other context it would be difficult to regard as other than licensed, contained, and perhaps despised. The articulation of desire involves not a public intelligibility, but a private linguistic space, constituted by a shying away, a fleeing from, in a momentary stability of relinquishment. The power of a phrase such as 'make us blest at last' ('The Mistress' (36)) lies in its very attenuation. In 'A Letter from Artemiza', 'Love' is 'The softest refuge Innocence can fynde' (41); in 'A Ramble in Saint James's Park', a 'humble fond beleiving mee' longs to be 'Wrapt in security and rest' (108, 131); and even amongst the cosmological orotundities and throwaway vignettes of 'Upon Nothing' comes the unmistakable poignancy of 'And when reduc't to thee are least unsafe and best' (36). A Rochester lyric is not an assertion of power but a desire for powerlessness.

In 'Absent from thee', the lines, 'When wearied with a world of Woe,/To thy safe Bosom I retire' (9-10), have obvious infantile resonances, but perhaps more striking is their senescence, if not senility. 'Wearied' and 'retire' activate a kind of double bluff in the following lines: 'Where Love and Truth and Peace doth flow,/May I contented there expire' (11-12). 'Flow' implies not so much imbibe, breast to child, as flow out of, drain. The erotic sense of 'expire' is subordinated to the funereal, if not sepulchral, resonance of the final line: 'And lose my Everlasting rest' (16).

There is no ecstasy in Rochester: sexual pleasure tends to be present through its own negation. The 'Happy Minute' is inscribed within scenarios of transience, failure, that which will have been experienced (see Thormahlen 1993: 1, 29). The complex time-scheme of 'The Disabled Debauchee' posits a future nostalgia for the very past activities which will have compelled the present cessation of pleasure. Human beings are ontologically deluded, but momentarily entranced in Rochester, and the ultimate absence of transformative power does not detract from the value of the 'Joys' of these 'fleeting Dreams' ('Dialogue' (27)).

'Love and Life' famously asserts the impossibility of assertion. The speaker of the poem, unable to get a hearing *sub specie aeternitate*, must make do with a female auditor, whose status is both enhanced and superseded by his address. Yet she cannot serve as more than a momentary substitute. Constancy is as much a question of matter as of soul, of the reshufflings of atomic particles as the verbal proclamation of an emotional bond. (As the courtier Pricket proclaims in *Sodom*: 'yet I still desire/And turn my freezing atoms into fire' (III.i.27).) The sincerity of the pledge of love can only be guaranteed by restricting it to the almost infinitesimal point of the 'present Moment', which is 'all that Heav'n' (in the sense of both pagan destiny and sexual climax) 'allows' (8, 15). The poem is uttered from a stance which can invoke but never inhabit the 'livelong Minute' (14). Where Donne tersely proclaims 'let mee/ Allow her change, then change as oft as shee' ('Change' (25-6)), in Rochester, similar claims, '"tis Nature's Law to Change,/Constancy alone is strange' ('Dialogue' (31-2)), become not an authorisation but an appeal: 'be kinder then, for I,/Cannot change, and wou'd not dye' ('Song' (7-8)).

There is a residual argumentative framework, but none of Donne's 'masculine perswasive force' ('On his Mistris' (4)). There is no specific mistress, and the markers of courtship, assent, and consummation, are seldom visible. These are not poems of seduction: no attempt is made to emulate Sedley's 'prevailing gentle Art,/ That can with a resistlesse Charme impart,/The loosest wishes to the Chastest Heart' ('An Allusion to Horace' (64-6)).

Pleasure is not a realm, but a moment: a paradisal entrancement that leads not to bitterness and disillusion, but to a distinctively self-reflexive stoicism. Rochester does not deal in before and after, delusion and recrimination: certain kinds of rational structuring are almost eerily absent. 'To see a wretch pursuing,/In raptures of a blest amaze/His pleasing happy Ruin' ('Song' (2-4)) is not a narrative undergone by the speaker, who retains the capacity to speak from outside the frame. Yet the tone is anything but condemnatory: it remains an open question whether 'blest amaze' should be regarded as cheap at the price. The counter-possibility always remains of, as Artemiza puts it, 'The perfect Joy of being well deceaved' (115). 'Though all Mankinde/Perceave Us false', the 'searching Wisedome' is of little value since not merely illusion but also 'Wonder by cleare knowledge is destroy'd' (131-2, 108, 120). The same point is made more discursively in 'A Satyr against Reason': 'His wisdom did his happiness destroy,/Aiming to know that *World* he shou'd enjoy' (33-4).

In Swinburne, pain comes to stand for things other than itself: adoration, tribute, initiation. In Rochester, it has the brute recalcitrance of a raw sensation, but as such is no less gratefully received. 'I have some pleasure in my pain' ('Woman's Honor' (15)) becomes a means of authenticating rather than dispelling illusion. 'Sacred Jealousie' becomes the 'only Proof... We love, and do not dream' ('The Mistress' (25, 27–8)); 'False Pleasure' may be mistaken 'for true Love;/But Pain can ne'er deceive' (31–2). The speaker of 'Absent from thee' implores that his 'Fantastic mind may prove, in the sense of both approve and confirm the reality of 'The Torments it deserves to try' (6–7). The 'Torments' are deserved as both punishment for his desertion and reward for his resolution: thus 'To wish all Day, all Night to Mourn' (4) implies not successive states, but a continuous desire to lament.

In Rochester, there is a refusal of retrospection in favour of a simultaneous vantage of apartness. In 'A Satyr against Reason', the voice is not merely disenfranchised, but disembodied, positing its ideal state as 'A Spirit free, to choose for my own share,/What Case of Flesh, and Blood, I'd pleas'd to weare' (3–4)); in 'The Mistress' the narrator, 'no more a Soul but shade', continually 'haunts my Breast, by absence made/The living Tomb of Love' (9, 11–12); and the narrator of 'The Disabled Debauchee', characterises himself as 'the *Ghost*, of my departed *Vice*' (27). (The convention is taken up in numerous subsequent elegies of Rochester, for example Tom Durfey's 'A Lash at Atheists' ([1690] Farley-Hills 1972: 163–5).) There is a kind of absolute presentness to the voice: not merely 'Youth' but utterance itself is 'a stuff will not endure' (*Twelfth Night* II.iii.51): 'There's Time for Rest when Fate hath stopped thy Voice' ('To Love' (46)).

Yet this evanescent poignancy coexists alongside a biological determinism. It is predicted of Charles that 'thy Prick ... Will governe thee' (16–17); perhaps more strikingly the exhortation of 'On Mistress Willis' is directed not against female seduction but 'Against the Charms our *Ballox* have' (1). Women in contrast are 'Framed by some Cruel Powers above', the 'Gods' which 'ever place,/To guard the Glories of a Face,/A Dragon in the Heart' ('Pastoral Dialogue' (11, 18–20)). The result is an intractable conflict between desire for and possession of:

> Since she's insensible of Love,
> By Honour taught to hate,

If we, forc'd by Decrees above,
Must sensible to Beauty prove,
How tyrannous is Fate?
('Pastoral Dialogue' (26–30))

Female 'Honour' is treated as an imposition rather than an affectation. Artemiza's sharpest criticism is reserved for those women whose 'private wish obeys their publicke Voyce' (61, 66), and so 'Forsake the pleasure, to pursue the Vice' (61). An exasperated protest against cultural constraints as a 'forc'd disguise', under whose compulsion men as well as women lead 'a tedious life in Misery,/Under laborious, forced *Hypocrisie*' (150–2), is combined with a self-reflexive awareness that the definition offered by the poem itself contributes to this process of manufacture. ('Upon his leaving his mistress' leaves the same issue delicately poised: 'You whom some kinder *Pow'r* did fashion' (5).)

In comparison to the traditions in which Rochester may be situated, there is remarkably little scopophilia, blazoning of the body in anatomical inventory. There is no interest in concealment and exposure of the body, or fetishistic substitutes for it. 'With Mouth screwd up, conceited winking Eyes,/And Breasts thrust forward' in 'Tunbridge Wells' (110–11) is virtually the only descriptive vignette of a woman; and even here it is more than counterbalanced by the portrait of 'Sir Woud-be-Wit, whose bus'ness was to wooe' (95). As Pope observes ([1743] Osborn 1966: i, 471), Rochester does 'Characters of Men'. Satiric abuse is primarily directed at the male community ('None had modesty, enough to 'plaine,/Their want of Learning, Honesty and Braine' ('Tunbridge Wells' (59–60; see also 21, 50)), a point that I will develop later.

The powerful presence of women in the poems is seldom if ever directly described: they are appealed to, challenged or narrated, but not from a position of the stable mastery of a predatory gaze. In contrast to Cowley's sneer at 'Vain Idol-Gods that have no sense or mind' ('Women's Superstition' (14)), women think in Rochester. Chloris is 'full of harmless thought' ('Song' (1)); the Gods 'Make a sweet Form divinely Fair,/And add a Cruel Mind' ('Pastoral Dialogue' (24–5)); in 'A Ramble in Saint James's Park', Corinna, though denounced as a 'Whore in understanding' is still acknowledged to possess a 'Mind' (101, 136). Rochester offers a 'Fragment of a Satire' (rather than 'An Essay') 'on Men'. Ridicule is no longer an exclusively masculine prerogative: 'You Men would think it an ilnatur'd Jest,/Should we laugh at you when you did your best' ('Second Prologue' (7–8)). Artemiza possesses a 'discerning Witt' (164); in 'Fair Chloris', the 'swain' laments 'I am so abhorr'd by thee' (18); in 'The Fall', the narrator appeals 'Be you not so severe' (15). There is perhaps something suspiciously neat about the analogy repeatedly employed between '*Women* and *Men* of *Wit*' ('A Satyr against Reason' (37)): at best it is a tactical alliance, designed as much to emphasise the insecurity of wits as the oppression of women. Nevertheless there is no compunction in admitting the viewpoint of an arrogant, volatile, and defiant female desire: 'Woman-kind more Joy discovers/Making Fools, than keeping Lovers' ('Dialogue' (71–2)).

It remains to be resolved, however, whether this sensitivity to 'that meane submissivness wee finde/This ill-bred age has wrought upon woman-kinde' ('Fragment of a Satire on Men' (3–4)), amounts to any more than an accidental by-product of an underlying hostility. If there is a female voice, it may be restricted to Corinna's response to the fop's courtesy in 'A Ramble in Saint James's Park': 'Permitt me your fair hand to kiss;/When at her Mouth her Cunt cries yes' (77–8). In order to clarify this issue, it will now be helpful to examine the relative degree of 'progressiveness' of Rochester's libertinism.

The perennial problem of Rochester criticism has been to link his satirical and lyric modes; and Hobbesian individualism has regularly been invoked to perform this generic unification. The only truth is that provided by the none too reliable senses: the only legitimate ethics must be founded on their possibilities and limitations. In Lockian epistemology, awareness of the 'flying Houres ... Whose Images are kept in store/By Memory alone' ('Love and Life' (2, 4–5)) produces an imperative to conserve, hoard, protect a finite and dwindling 'stock of ideas': in fairly simplistic terms, a bourgeois philosophy of accumulation. The libertine recuperation of Hobbes, in contrast, provokes a spendthrift pursuit of immediate and intense sensation: 'The Pleasures of a Body, lam'd with lewdness,/A neer perpetual motion makes you happy' (*Valentinian* V.ii.61).

It has frequently been argued that the libertine ideal of mutually reciprocated desire ('For did you love your pleasure lesse,/You were not fit for me': 'Song' (19–20)) has implications for the social and political domain: as Sarah Wintle puts it, 'pleasure through sexual variety' may 'lead to an attitude which grants rights of equal pleasure and promiscuity to women' (1982: 134). This potentially emancipatory aspect is, however, embedded by and impeded in a matrix of reactionary attitudes. Rochester's poetry 'oscillates' (1982: 148) between the two, providing an empirical confirmation of their continued incompatibility.

Several immediate objections may be lodged against such an approach. First, it divests Rochester's poetry of cognitive status by treating it as a secondary manifestation of intellectual debates that precede it, and so reduces it to a merely symptomatic status. Second, the ameliorative nature of an atomistic individualism may be questioned. Even celebration of female sexual desire defines the gender in terms of an innate eroticism rather than an autonomous subjectivity. It requires immediate reconstitution in terms of contract, which in Hobbes simply underwrites an authoritarian *status quo*. It is simple enough to regard the variety of relations women have with men – sexual, familial, economic – as entered into at a formal if unspecified point. Hobbes may point out in *Leviathan* that 'If there be no Contract, the Dominion is in the Mother' ([1651] 1991:140), but this is surely one reason why one always seems to exist. Third, the relative equality of 'In Love 'tis equal measure' ('Song' (14)) relies on a fictitious balance, disregarding the actual financial and political status underlying the 'nice allowances of Love' ('A Ramble in Saint James's Park' (110)), such as those made by, for example, Rochester to his mistress, Elizabeth Barry. 'For none did e're soe dull, and stupid prove,/But felt a God, and blest his pow'r in Love' ('A Letter from Artemiza' (48–9)); but that 'pow'r' manifests itself in a variety of cultural forms unavailable to women.

Mastery is not so much absent in Rochester as reversible: to be enslaved is quite as appealing an option as to enslave, though the question of who ultimately stages the scenario remains. In 'Fair Chloris', the swain, although 'Lustfull', remains a 'Slave' (26). The language of decorous sado-masochism abounds in the early lyrics: 'To see my Tyrant at my Feet;/Whil'st taught by her, unmov'd I sit/ A Tyrant in my Turn' ('Pastoral Dialogue' (53–5)). 'Kindness' itself 'guilds the Lovers Servile Chaine/And makes the Slave grow pleas'd and vaine' ('Song' (15–16)). In 'Insulting *Beauty*', it is boasted, 'I triumph in my Chain' (14); and the speaker of 'The Discovery' goes so far as to regret 'dying' only because 'I must be no more your Slave' (44). In this context it is even possible to put a positive gloss on the power of the testicles to 'make a Man a Slave/ To such a Bitch as *Willis*' ('On Mistress Willis' (3-4)).

Mutuality, equality, in Rochester, tends to be achieved in terms of stand-offs, explicit negotiation, rather than persuasion, consummation. This need not be reduced, as Wintle does, to a 'bleak notion of contract: I use you, you use me' (1982: 155). There is an unusual (if not unprecedented) sense of considering one's mistress worth talking to even after sleeping with her. There is no influx of power through casual disparagement, in the manner characteristic of Donne (see Ricks 1988b: 33-69). Whatever hostility there is seems primarily self-directed, a point to which I wish to return.

Adult equals are by no means the automatic paradigms for sexual encounters. Rochester's erotic landscape is inhabited by a broad and varied cast, including Signior Dildo, the oceanic Duchess of Cleveland and a herd of grunting pigs. It is mistaken to presume condemnation of or repulsion from grotesquerie. There remains something uniquely calm, unflustered, practical, about the attitude of the 'Young Lady' towards her 'Ancient Lover', whatever the relative proportions of nature and 'Art' in the 'reviving hand' (25, 19). 'Her Teeth being rotten, she Smells best below'('Signior Dildo' (55)) is as permissible as 'Mee-thinkes I long, to smell you stinke of Wine' ('A Letter from Artemiza' (88)) within this social register. 'I'le write upon a double Clowt/And dipp my Pen in Flowers' ('Song' (7-8)) relishes rather than recoils from the menstrual cycle, and 'The savoury scent of salt swoln Cunt' ('A Ramble in Saint James's Park'(86)) is first and foremost tangily appealing. Even Timon's equation of beef and carrot with arse and dildo can acquire a momentary beauty: the sexual toy 'Which her small *Pillow* cou'd not so well hide,/But *Visiters*, his flaming Head espy'd' (81-2), acquires via 'flaming Head' an association with passion and renewal, and even perhaps a mythological resonance of the sun-god, Apollo.

In Rochester there is an unmisgivingness about a wide variety of sexual scenarios that extends far beyond the point of simple amoralism: 'Things must goe on in their Lewd naturall way' ('Fragment'). This quality has been much praised in Keats but usually in the context of amiably passive voyeurism. (Byron commented on 'Johnny Keats *p-s-a-bed* poetry' that 'such writing is a sort of mental masturbation – he is always fr-gg-g his own *Imagination*' ([1820] 1977: 200, 222).) There is little problem with autoeroticism within or outside the parameters of the text. The lines, 'There's a sweet soft

Page, of mine,/Does the trick worth *Forty Wenches*' ('Love a *Woman*' (15–6), not merely establishes a rate of exchange between rival objects of satisfaction, but offers the poem itself as a superior means of fulfilment to having to 'Drudge in fair *Aurelia's* Womb' (4). 'Frigging' is an activity in its own right, recounted wryly, fondly, and temperately. Compared to other by-products of the 'Fantastick mind' ('Absent from thee' (6)), it is undoubtedly benign: Chloris emerges 'Innocent and pleased' (40). Where Keats's proclamation 'even now,/A clammy dew is beading on my brow' (*Endymion* iii. 567–8) implies solitude and self-absorption, in Rochester the 'clammy joys' ('The Imperfect Enjoyment' (20)) seem to involve actual and specific modes of conduct.

Restoration anti-feminist satire habitually denounces women for both harbouring animal lust and then pretending to restrain it: 'Poor helplesse Woman, is not favour'd more/She's a sly Hipocryte, or Publique Whore' ('An Epistolary Essay' (95–6)). In Rochester, the *grande dame* becomes a figure of urgent self-gratification: in 'Mistress Knights Advice to the Dutchess of Cleavland in Distress for a Prick', despite the demurral, 'Though Cunt be not Coy, reputation is Nice', the Duchess states a forthright preference for being 'Fuct by Porters and Carmen/Than thus be abus'd by Churchill and German' (4, 11–12), a contest between female desire and male hypocrisy that recurs throughout Rochester. In 'Signior Dildo', 'Her Grace of Cleaveland,/Has Swallowed more Pricks than the Ocean hath Sand' (37–8), and so, as Claude Rawson points out, becomes a figure of enormous power, even grandeur (1985: 335–6). The court ladies of *Sodom*, the inimitable Fuckadilla and Cuntigratia, offer a similar proclamation of 'cunt's omnipotence' (IV.i.33): 'We who for pleasures and great joys were born' (Epilogue, 56).

The ethic of 'generosity' is espoused in numerous contexts: in addition to the 'something Genrous in meer lust', 'Be generous, and wise, and take our part' ('Second Prologue' (38)); be not 'Generous and grateful never' ('Dialogue' (26)); seek 'true gen'rous *Love*' ('Woman's Honor' (11)); praise those 'Whose Principles most generous are, and just' ('A Satyr against Reason' (125)); 'In a generous Wench theres nothing of Trouble' ('Against Marriage' (10)); and 'Love, the most gen'rous passion of the mynde' ('A Letter from Artemiza' (40)).

From here it would seem a short step to celebration of a universal principle of fecundity: the Lucretian Venus. This, it seems, is provided in 'Upon his leaving his Mistress':

> Whilst mov'd by an impartial Sense,
> Favours like *Nature* you dispense,
> With Universal influence.
>
> See the kind Seed-receiving Earth,
> To ev'ry Grain affords a *Birth*;
> On her no Show'rs unwelcome fall,
> Her willing *Womb*, retains 'em all,
> And shall my *Celia* be confin'd?
> No, live up to thy mighty *Mind*,
> And be the Mistress of *Mankind*. (12-21)

'Confin'd' expands beyond possession by an individual male ('To damn you only to be mine' (4)) to a vision of unlimited universal access. The problem, however, with such a celebration of impassive abundance is that the iconography cannot be kept on a solely mythological level: it must necessarily become involved in narratives of contact and estrangement. In 'Song', 'She's my delight, all Mankinds wonder;/But my Jelous heart would break,/Should we love one day asunder' (14–16), the speaker fears being 'asunder' from 'Mankind' as much as from his mistress. To be included is always to be included alongside, amongst: the most forceful assertion of female autonomy is simultaneously the strongest confirmation of the social bond between men. Thus the 'Mistress of *Mankind*' (typically endowed with a 'mighty *Mind*') fuses personal with cultural libido: 'By merit, and by inclination,/The joy at least of one whole *Nation*' (6–7). Or, more crudely, 'Each Man had as much room, as *Porter, Blunt*, /Or *Harris*, had, in *Cullens*, Bushel Cunt' ('Timon' (93–4)).

A graphic illustration of this process can be found in Sedley's 'In the Fields of Lincoln Inn', attributed to Rochester in *Poems on Several Occasions* (1680), the first compilation of his verse. Phillis, faced with two gallants, acts decisively: '*Coridon's* Aspiring Tarse, she fitted/To her less frequented *Arse*' while Strephon 'into her *Cunt* she thrust':

> Now for Civil Wars prepare,
> Rais'd by fierce intestine Bustle.
> When these Heroes meeting Justle
> In the Bowels of the Fair.

> Nature had 'twixt *Cunt* and *Arse*
> Wisely plac'd firm separation,
> God knows else what desolation
> Had insu'd from warring *Tarse.*

The female body both allows contact and preserves 'separation' between men. A more contemporary example of this communalising function would be Gloria's declaration in *The Devil in Miss Jones* whilst similarly circumstanced: 'can you feel his cock against yours can you feel it' (cited McClintock 1992: 126).

The nearest equivalent in Rochester is undoubtedly the middle section of 'A Ramble in Saint James's Park', a conjunction of satiric commentary on sexual mores, specific, empirical, concrete, with the apostrophic mode, more usually delivered from an unspecified vantage to an unidentified mistress:

> Gods! that a thing admir'd by mee
> Shou'd fall to so much Infamy.
> Had she pickt out to rub her Arse on
> Some stiff-prickt Clown or well-hung Parson
> Each jobb of whose spermatique sluce
> Had fill'd her Cunt with wholesome Juice
> I the proceeding shou'd have praisd
> In hope she had quench'd a fire I'd raised.
> Such naturall freedomes are but Just
> There's something Genrous in meer lust . . .   (89–98)

Corinna retains initiative, choice, the power of 'picking out': the speaker bewails his exclusion from her 'Divine Abode' (39). (The initial 'Consecrate to Prick and Cunt' (10) and final 'dares prophane the Cunt I swive' (166) gives a religious framing to the whole poem.) Everett describes the poem as a 'savage, dangerous, yet obscurely innocent fantasy – innocent from the sensed rectitude which its upside down fury violates, the contained and quashed romantic idealism' (1982: 25); and she is correct, I believe, to see the poem as 'an actual if finalizing perpetuation (for all its grossness) of earlier Renaissance modes of idealism' (1982: 37). Corinna enters having 'dropt from Heaven that very Hour/. . . In scorn of some dispairing God' (38–40). The sexual 'thing' is initially 'admir'd', and the note of limpid self-pity retains a sense of etiquette, humility, deference ('praised'). The 'Infamy' to which it is opposed remains indeterminate. The capacity of the narrator to make such a judgement is uncertain after his initial departure from the 'grave discourse' (1). Hence the oddness of the subsequent accusation, 'To bring a blott on Infamy' (104): not so much to exceed the bounds of shame as bring the category itself into disrepute. 'Thing' can also be read as penis (with a play on 'fall'), and it is tempting to make the extrapolation that Corinna herself now represents the virility that the speaker lacks.

There is a querulous comic note in the feminine rhymes; and also an absence of hierarchy recalling the social as well as sexual dimensions of the 'all-sin-sheltering Grove': 'And here promiscuously they swive' (25, 32)). The 'spermatique sluce' of 'stiff-prickt Clown' and 'well-hung Parson' provides not corruption or disease but a 'wholesome Juice'. 'To rub her Arse on' continues the 'proud bitch' image: but as with the later 'longing Arse' (141) has a potential homoerotic dimension. 'Quench'd the fire' is a typical literalisation of a *précieux* diction, dousing the 'flame' with other men's semen. (Compare 'Dialogue' (39–40), 'the Show'rs that fall/ Quench the fire, and quiet all'; and 'The Advice' (23–4), 'for even streams have desires,/Cool as they are, they feel Love's powerful fires'). 'I'd raised' suggests the arousal of the 'knight errant Paramours' by the speaker himself. The 'natural freedomes' represent not liberation from but facilitation of exchange between men: 'meer lust' is not an underlying impulse, basic motivation, but an unattainable, longed-for, standard.

> But why am I of all Mankind
> To so severe a Fate design'd
> Ungratefull! Why this Treachery
> To humble fond beleiving me
> Who gave you Priviledge above
> The nice allowances of Love?
> Did ever I refuse to bear
> The meanest part your Lust could spare
> When your lewd Cunt came spewing home
> Drench't with the seed of halfe the Town
> My dram of sperm was suppt up after
> For the digestive surfeit water.
> Full gorged at another time
> With a vast meal of nasty slime
> Which your devouring Cunt had drawn
> For Porters back and Footmens brawn

SORDID IMAGES

> I was content to serve you up
> My Ballock full for your Grace cupp
> Not ever thought it an abuse
> While you had pleasure for excuse
> You that cou'd make my heart away
> For noise and Colour and betray
> The secretts of my tender houres
> To such knight errant Paramours
> When leaneing on your faithless breast
> Wrapt in security and rest
> Soft kindness all my powers did move
> And Reason lay dissolv'd in Love.   (105–32)

The relation of 'I' to 'all Mankind' initially seems antithetical, but in the course of the passage undergoes a physical assimilation. There is a typically determinist note in the severity of 'Fate'. 'Priviledge above' and 'nice allowances' attribute a certain authority to the speaker, but this is immediately compromised by the infantile dependence of 'humble fond beleiving me'. The 'meanest part' could be genitals of either sex or a role in 'loves Theatre the Bed' ('Leave this gawdy guilded Stage' (5)). 'Ungratefull' most immediately refers to the flouting of contract by Corinna, but can be extended on to the speaker's own behaviour or the reader, pre-emptively rebuked for simultaneously witnessing and violating the erotic intimacy. There remains a sense of decorum, almost gentility, in the 'digestive surfeit water' served up; and an infinite poignancy in 'content', whose obvious sexual play cannot detract from the peculiar resonance of 'Grace'.

'Pleasure for excuse' seems to ascribe a libertine autonomy, 'naturall freedoms': 'abuse' refers to the narrator's own 'dram of sperm' as much as Corinna's behaviour. 'Meer lust' cannot be taken as simply an anti-inflationist view of 'pleasure' as a secular pastime. (Though there is no compunction about describing Corinna as 'joyfull and pleas'd' (80) at her liaison.) The poem would be much simpler and more manageable if this was a clearly available standard. Yet the 'pleasure' of the speaker lies more in his relation with Corinna's other lovers than in any momentary spasm of ejaculation. Indeed, orgasm as an entity in itself is immediately redefined in terms of two overlaid relations: an apostrophic address to Corinna, and an indirect communion with 'halfe the Town'. 'Spewing home' seems more appropriate to the behaviour of the narrator himself; and if one pursues this somewhat lurid transference, he receives as well as adds to the 'seed' within. The voracity of the 'devouring Cunt' seems part of its attraction rather than a cause of repulsion. 'Full gorged' would seem attached to 'Cunt', but transfers itself to the speaker in both active and passive senses: he is himself swallowed up but also bloated by receiving the 'vast meal'. (Compare *Sodom*, where Flux comments 'Men's pricks are eaten of the secret parts/Of women' (V.ii.51)). The 'nasty slime' is displaced from the juices of female arousal onto the male ejaculate; but the point is that the two are inseparable, and satisfaction is received from contact with both.

One might go so far as to say that the affair is only fully consummated in the moment of infidelity. The term 'betray' comes to represent both revelation and exposure. The expression that gives public significance is brought into existence by a movement inseparable from fickleness and duplicity. The lyrics offer a host of examples of this usage: 'To betray, and engage, and inflame my Desire' ('The Submission' (6)); ('Dialogue' (6–7)); 'my unfaithfull eyes/Betray a kinder story' ('Song' 7–8); and 'But Virgins Eyes their hearts betray,/And give their Tongues the lie' ('Song' (19–20)). (Even in 'A Satyr against Reason', the line, 'But Savage *Man* alone, does *Man* betray' (130), allows, by the logic of its own argument, the reading that the primitive impulses are superior because closer to the spontaneous behaviour of the animal kingdom.) As Everett says, the narrator of a Rochester poem is always hoping 'that he will betray love enough' (1982: 19). Logically Corinna cannot reveal 'secrets' until they have been confided in her, but the implication seems to be that she already has been 'faithless'. This of course conforms to the argument for mutable desire espoused in some of the lyrics. Nevertheless the implication is that she is attractive precisely because of, not in spite of, her 'Treachery'. 'When leaneing' refers both backwards to the 'Paramours' engaged in lovemaking and forward to the narrator seeking comfort: the two are telescoped into being simultaneously present. 'And Reason lay dissolv'd in Love' is not the prelude to disaster, Samson in Delilah's lap, but the desired outcome, the culmination of the preceding accelerated pattern of inversions.

The primary tension of the passage lies in its conflation of third-person satire with second-person apostrophe: 'But mark what Creatures women are/How infinitly vile when fair' (41–2). The definition is not the result of taxonomy, categorisation, but of the movement between vileness and fairness: the apparent stability containing progressively more estranged extremes. There is a summoning and making-present of physical residue, an inverted and arguably perverse idealisation of a gluttonous absorption of the male body. The hostility towards the male rivals is merely an inversion of the attraction towards physical contact via the 'devouring Cunt'.

Such a reading would suggest that the sphere of female autonomy is largely illusory. Certainly the generosity of Rochester's verse cannot be directly equated with his libertinism. Instead, I would suggest, attention should be directed towards the issue of masculine bonding, and in the next section I shall examine its various dysfunctions.

Nussbaum comments that 'the satirist's stance is one of enraging the audience in a shared feeling of disgust' (1984: 23): his purpose is at least as much communal reinforcement as rectification of abuse. 'The satirist reassures the male sex; he employs a rhetorical stance of providing other men with the powerful word to fend off impotence and passivity' (1984: 42). The bonding of the satirist with his audience through eroticised abuse may perhaps be taken as a given: it remains to be explained why this transaction requires a display of 'impotence'. Ober (1979: 234) notes that the subject of *chagrin d'amour* tends to be shied away from as a source of discomfort and embarrassment; yet in Rochester it is insisted upon to the virtual exclusion of empowerment (though arguably the energy of abuse unleashed, what Rawson dubs the 'machismo of sexual debility', is experienced 'not as a cessation of erotic energy, but as an energy in its own right – a vigour generated in reverse' (1985: 335)).

Critics adopting the model of homosocial bonding commonly assume that male writers must inevitably endorse the system from which they benefit. According to Harold Weber, for example, the libertine economy is based upon the exclusion of women. Female desire is erased in the movement from the homosocial to the homosexual, which is designed 'to obscure and erase, even to banish the female body in order to realise a masculine fantasy of self-contained and omnipotent power' (Weber 1992: 111). (Or, as 'Fragment of a Satire on Men' puts it, 'the Beastly men wee dayly see/ Can Please themselves alone as well as wee' (33–4).) Rochester's poetry, I would suggest, is motivated by a precisely antithetical impulse: it attempts to escape from its entrapment within this system through a kind of implosion of the desiring body.

One by-product of the foregrounding of the instance of utterance in Rochester's lyrics is the reduction of the masculine community to 'The false Judgement of an Audience/Of Clapping-Fooles' ('An Allusion to Horace' (13–14)). 'The Mistress', for example, offers a series of outward addresses: 'You Wiser men despise me not'; 'Had you not been profoundly dull,/You had gone mad like me'; 'Nor Censure us You who perceive/My best belov'd and me' (13, 19–20, 21–2). These are not apologies or appeals for social endorsement so much as a kind of pre-emptive debunking. Yet there is no corresponding idealisation of the lovers: where Donne's 'The Good Morrow' celebrates the power which 'makes one little roome an every where' (11), the lines, 'To make the old *World*, a new withdrawing Room,/Whereof another *World* she's brought to *Bed*!', provoke nothing but mockery in 'Timon' (148–9).

The testimony of the isolated speaker is displaced on to an almost phenomenological emphasis on the personal body; it articulates not the authority of collective experience but an estrangement from and within it. In Rochester, there is never any sense of transmission of a received and proven wisdom. The generational axioms of 'some formal Band, and Beard' receives short shrift in 'A Satyr against Reason', and the self-undermining paradoxes of the poem's discursive stance suggest the possibility of an uninhabited language rather than one authenticated in its public circulation. The occasional hints of competition prompt not fury but incredulity at the quality of the co-suitors: ''Tis some relief in my extreme distress/My rivall is Below your power to Bless' ('Could I but make my wishes insolent' (26)). In the competition between 'Rivall Bottle' and 'Rivall Fop', it goes without question that 'the heads of your Admirers' must be 'empty' and 'dull' ('Song' (7–8, 22–3). This does not lead to a proclamation of superiority. In 'Sab: Lost', the scepticism extends to the speaker himself: 'Could you submitt to Lett this Heavy thing/ Artless and witless, noe way merriting' (11–12). The most vitriolic and impassioned invective is directed against Scroope and Mulgrave, the only aristocrats at court younger than Rochester himself, and so paradoxically closest to him.

There is no protective persona of a public self, but equally no post-romantic subjectivity conflating the two spheres. Not merely Rochester but also Sedley, Dorset and the rest seem almost devoid of political and social identities in their verse. The privacy of the cavalier lyric does not preclude the elevation of personal ethics as substitute and rebuke for political actualities. No such analogical transference is attempted in Restoration lyric. It has often been noted how little public sphere there is in Rochester: attempts such as Paulson's to read the obscene as 'the private half of a basic analogy between public and private life' ([1978]1988: 48) have little purchase compared to the reverse movement that transforms Charles II into an alter-ego and displaced father-figure, and his mistresses into demonic maternal presences.

This may, of course, be linked to the volatility of personal status in the politics of the Restoration court, but the degree of exposure and inability to exploit this power of disparagement remain striking. This would seem to be contradicted by such contemporary testimony as Marvell's 'merry gang' ([1677] 1961: ii.329), Dryden's 'men of pleasant conversation ... ambitious to distinguish themselves from the herd of gentlemen, by their poetry' ('Preface' to *All for Love*, [1678] 1973: 18), and Pope's 'Mob of Gentleman who wrote with Ease' (*Imitations of Horace* II.i.108). 'An Allusion to Horace' recommends

> Scorne all Applause the Vile Rout can bestow,
> And be content to please those few, who know ...
> I loathe the Rabble, 'tis enough for me,
> If Sidley, Shadwell, Shepherd, Witcherley,
> Godolphin, Buttler, Buckhurst, Buckingham,
> And some few more, whom I omit to name,
> Approve my Sense, I count their Censure Fame.
>
> (102–3, 120–4)

There is a predictable hauteur in the roll-call perhaps, but the 'few, who know' have scarcely any significant presence in Rochester's verse. There is a peculiar solipsism, a sense of self-directedness, with little or no sense of a Rochester poem being for anyone, whether wife or mistress, specific confidant or broader circle.

In Shakespeare's sonnets, there is a continuous drama of compromise, renegotiation and assimilation of the lyric voice to that of 'vulgar scandal' (112.2). In Rochester, this adjacency of third-party opinion is conspicuous by its absence: we must either presuppose the communal values of an implied audience, or respond to the eerie weightlessness, the sheer space around the words in a Rochester lyric. Otherworldliness is an unexpected quality for a Hobbesian libertine, but luminescence in a void, as Everett says, is undoubtedly the distinguishing feature of his lyrics (1982: 7; compare Thormahlen 1993: 83).

'Love a *Woman!* y'are an *Ass*' advises staying home with a 'lewd well-natur'd *Friend,*/Drinking, to engender *Wit*' (11–12). Yet there is no equivalent to the cheerfully *louche* exchanges between Buckhurst and Etherege. Where their verse-letters celebrate a benign itinerary of collective indulgence ('Then the next morning we all hunt/To find whose fingers smell of cunt', 'Etherege's Answer II'), Rochester's 'Regime d' viver' offers an irascible filofax of cyclic, solitary debauchery: 'Then crop-sick, all *Morning,* I rail at my *Men,*/And in Bed I lye Yawning, till Eleven again' (13–14). The poem includes a familiar cast of 'Whore' and 'Page', but its culminating animus expands out from servants in the immediate vicinity on to a whole gender: '*Men*' in general.

Even in Sade, as has often been noted (de Beauvoir [1951–2] 1989: 60; Carter 1979: 90), there is an ethic of friendship; and a certain clubbability has accompanied most outbursts of ethical antinomianism and romantic diabolism. In contrast, Rochester finds in 'On Poet Ninny': 'The worst that I cou'd write, wou'd be noe more,/Than what thy very Friends have said before' (27–8). 'A Satyr against Reason' warns

> You'le be undone –
> Nor can weak truth, your reputation save,
> The *Knaves,* will all agree to call you *Knave.*
> Wrong'd shall he live, insulted o're, opprest,
> Who dares to be less a *Villain,* than the rest.   (163–7)

The feminised victim is 'undone' by vindictive gossip rather than communal judgement, prefiguring Pope's 'At ev'ry word a Reputation dies' (*The Rape of the Lock* iii.16). The masculine 'grave discourse/Of who Fucks whom and who does worse' ('A Ramble in Saint James's Park' (1–2) compares extremely unfavourably with Artemiza's vivacious and compassionate desire 'To heare, what Loves have past/In this Lewd Towne' (32–3). The monkey that she addresses as a 'curious Miniature of Man' is a 'dirty chatt'ring Monster' (143, 141)); and while 'dirty' may do no more than reflect contemporary standards of hygiene, 'chatt'ring', gossipy, empty-headed, neatly and decisively reverses the stereotype of feminine volubility.

The 'dull dining *Sot*' pursues Timon, 'but as a *Whore,*/With modesty enslaves her *Spark,* the more' (9–10), a comparison that both refuses to differentiate between male honour and female modesty, and gives an explicitly sexualised dimension to male social intercourse. After attributing a libel to Timon (which may or may not be the poem itself, yet to be written), he is left 'to his dear mistake/Which he, by this, had spread o're the whole Town,/And me, with an officious Lye, undone' (28–30). This vulnerability to public opinion, again feminised ('undone'), is powerfully prefigured in Strephon's early dialogue with Alexis:

> As Trees are by their Barks embrac'd,
> Love to my Soul doth cling;
> When torn by th' Herd's greedy taste,
> The injur'd Plants feel they're defac't,
> They wither in the Spring.
> ('Pastoral Dialogue' (61–5))

The arboreal 'Soul' is divided into 'Tree', 'Bark' and the 'Herd's greedy taste': 'Love' serves the function of protective surface, but is itself 'defac't', 'torn', and 'injur'd'. The 'Soul' is left quiveringly vulnerable after the world's attentions: 'Lamenting, frighted, and alone,/I fly from place to place' ('Pastoral Dialogue' (9–10)). Rochester's hyper-sensitivity to public exposure extends his sympathy to unlikely or previously decried personages. There is a curious empathy with Corinna, 'Now scorn'd by all, forsaken, and opprest', who 'unheard off, as a Flye/In some darke hole must all the Winter lye' ('A Letter from Artemiza' (201, 205–6); and the culminating tirade from 'A Ramble in Saint James's Park' acquires a sudden pathos when envisaging the mistress as 'Loath'd, and despis'd, Kick't out of town/Into some dirty Hole alone' (161–2).

In 'Timon', the congregation of 'all brave *Fellows*', the rompish camaraderie of the 'tough *Youth*', provokes a fastidious shudder (37, 86):

> Their rage once over, they begin to treat,
> And Six fresh *Bottles*, must the peace compleat.
> I ran down Stairs, with a Vow never more
> To drink Bear Glass, and hear the *Hectors* roar. (174–7)

The persona never dominates, seldom interjects, but rather witnesses with varying degrees of tacit fascination and contempt. There is no single *adversarius*, but rather a whole social group, and Timon hates himself for being unable to differentiate himself from them: 'No means, nor hopes, appear of a retreat' (42). The speaker of 'Tunbridge Wells', despite frequent protestations of distance, remains immersed 'amidst the crowd':

> Endeavouring this irksome sight to Balke,
> And a more irksome noyse, their silly talke,
> I silently slunke down to th' lower Walke: (35–7)

The narrator repeatedly attempts to absent himself from his own poem: 'th' hearing what they said,/I did myself the kindnesse to evade' (84–5), and 'Tir'd with this dismall Stuffe, away I ran' (126). But there is nowhere to move on to, only a repetition of departure. Even the speaker of 'Upon His Drinking a Bowl' defines himself in terms, not of belonging to, but of separation from: 'I'm none of those that took *Mastrich,*/Nor *Yarmouth Leaguer* knew' (11–12): 'For I am no Sir Sydrophell,/Nor none of his *Relations*' (15–16).

Given a masculine community as brutish and rapacious in its pleasures as one could wish (or perhaps envy), it still remains to be explained how Rochester speaks (or appears to be speaking) from a point outside this collectivity. In the final section of this chapter, I wish to relate this disengagement to his dramatisation of bodily failure.

'For here walke Cuffe, and Kick,/With Brawney Back, and Leggs, and potent Prick' ('Tunbridge Wells' (155–6)): the healthy bodies of other men populate Rochester's verse. Appetite is continuously displaced from the speaker on to those whom he describes. 'The *Porter,* and the *Groome*' are not merely 'dirty *Slaves*' ('Love a *Woman*!' (5–6)) but sturdier performers: 'good Assistants unto Generation' ('Tunbridge Wells' (160)). It has often been noticed (by Fabricant 1974: 346–50, Nussbaum 1984: 75, Griffin 1988: 61, amongst others) that Rochester's poems are preoccupied not with dominance, reinforcement of power, but with male powerlessness. This is imaged most vividly in the famous scenarios of impotence, but can be paralleled in the satires by what Everett calls Rochester's 'radical self-undercutting, an intelligence almost self-destructive' (1982: 10). There is little reference to the female body, whether descriptive, idealising, or defamatory. Yet the male body that supplants it is one that fails; and the foregrounding, rhetorical liberation, inaugurated by its very conspicuous deficiency, is, I would argue, crucial to Rochester's verse.

One tradition of feminist reading would stress the residual

equality of desires: 'When neither overcomes Loves triumph greater is' ('Leave this gawdy guilded Stage' (10)). There is undoubtedly a willingness to allow independent female voices into the poems. Satiric modes are directed as, if not more, frequently against men than women; and the conventions of cavalier lyric themselves become transposable. The final stanza of 'Against Constancy', for example, applies the rhetoric of both *carpe diem* and epithalamium to the narrator himself: 'Then bring my Bath, and strew my bed,/as each kind night returns,/Ile change a Mistress till i'me dead,/and fate change me for worms' (17–20). Even 'The Platonick Lady' sees it as her prerogative to initiate foreplay ('I love a youth, will give me leave/His Body in my arms to wreath' (12–13)); and the 'Young Lady' promises her 'Ancient Lover' to inseminate 'thy withered Lips and dry,/Which like barren Furrows lye' with 'Brooding Kisses' like 'Kind Showers' (7–11).

The presentation of the host's wife in 'Timon' is entirely devoid of the callous mockery characteristic of similar pieces by Rochester's contemporaries (for example, Dorset's 'The Antiquated Coquette'):

> In comes my *Lady* strait, she had been *Fair*,
> Fit to give love, and to prevent despair.
> But *Age*, *Beauties* incurable Disease,
> Hath left her more desire, than pow'r to please.
> As *Cocks*, will strike, although their *Spurrs* be gone,
> She with her old bleer *Eyes* to smite begun:
> Though nothing else, she (in despight of time)
> Preserv'd the affectation of her prime;
> How ever you begun, she brought in love,
> And hardly from the Subject wou'd remove.   (49–56)

The Lady has scarcely worn worse than Timon himself; and the passage reflects the same ambivalence towards its object as the reader feels towards its narrator. '*Age*' is the 'incurable disease of others beside '*Beauty*'; and the gap between 'desire' and 'pow'r to please' is famously commented upon by Rochester himself: 'soe greate a disproportion 'twixt our desires and what has been ordained to content them' (1980: 241–2). '*Cocks*' gives a momentary masculinity, force, not wholly retracted by 'old bleer *Eyes*', no less to be respected than the disabled debauchee; 'smite' has overtones of both heroic endeavour and social flirtation. There is a note of admirable defiance, 'in despight of time'; 'affectation' also acquires a certain dignity as a conscious role-playing. She shares her preoccupation with love with Rochester himself; and the resulting dialogue is closer to Eliot's 'Portrait of a Lady' than to the witches' sabbath of Pope's 'Ghosts of Beauty' (*Epistle to a Lady* (241)). 'Fit to give love' is almost the finest compliment that can be paid; 'prevent despair' a notably unrecriminative term for sexual availability. Her tone is gently reproachful, unflustered, graceful, with a note of disdain towards the 'Hair-brain'd *Youth*', deemed 'Too rotten to consummate the Intrigue' (104, 106). In perhaps the morally finest line in Rochester, and certainly the most understated epithet, she is allowed to depart undisparaged, undiminished: 'And decently my *Lady*, quits the Room' (110).

Wintle dismisses this persistent tactic of gender-reversal as simply offering a 'parody of a woman' (1982: 151), but this is to underestimate the slitheriness of role-playing in Rochester. The demand for 'mutual Love' ('The Advice' (16)) precludes full appreciation of the instability, the solipsism, and the impassioned lyricism of sexual failure in his verse. Sex is ethical, even conceptual, before it is erotic; and the key instances to be debated are not those of ecstasy and fulfilment but of disappointment and inadequacy. There is a truth of the body to be found through its very humiliation, in the pursuit of a pleasure known to be insufficient beforehand.

In 'The Women about Town', 'a Fate which noe man can oppose;/ The losse of his heart and the fall of his Nose' ('Lampoone' (9–10)) refers to not merely possible infection, but extends to a whole betrayal by the body. There is no specific guilt or punishment for indulgence beyond the acceleration of an inevitable decline. There is little or nothing of the *poète maudit* in Rochester, seeking transgression as an end in itself. Despite the deathbed conversion to Catholicism, there is similarly little sense of blasphemy as an inverted mode of belief. Physical corruption is not the correlative of sin; and, as previously noted, there is no sense of the disgusting as in itself arousing. Instead there is a certain stoic dignity in conscious acceptance, even pursuit, of this corporeal transformation. The 'old faithfull Souldier' (3) of 'To Love', 'me then, who hath freely spent my blood', claims to deserve 'E'en to retire, and live at peace at home' (23, 26); the disabled debauchee boasts of the 'Honourable scars/Which my too forward valour did procure'; and in 'To the Post Boy', even the more graphic 'Sear cloaths and ulcers from the top to toe' remain 'Heroick scars' (8–9).

The 'Satire on Charles II' is concerned with the obvious political dimension to virility in terms of the royal succession, but what is striking is his more universal masculine ungainliness: 'Yett his dull graceless Ballocks hang an arse' (27). There is no political respect, but a biological empathy. A displaced self-loathing and curious solicitation are directed towards the bodily imperatives of the ageing debauchee: clapped out in every sense.

Mistress Willis, like Charles, represents a persona to be occupied. She 'Rails and Scolds when she sits down,/And Curses when she Spends' (15–16), terms with both a generic and psychological appositeness to Rochester and Restoration satire in general, with its close conjunction of arousal and abuse. Further points of connection are the odd poignancy of 'And yet with no man Friends'; in what might be seen as a lucid summation of Rochester's own style, 'Bawdy in Thoughts, precise in Words'; and even perhaps an oblique glance at the poet's constipation, the 'Belly' which is 'a Bagg of Turds' (13–14, 17, 19–20). There may also be a play on 'will is', which would further identify her with the impulses of the male narrator.

'So charming Oyntments, make an Old *Witch* flie,/And bear a Crippled Carcass through the Skie' ('A Satyr against Reason' (86–7)) also has something of this last-standness. There is a stark pathos to 'Old', an unsparing naturalism but no disgusted recoil in 'Carcass', and an immense respect for the refusal of the '*Witch*' to capitulate to the state of 'Crippled'. The 'Oyntments' are 'charming' because casting a spell, but also felicitous, because successful in doing so when there is no alternative but to inculcate an illusion.

In the rivalry between Count Cazzo and Signior Dildo, there is only one winner: the substitute clearly surpasses the original, a situation which 'Flesh and Blood cou'd not bear' (80). Witnessing the subsequent ambush and pursuit by 'A Rabble of Pricks' (83),

> The good Lady Sandys, burst into a Laughter
> To see how their Ballocks came wobbling after,
> And had not their weight retarded the Fo
> Indeed 't had gone hard with Signior Dildo. (89–92)

'Retarded' is delayed, but also rendered imbecilic; and 'gone hard' merely reinforces the superiority of the intruder, and the dispensability of the original. Weber astutely notes how the poem demonstrates that 'from the female point of view the male body provides an essentially comic spectacle' (1992: 110). 'Reducing men to their pricks' makes them '*objects of derision*', and there is unsparing indictment of the 'anatomical insufficiency of the male body', in particular the ballocks as 'the male body's betrayal of itself' (1992: 108). (As Weber points out, feminist models based upon the unitary phallus uniformly fail to accommodate the testicles, in all their queasy dangling vulnerability.)

The poems represent, Weber goes on to claim, 'an attempt to transform the penis into the phallus, to recapture an edenic wholeness which would banish death'. It is 'their inability to effect this transformation' which 'generates the rage and anxiety that so often disfigure the verse, marking the moment when the male will discovers the limits of its own power and authority' (1992: 110). Like Robinson, Weber is reluctant to acknowledge that 'rage and anxiety' might be what we read for. That which 'disfigures the verse' might be what produces it in the first place.

In Rochester, however, there is not a failed attempt to 'transform the penis into the phallus', but often a strikingly literal dramatisation of the reverse process: what is sought is not power, but powerlessness. Timon's claim to have 'never Rhym'd, but for my *Pintles* sake' may imply the opposite of self-aggrandisement.

'The Imperfect Enjoyment' offers the most complex display of this provocative self-deprecation. Weber argues that 'the failure to control desire, to overcome the gap between the mind and the body, transforms a genuinely erotic moment into a bitter litany of foul complaints' (1992: 103). Exposing this 'gap' may, however, be precisely what is at issue. The 'genuinely erotic' cannot be simply opposed to the 'bitter litany': the one is implicit within and generated out of the other. The speaker's inability to respond to his mistress's desires with 'wisht Obedience', what 'The Advice' dubs 'the Freedom to Obey' (12), prompts the final outburst of '*Rage*' (25):

> Trembling, confus'd, despairing, limber, dry,
> A wishing, weak, unmoving lump I ly.
> This *Dart* of Love, whose piercing point oft try'd,
> With *Virgin blood, Ten thousand Maids* has dy'd;
> Which *Nature* still directed with such *Art*,
> That through it ev'ry *Cunt*, reacht ev'ry Heart.
> Stiffly resolv'd, twou'd carelessly invade,
> *Woman* or *Man*, nor ought its fury staid,
> Where e're it pierc'd, a *Cunt* it found or made.
> Now languid lies, in this unhappy hour,

> Shrunk up, and Sapless, like a wither'd *Flow'r.*
> Thou treacherous, base, deserter of my flame,
> False to my passion, fatal to my *Fame*;
> Through what mistaken *Magick* dost thou prove,
> So true to lewdness, so untrue to Love?   (35–49)

The speaker appears not merely to address but actually to become his penis. The vainglorious boast of previous exploits is delivered from the point of minimum performance, leading to the suspicion that they are purely verbal and compensatory. Yet it should be stressed that erotic failure is the condition rather than the cessation of this indiscriminate assault, which, as in 'Mock Song', subjects an infinitely penetrable body to a random incision that verges on the sadistic and grotesque. It is noteworthy that the previous description of ejaculation might easily be transposed into female orgasm: 'In liquid *Raptures*, I dissolve all o're,/Melt into Sperme, and spend at ev'ry Pore' (15–16). 'Stiffly resolv'd' reverses the relation of conscious purpose to sexual arousal from one of prohibition and restraint. The '*All-dissolving Thunderbolt*' (10) becomes a display of authority, the antithesis of the yielding assimilation of the 'wishing, weak, unmoving lump'. Yet this state is broadly continuous with the ideal of protective enclosure prevalent elsewhere, An obvious parallel may be found in the masturbatory passivity of Bloom's 'languid floating flower' in *Ulysses* (Joyce 1984: vol. 1: 175), suggesting that the 'wither'd *Flow'r*' that 'languid lies' might be truer 'to Love' than the rampaging virility with which it is contrasted.

> Worst part of me, and henceforth hated most,
> Through all the *Town*, a common *Fucking Post*;
> On whom each *Whore*, relieves her tingling *Cunt*,
> As *Hogs*, on *Gates*, do rub themselves and grunt.
> Mayst thou'st to rav'nous *Shankers*, be a *Prey*,
> Or in consuming *Weepings* waste away.
> May *Strangury*, and *Stone*, thy *Days* attend,
> Mayst thou ne're Piss, who didst refuse to spend,
> When all my joys, did on false thee depend.
> And may *Ten thousand* abler *Pricks* agree,
> To do the wrong'd *Corinna* right for thee.   (62–72)

Abuse of the penis seems a more than adequate substitute for utilisation of it. A dismemberment of the body is performed through a series of violently repudiatory apostrophes; a making present of that which, as it were, had been gouged out of himself.

Rancour is drained away from all other possible targets: the unqualified intimacy of the opening lines paradoxically presupposes this eventual outlet. There is, as Treglown points out (1982: 85), a disconcerting urbanity to the pun on 'depend' (and on the previous 'confirm me impotent' (28)), ushering in a final compliment to the 'wrong'd *Corinna*'. The 'Worst part' is not so much expelled as expanded to fill the narrative present of the poem. It is then denounced for precisely what it is manifestly failing to do: providing 'a common *Fucking Post*'. The ferocity of invective is thus displaced from the state of powerlessness on to the state of potency apparently only invoked as a negative contrast. The punishment becomes a jubilant kind of release: not from the 'drudgery' of heterosexual intercourse, but from the necessity to 'agree' with, conform to, the hallucinatory array of 'abler *Pricks*'. Belief, opinion, scandal, are all set aside in favour of a reiteration of common physical limitation, whose buoyant explicitness refuses the grotesque or macabre. The 'consuming *Weepings*' of venereal sores might be seen as Rochester's version of *lacrimae rerum*; and in their more restricted fashion partake of some of the grandeur of the Virgilian pathos.

In the context of my original concern, misogyny, it is possible to offer a provisional conclusion. The intermittent continuities with anti-feminist satire, and inventive, occasionally horrifying, results of generic inversion of lyric, are of little consequence compared to the foregrounding and evacuation of masculinity as a cultural bond. The continual recourse to a negative testimony of the body represents a kind of obdurate refusal of a culturally endorsed mastery. Rochester may be seen as the great articulator of the malfunctioning body, a typology superimposed upon its most flagrant and ostentatious debaucheries.

In my next chapter I wish to explore the notably different outcome of Alexander Pope's attempts to 'Rhyme with all the *Rage* of *Impotence*' (*Essay on Man* (533)).

4

'LET BLOOD AND BODY BEAR THE FAULT'
Pope's exorcism of desire

Until recently, the issue of misogyny had received little attention in Pope studies. Even when addressed, it tended to be relegated to a minor aspect of a more general misanthropy. On the debit side, Pope is perceived as harbouring an ultimately disdainful condescension towards Belinda in *The Rape of the Lock*; he produces some consistently unflattering portraiture in *Epistle to a Lady*; and attaches some murkily foetal imagery to the 'Mighty Mother' of Dulness in *The Dunciad* ('How hints, like spawn, scarce quick in embryo lie' (i.59)). Against this is set the interest in a specifically female sensibility, shown in his excursions into elegy and heroic epistle; the affectionate and respectful intimacy of his addresses to the Blount sisters; and his wide-ranging awareness of the forms and conventions through which the women in his culture were 'by Man's Oppression curst' (*Epistle to a Lady* (213)).

This consensus has been forcefully challenged in recent books by Laura Brown, Felicity Nussbaum and Ellen Pollak. Nussbaum's *The Brink of All We Hate* provides an illuminating generic study of anti-feminist satire between 1660 and 1750. She convincingly demonstrates that this is an appropriate context (though not perhaps the only one) in which to situate such poems as *The Rape of the Lock* and *Epistle to a Lady*. No attempt is made, however, to break with the canon as traditionally conceived: it is assumed that the virulence of this tradition is mitigated through the capacity of literary artistry to 'add nuance to convey the ambivalence inherent in the female sex' (Nussbaum 1984: 2). Thus Pope's verse need not be condemned as 'finally misogynist' but can be partially redeemed as 'ambiguous and complex in its use of eighteenth-century conventions and commonplaces about the sex' (1984: 40). In contrast, Brown's *Alexander Pope* and Pollak's *The Poetics of Sexual Myth* adopt a more strongly iconoclastic position: 'Pope must be scrutinised, doubted, and demystified' and his 'explicit values . . . critically and remorselessly questioned' (Brown 1985: 3). Each accepts 'the premise that both the aesthetic and the mythic or conventional are functions of ideology', so that within the literary text 'the illusion of complexity' may be no more than 'a sophisticated rhetorical strategy for obscuring an ideological simplicity' (Pollak 1985: 194, 218). One may undoubtedly hold reservations about aspects of their respective approaches (which must of course be seen not as a single homogeneous entity but as a diverse context of argument). Briefly, Nussbaum's lack of a clear oppositional voice (rectified in her later work: see Nussbaum and Brown 1987; Nussbaum 1990) leads to numerous local collusions (Martha Blount, for example, becomes 'both the subject of panegyric and precariously like the sisters whom *we* all find morally repugnant' (1984: 156)). Brown presents Pope 'as a consistent advocate of the beliefs and ambitions of the capitalist landlords and of an imperialist consensus' (1985: 3), thereby positing a monolithic mercantilist ideology that wholly subsumes the actual political divisions between Walpole's government and the Tory opposition; and Pollak never satisfactorily reconciles the considerable finesse of her rhetorical criticism with the ponderous determinism of a globally conceived patriarchal order. Nevertheless, the cumulative impact of their work makes it impossible to regard Pope as writing poems 'about women' which establish an impartial taxonomy of an external object of study; it must now be acknowledged that the masculine attitude of ratiocination is necessarily bound up with issues of desire and control. Statements about women are best read as statements by men, with the ultimate function of reconfirming the authority of a masculine poetic voice. I wish to take this new stringency of assessment for granted and try to move beyond the issue of Pope's reinforcement or qualification of cultural stereotype. I shall begin by examining the ambivalence provoked by his body in the critical reception of his work, and go on to look briefly at its presence in his own writing; then analyse the depiction (or more accurately annulment) of the female mind in *The Rape of the Lock* and elsewhere; and conclude by considering the covert reinstatement of a vocabulary of gratified desire in *Epistle to a Lady*.

In 1759, W. H. Dilworth appended to his biography of Pope an itemised balance sheet, fourteen pages long, entitled 'A Parallel of the Characters of Mr. Dryden and Mr. Pope' (1759: 138–51); and such a comparison has been a virtual set-piece of English criticism for over two hundred years. The sub-genre possesses its own distinctively sexualised co-ordinates. Matthew Arnold compares these 'two men of such admirable talent, both of them, and one of them, Dryden, a man on all sides, of such energetic and genial power' (1880: xxxviii): notice the stress on 'man' (the lack of any parallel term sets up an implicit opposition to non-man or sub-man) and also on 'genial'. Johnson defines the primary meaning of the term as 'that which contributes to propagation', a sense vividly brought out in De Quincey's remark that, 'Dryden followed, genially, an impulse of his healthy nature. Pope obeyed, spasmodically, an overmastering febrile paroxysm' ([1851] 1889–90: vol. xi, 119). The contrast is between an essentially virile verse (Saintsbury talks of Dryden's 'infinite "body"' (1908: vol. ii, 456)) and an emasculated, though fastidious, dexterity; or, in Johnson's illustration, between the 'varied exuberance of abundant vegetation' and a 'velvet lawn, shaved by the scythe' (1905: iii, 222–3). The image of tumescence underlying the spatial metaphors in such formulations as T. S. Eliot's, 'When Pope alters, he diminishes ... But the effect of the portraits of Dryden is to transform the object into something greater' (1951: 310) becomes at times almost comically explicit. Leigh Hunt, for example, contrasts the 'delicate pungent nature' of Pope, 'a genius of a less masculine order', to the 'robuster' Dryden whose 'trenchant sword ... demanded stoutness in the sheath' (1846: 281; 1832: xxiii). In this context it becomes hard not to see a specifically sexual allusion in Leslie Stephen's comment, 'his emotion came in sudden jets and gushes, instead of in a continuous stream' (1880: 189). (De Quincey also remarks, 'all his thinking proceeded by isolated and discontinuous jets' ([1848] 1889–90: vol. xi, 63).)

Even taking historical fluctuation into account, there has been a remarkably consistent gender-reversal in the characterisation of Pope's poetic voice. In 1747, Thomas Gilbert praised his 'Female lines' (1747: 110); in 1759, Edward Young claimed that the 'masculine melody' of Homer had been betrayed by Pope's '*effeminate* decoration', which 'put *Achilles* in petticoats a second time' (1759: 59); in 1856 George Gilfillan mentioned the '*feminine* element' that 'mellowed and modified his feelings' (1856: 22); and Maynard Mack's 1985 biography referred to 'that quality of his sensibility that some critics have called feminine for lack of an exacter term'

(1985: 29). The *locus classicus*, or perhaps *reductio ad absurdum*, is supplied by Francis Thompson

> The gods are in pairs, male and female; and if Dryden was the Mars of English satire, Pope was the Venus – a very eighteenth-century Venus, quite as conspicuous for malice as for elegance. If a woman's satire were informed with genius and cultivated to the utmost perfection of form by lifelong and exclusive literary practice, one imagines it would be much like Pope's. His style seems to me feminine in what it lacks: the absence of any geniality, any softening humour to abate its mortal thrust. It is feminine in what it has, the malice, the cruel dexterity, the delicate needle point which hardly betrays its light and swift entry yet stings like a bee. Even in his coarseness – as in *The Dunciad* – Pope appears to me female. It is the coarseness of the fine ladies of that material time, the Lady Maries and the rest of them. Dryden is a rough and thick-natured man, cudgelling his adversaries with coarse speech in the heat and brawl and bluntness of his sensibilities; a country squire, who is apt to use the heavy end of his cutting whip; but when Pope is coarse he is coarse with effort, he goes out of his way to be nasty, in the evident endeavour to imitate a man. It is a girl airing the slang of her schoolboy brother.
>
> (Thompson 1910: 197–9)

The direct link is via his preceding comment on 'that sense of unrelieved cruelty which repels one in much female satire'. Thus Pope is cast as our Lady of Pain.

In terms of the inherited critical iconography it becomes appropriate to think of him as as much the victim as the perpetrator of sexist stereotyping. His attention to the nuances and conveniences of domestic life (Saintsbury describes his verse as 'swept, garnished, polished' (1908: vol. ii, 451)) is regularly denigrated as testimony to a restricted range of experience. Johnson says of *The Rape of the Lock*: 'the whole detail of the female-day is here brought before us', a somewhat mixed blessing as this is a routine 'from which we have a thousand times turned fastidiously away' (1905: vol. iii, 234, 197). (The idleness, consumption and display of Belinda's daily itinerary are unhesitatingly regarded as wholly representative of women of all classes.) In discussing Pope the invalid's 'perpetual need of female attendance', Johnson even transforms his sex: 'he expected that every thing should give way to his ease or humour, as a child whose parents will not hear her cry has an unresisted dominion in the nursery'. This is immediately preceded by a reference to Pope's will as 'polluted by a female resentment', and followed by a phrase adapted from Young's satire on women: 'He hardly drank tea without a strategem' (1905: vol. iii, 234, 197, 198, 200, see also Rumbold 1989: 5). Hazlitt seems more generous: though 'his Muse ... grew somewhat effeminate through long ease and indulgence', Pope's 'retired and narrow' life-style also helped produce a refined sympathy for the 'sentiments and habitudes of human life, as he felt them within the little circle of his family and friends'. Yet this effectively reinforces the association of femininity with illness, and therefore malice: 'his enmity is effeminate and petulant from a sense of weakness ... his delicacy often borders on sickliness' (1930–34: vol. v, 71, 69).

'Sickliness' should be understood in the sense of 'disposition to sickness; habitual disease' (Johnson, no. 1). Pope suffered from tuberculosis of the bone, known as Pott's disease, probably contracted from his nurse's milk. He consequently suffered bouts of high fever; severe eye inflammations, which impaired his sight from his mid-teens; coughing fits; abdominal pains; and eventual loss of use of his legs. Respiratory problems in turn caused cardiac difficulties: contraction of the spine and vertebra resulted in a condition called kyphoscolioscis. He was about four feet six tall, approximately the stature of a twelve-year-old boy. Complications developed in virtually any minor ailment: Pope endured constant headaches; frequent pain at the bone and muscle joints; shortness of breath; incapacity to take exercise; and recurrent fevers. Thus there is no exaggeration in his reference to 'this long Disease, my Life' (*Arbuthnot*, 132). (For a detailed analysis, see Nicholson and Rousseau 1968: 7–82; and for shorter discussions, see Mack 1982; Hammond 1986: 9–13; and Damrosch 1987: 19–24.) Until recently, twentieth-century criticism had given Pope's physical condition little attention, in contrast to the kind of psycho-biography that has seized upon Swift; and we should perhaps be grateful for the paucity of studies on Pope's excremental vision. This appears to be due in roughly equal measure to the residual force of the New Critical criteria so successfully applied to his verse by Mack, Wimsatt and Brooks; and to the assumption that to categorise him as the cripple-poet would necessarily deflect attention away from his poetic achievement on to such demeaning psychological blind-alleys as inadequacy, compensation and resentment.

The formalist demand for impersonality can be countered by an appeal to the wry, rueful defiance in such asides as 'In Tasks so bold, can little Men engage' (*The Rape of the Lock* i.11); in the supremely distasteful effect of lines such as 'See the blind Beggar dance, the Cripple sing' in *An Essay on Man* (ii.267); or in the curious erotic pathos of 'The lamentation of Glumdalclitch' over the departed Gulliver, who 'of Stature scarce a Span' could only 'Mimick the Actions of a real Man' (63–4).

In 'A Century of English Poetry', Swinburne elaborates this line of thought into:

> instinct or impulse had practically the upper hand of principle. The instinct of a deformed invalid, with a bitter wit and most irritable nerves, are of course more likely than the impulses of a strong man, with healthy blood and hot passions, to seem rather intellectual than physical energies or infirmities, yet in Pope's case the body was perhaps as liable to mislead the mind, and emotion to get the start of reflection as in the case of any hot-brained lyricist – even of any brainless athlete. ([1880] 1926: vol. iv, 133)

There are always problems in trying to verify the existence of such a direct expressiveness, an authenticity dependent on the direct coincidence of 'instinct and impulse' with verbal articulation. Paradoxically, a renewed emphasis on Pope's suffering body restores the presence of 'sensual passion', a kind of physical spontaneity, and through it a certain dignity, to the verse habitually characterised, if not caricatured, as the product of the presiding deity of a mythical age of reason.

Eighteenth-century biographers do not evade Pope's 'misshapen figure and direct deformity', but instead try to present it as emblematic of the triumph of genius over physical circumstances, spurred on to 'atone for the defects of an ungracious figure' (Ruffhead 1769: 21). His adversaries, predictably enough, were not slow to seize upon his disabilities. An early biography notes how hostile polemicists 'attacked his make, his shape, calling him an Ape, an Ass, a Frog', and thoughtfully included an index of insults (Ayre 1745). The principle enunciated in his own description of Thersites – 'His figure such as might his Soul proclaim' (*The Iliad* II.263) – was repeatedly turned against him, most witheringly by Lady Mary Wortley Montagu, who wrote of 'that wretched little Carcase':

And with the Emblem of thy crooked Mind,
Mark'd on thy Back, like *Cain,* by God's own Hand;
Wander like him, accursed through the Land.
(Montagu [1733] 1977: 70, 110–12)

Given the general tenor of anti-Pope polemic, his sexual capacities were unlikely to pass unremarked. Ruffhead tried desperately to hold the line: 'his constitution was too infirm and delicate to sustain the violent agitations of licentious pleasures: so that his tender frame preserved him from those modes of intemperance, to which genius, in particular, has often proved a victim' (1769: 20). But this in turn simply provides further ammunition: Edward Ward sneers in *Apollo's Maggot in his Cups* that the muses 'dab'd on just an Inch of Stuff/Enough to show the Gender' (1729: 19); the anonymous writer of *Sawney and Colley* adds 'As impotent in *Spite* as *Love* (1742: 7); and Lady Mary Wortley Montagu cruelly reverses his own line from *Epistle to a Lady* (166): 'No more for loving made, than to be lov'd' ([1733] 1977: 49).

'There is very little to say about his loves, and that little not pleasant': over a century later, Thackeray was still reworking the same sneers at 'the little pert prurient bard' (1853: 158). The most vivid and notorious instance of 'the delicate little creature' being 'sickened at habits and company which were quite tolerable to robuster men' (Thackeray 1853: 182) occurs in Colley Cibber's *Letter to Mr. Pope.* In response to the line, 'And has not *Colley* still his Lord, and Whore' (*Arbuthnot,* 97) Cibber recounts his visit to 'a certain House of Carnal Recreation, near the *Haymarket*' in the company of Pope and a 'young Nobleman' (1742: 47–8):

> where his Lordship's Frolick propos'd was to slip his little *Homer,* as he call'd him, at a Girl of the Game, that he might see what sort of Figure a Man of his Size, Sobriety, and Vigour (in Verse) would make, when the frail Fit of Love had got into him; in which he so far succeeded, that the smirking Damsel, who serv'd us with Tea, happen'd to have Charms sufficient to tempt the little-tiny Manhood of Mr. *Pope* into the next Room with her: at which you may imagine, his Lordship was in as much Joy, at what might happen within, as our small Friend could possibly be in Possession of it: But I (forgive me all ye mortified Mortals whom his fell Satyr has since fallen upon) observing he had staid as long without Hazard of his Health he might, I,

POPE'S EXORCISM OF DESIRE

> *Prick'd to it by foolish Honesty and Love,*
>
> As *Shakspear* says, without Ceremony, threw open the Door upon him, where I found this little hasty Hero, like a terrible *Tom Tit,* pertly perching upon the Mount of Love! But such was my Surprize, that I fairly laid hold of his Heels, and actually drew him down safe and sound from his Danger.

A fine comic anecdote, and a palpable hit for Cibber (see Straub 1991). But the episode must also have possessed a powerful emblematic significance to justify being illustrated in four separate broadsheet engravings. It brings out the double nature of the 'Figure' of Pope, his 'Size, Sobriety, and Vigour (in Verse)' belied by an actual 'little-tiny Manhood', subject to the officious intervention of nurse-surrogates. What should be stressed is that tributes to Pope's erotic charisma have been by no means uncommon. John Dennis comments that 'The grosser part of his gentle Readers believe the Beast to be more than Man: as Ancient Rusticks took his Ancestors for those Demy-Gods they call *Fauns* and *Satyrs*' (1939–43: vol. ii, 103–4); and more recently Allen Tate has sought to evoke this bestial potency in similar terms: 'Ladies leaned out more of fear than pity/For Pope's tight back was rather a goat's than a man's' ('Mr Pope', 3–4 [1928] 1977: 6)). In Cibber's description, 'fell Satyr' combines with 'fallen upon', to stress unexpectedly his poetic virility: '*Tom Tit,* pertly perching upon the Mount of Love' may be an absurd spectacle, but Pope can remain a 'Hero' in his verse provided it is able to repress, eradicate or transform all corporeal reference.

Pope took enormous care in constructing 'a willed highly controlled projection . . . of his person into posterity' through the medium of portraiture: of over sixty distinct types, only one (an unauthorised sketch by William Hoare) displays his bodily shape (see Piper 1982: 58). Within his verse a similar screening occurs. There is little or no sense of situated perspective even within the later, more elaborately developed, autobiographical persona. In *Eloisa to Abelard,* does the nun's voice emanate from her cell, from the convent, from the wilderness or from some realm of mystic meditation? Where (indeed who) is the speaker of the *Elegy to the Memory of an Unfortunate Lady* – lover, relation, or supposedly impartial onlooker? Is the tour offered in *Epistle to a Lady* of a supposedly real gallery or does it occur in a purely textual dimension? Everywhere in Pope, even in an explicitly topographical poem such as *Windsor Forest*, we find tricks of phantasmagoria through abrupt condensation and lack of syntactical connection.

The opening of the second canto of *The Rape of the Lock* provides a well-known example:

> Not with more Glories, in th'Etherial Plain,
> The Sun first rises o'er the purpled Main,
> Then issuing forth, the Rival of his Beams
> Launch'd on the Bosom of the Silver *Thames*.
> Fair Nymphs and well-drest Youths around her shone,
> But ev'ry Eye was fix'd on her alone.
> On her white Breast a sparkling *Cross* she wore,
> Which *Jews* might kiss, and Infidels adore. (ii.1–8)

Belinda's role as 'Rival' of an (absent) sun both enlarges her and threatens to extinguish her, as she is 'Launch'd' upon the river. The surrounding 'Nymphs' and 'Youths' contract to 'ev'ry Eye', a viewpoint with no specific location (see Ferguson 1992). Though Belinda (unnamed till line 52) is reduced to 'her white Breast', she is simultaneously expanded through identification with the 'Bosom' of the river, and nine lines later will be restored to solar scale ('Bright as the Sun, her Eyes the Gazers strike' (ii.13)). There is no attempt at spatial grouping apart from the onlookers being 'around her': the only preposition attached to Belinda, being 'on' the water, far from stabilising her location, sets off another chain of substitutions through identifying her with the 'painted Vessel' (ii.47). As Hazlitt says: 'the little is made great and the great little' (1930–34: vol. v, 72), primarily through rapid transitions of scale which make it virtually impossible to establish a fixed centre of sentience.

The later satires introduce a new tactic of brandishing 'the libel'd Person, and the pictur'd Shape' (*Arbuthnot*, 353). The pre-emptive poignancy of lines such as, 'In me what Spots (for Spots I have) appear' (*Satire* II.i.55), 'I cough like *Horace*, and tho' lean, am short' (*Arbuthnot*, 116), and 'Weak tho' I am of limb, and short of sight' (*Epistle* I.i.49) heightens the impact of the pervasive vocabulary of martial valour, and Pope's repeatedly declared willingness to 'perish in the gen'rous Cause' of moral and literary ideals (*Satire* II.i.117). The effect is well caught in a line from Statius quoted in one of Pope's contributions to *The Guardian* ([1713] 1982: 328): *major in exiguo regnabat corpore virtus* (great courage was sovereign in that little frame), and lies behind the famous proclamation:

Ask you what Provocation I have had?
The strong Antipathy of Good to Bad.
When Truth or Virtue an Affront endures,
Th' Affront is mine, my Friend, and should be yours.
Mine, as a Foe profess'd to false Pretence,
Who thinks a Coxcomb's Honour's like his Sense;
Mine as a Friend to ev'ry worthy Mind;
And mine as Man, who feel for all Mankind.
Fr. You're strangely proud.
  P. So proud, I am no Slave:
So impudent, I own myself no Knave:
So odd, my Country's Ruin makes me grave.
Yes, I am proud; I must be proud to see
Men not afraid of God, afraid of me.
  (*Epilogue to the Satires*, Dialogue Two, 197–209)

The persuasiveness of this 'Heroical disposition' (1939–69: Appendix 1 vol. v, 205) depends in large measure on its capacity both to carry and to suppress a negative connotation of actual physical prowess. This is particularly evident in 'strong Antipathy', which perhaps can be glossed as 'the physically weak possess strength in the cause of good', but this sense must admit the counter-possibility of 'strong in antipathy, but in nothing else and therefore probably not even in that'. Similarly, 'I own myself no Knave' comes perilously close to activating, and so dissociating itself from, the primary meaning of the term: 'a boy; a male child' (Johnson, no. 1).

It is because this risk is faced so directly that the pose comes across as something other than ludicrous charade. But this proclaimed ethical virility can be turned inside out by stressing its powerful neo-platonic implications. Howard Weinbrot notes that, 'one essential aspect of Pope's self-defence both before and after *The Dunciad* was his insistence upon the brave and masculine spirit chained within his warped body' (1982: 143); the rhetoric of righteous corporeal struggle can easily be transposed to ascetic renunciation, with 'souls' becoming 'Dull sullen pris'ners in the body's cage' and 'purer spirits' distilled from their 'kindred dregs' (*Elegy to the Memory of an Unfortunate Lady*, 17–18, 25–6). Thus in *Eloisa to Abelard*, Abelard's situation becomes emblematic of that of the poetic voice, the castrated male as recipient of the tribute of female passion and hence deemed worthy of elevation into godhead. (As Dilworth puts it, 'Abelard's being rendered impotent by the cruelty of Eloisa's friends, did not in the least abate the warmth of her passion for him, but seemed rather to increase it' (1759: 33).) In *The Rape of the Lock*, the power of the Baron can be seen as deriving as much from a gesture of symbolic self-emasculation as from actual possession of the lock; and in *Epistle to a Lady,* Martha Blount will be idealised as a 'softer Man' (272). In Pope's satiric verse, the most vivid example of this repudiation of the desiring body is undoubtedly the portrait of Sporus in *An Epistle to Dr. Arbuthnot.*

One is immediately struck by how much of the detail is applicable to Pope himself. 'Ass's milk' (306) was fed to invalids; Johnson comments on Pope's difficulty with personal hygiene ('His weakness made it very difficult for him to be clean', and so a 'painted Child of Dirt' (310)) and his beautiful features as a child ('His face was not displeasing, and his eyes were animated and vivid'; ('A Cherub's face, a Reptile all the rest' (331)) (1905: iii, vol.197). The 'familiar Toad' (319) recalls the famous gibe of 'hunch-backed Toad' from Dennis, who elsewhere refers to 'that Angel Face and Form of his' (1939–43: vol.i, 415: vol.ii, 105). It is also difficult to see how Pope's own exploitation of 'Antithesis' can be distinguished from that for which Sporus is condemned. If anything, it would appear to imply an unlikely equality between their respective compositions:

> His Wit all see-saw between *that* and *this,*
> Now high, now low, now Master up, now Miss,
> And he himself one vile Antithesis.
> Amphibious Thing! that acting either Part,
> The trifling Head, or the corrupted Heart!
> Fop at the Toilet, Flatt'rer at the Board,
> Now trips a Lady, and now struts a Lord.
> *Eve*'s Tempter thus the Rabbins have exprest,
> A Cherub's face, a Reptile all the rest;
> Beauty that shocks you, Parts that none will trust,
> Wit that can creep, and Pride that licks the dust.   (323–33)

The original Sporus, Nero's slave boy and catamite, was castrated. Pope, in contrast, insists on the voluptuous prowess of the 'Amphibious Thing'. 'Thing' must necessarily have the habitual play on genitals, (*OED* 11c: 'privy member, privy parts'; this is repeated interminably in *Sober Advice from Horace* (90, 103, 136, 154), and taken up in Edward Ward's mockery of Pope's 'poor thingless body' (1729: 19)); 'amphibious' in that it partakes of opposed elements, and in 'acting either Part' possesses knowledge of the enjoyment of both 'Lady' and 'Lord'. The 'reciprocating motion' (Johnson 1) of 'seesaw' takes on a specifically erotic connotation, as do the chiming thrusts of 'now Master up, now Miss'. (Compare Lovelace on 'what can be done by the *amorous see-saw*' (Richardson [1747–8] 1985: 424).) Even 'Half Froth, half Venom, spits himself abroad', becomes a paradoxical tribute to ejaculatory capacity (320). '*Eve*'s Tempter', after all, engaged in a famously successful seduction. This is further reinforced both by 'trips', usually taken as a mannered gait, but also suggesting both a literal and metaphorical fall to the ground, and by the secondary erectile sense of 'strut': 'to swell, to protuberate' (Johnson 2). Wherein then lies Pope's superiority?

> Not Fortune's Worshipper, nor Fashion's Fool,
> Not Lucre's Madman, nor Ambition's Tool,
> Not proud, nor servile, be one Poet's praise
> That, if he pleas'd, he pleas'd by manly ways.   (334–7)

'Manly ways' may appear to set up an unequivocal opposition to Sporus's 'florid Impotence' (317) and so represent another example of what has been called Pope trying to pass himself off as 'the phallus for the poetry of the age' (Hammond 1986: 159). Yet the Sporus-figure is sufficiently indeterminate in gender to assimilate the erotic experience of both sexes: Pope seeks to establish not a virile but a wholly desexualised poetic voice, one whose authority depends on its own incapacitation, its distance from this carnally proficient simulacrum of his own bodily deformity. (For more on Sporus as an 'anti-self', especially the contrast between his 'perverted sexuality' and Pope's own 'virtual sexlessness', see Griffin 1978: 178–88 (187).)

This ambivalence of gender also extends to Pope's two most intimate renditions of female desire, the *Elegy to the Memory of an Unfortunate Lady* and *Eloisa to Abelard*. The Lady's suicide demonstrates, as Brean Hammond says, her 'essentially *virile*' character (1986: 173). In acting the '*Roman*'s part' she displays not 'too tender' but 'too firm a heart' (7–8) and an 'ambition' that elevates her to the rank of 'Kings and Heroes' (13, 16). It is the masculine narrator whose soul 'now melts in mournful lays' (77). Eloisa's monologue in fact incorporates numerous statements that Pope's direct source attributed to her emasculated lover (the significant adaptations are nearly all from Abelard's third letter). In Hughes it is Abelard whose passion 'grows furious by Impotence' in the 'dark

Cells of the House'; who laments 'the Tumult of my Senses, and the Contrariety which reigns in my Heart' through the power of the 'Jealous God'; who describes himself as 'a distracted Lover, unquiet in the midst of Silence and restless in this abode of Peace and Repose'; who finds it 'difficult in our Sorrow to distinguish Penitence from Love'; and who begs Heloise to 'thrust your self between God and me, and be a Wall of Separation' ([1713] 1982: 74–8). And leaving aside the possible biographical parallels in Pope's own correspondence, to Lady Mary Wortley Montagu and the Blount sisters (see Winn 1979: Spacks 1984: and Mack 1985: 326–31), the superimposition of voices in Pope's pert and impudent close – 'He best can paint 'em who shall feel 'em most' (366) – also insists on the function of female emotion as 'sad similitude' of the 'griefs' of a 'future Bard' (359–60), and by extension, any male reader.

Much of the critical argument surrounding *Eloisa to Abelard* – particularly on the questions of dramatic progression and ironic distance – has been triggered by a sense of Eloisa as a kind of conduit for a passion ultimately extraneous to her situation and character. In this, I would argue, she is wholly representative of Pope's characterisation of women: the 'craving Void' (94) becomes the site of a double movement – an annulment of mental activity and an introjection of uninhibited desire. My most contentious premise is that this displaced physical passion need not be seen as a specifically female attribute, and in fact is best understood in the context of Pope's more general repudiation of the desiring body. I will now attempt to substantiate these claims in relation to Pope's most explicit treatments of gender: *The Rape of the Lock* and *Epistle to a Lady*.

The Rape of the Lock immediately announces its subject as 'am'rous Causes' (i.1), but this is quickly broken down into a further division of spheres of volition:

> Say, what strange Motive, Goddess! cou'd compel
> A well-bred *Lord* t'assault a gentle *Belle?*
> Oh say what stranger Cause, yet unexplor'd,
> Cou'd make a gentle *Belle* reject a *Lord?*   (i.7–10)

The latinate puns – 'assault' or leap on (*adsulto*), 'reject' or push off (*reicio*) – appear to suggest that both parties are equally subject to the impulses that arise from 'Things below' (i.36). The Baron's behaviour, however, is dignified by 'Motive' ('that which determines the choice' (Johnson 1)), whereas Belinda is to be rendered intelligible by disclosing a 'Cause, yet unexplor'd'. The opposition has become one of the commonplaces of modern analytic philosophy: she is placed in a physical universe of predetermined cause and effect while he belongs to a human realm of free decision. (Dennis's objection, that 'the Word *compel* supposes the Baron to be a Beast, and not a free Agent', presupposes that, unlike Belinda, he initially possesses choice (1939–43, vol. ii 350).) According to the *OED*, 'cause' can still be used of human volition, although its primary meaning would be 'that which produces an effect' in the physical realm. Pope's psychological usages regularly imply determination by an external force: for example, Belinda's dream 'That ev'n in Slumber caus'd her Cheek to glow' (i.24); the Gnomes 'caus'd Suspicion when no Soul was rude' (iv.73); and Othello roars for 'the Handkerchief that caus'd his Pain' (v.106). (Other notable usages include 'The same Self-love, in all, becomes the cause' (*Essay on Man* iii.271); and 'Something as dim to our internal view,/Is thus, perhaps, the cause of most we do' (*Epistle to Cobham*, 49–50; for further discussion, see Ferguson 1986: 32–63.)

It may seem anachronistic to accentuate the opposition between these terms, but this distribution of intentionality is consistent throughout. For example, the coffee that dulls Belinda's alertness 'Sent up in vapours to the *Baron*'s Brain/New Stratagems' (iii.119–20), and in the second canto, he is endowed with more mental activity in two couplets than she displays throughout the entire poem: 'Th' Adventrous *Baron* the bright Locks admir'd,/He saw, he wish'd, and to the Prize aspir'd:/Resolv'd to win, he meditates the way,/By Force to ravish, or by Fraud betray' (ii.29–32).

The same point can be made with regard to conscious expressions of and unconscious desire. The erotic subtext of the poem tends to support masculine utterance while undermining the female voice. Ariel, the leader of the sylphs dedicated to the protection of Belinda, threatens that any spirit found 'careless of his Charge' (ii.123):

> Shall feel sharp Vengeance soon o'ertake his Sins,
> Be stopt in *Vials*, or transfixt with *Pins*;
> Or plung'd in Lakes of bitter *Washes* lie,
> Or wedg'd whole Ages in a *Bodkin*'s Eye:
> *Gums* and *Pomatums* shall his flight restrain,
> While clog'd he beats his silken Wings in vain;

> Or Alom-*Stypticks* with contracting Power
> Shrink his thin Essence like a rivell'd Flower.
> Or as *Ixion* fix'd, the Wretch shall feel
> The giddy Motion of the whirling Mill,
> In Fumes of burning Chocolate shall glow,
> And tremble at the Sea that froaths below!   (ii.125–36)

The envisaged 'Vengeance' involves three distinct levels of sexual anxiety: engulfment ('stopt in', 'plung'd in' and 'clog'd'; also 'the Sea that froaths below'), detumescence ('contracting', 'Shrink', and 'rivell'd'; 'Stypticity', the power of stanching blood (Johnson 1)); and castration ('sharp', 'Pins', 'Bodkin', and especially the 'whirling' blades of the coffee 'Mill'). (The transformative power of 'Alom' is also referred to in Rochester's *Sodom*: 'cunt washt with allom makes a whore a maid' (I.i.6)). Though the urbanely surreal lyricism of the passage may qualify these punitive undertones, it does not detract from the central point: Ariel's assertion of authority and delegation of duties is reinforced rather than undermined by the underlying sexual reference.

In contrast, female speech is continually demeaned through a presumably unconscious stratum of erotic innuendo, most blatantly perhaps in Belinda's lament, 'O hadst thou, Cruel! been content to seize/Hairs less in sight, or any Hairs but these!' (iv.175–6). Dennis complained that Pope 'could not forbear putting Bawdy into the Mouth of his own Patroness' (1939–43: ii.130; see also Wasserman 1966; and more sceptically, Wilson 1988), and this accurately reflects the sense, not of innate impulses surfacing through cultural repression, as some recent critics may have it, but of an insidious form of control exerted through the implanting of a conveniently submissive anatomical destiny.

Thalestris's choric lament is directed at a different kind of 'Care'.

> Was it for this you took such constant Care,
> The *Bodkin, Comb* and *Essence* to prepare;
> For this your Locks in Paper-Durance bound,
> For this with tort'ring Irons wreath'd around?
> And this with Fillets strain'd your tender Head,
> And bravely bore the double Loads of Lead?
> Gods! shall the Ravisher display your Hair,
> While the Fops envy, and the Ladies stare!
> *Honour* forbid! at whose unrival'd Shrine
> Ease, Pleasure, Virtue, All, our Sex resign.   (IV.97–106)

As Geoffrey Tillotson notes, 'the imagery is all from incarceration and torture' (1939–69: vol. ii, 188); and while this may be attributed in part to a mock-heroic idiom or strident hyperbole, a powerful sense of voyeuristic complicity remains. There is something almost gynaecological, for example, about 'display' ('spread wide', Johnson 1). The knowledge possessed by the 'Ravisher' is of the masochistic nature of female pleasure: the preceding four lines have revealed the essentially voluntary nature of Belinda's submission to sadistic bondage (see Wilson (1988: 68) on 'perverse self-mutilation'). (Thus Belinda's addressing the Baron as 'Cruel' can be read as a term of admiration rather than rebuke.) 'Strain'd your tender Head' equates the sexual act itself with a form of punishment, and while the primary meaning of 'Fillet' is a 'band round the head', the pun on maidenhead introduces a secondary connotation of 'the fleshy part of the thigh, commonly applied to veal' (Johnson, 1). And 'Honour' is rendered virtually synonymous with biological sex through the use of 'Shrine'. (In *Sober Advice from Horace* (46) '*hoary Shrine*' is used to translate 'cunni' or genitals.) Hence it is 'unrival'd' in the sense of 'having no competitor' in the male body.

The 'envy' of the 'Fops' for the successful lover is straightforward enough, but the 'stare' of the 'Ladies' is far more ambiguous: is it motivated by fear, dislike of their rival, or some kind of reluctant fascination and recognition of their own situation in her plight? Indeed the question remains open as to whether through either rarity of classical education or supposed delicacy of sensibility, the contemporary female audience of *The Rape of the Lock* was as excluded as the dramatic characters from this level of allusive innuendo. As Pope's dedicatory epistle to Arabella Fermor puts it, 'I know how difficult it is to make use of hard Words before a Lady' (Preface, 18). Though Belinda may 'inspire', it is nevertheless Caryll who is invited to 'approve my Lays' (i.6). Thus one way of analysing the misogyny of the poem would be to move out into the history of its reception to establish the gender demarcations of its strategies of exemption and complicity. I would like to return, however, to what I regard as a prior question, the degree of consciousness possessed by Belinda, and then go on to examine the kind of commentary generated by the way her behaviour is predetermined.

'*Belinda* smil'd, and all the World was gay', but only because a sylph is available to take on the burden of all 'careful Thoughts' (ii.52, 54). The implications of this recurrent deflection have generally been overlooked. Alastair Fowler, for example, stresses that Pope's machinery 'has the originality of being thoroughly interiorised'; and thus Pope's 'undeniable partiality for the sylphs' indicates a 'conspiratorial fellow-feeling for the poignantly mutable beauty' (1988: 152, 164–5). Felicity Rosslyn also finds 'a sense of wonder and something very like love' elicited by the qualities of light, colour and change associated with Belinda (1988: 53). At no time, however, is the opposite possibility considered: that the function of the sylphs is not to endow the heroine's mind with a lyrical grace and emotional complexity but to effect an elaborate displacement of volition which allows it to be presented as a virtual interior void. What is the residue once the machinery has been removed?

There are many examples of a curious double motion whereby episodes that should enlarge the range of Belinda's mental activity actually suggest its nullity. Ariel inquires somewhat doubtfully: 'If e'er one Vision touch'd thy infant Thought' (i.29), and his scepticism as to the attention span of his charge proves fully justified since his warning immediately vanishes from her head (i.120). The question, 'What guards the Purity of melting Maids' (i.71) is answered by ''Tis but their Sylph, the wise Celestials know' (i.77), and there is a similar denial of agency in 'oft, in Dreams, Inventions we bestow' (ii.99) or in Belinda's own inquiry: 'What mov'd my Mind with youthful Lords to rome?' (iv.159). This is neatly exemplified in the line, 'Her lively looks a sprightly Mind disclose' (ii.9), where an apparently unequivocal statement of Belinda's mental animation is undercut by the alternative sense of 'sprightly' as 'of spirits' (a play also made in *Windsor Forest*: 'And purer spirits swell the sprightly flood' (94)). The vivacity of her 'Mind' indicates its dependence on rather than freedom from the sylphs.

As Dennis noted, the 'Machines ... do not in the least influence that Action; they neither prevent the Danger of *Belinda*, nor promote it, nor retard it', citing in particular Umbriel's journey in the fourth canto: 'How absurd was it then for this *Ignis Fatuus* to take a journey down to the *central Earth*, for no other Purpose than to give her the *Spleen*, whom he left and found in the Height of it' (1939–43: vol. ii, 337). The sheer oddity of this procedure has been insufficiently acknowledged: Belinda is frozen in a histrionic tableau while her 'Rage, Resentment and Despair' (iv.9) are imported from elsewhere. In similar fashion, the poetic voice imperiously decrees when her fictive existence shall be terminated, 'Then cease, bright Nymph! to mourn thy ravish'd hair' (v.141), and commands that she shall be henceforth placated by the lock's stellification (though, in one last twist, into a constellation vulgarly known as 'Bernice's Bush' (Fowler 1988: 159)).

In consequence, critical commentary on Belinda has tended to be a perpetual speaking for. It is always someone else who stocks the 'moving Toyshop' of her heart (i.100). The absence of any assertive self-consciousness within the poem results in an almost irresistible impulsion for the reader to deflect agency away from her on to some other causal factor that precludes choice or dissent. David Fairer, for example, remarks that, 'Any censure of coquettish "levity" of heart is deflected onto the sylphs who "contrive it all" (i.104)' (1984: 64). The alternative candidate for this role of determining principle is what Cleanth Brooks calls 'congeries of biological processes' (1968: 74). Murray Krieger, for example, notes 'the unaesthetic world of biological and domestic facts always lurks beneath' (1961: 184); and Pat Rogers finds 'a profoundly physical, even biological, cast to many areas of the text', commenting that Belinda's 'outrage at the Baron's assault is all the greater because it represents what subconsciously she has been wishing for and inviting all along' (1975: 37, 39). Brooks surmises 'Pope knows the rape has more in it of compliment than of insult, though he hardly expects Belinda to interpret it thus' (1968: 82–3). There is a fair amount of textual support for such an emphasis: Ariel delegates the duty of protecting the 'fav'rite Lock' to Crispissa (ii.115); in the card game, the king falling on a 'prostrate' Ace results in the nymph 'exulting' (iii.98–100); before the assault, 'Thrice she look'd back, and thrice the Foe drew near' (iii.138), suggesting wilful disregard and perhaps deliberate enticement. Yet one need not endorse the tendency of recent feminist criticism to read the 'rape' as an actual 'violent defloration of chastity' (Johnson, 1) to find these comments injudicious. It is surely a mistake, however, to pillory individual critics for such remarks: instead what should be stressed is the way in which the poem itself solicits this kind of extrapolation. As Hugo Reichard puts it: 'Pope has established the conflict of his scene not in the consciousness of the coquette but in the insight of the reader' (1954: 894).

Restoration satire tends to be wholly unconcerned with the mental processes of women: John Oldham's *A Satyr upon a Woman*, Robert Gould's *Love Given O're*, and Richard Ames's *The Folly of Love*, for example, are all heavily reliant on a simple correlation between seductive appearance and inner corruption – 'Within a gawdy Case a nasty Soul' (Gould 1682: 72)). Pope, in contrast, introduces at least the possibility of a far more nuanced inference of female personality from exterior gesture. He is prepared to acknowledge that 'Motions, Looks, and Eyes' (*The Rape of the Lock* iii.15) might disclose 'Th' exactest traits of Body or of Mind' (*Epistle to a Lady,* 191), and something distinctive comes into English anti-feminist satire with this desire to master by explaining rather than by chiding, berating, denouncing. The tone adopted is one of judicious yet playful commentary, and this subtler attention to female psychology – 'with how much more perspicacity female nature is investigated and female excellences selected' (Johnson 1905: vol. iii, 245) – has generally been taken as a sign of sympathy. Certainly Pope omits the coarse and declamatory invective and the frequent scatological abuse of his predecessors. Along with this, however, goes an essentially apostrophic relation to the subject which in its volatile hyperbole can approach a kind of inverted adoration. Thus it is equally possible to argue that the portraitist's detached and third-person account of mind and desire offers a more complete form of domination by acknowledging no relation to the object of study and disparagement.

The oft-noted imagery of fragile enclosure in *The Rape of the Lock* – the 'painted Vessel' on the Thames (ii.47), the 'frail *China* Jar' (ii.106), and the 'Silver Bound' and 'wide Circumference' of the petticoat (ii.121–2) – implies that the female mind has no 'imprison'd Essences' to 'exhale' (ii.94), and many of the poem's most celebrated effects, such as the complex transformations between sun, eyes, and gaze, depend on the play between internal and external allowed by its luminous void. As Dennis puts it, 'there is no such thing as a character in the *Rape of the Lock*: *Belinda*, who appears in it most, is a Chimera not a Character' (1939–43: vol. ii, 331). The authorial privilege of absolute insight itself represents an internalisation of the recurrent injunction in anti-feminist satire to penetrate the boudoir's private space: most famously in Swift's 'A Beautiful Young Nymph Going to Bed', but perhaps most forcefully in Ames's injunction, 'Open her secet Boxes' (1691: 22). This is rewarded by the spectacle of a 'vacant Brain' crowded by 'gay Ideas' that are externally derived and controlled (i.83). This mental vacancy manoeuvres almost any critical commentary into a position of implicit condescension – of explaining what Belinda cannot comprehend, her own motives and desires –

and allows it the satisfaction of expounding them from the perspective of an omniscient masculinity.

It is worth turning, however, to the key dramatic moment of the poem in order to distinguish an alternative possibility:

> Just in that instant, anxious *Ariel* sought
> The close Recesses of the Virgin's Thought;
> As on the Nosegay in her Breast reclin'd,
> He watch'd th' Ideas rising in her Mind,
> Sudden he view'd, in spite of all her Art,
> An Earthly Lover lurking at her Heart.
> Amaz'd, confus'd, he found his Pow'r expir'd,
> Resign'd to Fate, and with a Sigh retir'd. (iii.139–46)

Like the author and reader, Ariel is gifted with total insight into 'the close Recesses' of Belinda's mind: he abandons her because she is no longer one who 'fair and chaste/Reject[s] mankind' in order to be 'by some *Sylph* embrac'd' (i.67–8). This signifies the end of his participation in the poem: the elaborate defence strategems of the sylphs are 'in that instant' disbanded out of a mixture of pique and recognition of necessity (another example of their failure to influence the action). But who or what is 'lurking at her Heart'?

The most obvious identity for the 'Earthly Lover' would be the sender of the morning's billet-doux: a second frequent reading takes the figure to be a subconscious anticipation of and desire for the Baron's assault (which thereby becomes equated with 'Fate'). Both these options underestimate the sudden prominence of this apparition in a 'Mind' otherwise wholly transparent. ('Ideas' could only be so clearly distinguished against a surrounding vacuum.) And 'lurking' is a term of considerable force in Pope: in *Summer*, 'This harmless Grove no lurking vapour hides,/But in my Breast the Serpent Love abides' (66–7); and more ominously, in *An Essay on Man*, 'As Man, perhaps, the moment of his breath,/Receives the lurking principle of death' (ii.134–5). What has Belinda's 'Art' been employed for? To deceive Ariel perhaps, but he has previously been presented as its source. To keep lovers at bay, but the same artifice was designed to attract them. To discipline the impulses of the 'Heart', but previously these had been conspicuously absent: for better or worse, Belinda is a creature of cultural artifice rather than natural emotion.

Another possibility is that the 'Earthly Lover' indicates the presence of a masculine desire within Belinda, or at least a kind of potency that operates at a different level from the flirtatiousness of the coquette or the anatomical determinism of the female body. This may seem a bizarre suggestion. It should be remembered, however, that the sylphs themselves were originally 'inclos'd in Woman's beauteous Mold' before undergoing their 'soft Transition' into a form capable of enjoying the 'most intimate Familiarities with the Fair Sex' (i.48–50; Preface, 30–1, 25).

This suggestion may perhaps also illuminate the famous couplet:

> The Peer now spreads the glitt'ring *Forfex* wide,
> T'inclose the Lock, now joins it, to divide.   (iii.147–8).

I would suggest that the *Forfex* becomes an image of Belinda, 'spread ... wide', (di)splayed for the Baron's pleasure (the term signifies sexual availability throughout the anti-feminist tradition: for example, in Dryden's 'What care our drunken dames for whom they spread' (1958: vol. iii 694–7)). Yet in this moment of apparent mastery, it is possible to discern a paradoxical transference of force. Insofar as the lock represents autonomy for Belinda, the rape is a deprival of her power, both in terms of an immediate slump of her value on the marriage market to that of a 'degraded Toast' (iv.109), and as emblematic of a broader cultural exclusion. But in so far as the 'Lock' becomes a phallic symbol, 'inclos'd' in her, the 'fatal Engine' threatens to 'dissever' it: 'Fate urg'd the Sheers', and the subsequent fate of the sylph, 'cut ... in twain' by the 'meeting Points' of blades, legs, vaginal lips, provides ample testimony to the risk of castration (iii, 149–53; for further discussion, see Pollak 1985: 100–2). So the Baron gains the lock through symbolic self-emasculation: and here as elsewhere in Pope, the loss or renunciation of sexual prowess becomes a source of discursive authority. The question remains is what (if anything) has the other party gained through the encounter?

It has frequently been noted, particularly in relation to the enervation of Sir Plume and the narcissism of the Baron, that Belinda is herself the most virile figure in the poem: 'an arrant Ramp and a Tomrigg', as Dennis puts it (1939–43: vol. ii, 331, 334). The best-known instance occurs in the Homeric parallels to the dressing table scene, where 'awful Beauty puts on all its Arms' (i.139). But similar power is evident in Belinda's authority to summon forth 'The various Off'rings of the World' (i.130); in her bellicosity at cards, where she 'Burns to encounter' her opponents and 'decide their Doom' (a prospect which 'swells her Breast with Conquests yet to come' (iii.25–8)); and in the readiness of the 'fierce Virago' to command 'To Arms' (v.37), an epithet linking her to the passion of 'fierce *Othello*' (v.105)). This aggressive energy can be usefully related to the famous couplet in *Epistle to a Lady*: 'Men, some to Bus'ness, some to Pleasure take;/But ev'ry Woman is at heart a Rake' (215–16). 'Rake' is emphatically a masculine term: Johnson defines it as 'a loose, disorderly, vicious, wild, gay, thoughtless fellow, a man addicted to pleasure', citing this usage from Pope. So the second line could be glossed as 'every woman is at heart a man' – or at the very least a potent desiring body. The force of this singular term overpowers the comparatively vague and etiolated 'Bus'ness' and 'Pleasure' of the anonymous mass of 'Men'. The more logical version of the same sentiment is strikingly weaker: for example, in Gould's line, 'Thus if they durst, all Women would be Whores' (1682: 5), or in the direct paraphrase offered in *Sawney and Colley*, 'For *ev'ry Woman*, you are sure,/Is in her *Heart* a *very Whore*' (Anon. 1742: 11).

The precedent of Rochester as rake and wit hangs heavily over Pope's erotic vocabulary ('we must with Wilmot own/The Cordial Drop of Life is Love alone' (*Epistle* I.vi.126–7)), a point which is neatly brought out in 'On lying in the Earl of Rochester's Bed at Atterbury':

> With no poetick ardors fir'd,
> I press the bed where *Wilmot* lay,
> That here he lov'd, or here expir'd,
>   Begets no numbers grave or gay. (1–4)

'I press' seems a sadly forlorn and solitary activity in a location far more suitable for expiring in 'ardors' of a different kind – an exclusion made poignantly explicit in the verb 'begets'. Pope's customary attitude to Rochester is more censorious. He is reported by Joseph Spence as calling him a 'holiday writer' and 'of a very bad turn of mind, as well as debauched' (1966: vol. i, 201). There is a characteristically affected disdain for the 'Mob of Gentleman' of the Restoration: 'No wonder then, when all was Love and Sport,/ The willing Muses were debauch'd at Court' (*Epistle* II.i.151–2): though even here it is not difficult to detect a scarcely concealed envy for the 'fat Age of Pleasure, Wealth and Ease' of Charles II (*Essay on Criticism*, 534).

Pope and Rochester may seem the embodiment of antithetical

qualities: reckless debauchery against perpetual invalidism. Yet in many respects, a contrast with traditional masculine robustness would place them on the same side of the equation: feminised, sickly, and malicious. It should not be forgotten that it was Pope who survived to a comparatively late age, while the 'Squeamish Stomach' of his more flamboyant predecessor ('Tunbridge Wells' (6)) led to an early death. Pope praised Rochester's 'delicacy', a term which extends beyond a fastidious choice of diction to a whole mode of bodily sensitivity to the world (Spence 1966: vol. i, 473). Pope's 'Manly ways' are of course, partly defined through strictures on the aristocratic bisexuality of Lord Hervey ('Amphibious Thing'), which might easily be turned against Rochester himself (see Means 1983). (Rochester himself shows no inclination to adopt a comparable stance of martial valour, to which he was, after his courageous naval exploits as a young man, eminently entitled.)

Biographically, Pope caught the fag-end of Restoration libertinism in the unappealing figure of Wycherley (see Mack 1985: 94–100; for details of Pope's annotations to Rochester's *Poems on Several Occasions*, see Mack 1982: 384–5). There are numerous, if somewhat incongruous, attempts in his correspondence and occasional verse to adopt the persona of 'The gayest Valetudinaire/Most thinking Rake alive' ('A Farewell to London' (39–40)). (For more detailed treatment, see Winn 1979; Spacks 1984: and Turner 1988.) The most sustained poetic exercise in this vein comes in *Sober Advice from Horace*, which prompted Thomas Bentley to comment: 'What an *Erection* of Wit, what a *Tentigo* of Parts in his Notes! How he triumphs, and dashes his Sp(erm) about him!' (1735: 16). A few couplets are sufficient to convey the general flavour:

> When sharp with Hunger, scorn you to be fed,
> Except on *Pea-Chicks*, at the *Bedford-head?*
> Or, when a tight, neat Girl, will serve the Turn,
> In errant Pride continue stiff and burn?
> I'm a plain Man, whose Maxim is profest,
> 'The Thing at hand is of all Things the *best*'. (149–54)

This is Pope playing 'Philosopher and Rake' (158) with some panache, though without quite living up to Bentley's billing. Whereas in Rochester, the penis is the 'frailer part' ('The Fall' (16)), in Pope, 'that honest Part that rules us all' is dubbed 'A Thing descended from the Conqueror' (87, 90). There are incessant reminders of the narrator's virility ('continue stiff, and burn') rather than a decrial of its absence. Pope continually locates his authority in speaking as a 'plain Man' propounding a traditional 'Maxim'. The exemplary narratives in *Sober Advice* are cruel, terse, with a kind of lapidary finality: 'Engaging *Oldfield*! who, with Grace and Ease,/Could joyn the Arts, to ruin, and to please' (5–6). (Rochester would have refused the stock association of whores with 'ruin'.) Pope complacently itemises parts of the female body: 'your judicious Eye/May measure there the Breast, the Hip, the Thigh!' (133–4) (or negatively, 'Goose-rump'd, Hawk-nos'd, Swan-foot'd' (122)). While Rochester shows no interest in either 'proud Trappings' (116), or the 'Charms more latent' (126) that they might conceal, in *Sober Advice* the most cutting disdain is reserved for those oblivious to these visual guarantees: 'All for a Thing you ne'er so much as *saw*?' (136).

'Love follows flying game' (139), Pope assures us, but his whole emphasis is on establishing 'bounds to wild Desire' (143). Its random force is comfortably assimilated to the banalities of the ruling passion: 'But diff'rent Taste in diff'rent Men prevails,/And one is fired by Heads, and one by Tails' (35–6). Pope wishes to combine composure and defamation rather than rise to a crescendo of abuse: he seeks a permanence of invective. There is no free space of unpredictable utterance in Pope's poem: powerful women are curtailed by the constraints of their discursive situation rather than, as in Rochester, anarchically liberated by them. Though Rochester himself claims at one point, 'Right *Reason* . . . bounds desires, With a reforming will' ('A Satyr against Reason' (99, 102)), his verse refuses to perform any such segregation. The criteria of 'Trouble and Expence' (67) are almost wholly disregarded: there are no exhortations to caution lest you 'lose your Credit and Estate' (76). If, as Pope claims, 'Women and Fools are always in Extreme' (28), for Rochester, this would be a point in their favour. In his poetry, even the customary barriers to seduction (father, brothers, servants) are notably absent, and erotic pleasure is invested with a degree of sacrosanctness whatever its immediate context. Pope, in contrast, urges sexual continence by pointing out 'obstacles by dozens!/Spies, Guardians, Guests, old Women, Aunts, and Cozens!' (128–9), and consciously degrades the 'Happy Minute': 'She turns her very Sister to a Job,/And, in the Happy Minute, picks your Fob' (21–2). Where a comparable process of spermatic interchange may be glimpsed ('What push'd poor *Ellis* on th' Imperial Whore?/ 'Twas but to be where CHARLES had been before' (81–2)), the compulsion is not so much analysed as trivialised. There is none of the personal risk, the plaintive vulnerability, the fear of betrayal by the body, which for Rochester is the condition of encountering another's desire. For all the implied camaraderie of the stews, the predominant tone is one of a certain star-struck gloating at the spectacle of self-destructive aristocratic excess:

> And pity Men of Pleasure still in Pain!
> Survey the Pangs they bear, the Risques they run,
> Where the most lucky are but last undone.   (50–2)

There is more to *Sober Advice*, however, than glib injunctions to debauchery in moderation. The 'Men of Pleasure' undergo some unexpected metamorphoses. Bentley observes that 'our *Sober Adviser*, finding *Fufidius* in HORACE, turns him into *Fufidia*, and then persecutes the poor imaginary Woman with the most *horrid* and *brutal ribaldry* for which there's not the least foundation in the original' (1735: 5). This is not an isolated instance. Even the 'tight, neat Girl' in the passage quoted above (151) preserves something of the original anal *frisson* of the catamite boy in Horace (116–17); and Pope himself draws attention to his consistent tactic of gender-reversal in his opening Benteleian footnote: 'Why Imitated? . . . A Metaphrast has not turned *Tigellius* and *Fufidius*, *Malchinas* and *Gorgonius* . . . into so many LADIES. Benignus, hic, hunc, &c all of the Masculine Gender: Every School-boy knows more than our Imitator' (1939–69: vol. v, 74).

In his preface to Juvenal's *Sixth Satire*, Dryden observes that 'my Author makes their Lust the most Heroick of their Vices', and that 'to bid us beware of their Artifices, is a kind of silent acknowledgement, that they have more wit than Men' (1958: vol. ii, 694–5). However lurid the description of female sexuality, it is nevertheless evoked in terms liable to make it an object of envy rather than of derision to a male audience: thus Juvenal 'makes a Complement where he meant a Libel' (1958: vol. ii, 694).

Hippia and Messalina, for example, show an admirable boldness, strength and determination in conducting their liaisons, and the orgy of 'rank matrons' (441) has an unexpectedly revivifying effect:

> Nothing is feigned in this venereal strife,
> 'Tis downright lust, and acted to the life.
> So full, so fierce, so vigorous, and so strong,
> That looking on would make old Nestor young.   (453–6)

The Roman women prove themselves 'viragoes' through their undisputed prowess at acting, wrestling, and gladiatorial exercises ('Of every exercise the mannish crew/Fulfils the parts, and oft excels us too' (355–6)). All that prevents their 'mimic lechery of manly loves' (351) becoming a complete usurpation is a reluctance to abandon the more intense satisfaction of the female: 'Yet to be wholly Man she wou'd disclaim;/To quit her tenfold Pleasures at the Game/For frothy Praises and an empty Name' (362–4).

Therefore it is necessary to modify Nussbaum's contention that anti-feminist satires serve as 'recognitions of the impotence of a narrator forced to confront his own desires as he assaults female autonomy' and as occasions 'to project whatever is most frightening or unsettling in his own psyche onto another person' (1984: 4). In Dryden's translation, cumulative denunciation transforms itself into a scarcely veiled compliment: 'Yet *homo* is the common name for all' (399). And in Pope, where the issue of impotence, as we have seen, has a far more direct bearing on discursive authority, the figure of the virile woman will become the focus for a simultaneous intensification and expulsion of the desiring body.

The central contradiction of *Epistle to a Lady* has been well documented. 'The Characters of *Women*' are said to be 'more inconsistent and incomprehensible than those of *Men*', yet in their '*General Characteristick*, as to the Ruling Passion' to be 'more uniform and confin'd' ('Argument', 44): this is duly summarised as the dual impulse of 'The Love of Pleasure, and the Love of Sway' (210). The principle of mutability, that in the *Epistle to Cobham* threatened to dissolve the discursive voice into an inchoate relativism, here reinforces rather than undermines its authority. The narrator who perceives change is never himself exposed to 'those foes to Fair Ones, Time and Thought' (112); the possibility that his own judgement might be subject to similar pressures, and therefore subject to a similar volatility, is never broached.

Thus, as Brown observes, the 'Contrarieties' of female behaviour become the grounds for 'extended satiric condemnation': 'the one thing Pope knows in a changeable world is that women are contemptible' (1985: 101–2). Her reading, however, brings out a more paradoxical movement: the 'eminently transparent, clearly despicable, characterlessness' of the female mind becomes the condition of a covert reinscription of 'the ghosts of men from a lost moral system' (1985: 106). (Support may be found in Johnson's comment, 'Some of the female characters may be found perhaps more frequently among men; what is said of Philomede was true of Prior' (1905: vol. iii, 245).) Thus Brown's initial verdict of the poem's 'unqualified misogyny' becomes difficult to sustain. 'If women stand for men in the poem, where are the 'real' women to be found?'; and if none are to be found, Pope cannot be said to regard them with contempt. Instead the crucial question becomes the relation of his satiric authority to these 'surrogates for male stability' (Brown 1985: 106).

> Ladies, like variegated Tulips show,
> 'Tis to their Changes half their Charms we owe;
> Their happy Spots the nice admirer take,
> Fine by defect, and delicately weak.
> 'Twas thus Calypso once each heart alarm'd,
> Aw'd without Virtue, without Beauty charm'd;
> Her Tongue bewitch'd as oddly as her Eyes,
> Less Wit than Mimic, more a Wit than wise:
> Strange graces still, and stranger flights she had,
> Was just not ugly, and was just not mad;
> Yet ne'er so sure our passion to create,
> As when she touch'd the brink of all we hate. (41-52)

'Ladies' initially 'show', passively present themselves to their 'nice admirer' who confidently expounds 'their Changes' from a detached and presumably atemporal viewpoint. In the second couplet the focus starts to blur: one recalls the admission, 'for Spots I have' (*Satire* II.i.55), and 'delicately weak' is evidently far more applicable to Pope himself than to the subsequent portrait. 'Heart' suggests a shift from a cognitive to a more fluidly affective relation, in which Calypso dominates through a succession of active verbs – 'alarm'd', 'Aw'd', 'charm'd' and 'bewitch'd'. The 'we' and 'our' of the final couplet would seem to reassert a stable perspective, but turn out to be oddly indeterminate. To whom do they refer – an impersonal social consensus, an exclusively male audience, the speaker and his addressee, Blount, or the speaker and Calypso herself? 'Our passion to create', supported by the suddenly physical 'touch'd', suggests a specifically physical arousal within the collective male response. Yet Calypso may also be seen as partaking of this virility, and 'sure' of her capacity to control it. 'Brink' obviously comes to stand for temptation, and by extension that which tempts. The passages may be illuminatingly compared to *The Folly of Love*:

Who without horrour or amazement, can
Survey that hideous *Precipice* of Man?
Or with his Pen sufficiently deplore,
That fatal Gulph we call a *Common Whore.*
(Ames 1691: 12-13)

In Ames's lines, the gender demarcations remain clear: in Pope, however, 'all we hate', though referring most directly to 'ugly' and 'mad', is also powerfully linked by rhyme to 'our passion to create'. Discursive authority again appears to be constituted through an exorcism of desire: in this case the object of repudiation has become a female body invested with a masculine potency.

The competitive and aggressive sexuality of the central sequence of portraits in *Epistle to a Lady* is likewise identified with this quality of wit-as-aggression: Calypso (48), Philomede (76), Flavia (87), and Atossa (127); even Narcissa seeks to 'pique all mortals, yet affect a name' (61). So 'Turn then from Wits' (101) may seem to be the central injunction of the poem. But what exactly does this entail? Should we regard 'Wit' here as a disastrous imbalance of the imaginative faculty, the scandalous appropriation of a masculine prerogative, or 'inexorably a sign both of its own absence and of the absence of the presence it usurps' and thus 'no wit at all' (see Fairer 1984: 99-106; Gubar 1977; Pollak 1985: 114)? I would prefer to relate the term in more direct fashion to Pope's Restoration predecessors: not in the Bloomian sense of insufficiently absorbed precursors, but as a vocabulary and precedent for the uninhibited display and performance of desire. Flavia's credo, 'While we live, to live' (90), is surely that of a libertine intellectual:

> Wise Wretch! with Pleasures too refin'd to please,
> With too much Spirit to be e'er at ease,
> With too much Quickness ever to be taught,
> With too much Thinking to have common Thought:
> Who purchase Pain with all that Joy can give,
> And die of nothing but a Rage to live.   (95-100)

(The attributes of 'Spirit', 'Quickness', 'Thinking', 'Pain', 'Joy', and 'Rage' make the preceding accusation of 'Impotence of mind' (93) almost ludicrously inappropriate.) Similarly Narcissa (53-68) is a 'fool to Pleasure' in whom 'Passion burns'; she is governed by whim, prone to debt, aristocratically disdainful of 'Good-nature', and drawn towards 'Atheism' and 'Heathen' behaviour. And it is tempting to see in 'Sin in State, majestically drunk', with a 'barren Bride' though 'frank to all beside' (69–72), at least a passing reference to Charles II (the name Charles occurs six lines later).

With Atossa (115–50), as with Sporus, the problem of duplication is particularly acute. It has often been observed that she occupies Pope's own position of satirist. Endowed with 'Fury', 'Rage', and 'Hate', she 'Shines, in exposing Knaves, and painting Fools' (recalling 'I must paint it' (16), and anticipating 'our Scorn of Fools' (276)); she 'Finds all her life one warfare upon earth', a line which powerfully, almost blatantly, echoes Pope's own words, 'The life of a wit is a warfare upon earth' ('The Preface of 1717' Pope 1939–69: vol. i, 6). Being 'Scarce once herself, by turns all Womankind' makes her ideally qualified to enlist in the ranks of 'Chameleons, who paint in black and white' (156). The attack mounted by the satiric voice comes to seem curiously self-directed.

Here it is worth considering the most famous of Pope's female portraits in greater detail:

> But what are these to great Atossa's mind?
> Scarce once herself, but turns all Womankind!
> Finds all her life one warfare upon earth:
> Shines in exposing Knaves, and painting Fools,
> Yet is, whate'er she hates and ridicules.
> No Thought advances, but her Eddy Brain
> Whisks it about, and down it goes again.
> Full sixty years the World has been her Trade,
> The wisest Fool much Time has ever made.
> From loveless youth to unrespected age,
> No passion gratify'd except her Rage.
> So much the Fury still out-ran the Wit,
> The Pleasure miss'd her, and the Scandal hit.
> Who breaks with her, provokes Revenge from Hell,
> But he's a bolder man who dares be well:
> Her ev'ry turn with Violence pursu'd,
> No more a storm her Hate than Gratitude.
> To that each Passion turns, or soon or late;
> Love, if it makes her yield, must make her hate: (115–33)

How can this tempestuous figure possibly be reconciled with the initial proposition, 'Most Women have no Characters at all' (2)? Perhaps because female 'character' as something *composed* (in the various senses of the word) is being ideally embodied in the malleable, mute, and somewhat abjectly acquiescent Martha Blount. For all the initial insistence on 'great Atossa's mind', she is depicted as incapable of any directed intellectual activity: 'No Thought advances' without being sucked back into the 'Eddy Brain'. The whirlpool image, common in misogynist satire, is superimposed on the vagina as 'fatal Gulph' (Ames 1691: 13); compare Gould, 'That Whirl-pool Sluice which never knows a Shore' (1682: 5). (A later example occurs in Rossetti's *Jenny*: 'Poor handful of bright springwater/Flung in the whirlpool's shrieking face' (16–17).) One may even, in the light of what was said earlier about Belinda, choose to regard her mental life as a series of quasi-allegorical forces manifesting themselves through, rather than possessed by, her. But once the key emotional and psychological terms of her portrait are assembled – 'Passion', 'Rage', 'Fury', 'Wit', 'Pleasure', 'Scandal', 'Revenge', 'Violence', 'Hate', 'Gratitude', 'Passion', 'Spirit', 'Warmth', and 'Wealth' – it surely becomes difficult to deny *her* the title of 'bolder man' (129).

Thus Pope's discursive authority ('Fine by defect' (44)) yet again appears to be constituted through an exorcism of desire: in this case the object of repudiation has become a female body invested with a competitive and aggressive sexuality. Female deviance, it should be stressed, is not employed in simple monitory fashion, in order to validate the masculine discourse that condemns it. Pope's satire is directed against what it most desires. It displaces its own illusory potency on to what it affects to despise, only to find that it remains embedded, recalcitrant, within the very discourse that disowns it. Whatever gender terms one chooses to apply to the process may now appear hopelessly indeterminate in relation to Pope's work. Perhaps we may come to regard this as one of its greatest strengths.

5

BLAKE AND FEMALE REASON

Considerable enthusiasm for Blake's work has regularly been shown in more broadly based feminist studies. In Susan Griffin's *Pornography and Silence* (1981: 11), he is hailed as an apostle of eros (despite the plentiful denunciations of the body and maternal fecundity in the later work), and in Gilbert and Gubar's *The Madwoman in the Attic* (1979: 200), he is identified with a utopian refusal of the existing patriarchal canon (though however far Blake has revised Milton, it is difficult to see him as representing an alternative tradition). The more specialist studies, however, have returned a somewhat dispirited verdict. The problems lie in several areas. The wide variety of creation myths reworked by Blake almost invariably identify the origin of the sexes with fall and division (in the *Book of Urizen*, 'Eternity shudder'd when they saw,/Man begetting his likeness/On his own divided image' (6: 16–17, E78)). Second, there is a repeated demand for a fundamental subordination from the female, simultaneously presented as an innate quality and a predestined role to be achieved. Virtually any passage on Beulah will bear out this restorative, supplicatory role, but it can also be vividly seen in the response of self-recrimination both in Ololon's encounter with Milton (*Milton* 41: 29–42; 6, E141-2), and England arising on Albion's bosom (*Jerusalem* 95: 22–4, E250)). Third, we are assured of the ultimate dispensability of all feminine qualities: 'In Eternity Woman is the Emanation of Man she has no Will of her own There is no such thing in Eternity as a Female Will' (*Vision of the Last Judgement* E552). This one-sided eradication is perhaps most powerfully dramatised in Enitharmon's 'great terror' in *Jerusalem* (92: 13, E250) when Los instructs her that 'sexes must vanish and cease' while reassuring his sons 'We shall not Die' (93: 19, E251).

Susan Fox, for example, concludes:

> Contraries are by definition equal, but the females in *Milton*, however crucial and powerful Blake intended them to be, are not convincingly equal to their male contraries ... Throughout the poem females are either passive or pernicious ... he does not say all females are weak, but he does say that all weakness is female ... Yet the more clearly the female roles are defined, the more circumscribed they are by male reality: female separateness is good when it permits communication among males, bad when it corrupts that communication, good when it passively awaits embrace, bad when it actively demands embrace. The more positive Blake's female becomes, the more passive, the more male-circumscribed she becomes. Jerusalem is better than Albion, but lesser ... The conflict between Blake's doctrine and the stereotypes of sexual relationship in which he expresses it remains.
> (Fox [1976–7] 1986: 84–5, 87–8)

This is echoed in Anne Mellor's comment that 'females at their best are nurturing... generous... compassionate... all-welcoming and never-critical emotional supporters', and that 'in Blake's metaphoric system, the masculine is both logically and physically prior to the feminine' (1982–3: 155); and in Alicia Ostriker's assessment that Blake though 'perhaps not quite a classic misogynist' was nevertheless 'someone who believes that the proper study of woman is the happiness of her man and who cannot conceive of a true woman in any but a supportive, subordinate role' ([1982–3] 1986: 229).

The archetypes so vigorously applauded by Frye and myth criticism are now seen as a kind of bottom line of cultural stereotype which Blake could not shake off however much he dramatised the internal dynamics of gender. 'The poet ... who more than any other writer of his time recognised the destructive effect of received attitudes toward women ... was nevertheless to some extent a victim of those attitudes' (Fox [1976–7] 1986: 88).

The essential complaint would be that Blake, by continuing to operate within a polarity of 'feminine indolent bliss' and 'active masculine virtue' renders the female intrinsically powerless (*The Four Zoas* 53: 6, 9, E322). Ololon asks, 'are we Contraries, O Milton' (*Milton* 41: 35, E142), but the answer is negative; she must be relegated to a separate level as bystander and perhaps ultimate booty in the 'great Wars of Eternity' (*Milton* 30: 19, E128).

There remains an element of externality in this treatment. It runs into the problems encountered by early representations of women criticism: the possibility of finite enumeration, that there seems little point in an exhaustive cataloguing of predictable deficiencies. But I think an interesting point is raised about the underlying polarities in Blake's thought on sexuality. If male and female tend to be defined in terms of active and passive, it would seem necessary for these at some level to be homologous with desire and reason, and there has been little compunction in mapping these terms onto an imaginative creativity continually threatened by entrapment within an alluring receptivity. But even this is more peculiar than it might at first appear. If man's 'pre-eminence', as Wollstonecraft insists ([1792] 1989: 81), lies in his faculty of reason, Blake immediately concedes this to the female half of the equation.

Furthermore, the 'received attitudes' deserve rather less perfunctory inspection. I would like to examine Rousseau's treatment of this issue in *Emile*, and briefly glance at Wollstonecraft's response. I shall then discuss three aspects of Blake's work in the context of this debate: sexual differentiation (or the absence of it) in his early writings; the potentially reactionary proclamation of joy in *Visions of the Daughters of Albion*; and finally the relation of desire and reason in the erotic dystopia of *Jerusalem*.

The relationship between Rousseau and Blake has yet to be illuminatingly explored. The studies to date have tended to subsume Rousseau into a collectively Deistic enlightenment, habitually coupled with Voltaire, initially greeted as liberator ('Over the head the soul of Voltaire shone fiery, and over the army Rousseau his white cloud/Unfolded' (*French Revolution* 283–4, E295)), later dismissed as one of 'two covering cherubs' guarding the temple of Natural Religion (*Jerusalem* 66: 12, E216; see Ackland 1989). At no point does Blake show interest in the enhanced subjectivism of *Confessions*, *La Nouvelle Heloise*, or *Reveries of the Solitary Walker*. Unlike Shelley, or indeed any of the other major romantics, Blake's affinity is with the genealogical mode of the *Second Discourse*, whose narrative of cultural progression as spiritual decline seems to have influenced the Lambeth Books, and *Emile*, the text with which I shall be predominantly concerned.

The most evident linkage appears in the sequence of images at the close of *Tiriel*:

> The child springs from the womb, the father ready stands to form
> The infant head while the mother idle plays with her dog on the couch.
> The young bosom is cold for lack of mothers nourishment & milk
> Is cut off from the weeping mouth. With difficulty & pain
> The little lids are lifted & the little nostrils opend
> The father forms a whip to rouse the sluggish senses to act
> And scourges off all youthful fancies from the new-born man
> Then walks the weak infant in sorrow compelld to number footsteps
> Upon the sand. &c   (pl. 8: 12–20, E281–2)

The passage dramatises Rousseau's discussion of midwifery, of obstetrics, of suckling and wetnursing, of maternal neglect and of excessive parental demands: 'From birth you are always checking them, your first gifts are fetters, your first treatment torture' (1974: 11). The psychology of the child in *Emile* – 'There is no middle course, he must rule or obey. Thus his earliest ideas are those of a tyrant or a slave' (1974: 15) – has obvious relevance to the *Songs*. Rousseau observes 'the most dangerous period in human life lies between birth and the age of twelve' (1974: 57) – which may or may not lie behind 'Into the dangerous world I leapt' ('Infant Sorrow' E78). 'The tendency to anger, vexation and rage' can be linked to Orc, as well as comments such as 'the work of destruction accords better with his eagerness', and his 'overflowing activity' remains 'the slave of anger, a prey to the fieriest passions' (1974: 33, 34, 51).

The insistence on the learnt nature of perception is close to Blake's numerous passages on constriction through the senses: for example, such remarks as 'we are now confined to a circle', and 'of all the senses, sight is that which we can least distinguish from the judgement of the mind; so it takes a long time to learn how to see' (Rousseau 1974: 129, 107). The lengthy interpolation, 'The Creed of the Savoyard Priest', seems to have influenced Blake's characterisation of Deism, both in its scepticism towards biblical revelation and its espousal of the 'selfish virtues of the natural heart' (52: 28, E199). (The characterisation in 'Mock on mock on

Voltaire, Rousseau' (E468) probably also draws on the treatment of 'civil religion' in the *The Social Contract*.)

Scant attention, however, has been paid to Rousseau's later re-emergence in *Jerusalem*. He first figures prominently in the preface to the third book as a 'preacher of Natural Morality or Natural Religion', and so 'in the state named Rahab' (pl. 52, E198). The 'religion of Satan' is vigorously characterised as 'the Worship of the God of this World by the means of what you call Natural Religion and Natural Philosophy, and of the Natural Morality or Self-righteousness, the Selfish Virtues of the Natural Heart'. This is a more accurate characterisation than may at first appear, running together Rousseau's insistence on the ontological primacy of feeling ('to exist is to feel' (1974: 253)) with the innate impulse of self-interest, described as the most fundamental human instinct in *The Second Discourse, The Social Contract,* and *Emile*.

Voltaire and Rousseau are adjudged 'Pharisees & Hypocrites, for you are constantly talking of the virtues of the human heart, and particularly of your own, that you may accuse others'. The *Confessions* are brusquely, though not altogether unfairly, dismissed as 'an apology & cloke for his sin & not a confession' (pl. 52, E199). More specifically, 'Rousseau thought Men good by Nature; he found them Evil & found no friend' (pl. 52, E199), appears to allude to the disastrous stay with Hume in England in 1766–7 and resulting acrimonious exchange of pamphlets (see Duffy 1979: 23–5).

Rather surprisingly, no one has bothered to follow up the connection, through Wollstonecraft, with the discussion of femininity in *Emile*. (For general background on the history of female education, see Martin 1985: 38–69.) Rousseau posits that the ideal education is conducted by a male tutor in almost continuous contact with his charge (obviously limiting the number of families through simple reasons of cost). The elevation of tutor to parent surrogate involves a corresponding down-grading of the role of female parent, to whom the text is explicitly addressd as simultaneous exhortation and accusation: 'Tender anxious mother, I appeal to you' (Rousseau 1974: 5); 'Good mother, be on your guard against the deceptions prepared for you' (1974: 164). On the one hand, it is assumed that she will be solicitous to the best interests of her child, on the other that she is responsible for its existing faults.

Somewhat anomalously, Rousseau lavishly apostrophises female power while retaining a model of citizenship based on classical city-states that entirely disenfranchises women. The identification of culture with the feminine is partly due to control over education, and partly to a more complex narrative of the origins of society. Men have the physical strength to be self-sufficient; women require a protector and provider while engaged in child-bearing, and so have a much greater interest in establishing family bonds. Hence the ambivalent status of the sexual impulse in Rousseau. It is the underlying motivation of society, in so far as it induces males to form bonds, and enter an ever more elaborate set of cultural ties; but it also represents a kind of fall from pristine solitude. Thus the structural significance of the ecstatic meditations on botany in the *Reveries* lies in its equation of perfect happiness with 'asexual anarchy' (Schwartz 1984: 8).

The ideal circumstances under which Emile is to be brought up preclude contact with girls, whether sisters or cousins, and a reduction of time spent under the tutelage of mothers or aunts to a minimum. When Sophie is eventually introduced, it is virtually as a different species. 'It is not good that man should be so alone' so Emile must be given his 'promised helpmeet'; but 'we can must know beforehand what she is and then we decide where to look for her' (Rousseau 1974: 321). The education of the girl, as with Milton and Freud, adopts the premise of the secondariness of the female. A paradigm is established for the male child which is then awkwardly transposed to explain an alternative pattern of development. ('Those who regard woman as an imperfect man are undoubtedly mistaken, but they have external resemblance on their side' (1974: 172).)

An opposition that presents itself as a confirmation of equality between the sexes is consistently weighted to endorse female subordination. There are plenty of illustrious precedents for such a procedure, dating back to the two rival creation accounts in Genesis; the first, 'male and female created he them' (1: 27), giving apparently joint dominion; the second, 'And the rib which the Lord God had taken from the man, made he a woman, and brought her unto the man' (2: 22), according a formal priority to the male. In *Paradise Lost*, as Wollstonecraft points out ([1792] 1989: 89), Milton conflates the two alternative narratives – 'unargued I obey' (IV.636) alongside 'among unequals what society' (VII. 383) – in order to insist upon the necessary subordination between equal companions. And famously in Freud, the bisexual components in each personality do not prevent the difficult, even blighted, development of the girl child. On a deconstructive model, there will always be a rhetorical supplement serving both to conceal and to accentuate the imbalance of, in Irigaray's elegant formulation, 'the blind spot of an old dream of symmetry' (see Parker 1987; and Jacobus, 1989: 241-50).

In Rousseau, this lies in the idealisation of difference: 'a perfect man and a complete woman should no more resemble each other in mind than in face' (1974: 322). Sophie in order to be 'as truly a woman as Emile is a man' must possess the appropriate 'physical and moral' features (1974: 321). Rousseau continually oscillates between difference as only a matter of degree and potentially culturally revisable, and attributing a wholly different ontological status (or lack of one) to women – 'nor is their perfection reducible to any common standard, (1974: 322).

Thus he continually makes statements such as 'en tout ce qui ne tient pas au sexe la femme est homme' (Rousseau 1762: vol. iv, 3: 'but for her sex a woman is a man' (1974: 321)) which can be read as supporting either position. When he approaches the contemporary distinction between biological sex and cultural gender – 'where men and women are like we have to do with the characteristics of the species, where they are unlike we have to do with the characteristics of sex' (1974: 321) – he reverses its customary application: biological similarity mitigates cultural difference. Indeed, the conclusions drawn from superior physical prowess are the reverse of what might have been expected: 'the stronger party seems to be master but is in fact dependent on the weaker' (1974: 323). It is not 'weakness which yields to force' but 'voluntary self-surrender'; the woman is 'proud' of her weakness, 'providing herself beforehand with excuses, with the right to be weak if she chooses' (1974: 323). Thus Rousseau claims that 'we rarely hear of violence' except in times of 'simplicity of nature'. It is now necessary to use 'gallantry' to achieve favours, hence 'woman reigns, not by the will of man, but by the decrees of nature herself' (1974: 323-4).

Rousseau's vocabulary is particularly slippery on this point; the general point of physical strength as distinction between the sexes emerges as a justification and even desirable mode of present conduct. As in Freud, description easily slides into prescription: 'the man should be strong and active, the woman should be weak and passive; the one must have both the power and the will; it is enough that the other should offer little resistance' (1974: 323). It is noteworthy that the French is far less conclusive – 'il faut nécessairement que l'un veuille & puisse, il suffit que l'autre résiste peu' (1762: vol. iv, 5). In itself this 'veuille & puisse' could be read as simply able and willing, or referring to the physical necessity of the man instigating intercourse.

It is useful to pay close attention to the problems encountered by the two contemporary translators of *Emile*: Thomas Nugent (1763) and William Kenrick (1767). Here 'veuille & puisse' become interior qualities: the phrase becomes 'necessarily have power and will' (Nugent 1763: vol. iii, 5)) and 'necessary that one should have both the power and the will' (Kenrick 1767: vol. iv, 4)). Generally, they try and reinforce the separation of genders – 'par-tout des rapports et par-tout des différences' (Rousseau 1762: vol. iv, 3), becomes 'differs entirely' (Kenrick 1767: vol. iv, 2) – and stabilise Rousseau's frequently entirely unillusioned analysis in a more euphemistic vocabulary. 'Elle le repousse & se défend toujours, mais non pas toujours avec la même force, ni par consequent avec le même succès' (Rousseau 1762: vol. iv, 9) which could describe simple physical resistance to force, acquires the adverb 'coyly' in Nugent (1763: vol. iii, 7); and in Kenrick is rendered as 'she is by nature constantly coy, and betrays a seeming reluctance to yield to his embrace' (1767: vol. iv, 7).

The greatest difficulties are caused by Rousseau's transposition of the vocabulary of violence: man has strength, but it is women who are dangerous. To give a couple of examples from many. 'Sa violence à elle est dans ses charmes' (Rousseau 1762: vol. iv, 6) is almost impossible to translate: literally his violence to her is one of his attractions or is the result of her charms. In Kenrick it becomes 'the violence of his desires depends on her charms' (1767: vol. iv, 4); in Nugent 'her violence depends on her charms' (1763: vol. iii, 5). Another example of this kind of slippage can be seen in 'if the siege is to be successful the besieged must permit or direct the attack' (Rousseau [1911] 1974: 323); in the original, this is 'pour que l'attaquant soit victorieux, il faut que l'attaqué le permette ou l'ordonne', with a masculine case for 'l'attaqué' (Rousseau 1762: vol. iv, 9–10).

This is essentially a patristic argument: because woman has 'la facilité d'exciter les desirs' (Rousseau 1762: vol. iv, 11), specifically the irrational power of erection, she is deemed responsible for man's arousal, and therefore requires strict control. There are pragmatic grounds offered for this restraint, but *the jurisdiction* envisaged is in excess of the pretexts given: the ultimate justification is this prior affront. (This is neatly brought out by the way that the dismissal of female complaint with 'elle a tort' (1762: vol. iv, 16) is translated by Nugent not as 'she is wrong' but as 'she is to blame' (1763: vol. iii, 19).)

Male desire is conveniently curtailed by a notably unspecific 'nature', which is later identified with the power of reason. It should be stressed that Rousseau's treatise on education offers no simple irrationalist celebration of childhood. It is urged that the relentless accumulation of knowledge implied by the Lockian 'stock' of ideas in the memory be postponed until puberty at least: 'keep his mind idle as long as possible' in order to 'prolong the innocence of childhood' (Rousseau 1974: 58, 177). Wollstonecraft is, however, incorrect when she claims Rousseau wished 'to stop the progress of reason in both sexes' ([1792] 1989: 89). The amount of practical expertise and gratified curiosity acquired by the child in itself represents a considerable achievement. Reason is hailed as the 'last and choicest growth' (Rousseau 1974: 53), the mark of participation in the adult world; the deferral of responsibility is 'retarding nature to the advantage of reason' (1974: 280).

The key question becomes: 'are women capable of solid reason; should they cultivate it, can they cultivate it successfully? Is this culture useful in relation to the functions laid upon them? Is it compatible with becoming simplicity?' (Rousseau 1974: 345). Arguments are made on the side of female reason. The girl is conceded to show earlier development. To lack reason involves a 'loss of esteem', makes the woman unable to reconcile conscience and opinion, and prevents her from being 'the judge of her own judges' (1974: 339, 346, 355). Husbands are easily bored with uneducated wives, who are unable to distinguish between fops and virtuous men, and are easily led into adultery, resulting in the dissolution of marriage and the breakdown of hereditary transmission of property.

Yet the demand for equality is described as 'quelle étrange dépravation de jugement' (Rousseau 1762: vol. iv, 6). This is usually translated as 'error', yet retains the force of 'depravity', and so can be linked to the continuous subtext of 'passions immodérées' and 'désirs illimités' (1762: vol. iv, 9). The linkage is further reinforced by the comment, 'in our great towns depravity begins at birth, in our small towns it begins with reason' (1974: 352). Where

Wollstonecraft urges the acquisition of rationality as a means of curbing the female 'propensity' for sexual pleasure, Rousseau regards it as a similar potentially uncontrollable excess. Woman must not be endowed with reason for this would undermine the priority of the male in the precarious equilibrium of the sexes: 'the result would be the destruction of both' (1974: 322).

Such a circumscription is regarded as no injustice because 'woman weak as she is and limited in her range of observation, perceives and judges the forces at her disposal to supplement her weakness, and those forces are the passions of men' (Rousseau 1974: 350). What Blake calls 'subtil modesty' (*Visions* 6: 7; E48) is therefore simultaneously an innate impulse ('cunning is a natural gift of woman') and cultural recompense ('a fair equivalent for her lack of strength' (Rousseau 1974: 334)). 'Her beauty and her wiles are all that she has' and must therefore be regarded as 'skill, not duplicity' (1974: 335, 348); therefore, 'in the genuine inclinations of their sex', women 'are not false even when they tell a lie' (1974: 348). (Thus the self-contradiction within the space of a few lines is only apparent: 'moreover our clumsy systems of education have made women so deceitful and so over-stimulated their appetites that you can no longer rely on the most clearly proved affection', followed by a footnote, 'just the opposite of that deceit becoming in a woman' (1974: 393).)

Rousseau contrasts 'female animals' whose desires are finite compared to the 'boundless' ones of woman who therefore must be 'curbed by this shame' (1974: 322). Man possesses reason as 'the curb of strength', but 'what would take the place of this negative instinct in woman if you rob them of their modesty' (1974: 54, 322)? In the original, this is 'où sera le supplément de cet instinct négatif dans les femmes, quand vous leur aurez ôté la pudeur' (1762: vol. iv, 8). 'Supplement' is translated as substitute by both Kenrick and Nugent, but can also be read as in addition to. (As in the earlier quotation, woman 'judges the forces at her disposal to supplement her weakness' (1974: 350); reinforced by the comment that 'the first lessons come by virtue, art only supplements them' (1974: 339)). Modesty both restrains and completes desire: it cannot be charged with hypocrisy because deceit is expected, the culturally manageable variant of an otherwise unlimited desire.

So Rousseau's analysis of existing social arrangements is essentially a justification of a lavishly praised natural order on grounds which he makes little effort to distinguish from cynical expediency. It should be stressed that this is often more incisive than Blake, because of its alertness to the formative power of social institutions; indeed Blake could be said to naturalise its more dubious aspects.

Rousseau is very perceptive about the deforming effects of social conditioning, freely acknowledging the 'inequality of man-made laws' and the calculated instillation of much of what Blake asserts to be innate: 'they must be trained to bear the yoke from the first, so that they may not feel it, to master their own caprices and to submit themselves to the will of others' (Rousseau 1974: 359). Consequently, 'the life of a good woman is a perpetual struggle against self', but 'il est juste que ce sexe partage la peine des maux qu'il nous a causé' (Rousseau 1762: vol. iv, 47): the final clause is translated by Kenrick as 'which it has caused us' and by Nugent 'of which we are the cause' (1767: vol. iv, 30; 1763: vol. iii, 27). The possibility that 'she should early learn to submit to injustice' (Rousseau 1974: 333) never arises on the Blakean model of intrinsic harmony ('let the men do their duty & the women will be such wonders' (E585)). The insistence on 'naked beauty' becomes a means of refusing analysis of what Wollstonecraft calls the 'drapery of factitious sentiments' ([1792] 1989: 220).

Rousseau's propositions on female reason are at best paradoxical. Women are incapable of abstract thought; nevertheless they have an astuteness and capacity for manipulation which in their position is not merely a necessary defence but rational for them to adopt. Women cannot desire as subjects, merely present themselves as objects of desire; but in so far as it is their craft that instigates male arousal, they can be said to control it by means of a courtship ritual of feint and resistance. The consequence is that women can be seen as possessing either both or neither qualities of desire and reason in their socially induced cunning; it is both that which makes them desirable, and the form of desire which it is rational for them on their own terms to pursue.

Rousseau's analysis lies behind Wollstonecraft's basic thesis in *A Vindication of the Rights of Women*: in the contemporary education of women, 'strength and usefulness are sacrificed to beauty', and this 'barren blooming' was produced through a 'system of education' that was more 'anxious to render them alluring mistresses than affectionate wives and rational mothers' (Wollstonecraft [1792] 1989: 73). Thus the minds of women are 'enfeebled by false refinement' leading to them being 'treated as a kind of subordinate beings and not as part of the human species' ([1792] 1989: 73). Women become the victims rather than beneficiaries of sensibility; pleasure itself is a form of social indoctrination. Here the recent charge is that Wollstonecraft not merely concedes but even grotesquely exaggerates the erotic preoccupation of women. All female desire becomes a learned response to a prior male demand for which women are held responsible as 'slaves of casual lust' ([1792] 1989: 208).

What is less to be expected is the intense hostility repeatedly directed against women within the text: 'all those who view them with a philosophic eye must, I should think, wish with me that they may grow every day more and more masculine' (Wollstonecraft [1792] 1989: 74). The paradigm of human maturation, as exemplified in the authorial voice, is 'to obtain a character as a human being, regardless of distinction of sex'; a disconcerting reminder of the Blakean 'Humanity knows not of Sex' (*Jerusalem* 44: 33, E191). This stance has produced a trend in recent feminist criticism, after a period of hagiography for both text and author, to see *A Vindication* as much as a betrayal as a proclamation.

The text is undeniably class-circumscribed: as Wollstonecraft herself says, 'the instruction which has hitherto been addressed to women has rather been applicable to *ladies*' ([1792] 1989: 74); and working-class women appear only in tart asides on the corrupting influence of maid-servants ('the square-elbowed family drudge' ([1792] 1989: 136)). No attempt is made to establish or define a group-consciousness: instead there is an explicit distaste for the 'gross degree of familiarity' of female company ([1792] 1989: 197–8) and hints of 'nasty indecent tricks' when women 'pig together in the same bedchamber' ([1792] 1989: 236)). No capacity to generate social change is located in women; direct exhortation tends to be addressed towards male attitudes – 'would men but generously snap our chains' ([1792] 1989: 220), 'be just then, O ye men of understanding' ([1792] 1989: 266).

Virtually nothing within the feminine realm is considered admirable; the authorial vantage aspired to is that of the' disinterested spirit' (Wollstonecraft [1792] 1989: 65), which if anything is more unsparing than that of the male satirist. Hamlet's 'they dress; they paint, and nickname God's creatures' ([1792] 1989: 76) and 'seems! I know not seems' ([1792] 1989: 168) are cited approvingly, and the text is laden with uncontested Popean maxims: 'fine by defect and delicately weak', 'the brink of all we hate', 'Matter too soft a lasting mark to bear' ([1792] 1989: 131, 96, 260; see Matthews 1990)). All is 'false refinement, immorality and vanity' ([1792] 1989: 74): the vices of a privileged leisure class are projected down the social scale as universal characteristics. Despite her earlier and subsequent enthusiasm for Rousseau's work, he is here unsparingly condemned for the 'sensibility that made him degrade woman by making her the slave of love' ([1792] 1989: 161). Nevertheless the major premises of this 'philosophy of lasciviousness' ([1792] 1989: 117n) are not merely adopted but intensified. Wollstonecraft moves from Rousseau's insistence that women's education must be 'relative' to men, 'le femme est faite spécialement pour plaire a l'homme' (1762: vol. iv, 5) 'woman is specially made for man's delight' (1974: 322)), to an insistence that pleasure is constitutive of the feminine *per se*, in a way that contradicts Rousseau's alternative characterisations of desire as an illusion best sustained by absence, as she herself notes elsewhere (Wollstonecraft [1792] 1989: 100).

Little attention is paid, for example, to women's lack of legal rights compared to their 'over-stretched sensibility': 'to their senses women are made slaves' (Wollstonecraft [1792] 1989: 130). One area in which Blake is noticeably more acute than Wollstonecraft is in acknowledging female labour. This is evident not only in Vala's great lament, 'We are made to turn the wheel for water/To carry the heavy basket on our scorched shoulders' (*The Four Zoas* 31: 6–7, E314), and the tableau of the spinning-girls, 'Endless their labour, with bitter food, void of sleep/ Tho hungry they labour' (*Jerusalem* 59: 30–1, E207), but also in Oothon's vision of utopia in which she relaxes 'wearied with work' (*Visions* 7: 1; E49).

The political analogy frequently employed insists upon women's 'illicit sway' rather than their powerlessness (Wollstonecraft [1792] 1989: 109): 'the slavery to which the pride and sensuality of man and their short-sighted desire of sway, like that of dominion in tyrants, has subjected them' ([1792] 1989: 113). The linkage of beauty, duplicity, and power that emerges in Blake's Notebook poems ('Soft deceit & idleness/These are Beautys sweetest dress' (E466)) and continued in *Europe* ('That Woman, lovely Woman! may have dominion' (6: 3, E61)) is already implicit in Wollstonecraft's text. Pleasure, actual, tangible, and immediate, leads to a degree of control: 'this artificial weakness produces a propensity to tyrannise, and gives birth to cunning, the natural opponent of strength' (Wollstonecraft [1792] 1989: 77). So why the necessity to obtain reason? Wollstonecraft claims 'it is a farce to call any being virtuous whose virtues do not result from the exercise of its own reason' ([1792] 1989: 90); as for men and women, 'the nature of reason must be the same in all, if it be an emanation of divinity ... the inquiry is whether she has reason or not' ([1792] 1989: 122). The faculty is defined in strict Lockian terms: 'the power of generalising ideas, of drawing comprehensive conclusions from individual observations, is the only acquirement, for an immortal being, that really deserves the name of knowledge' ([1792] 1989: 123). 'Children cannot be taught too early to submit to reason' ([1792] 1989: 227), and there is a brusque dismissal of any specifically feminine intuition. Anything less than the axiomatic demonstration of 'clear and vigorous judgement' is dismissed as a 'negligent kind of guesswork' designed to 'enslave women by cramping their minds and sharpening their senses' ([1792] 1989: 91).

Such statements appear to lend support to the recent tendency to turn her charge against Rousseau, that the 'voluptuous tyrant' projected his own desire as 'natural law' (Wollstonecraft [1792] 1989: 160–1), against the 'dynamics of repression and compensation' of her own text. Cora Kaplan remarks that Wollstonecraft 'offers a puritan sexual ethic with such passionate conviction that self-denial seems a libidinized activity' (1986: 36). There are a striking number of asides on 'the depravity of the appetite that brings the sexes together' (Wollstonecraft [1792] 1989: 208) and perhaps most graphically 'what are the cold, or feverish caresses of appetite, but sin embracing death' ([1792] 1989: 264). The ideal of a genderless rationality involves a systematic repression of pleasure; or, if read biographically, a therapeutic asceticism designed to counteract the unhappiness of her attachment to Fuseli at the time of composition (see Poovey 1984: 48–81).

Wollstonecraft sternly insists 'love, from its very nature, must be transitory': one can only be 'degraded' by the 'propensity to enjoy the present moment' ([1792] 1989: 121); The Supreme Being is conceived in deistic terms as accessible through reason; adherence to rational faith necessitates a continuous renunciation of immediate pleasure. Yet the 'salutary, sublime curb of principle' ([1792] 1989: 105) inherits some of Rousseau's ambivalence towards shame as 'frein' for 'desir illimite'. Thus the question in *Thel* – 'Why a tender curb upon the youthful burning boy?' (6: 19, E6))

– may be answered: in 'curbing a sensual fondness' ([1792] 1989: 195), the means of repression itself becomes the object of desire, which could not subsist without it.

Reason is not merely a 'curb', but a post-mortem perspective, 'the stamen of immortality' (Wollstonecraft [1792] 1989: 122). Wollstonecraft's concern for the plight of the vacant female soul after death – denied 'a proper education, or to speak with more precision, a well-stored mind' ([1792] 1989: 101) – leads her to agonise on 'where is that store laid up to clothe the soul when it leaves the body' ([1792] 1989: 123). There are plenty of parallels in eighteenth-century theology, notably Addison and Butler, but there is something peculiarly sexualised about this disengagement. What Wollstonecraft offers as 'an emphatical description of damnation: – when the spirit is represented as continually hovering with abortive eagerness round the defiled body, unable to enjoy any thing without the organs of sense' ([1792] 1989: 130) can equally well stand as an emblem of the relation of her own discursive voice to that which it repudiates. Hence Blake's repeated insistence in *Visions* on Oothon hovering over the breast of Theotormon; and it is surely no coincidence that the famous phrase, 'the self-enjoyings of self-denial' (7: 9, E49) is a reworking of Wollstonecraft's 'they cannot submit to resign the highest sensual gratification, nor even to relish the epicurism of virtue – self-denial' ([1792] 1989: 196). If Wollstonecraft must be allotted a role in *Visions*, it is as least as much Theotormon as Oothon, spurning 'the moment of desire' in favour of 'the rewards of continence' (7: 8, E49).

So reason is seen as synonymous with emancipation in terms of rights, equality, the better performance of duty; but in its structural function comes to resemble Rousseau's technique for sustaining an otherwise transient impulse: the ethic of deferral that reaches a *reductio ad absurdum* in *La Nouvelle Heloise*. Even in *Emile* there is no consummation: the lovers are separated at the end of the book; desire is an inculcated illusion that requires distance to thrive.

It is usually assumed that Wollstonecraft figures only briefly as a significant influence on Blake, dropping by the wayside after the revolutionary epicentre of the early 1790s. She is allowed only one reference in the annotated Blake, and that is coupled with Godwin (Stevenson 1989: 181n); and more detailed studies have almost uniformly concentrated on how Blake has 'relentlessly exposed' the limitations of her work (Ackland 1983: 192; see also Mitchell 1984; Lee 1983). This may be refuted by simple textual detail. The influence of her previous *A Vindication of the Rights of Men* is evident in the denunciation of enclosure, tithes, game-laws, and the press-gang in *Visions*, and perhaps its reference to parents seeking to imprison their child, Orc-like, with an 'ignoble chain' ([1790] 1989: 14). In the *Vindications of the Rights of Women*, we are also told 'parents often love their children in the most brutal manner' as a 'pretext to tyrannise' ([1792] 1989: 221). The influence of Wollstonecraft's text is neither insignificant nor localised to a brief period. 'In the world few act from principle; present feelings and early habits are the early springs; but how would the former be deadened, and the latter rendered iron-corroding fetters if the world were shown to young people just as it is' ([1792] 1989: 176) obviously may be linked to the 'mind-forg'd manacles' of 'London' (E27); 'specious poisons, that encrusting morality eat away the substance' ([1792] 1989: 201) to the 'Incrustation over my immortal/Spirit' in *Milton* (40: 35–6, E141); and 'religion will not have this condensing energy, unless it be founded upon reason' ([1792] 1989: 184) to Urizen's action in *The Four Zoas* of 'condensing the strong energies into little compass' (30: 5, E313).

The central myth of *The Four Zoas*, the seduction of the Universal Man by Vala, conforms neatly to Wollstonecraft's 'To see a mortal adorn an object with imaginary charms, and then fall down and worship the idol he himself hath set up' ([1790] 1989: 180); and also recalls the 'Idol-Virtue of the Natural Heart' denounced in *Milton* (38: 46, E138). In the opening sequence of *The Four Zoas*, Enion's reweaving of the body of Tharmas into the spectre, 'in every man most insane & most/Deformed' (6: 38–9, E299), culminates in the production of a rapacious and devouring sexuality ('mingling together they join in burning anguish') which transforms her into both a 'bright wonder' ('Beauty all blushing with desire') and insatiable demon ('Half Woman & half beast' (7: 1–4, E299)). Vala herself is defined primarily in terms of erotic bonding with Luvah, Enitharmon claims power through her right to withhold sexual access, and Urizen declares to Ahania that 'Thy passivity thy laws of obedience & insincerity/Are my abhorrence' (43: 10–11, E322).

I shall go on to argue that terms established in the debate between Rousseau and Wollstonecraft continue to be powerfully relevant to the sexual psychology of *Jerusalem*. First, however, I wish to establish some connections with Blake's earlier work, and then look more closely at *Visions of the Daughters of Albion*.

In *Studies in Classic American Literature* Lawrence compares Blake to Poe as another 'one of those ghastly, obscene "Knowers"' (1956: 338). This identification goes against a massive weight of critical commentary presenting his work as a continuous repudiation of reason. Yet from a very different perspective, Eliot also stresses Blake's 'extraordinary labour of simplification' and refusal to be distracted from 'exact statement' (1951: 317). This is attributed, however, to a 'mind unclouded by current opinions' rather than to an extreme precision in the use of a dominant contemporary psychology. Since the lexical studies of Josephine Miles (1957, 1973), it has been clear that Blake's core vocabulary remains reasonably constant: despite the rampant proliferation of mythological entities his work continues to depend on a finite cluster of sentimentalist terms: love, pity, wrath, joy, sorrow, and, from a slightly different idiom, desire.

The characteristic Blakeian vocabulary can look like a modified prosopopoeia, distinguished only by its unusual degree of animism. Abstract terms are certainly more sprightly than in the run of eighteenth-century personification. But it is not so much this that is distinctive as the tightly bound causal sequences: internalised emblematic narratives witnessed by a curiously inert bystander. Albion's plight in *Jerusalem* is indicative of a continuous procedure: 'All his Affections now appear with outside' (19: 17, E162).

In very general terms, Blake may be said to be the most propositional of writers on sexual desire: as Los harangues his opponents in *Jerusalem*, 'Tell him to be no more dubious: demand explicit words' (17: 61, E161). At times he seems to believe not merely, as Mallarmé suggested, that the world exists to end up in a book, but that the human psyche could be explained in a single line decisively enough phrased.

In more technical terms, Blake offers not inductive generalisations, but posits a thesis of essential though defining potentiality, giving *a priori* suppositions that cannot be refuted by any particular instance. The opening sentence of Rousseau's *The Social Contract* provides a famous example of the same structure: 'Man is born free, and yet we see him every where in chains' (1761: 3). Leaving aside queries about whether this includes women, or indeed whether 'man' is born at all rather than individual children, if he is everywhere imprisoned, freedom can only be defined in terms of the opposite of a present condition.

A potential dualism is opened up even within the simplest terms.

A genuine emotion situated within an eternal present unavailable to us becomes the grounds for the dismissal of its empirically experienced fallen counterpart. So it should cause no surprise that as early as the annotations to Lavater, hell may be defined as 'being shut up in the possession of corporeal desires which shortly weary the man' (E579).

There seems little or no element of personal testimony in such utterances, or performative force, to adopt Austin's terminology. To quote a famous quatrain:

> Never pain (seek) to tell thy love
> Love that never told can be
> For the gentle wind does move
> Silently invisibly. (E458)

The ambiguity of the first two lines neatly underlines their function as speech-act: do not seek to articulate a love that can never be communicated, or do not tell your lover that love can exist without being expressed. This is not a telling of love, but a statement about the telling, in which the internal emotion is readily conflated with its supposed recipient. It is a description of an adequately encapsulated consciousness from an almost eerily detached vantage. There is no difficulty, for example, in switching the line 'Why was I born with a different face' from a confessional lyric (E700) to a speech in the ballad 'Mary' (E479), and all through the Notebook poems a similar objectification occurs: 'But once alas committing a Mistake/He bore the wretched Soul of William Blake' (E495).

To give a trivial and probably apocryphal example from Cunningham's biography:

> he was describing one evening in company the pains he had suffered from some capricious lady or other, when Katherine Boucher said, 'I pity you from my heart'. 'Do you pity me?' said Blake, 'then I love you for that'. 'And I love you', said the frank-hearted lass, and so the courtship began.
> (1975: 174)

What is distinctively Blakeian in this exchange is the status of 'then' as a third-person description of a mental state; pity is not an act or a moment but a continuous state of relation. The narrative orthodoxy would be typified by the echo of Othello's speech to Desdemona – 'She loved me for the dangers I had pass'd/And I lov'd her that she did pity them' (I.iii.167–8) – where past narration allows the confident enunciation of a resultant emotion. Blake, however, depicts present emotion in what Donald Davie dubs the 'syntax as of the proposition' (1976: 81). If x, then y; if pity then love, and conversely, if no pity, then no love.

This peculiar clarity of definition concerning mental events contributes to the extreme difficulty of reading in a centre of sentience or pursuing any kind of associative linkage. Blake's work is almost entirely unresponsive to such an account of imagination, although substantial elements of his aesthetics emerge out of the same tradition.

There is also a conspicuous absence of erotic innuendo, inflection. It should be stressed that Blake has no interest in the unconscious as source of either artistic creativity or libidinal drives: Plato's claim that 'Poets & Prophets do not know or Understand what they write or Utter' is denounced as a 'most pernicious falsehood' (*Vision of the Last Judgement* E544). When Oothon pleads 'And then tell me the thoughts of man, that have been hid of old' (3: 13, E46), she receives a highly technical set of inquiries on the nature of memory rather than an expression of repressed desires. So the frequent mapping of 'energy' on to a cathectic model of the psyche, as when Auden, for example, claims that the *Marriage* anticipates the entire teaching of Freud ([1935] 1977: 339), is not merely reductive but profoundly misguided; and the same point can be made against Reichian or Marcusian readings of *Jerusalem* in terms of repressive desublimation.

This refusal of blurring, which gives the early work its invigorating trenchancy and concision, may however be more problematic than it appears. To look briefly at the two series of aphorisms, 'There is no Natural Religion'. The first series works by progressive contraction producing an ultimate exemption: 'If it were not for the Poetic or Prophetic character the Philosophic & Experimental would soon be at the ratio of all things, & stand still unable to do other than repeat the same dull round over again (E1). The second series treats the impasse reached in the first as sufficient grounds for the assertion of an opposed psychology. The fourth proposition, 'The bounded is loathed by its possessor', allows the culminating assertions.

VI If any could desire what he is incapable of possessing, despair must be his eternal lot.
VII The desire of Man being Infinite the possession is Infinite & himself Infinite.

Application. He who sees the Infinite in all things sees God.
He who sees the Ratio only sees himself only.
Therefore God becomes as we are, that we may be as he is. (E2)

The assumption that despair is man's eternal lot is not empirically refutable: the pursuit of more may be doomed to unfulfilment and this unfulfilment may turn to despair, but this may be merely a just assessment. The pessimism of an argument is no proof of its falsity. (Compare Shakespeare's Troilus: 'This is the monstruosity in love, lady, that the will is infinite and the execution confin'd; that the desire is boundless, and the act a slave to limit' (*Troilus and Cressida* III.ii.77-80).) Blake, in contrast, baldly asserts that because despair is not man's eternal lot (unproven), his desire must be infinite; with the corollaries that to desire the infinite involves its possession, and possessing the infinite means man himself is infinite. The desire of the infinite is treated as synonymous with desire being infinite.

So, on a very general level, Blake resists defining desire in terms of need, lack, insatiability – what Locke calls uneasiness and Hegel the restlessness of life. Genuine desire is always gratified: the absence of gratification merely shows the inadequacy of the mode of desiring.

> such is that false
> And Generating Love: – a pretence of love to destroy love:
> Cruel hypocrisy unlike the lovely delusions of Beulah
> (*Jerusalem* 17: 25-7, E160)

Even such an apparently unequivocal pronouncement such as 'every thing that lives is Holy' (E44) can be read as everything that is not 'Holy' is not living and therefore worthy of nothing but contempt.

So whatever the appeal of 'infinite desire', like the 'soul of sweet delight', and innocence itself, it remains a state rather than an act. And as the annotations to Lavater point out, 'weak is the joy that is never wearied' (E573): an emotion defined as continuous and unvarying becomes ultimately tedious. The exceptional force of phrases such 'Joys in anothers loss of ease' in 'The Clod & the Pebble' (E18) or 'it joyd' in the *Preludium to America* (2: 4, E51), is partly owing to the remarkable scarcity of verbal usages in Blake's core vocabulary. This is evident in the Notebook epigrams:

> In a wife I would desire
> What in whores is always found
> The lineaments of Gratified desire.   (E465)

It must be considered highly dubious whether whores display any such enthusiasm for their trade; but apart from that, I would stress how the subjunctive, 'would desire', weakens what is already a somewhat enfeebled request, scarcely more forceful than the social usages in the letters. The use of 'in' combined with 'lineaments' is repeated in the famous quatrain:

> What is it men in women do require
> The lineaments of Gratified Desire.
> What is it women do in men require
> The lineaments of Gratified Desire.   (E466)

It may be unwise to put too much weight on a single preposition, but the absence of 'from', interpersonal recognition, is surely significant: instead of reciprocated emotion there is an attributed abstract state.

Furthermore there is no attempt at particularisation: no distinction between the unfocused impulse and the specific object of desire. As Rousseau puts it, 'Love does not spring from nature, far from it; it is the curb and law of her desires; it is love that makes one sex indifferent to the other, the loved one alone excepted' ([1911] 1974: 175). A crucial distinction is made between need and desire; needs are fulfilled by the consumption of their object, desire always surpasses and exceeds that which ought to satisfy it. For thinkers in this tradition, a gratified desire is no desire at all. The unfulfilled yearning itself becomes an image of transcendence, whether intimation of immortality, as Diotima argues in Plato's *Symposium*; the eroticised reverie made possible by absence in Rousseau; or the forever-denied reunion with the other in Lacan. On a somewhat elementary level, I would stress the remarkable absence of 'you', epideictic address, in Blake's poetry: even the Zoas, the most domesticated of the mythological figures, desire in a wholly unparticularised way. Enion, for example, announces to Tharmas, 'All Love is lost Terror succeeds & Hatred instead of Love' (*The Four Zoas* 4: 17, E301), rather than simply saying 'I no longer love you'. There is no suggestion that the relation to a specific individual might be qualitatively different from an undifferentiated biological compulsion.

Blake's early work has often been lavishly praised for its great utopian ideal of fully gratified desire: the 'improvement of sensual enjoyment' (*Marriage* pl. 14, E38), however, offers no recognition of sexual difference. The same analytic vocabulary is deemed appropriate to both sexes; desire is presented as a unitary impulse struggling against social and psychological repression.

In *The Marriage of Heaven and Hell*, however, it is 'Man' who 'has no body distinct from his soul' (4: 8, E37). This revolutionary manifesto on behalf of desire contains no use of the pronoun 'she', and only one, scarcely flattering, occurrence of 'her': 'as the catterpillar chooses the fairest leaves to lay her eggs on, so the priest lays his curse on the fairest joys' (5: 55–6, E37). The only passing references are to Prudence as a 'rich ugly old maid' (5: 4, E35); to 'the nakedness of woman' which like the 'pride of the peacock', the 'lust of the goat', or the 'wrath of the lion', is a manifestation of the 'glory of God' (8: 22–5, E36); to the desirability of women wearing 'the fleece of the sheep' rather than 'the fell of the lion' (8: 30, E36); and to the forgiveness offered by Jesus to 'the woman taken in adultery' (pl. 23, E42). In addition to this, there are a series of implicitly sexual oppositions such as 'the thankful receiver bears a plentiful harvest' (9: 52, E36), and 'where man is not nature is barren', (pl. 10, E37); and a residual female presence in the imagery of images of caverns, voids, and chambers. The 'Eternal Female', whose groans open the coda, *A Song of Liberty*, simply vanishes once the 'new born terror', Orc, has appeared (1: 7, E43).

At times the imbalance in Blake's propositional habit of mind is so pronounced that both terms are dubbed masculine: the fecundity of the 'Prolific' might seem to be feminine, but 'the Devourer as a sea received the excess of *his* delights' (pl. 16, E39, my italics). This cannot but effect the way in which the famous central declaration is received:

> Without Contraries is no progression. Attraction and Repulsion, Reason and Energy, Love and Hate, are necessary to human existence. (pl. 3, E34).

If one takes the terms as parallel, one already gets the slightly perplexing superimposition of 'Reason', 'Attraction', and 'Love'; although the 'Governor, or Reason' is later an explicitly masculine 'Messiah' who 'formed a heaven of what he stole from the Abyss' (pl. 5, E38), its 'Contrary', 'Energy', is also located in the male body. The opposition is always between 'two classes of men' (pl. 16, E39).

In Blake's early work, therefore, the sentimentalist vocabulary is employed as a uniform language to cover the erotic experience of both sexes. The more gender differentiation is emphasised, the more desire is depicted as primarily destructive.

This is evident in the Notebook poems, where the monologic idiom of the *Marriage* begins to fracture into distinctive gender polarities. Some curious pronoun play results, for example, in 'The Sick Rose':

> O Rose, thou art sick;
> The invisible worm.
> That flies in the night,
> In the howling storm,
>
> Hath found out thy bed
> Of crimson joy;
> [O dark secret love
> Doth life destroy]
> And [his] her dark secret love
> Does thy life destroy.
> (Erdman and Moore 1973: N107)

The masculine variant, reinstated in *Songs of Experience*, is in many ways the least interesting characterisation of the 'invisible worm': it becomes readily identifiable with a demon lover, or if one prefers, a myth of Cupid and Psyche. At the very least, the 'worm' is that which threatens the rose, and through force of emblematic convention necessarily masculine. (See Langland 1987: 231-7, for a fine analysis of the reception history of the poem.) It is presumably 'invisible' to both the 'rose' and the narrator because secreted within the 'bed of crimson joy'. Yet if this is taken as an an image of sexual penetration, it is felt by both of them as an intrusion into a bodily interior. 'Dark secret' can be transposed on to both the 'worm' and the 'bed'; 'found out' (the secret) makes the second reading slightly stronger; and the faint echo of secretions, bodily enclosure, supports this. The move from present to past tense also allows the reading that the 'worm', having discovered the 'bed', 'flies' *from* it in terror. In the variant apostrophe, 'O dark secret love', 'love' becomes a force equally destructive to both parties (assuming both 'rose' and 'worm' qualify as living, though the 'worm' thrives by feeding on and so destroying the bud). The parallel with the opening apostrophe, 'O Rose', makes it possible even here to see this destructive 'love' as feminine. One could also read the ordering as object, verb, subject: 'life' destroys 'dark secret love' by exposing it to morning light. 'Her' refers back most immediately to 'bed/Of crimson joy'; but may also be taken as referring to the 'worm', in which case the role reversal renders the rose itself implicitly masculine. Certainly, if 'dark secret love' is taken as an objectification of the 'Rose', the warning seems primarily directed towards the 'worm': the 'Rose' is addressed but the 'worm' is at risk. (In this case 'sick' can be taken as contagious rather than simply ill.)

Throughout the Notebook poems of 1791–2, we can see gender polarities developing between conceptual terms and a strange triangular mode evolving where desire is dramatised as an external agent (for example, the mysterious 'traveller' who passes like the 'gentle wind' (E458)). In 'Silent Silent Night' (E462), the triplet, 'But an honest joy/Does itself destroy/For a harlot coy', pivots very precisely on 'itself', which is interposed between the powerful semantic bonding of 'honest'/'harlot' and 'joy'/'coy'. The 'joy' is 'honest', unlike the preceding ones that are 'sweet' because 'used with deceit', to the extent that it can present itself as simultaneously impersonal and the masculine opposite of 'harlot'. It is in such verbal niceties that we find the gradual disintegration of the bold certitudes of the early work, and the emergence of a more complex and agonised view of human sexuality.

Usually it is simply assumed that unless explicitly signalled the narrators of the lyrics are necessarily male. Yet there seems no reason why there should not be a female narrator of 'I saw a chapel all of gold' (E458); taking the chapel as vagina is no more awkward an estrangement of body from consciousness than that demanded by 'I saw a serpent rise between/The white pillars of the door'. This is supported by the response of the narrator: 'laid me down among the swine' can be taken as became sexually available, a reading supported by 'I askd a lithe lady to lie her down' (E459) on the previous page of the Notebook (Erdman and Moore 1973: N114–5).

Ostriker remarks of 'The Garden of Love' that 'the speaker might be of either sex: all repression is one' ([1982–3] 1986: 213). This is precisely what is at issue. Blake's propositional mode demands to be taken as absolute, disregarding the balance of power in any actual state of 'repression'. The repeated reworking of scenes of primal violation ('And binds her down for his delight' (E475)) in the *Preludium*, *The Mental Traveller*, and the first night of *The Four*

Zoas could be seen as a consequence of making desire transitive, an interpersonal relation rather than an intrinsic state.

The sentimentalist point of the goodness of spontaneous impulse is difficult to sustain in this area; and no argument is offered why sexual aggression should not itself be seen as learned behaviour, one of the 'errors of acquired folly' (E589), and self-protective recoil as innate. It is surely no coincidence that the two relevant aphorisms from the *Marriage* – 'He who desires but acts not, breeds pestilence' (5: 5, E35), and 'Sooner murder an infant in its cradle than nurse unacted desires' (10: 67, E37) – both contrast the fulfilment of impulse with the feminine activities of 'breed' and 'nurse'.

One could perhaps argue that Blake's mythological mode at least resists this naturalisation of physical coercion as inevitable and unblameworthy. Nevertheless the coalescence of sexual violation with euphoric rebellion remains disquieting. Usually the analogical transposition between libidinal energy and social rebellion is accepted without too much protest, but it is at least possible that the underlying impotence of the rhetoric of political radicalism is compensated for by the assertion of erotic dominance. (The same point can be made about the later imagery of Vala as the Scarlet Whore of *Revelations*: in *Milton*, for example, denunciation of 'A Female hidden in a Male' as 'A Dragon red & hidden Harlot' is the prelude to tearing and rending the 'Sexual Garments' as an 'Abomination' (40: 20, 22, E140; 41: 25, E141).)

In the *Preludium* to *America*, it remains ambiguous whether Orc's 'fierce embrace' liberates the 'virgin cry' or merely instigates another cycle of repression (1: 10; 2: 6, E50–1). (The nameless 'shadowy daughter of Urthona', far from acquiring a fixed identity, passes through being a 'panting struggling womb' to the total anonymity of 'it joyd' (1: 1; 2: 3–4, E50–1)). Blake's account of rebellion against the 'father stern abhorr'd' arguably collapses back into a more insidious form of sexism, the final cry of triumphant possession: 'I know thee, I have found thee, & I will not let thee go' (1: 11; 2: 7, E50–1). As in Rousseau, the initial resistance of the 'daughter' is presented as a strategy to arouse the 'power of desire' (1974: 322). Indeed the only reason for restraining phallic mastery appears to be not that it violates women but that they might gain power through it.

The absence of, if not 'modesty', appropriately Beulahesque qualities of self-effacing adoration, produces rampant and destructive desire. Enitharmon's 'The joy of woman is the Death of her most best beloved' (34: 63, E317) is generally taken to mean that she takes pleasure in withholding consummation, in the fashion of a Petrarchan mistress; but the line can also be taken in a literal sense – the pleasure of woman destroys her beloved. And in *Jerusalem*, it is repeatedly insisted, 'no one can consummate Female bliss in Los's World without/Becoming a Generated Mortal, a Vegetating Death' (69: 30–1, E221). In the light of such statements, I shall now go on to examine Blake's apparently most unequivocal endorsement of 'Female bliss', *Visions of the Daughters of Albion*.

One can look at *Visions* in terms of transitivity of desire (or lack of it); there is a curious stasis in these interlocking monologues accentuated by the peculiar tempo of the poem: a day, a night, more lamentation, more silence.

The condition of the daughters of Albion as 'Enslav'd' in *Visions* (1: 1, E44) obviously picks up a key motif of Wollstonecraft's *Vindication*, but it is important to be clear about the oppositional relation of the texts. For better or worse, Blake defines Oothon in terms of her sexuality, and far from demanding respect for a rational equal, separates her off into an alternative mode of being. The utopian demand plays the same structural role as a distinctively feminine mode of expertise in Rousseau: an apparently generous concession resulting in a permanent segregation. From Wollstonecraft's point of view, the problem is not sexual repression but the wrong kind of eroticism routinely extorted in social relations. It is not a possibility raised by Blake, that energy is not enslaved enough, and 'chastity must more universally prevail' (Wollstonecraft [1792] 1989: 67); and until then, 'subtil modesty' (6: 7, E48) might be a necessary pragmatic response to a cultural disenfranchisement.

Wollstonecraft's emphasis falls on the enslavement of women to pleasure, and a whole resultant psychology of cunning and manipulation. Blake adopts this analysis, while insisting that genuine desire is the appropriate mode of liberation. This causes no problem while kept on the level of aphorism or utopian proclamation. But immediately it is dramatically situated, Blakean delight simply becomes a more insidious form of entrapment on a higher level. As Wollstonecraft warns, 'the sensualist, indeed, has been the most dangerous of tyrants' ([1792] 1989: 93).

Visions opens with a dialogue between Oothon and a 'Marygold' (with a possible play on 'Mary' (Hilton 1986: 81–2), in which she is urged to 'pluck the flower'. The subsequent 'wing'd exulting swift delight' (1: 14, E45) can, however, be read as synonymous with rather than opposed to the subsequent rape: 'Bromion rent her with his thunders. On his stormy bed/Lay the faint maid' (1: 16–17, E45). Rousseau's psychology of involuntary consent seems comparable; this is the only sexual act of the poem, and the whole vocabulary of joy seems evacuated in comparison, deracinated from any dramatic encounter, a purely verbal release. A 'stormy bed' is by no means unarousing, and a 'faint maid' could be satiated as well as 'appalld' (1: 16, E45). The initial act can be read as a cruel dispelling of illusion, if read consecutively, or a longed-for consummation, if read as simultaneous.

So there is a certain justice in and verification of Bromion's prognosis: 'They are obedient, they resist not, they obey the scourge:/Their daughters worship terrors and obey the violent' (1: 22–3, E45). The subsequent usage of 'terror & meekness' (2: 5, E45) raises the possibility of the rapist and his victim being allegorised into uniquely compatible aesthetic complementarities. This is supported by Oothon's later comment that 'none but Bromion can hear my lamentations' (3: 1, E46); no mention is made of her putting up resistance, and her emission of 'woes' might be seen as motivated by the desertion of her assailant rather than by condemnation of his assault. Indeed her abrupt seduction and abandonment seem to confirm Wollstonecraft's diagnosis: 'allowing Pope's summary of their character to be just, "that every woman is at heart a rake", why should they be bitterly censured for seeking a congenial mind, and preferring a rake to a man of sense?' ([1792] 1989: 187). No-one contradicts Bromion, or even criticises him; and on certain Blakean lines of argument – gratifying desire, spontanous impulse – one suspects his action is implicitly condoned. Furthermore his offer to return 'Bromions harlot' to Theortormon (2: 1, E45) could be seen as representing the free circulation of women envisaged by Oothon later in the poem: a curious mixture of magnanimity and taunt.

As has often been remarked, Oothon seems to be offering something close to a masochistic frenzy (see Damrosch 1980: 197–201):

> I call with holy voice! kings of the sounding air,
> Rend away this defiled bosom that I may reflect.
> The image of Theotormon on my pure transparent breast.

The Eagles at her call descend & rend their bleeding prey.
Theotormon severely smiles. her soul reflects the smile;
As the clear spring muddied with feet of beasts grows pure &
smiles. (2: 14–19, E45)

There is an an obvious paradox in the 'holy voice' soliciting self-mutilation: Oothon not merely 'obeys the violent' but even summons them 'at her call'. At this point she insists upon her own status as 'flesh' (2: 13, E45), defined by Johnson as not only 'the body distinguished from the soul' but also 'carnality; corporal appetites' (1, 6). 'Grows pure' perhaps reverses the normal order of defilement, but only by reducing her to 'bleeding prey', a carcass. The later reference, 'the Eagle returns/From nightly prey' (2: 25–6, E46), has a grim irony in this context, suggesting a regularity to Oothon's torment, and also anticipating the later depiction of the 'frozen marriage bed' (7: 21). This ritual is apparently preferable to Theotormon's 'night of sighs' (2: 38, E46), though one should not forget that even a 'golden beak' (2: 27, E46) trails strands of intestines after feeding.

This self-abasement appears the precondition of achieving the emotional pellucidity of a 'pure transparent breast'. The full stop after 'reflect' (2: 15) seems to insist on its sense of thought, but the absence of a verb in the subsequent line immediately switches this to a passive mirroring. The second 'reflects' (2: 18) again implies pathetic acquiescence in Theotormon's right to severity, and the later demand, 'How can I be defild when I reflect thy image pure' (4: 16, E46), similarly appears to invite rather than protest against abuse.

The best case reading is that Oothon's very speech-act represents a performative emancipation; as in the *Marriage*, 'a firm perswasion that a thing is so' is sufficient to 'make it so' (pl. 13, E38). It is noteworthy, however, that she asserts 'I am pure' (2: 28, E46) rather than 'I am free', and Wollstonecraft has some caustic remarks on 'blind persuasion' ([1792] 1989: 14). 'Perswading him in vain' (2: 22, E46) gives an explicitly negative frame to her speeches. There is no appeal for release, and a total absence of protest as to her own situation, only an exhortation for Theotormon to 'arise'. The worst case, and this, one may reasonably assume, would be Wollstonecraft's position, is that Oothon, 'blown about by every momentary gust of feeling', whips up a self-deluding and ineffectual frenzy, 'the transient effusions of overweening sensibility' ([1792] 1989: 129, 94). She claims to have been 'obliterated and erased' by the enclosure of her brain in the 'narrow circle' of the five senses (2: 32–5, E46); but this can be read as a crucial exclusion from a Lockian vocabulary. Incapable of handling the abstractions of general ideas, Oothon is obliged to resort to a diffuse and unconvincing intuitionism: the result, as Wollstonecraft puts it, of 'the passions thus pampered whilst the judgement is left unformed' ([1792] 1989: 130).

Urizen is apostrophised as 'Creator of men' (5: 3, E47); and his influence is apparent in Theotormon's extremely technical questions on personal identity, and Bromion's strict induction from the evidence of the senses. But why is Urizen not the 'Creator of women' also? Perhaps he creates men who in turn create women; perhaps women create (and so condemn) themselves. Oothon claims distance, sceptical disengagement, from this process, but what seems a stance of empowerment can equally well be seen as a deprivation of autonomy.

Oothon's string of rhetorical apostrophes to the holiness of individual qualities ('yet are their habitations./And their pursuits, as different as their forms and as their joys' (3: 5–6, E46)) suffers from an immediate and fatal drawback: how can the 'chicken' and 'tame pigeon' inhabit the same world as the 'ravenous hawk' (3: 2–3, E46)? (The 'mouse' and the 'frog' are also potential prey; the 'fly' is hardly likely to relish an encounter with the 'still spider' (5: 3–8, E48); and the 'wild ass' and the 'meek camel' are going to have problems when they encounter the 'wolf and tiger' (3: 7, 9, E46).) The logic of Oothon's argument insists that the 'fat fed hireling' has experiences of equal value and authenticity to those of the 'giver of gifts' providing he is true unto his own nature (note the odd jubilation of 'sings upon the heath' (5: 14, 12, E47)). It also allows the slaver to have the innate quality of enslaving and the rapist of assault; the removal of the imperative to 'Reason & Compare' (*Jerusalem* 10: 21, E153) leads to an uncontrolled relativism.

Joys, moreover, cannot be said to exist apart from one another: the joy of the predator is the destruction of its prey. The doctrine of essential qualities – 'the rant about innate elegance', as Wollstonecraft puts it ([1792] 1989: 97) – presupposes an utter segregation of competing interests. 'Different joys' can only be regarded as 'Holy, eternal, infinite' (5: 5–6, E47) if one excludes lust, domination, and cruelty. 'And each joy is a Love' (5–6, E47) is a tautologous definition that precludes the possibility of unloving joy such as Oothon ascribes to Urizen, 'Thy joys are tears' (5: 4, E47).

It cannot begin to address the question posed in *The Four Zoas* by Urizen to Orc, 'is thy joy founded on torment which others bear for thee' (78: 41, E354).

Theotormon may be decried for brooding on the 'present moment of affliction' (4: 9, E47) but the tendency of Oothon's argument is to deny the reality of suffering in any form whatsoever. 'And are there other joys, besides the joys of riches and ease', Bromion asks (4: 21, E47): Oothon certainly thinks so but lacks the specificity of his definition, and remains unable to incorporate 'wars' and 'sorrow' into her world view. There is a certain elegance to Bromion's reversal: if one postulates 'eternal life', one can also postulate 'eternal fire – and eternal chains' as modes of exclusion from that state. To judge by this standard is to reduce all aspects of 'existence' to 'phantoms'; to posit eternity is to condemn oneself to the pain of exclusion (4: 23–4, E47).

'Tell me what is a joy?' (3: 24, E46) is therefore a perfectly sensible question to put to Oothon, in particular, the extent to which a 'lustful joy' might be compatible with one which is 'free born' (7: 6, 2, E49). 'Lust' entraps to a specific object, requires prior repression, in fact is inconceivable without it: the question remains whether joy can match it in intensity or plausibility, or whether it can only be unlustful in so far as it is unsexual. The problem is fundamental to Oothon's later prophecy:

Till she who burns with youth, and knows no fixed lot; is bound
In spells of law to one she loaths: and must she drag the chain
Of life in weary lust! must chilling murderous thoughts, obscure
The clear heaven of her eternal spring? to bear the wintry rage
Of a harsh terror driv'n to madness, bound to hold a rod
Over her shrinking shoulders all the day; & all the night
To turn the wheel of false desire: and longings that wake her womb
To the abhorred birth of cherubs, in the human form
That live a pestilence & die a meteor & are no more.
Till the child dwell with one he hates. and do the deed he loaths
And the impure scourge force his seed into its unripe birth
Ere yet his eyelids can behold the arrows of the day.
(5: 21–32, E48)

The opposition between 'burns with youth' and 'weary lust' cannot be sustained: logically the girl should 'burn with lust'. Good lust may perhaps be opposed to bad lust; but 'burning', with its Orc-like connotations of rebellion, has already been consigned to a pejorative sphere in the earlier reference to the slaves 'That shiver in religious caves beneath the burning fires/Of lust that belch incessant from the summits of the earth' (2: 9–10, E45). In this context, repression increases rather than frustrates desire.

'Bound' recalls 'Bound back to back' (2: 5, E46), and 'spells of law' captures magnificently the illusory yet inescapable force of ideology. Yet the question remains of how far Oothon's situation is to be identified with the sub-narrative of female subordination within these lines. There is a conspicuous fatalism in the repeated 'and must she' rather 'why should she', and the sequence of puberty, marriage, childbirth, indoctrination and further resentment, is presented very much as a closed circuit. What validity can the claim – 'but Oothon is not so' (6: 21, E49) – have in a social context that has already predetermined that pleasures may never be 'free born'? Critics have responded to the problem in a variety of ways: David Aers criticises the poem for being unable to account for Oothon's post-revolutionary consciousness (1981: 31); and Susan Fox surmises that Oothon urgently needs an injection of Female Will ([1976–7] 1986: 80). One can perhaps be more precise than this. Oothon's social diagnosis can only be judged on its persuasiveness and coherence according to rational criteria. Yet the logic of her position is that not merely 'chilling murderous thoughts' but any kind of mental activity whatsoever would sully the 'clear heaven of her eternal spring'. 'Chilling' recalls the 'cold floods of abstraction' (5: 19, E49), and hence the denial of female capacity to possess 'what deserves the name of intellect, the power of gaining general or abstract ideas' (Wollstonecraft [1792] 1989: 257). And to deny 'murderous' is perhaps to deny the legitimacy of not only revenge but even protest. In its place, Oothon offers absolutes with no positive content in their own right: a 'spring' that was 'eternal' would deny the existence of all other seasons, and a 'clear heaven', as with the later 'heaven of generous love' (7: 29, E50), can only be defined in terms of the absence of 'jealous cloud' and 'selfish blightings' (7: 28–9, E49).

The passage seems initially to respond to Wollstonecraft's outrage against Rousseau's exhortation to women passively to acquiesce in injustice. 'To bear the wintry rage/Of a harsh terror' refers back to both the earlier pairing of 'terror & meekness' and the 'child/Of

Bromion's rage' (2: 5, 1–2, E45). ('Rage' has the specific sense of sexual arousal (OED 4b).) To 'bear', to carry the child of, is also to endure a punishment: any positive representation of human fecundity is notably absent. There are no happy families in Oothon's vision. Both Bromion's rape and the narrated marriage involve conception and reproduction, something starkly absent from her rhapsodic celebration. 'False desire' leads to 'the abhorred birth of cherubs, in the human form' which 'live a pestilence and die a meteor & are no more'. This, supported by the final reference to forcing 'the seed into its unripe birth', recalls Wollstonecraft's 'weak enervated women' who 'either destroy the embryo in the womb, or cast it off when born' ([1792] 1989: 209); and also Rousseau's bleak response to the rate of infant mortality: if 'one half of the children who are born die before their eighth year' why should 'the age of harmless mirth' be 'spent in tears, punishment, threats, and slavery' (1974: 15, 43).

'Driv'n to madness' could refer either to 'she' or to the 'harsh terror'; the second 'bound' stresses the oppressiveness of the role of master. As Wollstonecraft says, women may be 'convenient slaves, but slavery will have its constant effect, degrading the master and the abject dependent' ([1792] 1989: 68). He too is condemned 'all the night/To turn the wheel of false desire': an image of male blindness and Samson in Gaza reminiscent of Rochester's 'drudgery' in 'fair *Aurelia*'s womb'. (Compare 'will he bind himself/Beside the ox to thy hard furrow' (8: 3–4, E49).) The phallus as instrument of punishment ('rod') becomes a mechanical addition to the 'wheel', which is inserted as a kind of pivot, an onerous duty. (On purely physiological grounds, one might enquire at what point 'weary lust' for the male ceases to be desire at all?) The second 'till' superimposes the final lines onto 'she who burns with youth', yet it is an explicitly male child. The oedipal resonance has often been commented on, yet the most obvious candidate for the 'one he hates' and with whom he must do 'the deed he loaths' is the original 'she who burns with youth'.

'Impure' seems to transfer on to the whole reproductive cycle, whose implicit corruption surfaces in the closing lines of Oothon's speech:

Does not the worm erect a pillar in the mouldering churchyard?
And a palace of eternity in the jaws of the hungry grave
Over his porch these words are written. Take thy bliss O Man!
And sweet shall be thy taste & sweet thy infant joys renew!
                              (pl. 5: 41–pl. 6:3, E48)

To 'erect a pillar' has obvious sexual connotations, although the 'blind worm' privy to the 'secrets of the grave' was previously female (3: 10, E47). The implicitly feminine 'mouldering churchyard' and 'jaws of the hungry grave' recall the sexually voracious 'Grave' of the *Song of Los*, which 'shrieks with delight, & shakes/Her hollow womb, & clasps the solid stem./Her bosom swells with wild desire' (7: 35–7, E69). Here the 'palace of eternity' seems oddly fragile, placed emphatically within mortality and putrescence: the offer has an air of desperate taunt, persuasive bluff, an assertion that cannot confidently surmount its funereal context. 'Sweet shall be thy taste' suggests, in a macabre fashion, both the 'bliss' which is to be sampled and the worm's feasting on rotten flesh in the cycle of mortality that permits the 'infant joys' to be renewed. (This may be compared to Oothon's previous offering of herself in terms of 'Sweetest the fruit the worm feeds upon' (4: 17, E46).) The most striking displacement, however, comes with the address not to other women but to 'Man', whose pleasures, one might have thought, were quite sufficient. The most immediate example within the poem of a character heeding the injunction to 'Take thy bliss' is, of course, Bromion.

The depiction of fallen sexuality is infinitely more erotic and particularised than the exhortations to transformed desire: 'hypocrite modesty' wins hands down over the 'eyes of honest morn' (6: 14–15, E48).

> Who taught thee modesty, subtil modesty! child of night & sleep
> When thou awakest wilt thou dissemble all thy secret joys
> Or wert thou not, awake when all this mystery was disclos'd!
> Then com'st thou forth a modest virgin knowing to dissemble
> With nets found under thy night pillow, to catch virgin joy,
> And brand it with the name of whore, & sell it in the night,
> In silence, ev'n without a whisper, and in seeming sleep:
> (6: 7–13, E48)

There is still an identification of the female 'child of night & sleep' with sexual culpability and deceit. 'Dissemble' is both to conceal and yet to brandish, dissemble with. ('To hide under false appearance' and 'to pretend to be what one is not' are Johnson's alternatives.) The female child both withholds her 'secret joys' and learns to offer them as genuine ones, 'in silence, ev'n without a whisper, and in seeming sleep' (6: 14, E48). 'When all this mystery was disclos'd' is equally ambivalent, suggesting both exposed as mystification and passed on as technique. 'Knowing to dissemble' similarly suggests how to dissemble and that one must dissemble, 'taught', presumably, by the schoolmaster Urizen. Blake is unwilling to concede even the possibility of these being necessary strategems for 'the crafty slave of selfish holiness' (6: 20, E48). Yet at the very least, the 'modest virgin' has greater negotiating power and autonomy if she has mastered the 'cautious craft of ignorant self-love' (Wollstonecraft [1792] 1989: 182) than the victim of the previous narrative of repression.

This may be seen in the curious neutrality of the rhetorical doubling in the poem. The 'nets found under thy night pillow' look back to the priest's 'nets & gins & traps' and forward to 'silken nets and traps of adamant' (5: 18, E48; 7: 23, E49). 'To catch virgin joy' anticipates to 'catch for thee girls of mild silver, or of furious gold' (7: 24, E49). Oothon's final exhortation: 'Is it because acts are not lovely, that thou seekest solitude,/Where the horrible darkness is impressed with reflections of desire' (7: 10-11, E49), would carry more weight if she showed any desire to participate in 'happy copulation' rather than simply procure and witness it: 'I'll lie beside thee on a bank & view their wanton play/In lovely copulation bliss on bliss with Theotormon' (7: 25-6, E49). (A position identical in kind to that of 'self-love': 'a creeping skeleton/With lamplike eyes watching around the frozen marriage bed' (7: 21-2, E49).) 'Open to joy and to delight' (6: 22, E49) sounds suspiciously like infinitely available; and Wollstonecraft's attitude to such tawdry speculations is suitably curt: 'if polygamy is necessary, woman must be inferior to man, and made for him' ([1792] 1989: 139). The 'virgin fancies' that Oothon prophecises (pl. 1: 5-6) seem attenuated compared to the later onanistic satisfaction of 'the virgin/ That pines for man . . . In the secret shadows of her chamber' (7: 3-5, E49). (In the probable source in Milton's *Paradise Lost*, Nature's 'virgin fancies' are synonymous with rather than opposed to 'enormous bliss' (V. 297)). Moreover, as Hilton points out, the opening interchange of the poem, between Oothon and her 'golden nymph' (1, 5-6, E44) is itself autoerotic: 'nymphae' is the eighteenth-century medical term for clitoris (Hilton 1986: 81-2). Oothon's own attempt to 'create an amorous image' (7: 6, E49) results in her being reduced to 'a solitary shadow wailing on the margin of non-entity' (7: 15, E49): she cannot compete with the 'enormous joys' experienced by her counterpart (7: 5, E49), both vast and monstrous in the intensity of her masturbatory pleasure.

'Acts are not lovely' is certainly borne out by Oothon's own narrative of existing sexual practices. To 'forget to generate' (7: 6, E49) seems in many respects the most positive option all round. Thus the castigation of 'Generation' in *Jerusalem* can be seen as latent within Blake's original utopian proclamations. The contradictions of *Visions* may, however, be more specifically located in the grounds of denunciation of Urizen: not for withholding reason from women but for failing to comprehend joy. 'Reflections of desire' are precisely what are required: reflections on rather than mirrorings of (see Hilton (1986: 92-3) for further discussion of 'reflection' in *A Vindication*). Oothon falls back on a series of fallacious arguments on natural instinct which undercut her incisive denunciation of sexuality as cultural construct. This expulsion of rational equality will have pernicious consequences for Blake's later characterisation of the female emanations. They will be restricted to two roles: a perpetual supplication to a lost lord ('I cannot kiss the place/Whereon his bright feet have trod' (*Book of Ahania* pl. 4 E89)) or a ruthless supplanting of him. The position enunciated in *Visions* is in this respect continuous with that of a less celebrated contemporary text, Richard Polwhele's 'The Unsex'd Females', where the 'female Muse' is seen as perverted when 'pale amidst the wild, she draws/Each precept cold from sceptic Reason's vase', so that she may 'o'er humbled man assert the sovereign claim' ([1798] 1810: vol. ii, 38). I now wish to examine the role the acquisition of reason plays in the usurpation of male authority in Blake's final epic, *Jerusalem*, in which, to borrow another phrase from Polwhele, 'unsex'd woman vaunts the imperious mien'.

Blake's work is generally regarded as moving from an ethic of revolutionary energy, libidinal release, to a transcendent account of redemptive imagination; both are seen as equally opposed to the common term of reason, that which oppresses and must be cast off. In *Jerusalem*, this takes the form of repeated denunciations of 'Patriarchal Religion' (27: 3, E169), and the 'cruel Patriarchal pride/Planting thy family alone,/Destroying all the World beside'; and a series of famous identifications of sexual violation, deist religion, and imperial expansion: 'Albions Spectre from his Loins/Tore forth in all the pomp of War' (4: 77-8, E145). Yet the previously noted complaints of feminist criticism are obviously immediately applicable to this most elaborate of Blakean mythologies.

Females are conspicuously absent from eternity, where reside 'As One Man all the Universal Family' (34: 19, E178). The possible female roles – 'Thy nurses and thy mothers, thy sisters and thy daughters' (4: 12, E143) – are all defined through adjacency to the male. (When the 'Male' is defined in terms of 'a breeder of Seed; a Son & Husband' (64: 12–13, E213), the response is outrage.) Los insists 'in Eternity Man converses with Man' by means of their emanations meeting to 'embrace & commingle' (88: 3, 5, E244).

> For Man cannot unite with Man but by their Emanations
> Which stand both Male & Female at the gates of each
>   Humanity
> How then can I ever again be united as Man with Man
> While thou my Emanation refusest my Fibres of dominion?
> When souls mingle & join thro all the Fibres of Brotherhood
> Can there be any secret joy on Earth greater than this?
>   (88: 10–15, E240)

Logically a spectre should be a male emanation, but the idea of women mingling through their reason, as we shall see, is regarded with abhorrence. The speech is curiously beside the point: why should Enitharmon sacrifice herself to facilitate a relation of 'Man with Man' when 'Brotherhood' is so explicitly equated with 'dominion'? The structuralist analysis of the circulation of women as social bonding between men is here not merely prefigured but virtually obligatory. To be 'mutual in love divine' (1: 7, E177) is a homosocial, if not homoerotic, condition, against which the 'secret joy' pales into insignificance. The 'fibres of love' that run 'from man to man' (1: 7–8, E145) are a commonplace of the sentimentalist vocabulary, but even here possess a bodily dimension, and later in the poem the 'milky fibres' (86: 39, E246) will become explicitly spermatic (see Hilton 1982–3: 166, and Hagstrum 1985: 140).

There are all too many problems of generic affiliation and narrative ordering in making sense of *Jerusalem*: 'a long season & a hard journey & a howling wilderness' sums up what most critics have felt about the poem pretty well (62: 27, E211). This is a long and extremely difficult text which remains formidable even to specialists. The two strands I would pick up on are the poem's outright equation of repressive rationality with the power of the female and its use of aphorism.

Blake's explicit repudiation of generalisation – 'Those who dare to appropriate to themselves Universal Attributes/Are the blasphemous selfhoods & must be broken asunder' (90: 31–2, E247) – is contradicted by the whole stylistic ethos of the poem. In *Jerusalem*, Blake returns to the aphoristic mode of his earlier work, notably the *Marriage*: 'He who will not commingle in Love, must be adjoind by Hate' (66: 55–6, E217); 'In Heaven Love begets Love! but Fear is the Parent of Earthly Love!/And he who will not bend to Love must be subdued by Fear' (81: 15–16, E236); 'She who adores not your frowns will only loathe your smiles' (95: 234, E252). A more general point may be made about the absence of specifically dramatic irony; such propositions retain their universalising force above and beyond the constraints of interlocutor and situation.

In the *Marriage*, aphorism was employed to confront the rationalist tradition with the weapons of its own stylistic armoury – trenchancy, concision, and bold declarative sweep. In *Jerusalem*, it is seen as gender-bound: 'when the Individual appropriates Universality/He divides into Male & Female' (90: 52–3, E248). The *Marriage* stressed exuberance, power, creativity, albeit from a patriarchal viewpoint; *Jerusalem* offers a series of interlocking propositions that produce absolute closure: 'when the Male & the Female/Appropriate Individuality, they become an Eternal death' (90: 53–4, E248). Reason produces repression which leads to perverse sexual gratification which in turn underpins reason. This was also inherent in Blake's earlier politico-sexual analysis: what has changed now is that the terms of analysis of desire are themselves implicated in the condition that they denounce.

I would like to stress one aspect in particular: the acquisition of reason by the daughters of Albion. In the early plates of the poem, reason and the female are diametrically opposed: 'Jerusalem is not! her daughters are indefinite:/By demonstration man alone can live, and not by faith' (4: 27–8, E145). The feminine is here a victim, 'scatterd abroad' while the heathen 'Receive her little-ones for sacrifices and the delights of cruelty' (4: 13; 5: 15, E146). The 'daughters of Albion' are defined as the 'emanation of Albion's sons': though subsequently 'united into Tirzah and her sisters, on Mount Gilead' or 'into Rahab in the Covering Cherub on Euphrates', they nevertheless remain 'beautiful' and 'lovely' (5: 37, 40, 42, E146). The argument seems to be that the daughters, though formed by division, immediately recoalesce; and in this collective form may be identified with a rationalist ideology. It is the

'Starry Wheels' who are said to feel 'anguish of maternal love' (5: 46–7, E147). Jerusalem and Vala are at this point indistinguishable in the 'pillar of smoke', both 'weeping' for the 'sons & daughters of Albion' (5: 51, E147).

> O what avail the loves & tears of Beulahs lovely Daughters,
> They hold the Immortal Form in gentle hands & tender tears
> But all within is opend into the deeps of Entuthon Benython,
> A dark and unknown night, indefinite, unmeasurable, without end,
> Abstract Philosophy warring in enmity against Imagination.
> (5: 54–8, E147)

'All within' has the sexualised quality of the encounter of Orc with the Shadowy Female. Glossing is clumsy, but obviously some kind of causal relation is asserted between 'loves & tears' and 'Abstract Philosophy'. The uncharted 'deeps' of the female are simultaneously the haunt of rationalism. In some ways this is an extension of the eroticised mystery of the earlier work, but the verse is crisp in its demarcations, offering a strikingly clear exposition of the indefinite.

The spectre seeks to 'lure Los: by tears, by arguments of science & by terrors/Terrors in every nerve, by spasms & extended pains' (7: 7–8, E148). The 'arguments of science' are a means of both seduction and intimidation: 'terrors in every nerve' prefigures the later vivisections by the daughters. This prompts the appearance of Vala, 'Albions Emanation', 'prolific upon the Chaos/Reflecting back to Albion in Sexual Reasoning Hermaphroditic' (29: 26, 27–8, E173). The 'prolific' is now feminine, reversing the previous identification in the *Marriage*: 'Reflecting' involves thought rather than Oothon's transparency. 'Sexual Reasoning' may probably be glossed as 'based on the experience of generation', but even so it fuses two previously antithetical concepts. Reasoning does not repress the sexual but articulates and even constitutes it.

Even the figure of Jerusalem is not exempt: 'She sat at the mills, her hair unbound, her feet naked/Cut with the flints: her tears run down, her reason grows like/The wheel of Hand' (60: 41–3, E208). Women are powerful not only because they are seductive and deceitful but because they are rational. As Wollstonecraft observes, 'has not a little rationality exposed many women to the severest censure?' ([1790] 1989: 248). On a simple empirical level, the most powerful declamation of the poem is directed against the power of women possessed with reason. Rousseau's 'those who desire to guide young people rightly and to preserve them from the snares of sense give them a disgust for love' (1974: 292) becomes in Blake 'That he who loves Jesus may loathe terrified female love' (88: 20, E244). These sentiments are resonantly endorsed by Los:

> What may Man be? Who can tell? But what may Woman be?
> To have power over Man from Cradle to corruptible Grave.
> There is a Throne in every man, it is the Throne of God.
> This Woman has claimd as her own & Man is no more! ...
> O Albion why wilt thou create a Female Will?
> (30: 25–8, 31, E175)

The initial question covers both what man 'is' and what he 'has the capacity to become'. The sheer abstractionism requires comment: there is not merely no division into types of the categories of man and woman, but no acceptance of even boy and girl. It is 'Man' in the 'Cradle'. The threatened usurpation of priority in which 'God himself become a Male subservient to the Female' (88: 21, E244) is ultimately Pauline: 'Look back into the Church Paul! Look! Three Women around/The Cross! O Albion why didst thou a Female Will Create' (56: 42–3, E204; see also Riede 1987). There are also strong Miltonic precedents: Adam's lament, 'Thus it shall befall/Him who to worth in woman overtrusting/Lets her will rule' (*Paradise Lost* IX.1182–4), and Samson's desire to be 'not swayed/By female usurpation' (*Samson Agonistes* 1059–60). The 'Female Will' could be 'a will under the domination of the female' or 'choosing to behave in a passive and demeaning way'; what remains to be explained is why either of these conditions, and indeed 'sexual love' in general, should be so readily equated with the 'rational power' (54: 16, E201).

The usual way of handling the 'Female Will', most famously and influentially in Frye's *Fearful Symmetry*, is by allegorical transposition (1947: 74–6): Blake's denunciations are to be treated as ultimately theological, directed against a materialistic concept of nature, which acquires maternal qualities through her entrapping nurturance. ('Art thou not Nature, mother of all' (30: 9, E174); Diana Hume George offers an extended defence along similar lines (1980: 185–207)). In *Milton*, Ololon surmises that 'those who contemn Religion' have 'Become in their femin(i)ne portions the causes & promoters/Of these Religions' (40: 9–10, E140); and in *Jerusalem*, this is amplified into a full-scale denunciation of the

'Deists' for 'worshipping the Maternal/Humanity; calling it Nature and Natural Religion' (90: 65–6, E248; see also 93: 23–5, E251). This position also gains considerable support from the late annotations to Wordsworth and Boyd, and the presentation of Beatrice as Vala in the Dante illustrations. I would like, however, to explore the consequences of mapping this issue on to the Rousseau-Wollstonecraft debate of the 1790s.

Though *Jerusalem* is customarily associated with a vocabulary of sin and forgiveness, 'Los's Halls' are also said to contain 'every pathetic story possible to happen from Hate or/Wayward Love' (16: 62, 63–4, E159). The key vocabulary of the poem remains sentimentalist: 'O love! O pity! O fear!/O pain! O the pangs, the bitter pangs of love forsaken' (67: 54–5, E219). However preoccupied *Jerusalem* may be with spiritual redemption, it should not be overlooked that Albion rises into 'Wars of mutual Benevolence' (97: 14, E254). In political terms, the major problem of the poem lies in the way Blake offers an ethic of personal transcendence – mercy, pity, love, kindness and forgiveness – as a remedy for a series of social ills. To define 'sin' as 'but a little/Error & fault that is soon forgiven' (20: 23–4, E165) will make little headway against institutionalised oppression.

Once Man was occupied in intellectual pleasures & energies
But now my soul is harrowed with grief & fear & love & desire
And now I hate & now I love & Intellect is no more;
There is no time for any thing but the torments of love & desire
(68: 65–8, E220)

'Intellectual pleasures & energies' (distinctly the prerogative of 'Man') blithely overrides the polarities of Blake's early work. It is not the mixture ('grief & fear & love & desire'), but only the final two terms that provide 'torments'. As Damrosch observes, these arise not out of 'the misuse of desire' but from its 'essential nature' (1980: 212; see also Ostriker [1982–3] 1986: 226; and Hagstrum 1985: 132; for an attempted rebuttal). What is new to *Jerusalem* is the sense that analysis by means of the core vocabulary of sentimentalism, which Blake had used with such decisive conviction in his earlier work, is an admission of guilt in itself, an abject submission to essentially non-human impulses (a point laboriously made when the daughters 'drew out from the Rocky Stones/Fibres of Life to weave' (67: 3–4, E217)). The animistic personifications in 'Auguries of Innocence' points to a more fundamental tension:

> Man was made for Joy & Woe
> And when this we rightly know
> Thro the World we safely go.
> Joy & Woe are woven fine
> A Clothing for the soul divine
> Under every grief & pine
> Runs a joy with silken twine.   (56–61, E491)

These gnomic riddles offer an elegant condensation of a sentimentalist psychology based on the hedonic scale of competing impulses of appetency and aversion. The rationalist origins of the idiom are acknowledged in 'rightly know' (though it remains unclear why this knowledge should necessarily enable us to 'safely go'). 'Woven fine' suggests nerves, conduits of sensation, but also the woven tissues of the fallen body, 'a Clothing'. 'Twine' suggests the nets that appear elsewhere, but it is not an uncommon idiom during the period; more contentiously, from the viewpoint of the 'soul divine', 'Joy & Woe' are indistinguishable. Commentary on the passage quoted from *Jerusalem* tends to gloss 'Intellect' as the harmonious balance of faculties, 'Co-operating in the bliss of man', as *The Four Zoas* puts it (126: 16, E395), but the poem no longer accedes to that essentially humanist accountability. The particularly fervent repudiation is due to the poem's insight that one can only feel as one has been taught, that the whole range of emotional responses, even those apparently positive and liberating, are ultimately entrapping. Erotic fulfilment necessarily involves an essential loss of freedom: we are 'bound in the bonds/ Of spiritual Hate, from which springs Sexual Love as iron chains' (54: 11–12, E201).

Psychoanalytic approaches to the poem have tended to show the same weaknesses as the application of somewhat schematic and popularised versions of Freudian repression-displacement mechanisms on to the early work. One tends to get a very simplistic version of the cathectic model, minus the hermeneutic aspects crucial to the talking cure.

The contexts of usage of 'desire' in the poem are unpredictably diverse. At various points it is undisguised, sweet, tormenting and so on, and there are still occasional indictments of prohibitions that 'are death/To every energy of man, and forbid the springs of life' (31: 11–12, E176). Yet libertarian protest against 'Drawing the free loves of Jerusalem into infernal bondage' could only apply if we had some clearer idea of what 'free loves' might mean, certainly when compared to the characterisation of 'the various Species of Contention/And Jealousy & Abhorrence & Revenge & deadly Murder' currently experienced (69: 9, 12–13, E221). The daughters 'wooe Los continually to subdue his strength', but where Blake once readily endorsed the taking of sexual initiative, here Los 'Dare not approach the Daughters openly lest he be consumed/In the fires of their beauty & perfection, and be Vegetated beneath/Their Looms' (17: 7–9, E160). If he does respond, they are 'terrified by undisguisd desire': 'Shuddring they flee: they hide in the Druid Temples in cold chastity' (17: 14–15, E160).

We are given a counter-vision of 'a translucent Wonder: a Universe within', but even this is ambiguous: 'Increasing inwards, into length & breadth, & height:/Starry & glorious'. The 'beautiful golden gate' still 'opens into the vegetative world', encrusted with 'rubies & all sorts of precious stones' of the kind formed out of Gwendolen and her cohorts earlier (14: 16–21, E158). Albion somewhat prissily shudders at 'Unnatural consanguinities and friendships/Horrid to think of when enquired into deeply' (28: 7–8, E172), but nevertheless has a point: it seems impossible to analyse existing sexual relations without revealing them to be 'crimes'. Albion's response is to 'condense them into solid rocks, stedfast!/A foundation and certainty and demonstrative truth:/That Man may be separate from Man' (28: 10–12, E172). Los claims to use 'the spiritual sword/That lays open the hidden heart' to draw forth 'the Pang/Of sorrow red hot', yet the outcome is essentially identical: 'I behold the soft affections/Condense beneath my hammer into forms of cruelty' (9: 18–19, 26–7, E151). This in turn is impossible to distinguish from Hand on the same plate, who, we are told, 'Condensed his Emanations into hard opake substances;/And his infant thoughts & desires into cold, dark, cliffs of death' (9: 1–2, E150). On certain lines of Blakean argument, such as giving a body to falsehood, an outline to error, or definite form to the impalpable, this must be regarded as an unequivocal positive, and his own rhetoric can be seen as performing a similar function: no other writer in English is so confidently analytic, aphoristic, propositional in his treatment of desire.

'Such is the nature of the Ulro: that whatever enters: /Becomes Sexual, & is created, & vegetated, & born': this 'Sexual Machine' most immediately refers to the body, but is inevitably transferred on to the closed set of interlocking propositions characterising mortal life (39: 21–3, 25, E184–5; see also Frosch 1974: 161, for a remarkably sanguine exposition).

This is prefigured in the savage cycle of patterned retaliation in 'The Mental Traveller'. The poem constructs a series of gender power relations – mother/son, man/wife, father/daughter – that are all equally characterised by mutual parasitism – 'She lives upon his shrieks & cries/And she grows young as he grows old' (19–20, E475). The poem seeks to render desire systematically intelligible, and as such has proved irresistible to the geometrical/cabbalistic school of Blake criticism stemming from Yeats. The stance of passive disengagement characteristic of the *Songs* here attempts to separate from the very 'cycle of generation' itself; and this curious interplay of abstract determinism and sadistic voyeurism becomes constitutive of the poetic voice in *Jerusalem*.

The poem offers a continuous dramatisation of the anguish of a body entrapped within the 'cycle of generation'. 'The whole creation', throughout the poem, 'groans to be delivered': from the throes of labour, but also to be 'delivered' from delivering, released from the whole realm of generation. 'I hear the screech of Childbirth loud pealing, & the groans/Of Death' (30: 23–4, E175): giving birth to death, dying in birth, groaning as if dying. 'The passage through Eternal Death' suggests a birth-trauma (1: 1–2, E145); and the poem opens with a sense of absolute origin, a new awakening to see 'the Saviour over me', maternally, 'Spreading his beams of love, & dictating the words of this mild song' (4: 4–5, E145), a lullaby that turns out to be the poem itself. In another enunciation of the dream of male parthenogenesis – as Wollstonecraft puts it, to 'kindly restore the rib' ([1792] 1989: 102) – Los gives birth to the spectre 'divided from his back' (6: 1–2, E147): and later in the poem, Enitharmon becomes a 'Trembling globe' which 'shot forward self-living & Los howld over it:/Feeding it with his groans & tears' (17: 55–6, E162).

'Mighty Hand' gives a parody birth to the 'Giant-brood' of Bacon and Newton and Locke: 'the key-bones & the chest dividing in pain/ Disclose a hideous orifice' (90: 11–12, E222). It is not merely a hole in the torso which is 'hideous', but the 'orifice' which gives birth in a more orthodox fashion. In an explicitly vulval image, 'Satan withered up Jerusalem's Gates/And in a dark Land gave her birth' (27: 51–2, E171), though quite what the lips of the unfallen vagina would look like is unclear (the vampire-vulva of plate 58 gives its present condition). The 'dark Land' is simultaneously inside and outside the body; the power of birth itself, rather than the pains of labour attendant upon it, is the object of denunciation. The momentary intimation of an Amazonian idyll, with 'Breeding women walking in pride & bringing forth under green trees/With pleasure, without pain' is instantly rescinded: 'for their food is: blood of the Captive' (68: 36–7, E210). Even the figure of Christ is not exempted from condemnation:

> by his Maternal Birth he is that Evil One
> And his Maternal Humanity must be put off eternally
> Lest the Sexual Generation swallow up Regeneration.
>
> (90: 35–7, E247)

The 'religion of generation' has replaced the repression of generation by religion, and is itself seen as a source of potential destruction. The paradoxes of the garment motif are brought into play: a language of unclothing the body is transposed on to the uncovering of the soul by stripping off the 'sexual garments' of the body itself (see Paley 1973).

Nature is to man as mother is to child: the origin, the provider, the encompassing reality. Knowledge of nature comes through experiment and analysis. Woman, in her guise of nature, performs a reciprocal dismemberment and sacrifice of the male body. And this somewhat tendentious leap gives us the distinctive strain of biological sadism in the poem: the 'daughters of Albion' delight in cutting 'asunder his inner garments, searching with/Their cruel fingers for his heart' (66: 27–8, E218). Woman triumphs over the body that she has borne by ruthlessly exposing its frailty, relishing its pain. Famously in 'The Mental Traveller', 'And if the Babe is born a boy/He's given to a Woman Old/Who nails him down upon a rock,/Catches his shrieks in cups of gold' (9–12, E475). (This theme can be traced back through the peculiar ways in which Blake's characters get born – being woven, hammered into shape, released by earthquake – anything rather than the relatively simple expedient of coming out of a womb. (See Hagstrum 1985: 109–45, for an ultimately unconvincing attempt at rehabilitation).)

'I breathe him forth into the Heaven from my secret Cave/Born of the woman to obey the woman O Albion the mighty' (29: 51–2, E174). Such statements suggest that woman's power derives primarily from the fecundity of her flesh. But *Jerusalem* also depicts a world 'Where the Masculine & Feminine are nursed into Youth & Maiden/By the tears & smiles of Beulah's daughters' (79: 76–7, E233). The reference is more significant than it looks in the kind of control attributed to the female over the child: Gwendolen boasts 'I have *educated* you' (my emphasis) with, rather than initiating into or intimidating with, 'the crucifying cruelties of demonstration'. Lines such as 'England: nursing Mothers/Gives to the Children of Albion & to the Children of Jerusalem' (16: 23–4, E158) strike an oddly Rousseauesque note on breast-feeding and wet-nursing. Gwendolen asks 'what shall we do to keep/These awful forms in our soft bands' (80: 84–5, E235) and in Book IV there is a narrative of reverse development in which Hand reverts to a 'weeping infant': 'Let us look! let us examine! Is the Cruel become an Infant/Or is he still a cruel Warrior?' (81: 8–9, E236). The emphasis consistently falls on control of the child rather than the lover: 'Bring your Offerings, your first begotten: pamperd with milk & blood/Your first born of seven years old: be they Males or Females' (68: 30–1, E220). The mother instills and controls the infant's sexuality: 'looking on Albion's dread Tree,/She wove two vessels of seed, beautiful as Skiddaw's snow;/Giving them bends of self interest & selfish natural virtue;/She had them in his loins' (80: 73–6, E237–8). (Though it remains difficult, however, to see how a testicle can be a deist.)

Maternal dominance lasts 'from cradle to corruptible grave'; the Daughters of Beulah whilst they 'feed the human vegetable' delight in

> Cords of affection thrilling exstatic on the iron Reel:
> To the golden Loom of Love! to the moth-laboured Woof
> A Garment and Cradle weaving for the infantine Terror!
> (56: 12–14, E206)

Los pleads

> O daughters of despair!
> Rock the Cradle, and in mild melodies tell me where found
> What you have enwoven with so much tears & care? so much
> Tender artifice:
> (56: 21–4, E206)

'Tender artifice' is the key phrase: what is most role-defined, naturalised, is ultimately manipulative and manipulated.

> Men understand not the distress & the labour & sorrow
> That in the Interior Worlds is carried on in fear & trembling
> Weaving the shuddring fears & loves of Albion's Families
> (59: 50–2, E207)

This is normally understood in neoplatonic terms, but if one accepts a gender-specific 'Men', 'Interior Worlds' is far better read as female sphere of domestic relations. Rousseau's sense of the corrupting domination of the child ('the early education of man is in woman's hands: his morals, his passions, his tastes, his pleasures, his happiness itself depends upon her' (1974: 328)) becomes increasingly prominent in Blake. In Innocence, the maternal figure is customarily protective – 'When my mother died I was very young' ('The Chimney Sweeper', E9), 'My mother bore me in the southern wild' ('The Little Black Boy, E10) – contrasted with the frequently absent or ambiguous paternal authority. In *Europe*, however, Enitharmon's 'dominion' lies in promulgating strategems of erotic manipulation; 'Forbid all joy, and from her childhood shall the little female/Spread nets in every secret path' (6: 40–1); and in *Jerusalem* female control of education has become central to the whole presentation of sexual roles: 'O Woman-born/& Woman-nourishd & Woman-educated & Woman-scorn'd' (64: 16–17, E213).

Rousseau's warning, 'the men tyrannised over by the women would at last become their victims and would be dragged to their deaths without the least chance of escape' (1974: 322), provides a succinct summary of the narrative action of *Jerusalem*, and I would suggest that the sexual analysis offered by the poem continues to work within terms established by his work. Put schematically, women control culture: 'their Daughters govern all/In hidden deceit' (37: 46–7, E177). The convergence of female reason and female desire in the third book produces a scenario in which, as Ostriker says, 'an array of passive males' are 'subject to females who seduce, reject, betray, bind, lacerate, mock and deceive them' ([1982–3] 1986: 229).

Throughout the poem, the Wollstonecraftian idiom of 'deadly cunning & mean abjectness' (88: 38, E245) is regularly transposed on to the male figures. Hand, oddly, employs 'sweet deceits'; and Albion is 'dissembling/His jealousy before the throne divine' (4: 33–5, E147), both concealing and flaunting, as in 'hypocrite modesty'. 'O Shame O strong & mighty Shame I break thy brazen fetters' (10: 34, E151); 'brazen' is cast strong, but also sluttish. 'I have no time for seeming; & little arts of compliment', Los declares (42: 27, E189), and if, as Erin laments, 'deep dissimulation is the only defence an honest man has left' (49: 23, E198), his situation is very close to that of an honest woman.

The 'infernal Veil' that 'grows in the disobedient Female' (69: 38, E221) necessitates a reversion to physical violence. 'If you dare rend their Veil with your Spear you are healed of Love' (68: 42, E220); but only at the expense of inflicting a wound. 'When Albion rent thy beautiful net of gold & silver twine' (20: 30, E164) is described as 'a time of love' (20: 41, E164); though sufficiently far from 'beauty & perfection' to require that 'thou forgavest his furious love' (20: 37, E164). It is almost impossible not to put a starkly sexual reading on to such imperatives as 'Arise O Lord & rend the veil' (44: 40, E194), combining an iconography of phallic tumescence, weaponry, conception and mortality (for fuller discussion, see Riede 1981). It is perhaps unwise to read too much into the single reference in *Vindications* to the 'artful veil of wantonness' (Wollstonecraft [1792] 1989: 265); taking up, perhaps, Rousseau's comment that without illusion, 'the magic veil drops, and love disappears' ([1911] 1974: 354), but at times the reminiscence, supported by various Miltonic contexts (for example *Paradise Lost* V.379, IX.1054; *Samson Agonistes* 1035), seems direct: 'that Veil which Satan puts between Eve & Adam/ By which the Princes of the dead enslave their Votaries' (55: 11–12, E202). Enitharmon manages neatly to combine modesty with maternity:

> here is the lovely wayward form
> That gave me sweet delight by the torments beneath my Veil
> By the fruit of Albions tree I have fed him with sweet milk
> (82: 38–40, E240)

The daughters similarly 'refuse liberty to the Male'

> not like Beulah
> Where every Female delights to give her maiden to her husband
> The Female searches sea & land for gratifications to the
> Male genius: who in return feeds her in gems & gold
> And feeds her with the food of Eden.
> (69: 14–18, E223)

It is unnecessary to recapitulate the widely felt dissatisfaction with the allotted roles; but I would point out that the parenthesis is strictly according to a Wollstonecraftian analysis. (The reference to imperial trade also suggest some relation to Pope's Belinda, cosmetics and imports.) The female is corrupted by a preoccupation with 'gratifications' for which she receives ornaments ('gems & gold', more usually part of the whore iconography) and economic support (reversing the dependence on nurturance from the female body). At one or two points, the possibility of social conditioning is raised: prior violence produces deceit. In the annotated Blake, Stevenson (1989: 784n) glosses 'they' as male in the line, 'Till they have had punishment enough to make them commit Crimes' (69: 27, E220) yet it must apply equally well to the greater degree of cultural determination of femininity. 'Shriek not so, my only love', Gwendolen croons, 'I refuse thy joys: I drink/Thy shrieks, because Hand & Hyle are cruel & obdurate to me' (67: 61-2, E221): an explicit attribution of blame to prior male repression. It is after all Albion, we are repeatedly told, who seeks to 'Create a Female Will' (30: 31, E175).

Under such circumstances it should not be surprising that Enitharmon resists:

No! I will seize thy Fibres & weave
Them; not as thou wilt but as I will, for I will Create
A round Womb beneath my bosom lest I also be overwoven
With Love; be thou assured I never will be thy slave
Let Man's delight be Love; but Woman's delight be Pride.
In Eden our loves were the same here they are opposite
I have Loves of my own I will weave them in Albions spectre
                              (89: 12-18, E244)

'Fibres' again stresses emotional control over the male: 'round Womb' is presumably pregnancy, an emotional investment in the child at the expense of its father. The unwillingness to be 'overwoven/With Love' is followed by the refusal to 'be thy slave': as Wollstonecraft would recommend, the woman must be prepared to 'weave' her emotions 'in Albions spectre' rather than resort to a predictable strategy of 'secret places'. Enitharmon declares her motivation to be 'Pride' whilst it is the male who is defined through his sexuality. There should be no lament for a putative state in which 'our loves were the same', but rather active commitment to 'separation': from her point of view, 'Two Wills they had; Two Intellects: & not as in times of old' (86: 61, E245) becomes an ideal to be achieved rather than a condition to be lamented.

The putative consequences of this position, however, are dramatised in the third book:

SORDID IMAGES

> In beauty the Daughters of Albion divide & unite at will
> Naked & drunk with blood, Gwendolen, dancing to the timbrel
> Of War: reeling up the street of London
> (58: 1-3, E205)

In a Rousseauesque transposition, the violence of the 'stern Warriors' is enacted by the female: 'lovely sport the Daughters round their Victims./Drinking their lives in sweet intoxication' (65: 4-5, E215). Their orgiastic rites, however, do not distract them from erecting 'a Wondrous rocky world of cruel destiny', a 'feminine tabernacle 'with 'Two Covering Cherubs afterwards named Voltaire & Rousseau (66: 6, 14-16, E216). They are simultaneously both torturers and victims: stripping off their 'garments of needle work ... they sit naked upon the Stone of trial' (which may or may not be the same as the preceding 'Cove & Stone of Torture').

> The Knife of flint passes over the howling Victim: his blood
> Gushes & stains the fair side of the fair Daughters of Albion.
> They put aside his curls, they divide his seven locks upon
> His forehead: they bind his forehead with thorns of iron
> They put into his hand a reed, they mock: Saying: Behold
> The King of Canaan whose are seven hundred chariots of iron!
> They take off his vesture whole with their Knives of flint:
> But they cut asunder his inner garments: searching with
> Their cruel fingers for his heart, & there they enter in pomp,
> In many tears; & there they erect a temple & an altar:
> They pour cold water on his brain in front, to cause
> Lids to grow over his eyes in veils of tears, and caverns
> To freeze over his nostrils, while they feed his tongue from cups
> And dishes of painted clay. Glowing with beauty & cruelty:
> They obscure the sun & moon; no eye can look upon them.
> (65: 20-34, E216)

The 'Knife of flint' might be seen as a curiously disengaged phallic entity (though in the Mexican context, used for circumcision). The victim is 'howling' more out of fear than desire, but there remains the possibility that he is crying out for his own blood; 'Gushes & stains' might be taken as an image of ejaculation over the 'fair side' of the female body. (Camille Paglia is, I think, correct to detect a vicarious relish for the depiction of suffering (1990: 498).) The horrific aptness of 'inner garments', paralleling the 'vesture whole', contrasts with the weaving performed by the Daughters of Los. From their perspective, nevertheless, the 'delights of revenge Earth-shaking' might well be seen as justifiable (66: 39, E216). Despite the violence of the physical penetration, the physical intimacy ('They put aside his curls') continues to suggest tending and nurturance. The daughters 'feed with their souls the Spectres of Albion': if 'the Warrior they adore', they still 'his revenge cherish' (67: 18–21, E218). The female-dominated education becomes an actual sacrifice.

> The twelve daughters in Rahab & Tirzah have circumscribed the brain
> Beneath & pierced it through the midst with a golden pin
> Blood hath stained her fair side beneath her bosom.
> (67: 41–3, E218)

The heroic self-curtailment of Urizen's compasses are replaced by a 'golden pin'. The Petrarchan mistress has, one might say, gone sado-rationalist.

In this chapter, I hope to have established that Blake's work cannot be reduced to a simplistic opposition between masculine activity and feminine passivity. At the very least this polarity needs be to read in the context of the contemporary debate between Rousseau and Wollstonecraft which significantly alters the relation of these terms. Women gain power through the exercise of reason: men lose it. These positions in turn are identified with luridly and at times grotesquely eroticised gender roles. Female pleasure in cruelty both complements and is solicited by male delight in submission. For both parties, rationality does not repress desire: it has become entirely synonymous with it.

Jerusalem, situated in the early stages of romantic decadence, has in abundance what T. S. Eliot called 'the unpleasantness of great poetry' (1951: 317). I now wish to examine the relation of his own poetry to the later stages of this tradition.

6

'TESTING THE RAZOR'
T. S. Eliot's *Poems 1920*

> One error, in fact, of eccentricity in poetry is to seek for new human emotions to express; and in this search for novelty in the wrong place it discovers the perverse. The business of the poet is not to find new emotions, but to use the ordinary ones and, in working them up into poetry, to express feelings which are not in actual emotions at all ... Poetry is not a turning loose of emotion, but an escape from emotion; it is not the expression of personality, but an escape from personality. But, of course, only those who have personality and emotions know what it means to want to escape from these things.
>
> T. S. Eliot, *Selected Essays*

The familiarity of *Tradition and the Individual Talent* breeds not so much contempt as staleness. Eliot's 'Impersonal theory of poetry', in which so much was invested by the New Criticism, now seems a known quantity, thoroughly absorbed and largely superseded, and his verse, so readily assumed to vindicate and be vindicated by this aesthetic, has tended, over recent years, to be greeted with a similar weary recognition. Anything so firmly lodged within the canon, it is supposed, can only represent an orthodoxy against which to rebel. I wish to dispel this complacency by stressing what is 'perverse' in Eliot's early poetry, in particular *Poems 1920*.

For over fifty years, the collection was subject to a virtual conspiracy of silence concerning its violently repudiatory sexuality. Eliot's 'persistent concern with sex, the problem of our generation' (Richards 1926: 292) was readily granted a representative and even heroically diagnostic status; Randall Jarrell's tribute, for instance, is entitled 'T. S. Eliot as International Hero' (Schwartz: [1945]

1970). Yet explicit sexual reference has been customarily recuperated as demonstrating a broader social degeneration, or simply ignored. As early as 1931, the formative influence of American Puritanism, with its 'dark rankling of passions inhibited', was noted by Edmund Wilson (1931: 102). Yet in *A Half-Century of Eliot Criticism*, compiled, it must be said, by a woman, Mildred Martin, in 1972, there are no entries under disgust, eroticism, female, femininity, impotence, misogyny, obscenity, sexuality or woman (compared to, for example, seven articles on the influence of Conan Doyle). And in 1980, Beatrice Ricks, in *T. S. Eliot: A Bibliography of Secondary Works* does little better, recording one article on impotence (Fitz 1971) one on disgust (Johnson 1969); and a solitary survey of his representation of women (Sampley 1968). Perhaps the decorum of such lacunae may be approved, but more is at stake than the occasional suppression of a lurid detail: I shall argue that the strength of this phase of Eliot's poetry lies in the virulence of its misogyny, and its capacity not only to shock and repel, but also to implicate.

The re-emergence of the drafts to *The Waste Land* in 1971 inaugurated a new perception of the 'personality and emotions' from which Eliot's poetry drew its power. Recent criticism has witnessed a strongly biographical emphasis, stemming from Lyndall Gordon (1977) and James E. Miller Jr. (1977), revealing the traumas of Eliot's life to have a fascination in their own right; a reappropriation of Eliot as a specifically American writer rather than a renegade and exile; and an increasing unwillingness to accept Eliot's own curtailed definition of his earlier writings in both poetry and prose.

It is not a question of the work having been dissolved back into the life, so much as the life having been reformulated in terms derived from his own poetry: pattern, quest, ordeal. Gordon states her guiding principle as being that 'Eliot wrote his own biography': her narrative, therefore, 'will follow his own formulation, testing that against the facts of his actual day-to-day life' (1977: 1–2). And while, as one might have expected, revelations about Eliot's marriage have stimulated discussion of the importance of gender in his poetry (e.g. Sicker 1984; Abdoo 1984), the challenge offered by this aspect of Eliot's poetry has not, as yet, been fully addressed.

The (male) critical consensus would seem to be, yes, he's screwed up, but aren't we all, with a corresponding reluctance to cast the first stone against him. I think the importance of this protective solidarity cannot be overrated. As Wayne Koestenbaum remarks, '*The Waste Land* has always been a scene of implicit collaboration between the male poet and his male reader', and as such invites 'collusive interpretation, by the reader's analytic listening' (1989: 138–9; compare Ricks 1988a: 7). Why has it been so important for all concerned to sustain the ideal of ontological autonomy specifically in relation to this poetry? What happens if the aesthetic contract that guarantees impersonality, immunity, to both poet *and* reader is transgressed? What does it mean to read Eliot not as an exegete but 'as a man', specifically responsive to the complicities and vicarious satisfactions offered by his texts?

Even in the short extract cited above, Eliot's terminology slips and slides: the relation between 'emotion' and 'feeling' must remain, I think, permanently insoluble. The gist is, however, reasonably clear: the 'medium' of poetry is uniquely attuned to experiences screened out by the 'personality'. It allows one's subtlest and most elusive perceptions to be articulated; and then, just as importantly, to be disowned. Three modes of 'escape' from the 'eccentricity' of the merely personal are suggested. First, and most famously, through submission to the discipline of a common heritage, 'the historical sense' which 'compels a man to write not only with his own generation in his bones' (Eliot 1951: 14). It should be noted, however, that the 'simultaneous order' to which such an aesthetic appeals is an exclusively masculine enclave. To participate in the 'mind of Europe' involves the perpetuation of a patriarchal authority stemming back beyond Homer to the 'Magdalenian draughtsmen' (1951: 16). The second rationale is less lofty and so more disturbing: by employing commonly available, even commonplace, emotions, the poet is able to escape out of perversity into the 'ordinary'. He may enforce a complicity of recognition, not as spokesman for an androgynous human condition, but for men, male sexual experience. Yet Bernard Bergonzi, for example, is wholly characteristic in his elevation of Eliot's 'intense sense of erotic failure and bewilderment' to 'a perennial aspect of the human condition' without seeing it as in any way gender specific (1978: 22).

The third option involves the adoption of an experimental detachment towards one's own mind. 'It is in this depersonalisation that art may be said to approach the condition of science' (Eliot 1951: 17); and the change of prefix is significant. The famous analogy between the creating mind and a catalyst is elaborated in order to establish art as a realm not of objectivity but of clinical anonymity. What is produced, though, is 'sulphurous acid', and I now wish to turn to the passage from Tourneur which Eliot offers as exemplifying this achieved impersonality:

> And now methinks I could e'en chide myself
> For doating on her beauty, though her death
> Shall be revenged after no common action.
> Does the silkworm expend her yellow labours
> For thee? For thee does she undo herself?
> Are lordships sold to maintain ladyships
> For the poor benefit of a bewildering minute?
> Why does yon fellow falsify highways
> And put his life between the judge's lips,
> To refine such a thing – keeps horse and men
> To beat their valours for her?

> In this passage (as is evident if it is taken in its context) there is a combination of positive and negative emotions: an intensely strong attraction toward beauty and an equally intense fascination by the ugliness which is contrasted with it and which destroys it. This balance of contrasted emotion is in the dramatic situation to which the speech is pertinent, but that situation alone is inadequate to it. This is, so to speak, the structural emotion, provided by the drama. But the whole effect, the dominant tone, is due to the fact that a number of floating feelings, having an affinity to this emotion by no means superficially evident, have combined with it to give us a new art emotion.
>
> (Eliot 1951: 20)

The 'attraction', 'affinity', and 'combination' of the 'balance of contrasted emotion' at the 'positive and negative poles' of beauty and ugliness give a precipitate of 'a new art emotion': presumably opposed to a merely human one. But even a cursory glance at the passage cited will confirm the complete absence of any such equilibrium. (If nothing else, this should be compared with Eliot's fuller account of *The Revenger's Tragedy* in his essay, 'Cyril Tourneur' (1951: 812–92): 'its motive is truly the death motive, for it is the loathing and horror of life itself. To have rendered this motive so well is a triumph; for the hatred of life is an important phase – even, if you like, a mystical experience – in life itself' (1951: 190).)

To ask an obvious but neglected question, what is the 'structural emotion' that has been superseded by the 'dominant tone'? To restore the passage to its context: Vindice, who has sworn to avenge his poisoned betrothed, Gloriana, has just uncovered 'the masked skull of his love' and proceeds to contrast her past beauty and present mortality. (The prop is addressed at the opening of the play as 'Thou sallow picture of my poisoned love,/My study's ornament, thou shell of death,/Once the bright face of my betrothed lady' (I.i.14–16)). As an isolated verse extract, the repeated 'For thee' might be understood as addressing a still surviving spirit of loveliness. But the presence of the skull makes any such idealisation impossible. There is no attempt to evoke past happiness, no shared memories or lost future. Instead Vindice chides himself for 'doating', for having allowed himself to 'expend' and 'undo' himself in her service: his efforts to 'maintain' and 'refine such a thing' are acknowledged to be as futile as the 'yellow labours' of the silk-worm. (This is made explicit in the concluding lines omitted by Eliot: 'Surely we're all mad people, and they/Whom we think are, are not: we mistake those;/Tis we are mad in sense, they but in clothes' (III.vi.79–81).)

There are certainly 'floating feelings' drawn into the soliloquy, of pawned estates and hanging judges; they represent not the ugliness that destroys beauty, but the practical consequences of being seduced by its power. The speech marks a casting off of obligation: Vindice will henceforth participate freely and independently in the intricate choreography of the play's intrigue. And so a kind of aesthetic repletion becomes possible in contemplating the victim: she no longer has the deceiving beauty of the living, but an alternative and more potent allure in death. Here, as often in Eliot, fear of mortality can be tamed, utilised almost, through the violation and sacrifice of the female body: the propitiatory offering to a new spiritual or symbolic order.

I would suggest that Eliot reads the passage at least as much in the light of Rossetti's 'golden hair undimmed in death' ('Life-in-Love' (14)) as in Donne's 'bracelet of bright haire about the bone' ('The Relique' (6)); and I now wish to offer a brief examination of his debt to nineteenth-century poetry.

In his essay, 'The Philosophy of Composition', Edgar Allan Poe famously (or infamously) declared that 'the death of a beautiful woman is, unquestionably, the most poetical topic in the world'

([1846] 1965); and Eliot's poetry, as has often been noted, may be seen as fulfilling this injunction (Gordon 1977: 68; Mayer 1989: 18; Pinkney 1984: 18). The motif precedes the biographical explanation of difficulties in Eliot's marriage with Vivienne; and there is something chilling about both its explicitness and the equanimity with which it has customarily been received. It can be detected in 'Nocturne' (1909); in 'The Love Song of St. Sebastian' (1914); in the prose-sketch, 'Eeldrop and Appleplex' (1917); in the figures of Philomela and the rhine-maidens in *The Waste Land* (1923); and in the mid-ocean disappearance of Harry's wife in *The Family Reunion* (1939). I shall discuss the most notorious instance, Sweeney, in more detail later; but here it is sufficient to point out that even the previously unpublished contribution to *Cats*, 'Grizabella the Glamour Cat', given to Andrew Lloyd Webber by Valerie Eliot, repeats this motif: 'And the postman sighed, as he scratched his head:/You'd really ha' thought she ought to be dead' (Webber 1981: 35, ll. 5–6).

There are two inferences to be drawn from this. First, that the conjunction of the aesthetic, femininity and death is at the heart of Eliot's poetry; second, that it is consequently best regarded, despite his own protestations and polemics to the contrary, as the successor and arguably culmination of the tradition of romantic decadence (see Praz 1951; Dijkstra 1986; and Bronfen 1992).

The opening lines of *The Waste Land*, 'April is the cruellest month, breeding/Lilacs out of the dead land, mixing/Memory and desire' (1–3: 61) are often taken as epitomising the modernist break with Victorian poetry. Yet in the context of Eliot's immediate precursors, they may be seen as almost formulaic. Behind them lie, among many others, Tennyson's 'Is it, then, regret for buried time/That keenlier in sweet April wakes' ('In Memoriam' (116: 1–2)); James Thomson's 'the clamorous throng/Of thoughts that raged with memory and desire' ('Weddah and Om-el-Bonain' II.xix); and Coventry Patmore's 'Once more I come to Sarum Close,/With joy half memory, half desire' ('The Angel in the House' 1.3.1–2). Eliot's distinctive tone of fastidious alienation, and analytic preoccupation with the very absence of feeling, owes much to Arnold's 'The Buried Life' and Marguerite poems. The debt to Tennyson is varied and widely acknowledged: Eliot's interest in the figures of prophet and saint may be linked to 'Tiresias' and 'St. Simeon'; his despondent soliloquies on the entrapment of age to 'Tithonus' and 'Ulysses'; and the final section of *The Waste Land* to the phantasmagoria of *The Idylls* ('And solid turrets topsy-turvey in air' ('Gareth and Lynette'

(251)), for instance, becomes 'And upside down in air were towers' (382: 73)). The title of the poem itself probably derives from 'Morte d'Arthur': 'as if it were one voice, an agony/Of lamentation, like a wind that shrills/All night in a waste land, where no one comes,/Or hath come, since the making of the world' (200–3)).

There are, of course, plenty of Victorian precedents for Eliot's necrophilia, of which Browning's 'Porphyria's Lover' and 'My Last Duchess' are probably the best-known (see Pinkney 1984: 74–9). The form of the dramatic monologue allows us to regard these poems as case studies in morbidity, but also presents a world without moral bearings or culpability. The justification that the Duchess or Porphyria have been transformed into aesthetic icons, and thus improved, remains uncontested. No sanctions are taken against the Duke: the unnamed lover continues to sit unmolested with Porphyria's corpse. The response to the victim is synonymous with that to the poem: moral outrage is pre-empted by the fact that the spectacle of the dead woman is its occasion, motivation, and chief attraction.

The text most flagrantly indebted to this tradition is 'The Love Song of St. Sebastian', written in 1915, but only recently published in Eliot's correspondence. The speaker proposes to 'flog myself until I bled' until 'after hour on hour of prayer/And torture and delight' so that I might 'arise your neophyte' (4–6, 9, 1988: 46–7). As Gilbert and Gubar point out, the basic scenario is 'Swinburnian' (1988b: 30): the ordeal purifies through desecration. In the second stanza, the roles are reversed:

> I think that at last you would understand.
> There would not be one word to say.
> You would love me because I should have strangled you.
> And because of my infammy
> And I should love you the more because I had mangled you.
> And because you were no longer beautiful
> To anyone but me.   (32–8)

The initial flagellation entitles the speaker to love: the subsequent violence is a strategy of preserving it. The male's sexual desire is displaced on to the female: her consequent punishment serves as both the repression and fulfilment of that attraction. (The annotation inscribed after 'infammy' – '*not* to rhyme with mammy' – obviously lends itself to interpretation in terms of dependence on the maternal body.) What is characteristic of Eliot is the close connection of abasement and sacramental violence, and an elusive mobility of identification. Within his texts all the roles are potentially open: as a couplet from the drafts to *The Waste Land* puts it, 'I am the husband and the wife/And the victim and the sacrificial knife' (1971: 111). There are numerous direct textual links that could be explored between Eliot and Rossetti: as with many other precursors, Eliot's early 'rapture' is never subsumed in later 'revolt' (Eliot 1951: 261). Rossetti too invokes a 'hand' which 'taught memory long to mock desire' ('Supreme Surrender' (9–10)), and laments, 'So Spring comes merry towards me here, but earns/No answering smile from me' ('Barren Spring' (5–6)). More specifically, 'And the souls mounting up to God/Went by her like thin flames' ('The Blessed Damozel' (41–2)) becomes in 'Mr Eliot's Sunday Morning Service', 'Where the souls of the devout/Burn invisible and dim' (23–4: 54); 'stamped a memory all in vain/Upon the sight of lidless eyes in hell' ('Inclusiveness' (13–4)) becomes in *The Waste Land*, 'Pressing lidless eyes and waiting for a knock upon the door' (138: 65); and in the drafts to the poem, 'The lazy laughing Jenny of the Bard' (1971: 27) is directly adapted from Rossetti's 'Lazy laughing languid Jenny' ('Jenny' (1)).

Rather than pursue such connections further, however, I wish to offer an analysis of a pair of sonnets by Rossetti: 'For "Ruggiero and Angelica" by Ingres'. In the following analysis I shall be concerned not so much with stylistic indebtedness as with a common pattern of displacement built around oppositions between masculine and feminine.

> A remote sky, prolonged to the sea's brim:
> One rock-point standing buffetted alone,
> Vexed at its base with a foul beast unknown,
> Hell-birth of geomaunt and teraphim:
> A knight and a winged creature bearing him,
> Reared at the rock: a woman fettered there,
> Leaning into the hollow with loose hair
> And throat let back and heartsick trail of limb.
> The sky is harsh, and the sea shrewd and salt:
> Under his lord the griffin-horse ramps blind
> With rigid wings and tail. The spear's lithe stem
> Thrills in the roaring of those jaws: behind,
> That evil length of body chafes at fault.
> She doth not hear nor see – she knows of them.

The poem collapses its apparent triangulation – 'knight', 'winged creature', 'woman' – into a series of unstable oppositions. The 'remote sky' and 'sea's brim' are immediately set against the masculine symbol of 'One rock-point standing'. This is reinforced by 'Reared at the rock', which refers to both the process of education and arousal undergone by the 'knight', and the position of the horse on its hind legs. The 'foul beast unknown' at its 'base' is merged with 'a woman fettered there', whose 'loose hair' and proffered 'throat' suggests both sensuality and victimisation. (To 'trail' is 'to hang down or float loosely', but also 'to creep, crawl, as a serpent or other reptile' (OED 6, 7).)

The 'winged creature' initially might be taken as a periphrasis for the angel in the house: 'bearing him', both in giving birth to, enduring, and being physically under in love-making. The phrase is subsequently attached to the 'griffin-horse', also described as 'Under his lord', which 'ramps blind/With rigid wings and tail'. 'Ramps', rear up, and 'rigid' combine with 'stand' and 'prolonged' to produce an image of sexual arousal; and 'the spear's lithe stem' recalls the phallic image of the 'naked stem of thorns' in 'Jenny' (120)). 'The roaring of those jaws' refers back to 'beast', but is drawn through opposition to the 'spear' that 'Thrills' within them into a symbol of female sexuality. The 'evil length of body' also serves as a metonymy for the woman as well as the 'beast': 'chafes', whether taken in its primary sense of warms up (*chauffer*), or more familiar one of rubs, implies sexual pleasure. 'Chafes at fault' has the further intimation of being impervious to blame, resentful of condemnation.

Angelica's autistic response – 'She doth not see or hear' – implies not weakness but power. 'She knows of them': the pronoun may refer most directly to the 'knight', 'beast' and 'horse', but it also extends outwards to the audience of the poem itself. Angelica is presented both as an image, and responding to witnessing herself as a spectacle. This self-reflexive awareness is taken up in the second sonnet:

> Clench thine eyes now, – 'tis the last instant girl:
> Draw in thy sense, set thy knees, and take
> One breath for all: thy life is keen awake, –
> Thou mayst not swoon. Was that the scattered whirl
> Of its foam drenched thee? – or the waves that curl
> And split, bleak spray wherein thy temples ache?
> Or was it his the champion's blood to flake
> Thy flesh? – or thine own blood's anointing, girl?

Now silence: for the sea's in such a sound
As irks not silence: and except the sea,
All now is still. Now the dead thing doth cease
To writhe, and drifts. He turns to her: and she,
Cast from the jaws of Death, remains there, bound,
Again a woman in her nakedness.

The 'last instant' may be compared to Eliot's 'bewildering moment' of heightened sensation. 'Set thy knees', ominously close to setting a trap, gives this an obviously erotic dimension: 'One breath' links back to the previous 'jaws'. There is switch to the imperative mode. Yet the imperative to 'Clench thine eyes' (recalling the earlier 'blind') is equally directed towards the reader, and the repeated use of 'thy' may be taken as similarly outward addressed: 'Draw', in the sense of illustrate, refers back to the contemplation of a picture. 'Thou mayst not swoon' could be order, plea, demand, or prohibition: however it is understood, it presupposes an identification of the reader with the spectacle of female pleasure. One is invited to witness and participate simultaneously.

Rossetti's erotic imagery is almost dead-pan in its literalism: compare, for example, the fountains in 'Dante at Verona', 'Where wearied damsels rest, and hold/Their hands in the wet spurt of gold' (167–8). In the phrase, 'scattered whirl/Of its foam', 'its' should logically refer to sea, yet has no direct antecedent: it dramatises a response from outside the frame into the picture. The 'bleak spray' might appear a synonym for the 'foam', yet the 'waves that curl/And split' might be seen as implicitly feminine. The equation of woman and sea is commonplace in Rossetti (for example 'The Portrait', 'he who seeks her beauty's furthest goal/... may know/The very sky and sea-line of her soul' (5, 7–8)). The opposition is also supported by the subsequent contrast of 'his the champion's blood' and 'thine own blood's anointing'. 'To flake/Thy flesh' is to mark with streaks, but also suggests slake, flake out; the alternative scenario is for Angelica to be 'drenched' in self-arousal.

In the sestet, the 'dead thing' is opposed to 'thy life' which 'is keen awake'. It 'doth cease/To writhe', erotically, and 'drifts', postcoitally (another frequent Rossetti usage, for example 'Nuptial Sleep' (9–14)). Angelica is 'Cast from the jaws of Death' in the sense both of having escaped from and having been created out of. She 'remains there, bound', having been brought back under control rather than liberated, though 'there' suggests still within the 'jaws'. 'Again' raises the question of what she was before: 'in her nakedness' is suggestively parallel to the 'evil length' of the previous sonnet, and the transition from 'girl' to 'woman' suggests sexual maturation.

There are several reasons for selecting Rossetti as a representative text. First, these sonnets make a convenient bridge to the reading of 'Sweeney Erect' that will be offered later in this chapter. Obvious parallels can be drawn between their techniques of framing within mythic tableaux, the struggles of their respective male figures, and the interplay of eroticised oppositions throughout both texts. Second, there is a considerable degree of self-consciousness with regard to the underlying categories of the poem. This is most notable in the exotic parentage of the 'Hell-birth'. 'Teraphim' is 'a kind of idols or images, or an idol or an image, applied especially to household gods': 'geomaunt', one engaged in 'the art of divination by means of lines and figures'. The 'beast' is itself the product of an opposition between masculine and feminine, rationality and domesticity, analysis and icon. Third, there is an evident preoccupation with the woman's body as the site of sexual pleasure: the struggle to liberate her is simultaneously to overcome her. The highly sexualised imagery – 'spear's lithe stem', 'bleak spray', 'jaws' – is combined with a curious arrestedness. The poem starts from and returns to a 'remote sky', 'silence' and stillness. The male as 'champion' is both triumphant and deceived. Within the narrative, or succession of tableaux if one prefers, the point of repose comes with 'bound': the poem is more iconic than Sidney's 'Desire', but has something of the same self-generating emotion. The woman is desirable because she is monstrous: her pleasure stands for that of the male protagonist and reader, whose relation to her, however, is as much empathetic as voyeuristic.

In Rossetti, dependence on a dualistic iconography does not preclude unpredictable substitutions and complicities. The question is whether Eliot merely inherits a simplified version of this taxonomy. Gordon proposes that his 'automatic disgust' results from 'hardly seeing' women 'as they slot into given roles: inciters or prey of low desire' (1977: 14); Mayer finds only 'pallid wraith or mastering pariah' (1989: 37), and Pinkney, 'stereotypical juxtaposition – woman as saint or sinner' (1984: 27–8)). Such comments would suggest that Eliot's debt to his nineteenth-century forebears in this area is seen as amounting to little more than transmission of 'traditional and literary prejudices' (Gordon 1977: 76).

Eliot obviously may be fitted into what Bram Dijkstra calls 'the turn of the century male's fascination for, horror of, and hostility towards woman, culminating in an almost uncontrollable urge to destroy her, to do violence to that perverse, unPlatonic reflection of the Platonic beauty he was so eager to pursue' (1986: 149). This account catches the interdependence of idealisation and hostility; yet it underestimates, I believe, the ascription of power to the female image, and the degree to which the violence against it might also be regarded as self-directed, although perhaps not the less craved for that reason.

I now wish to explore the presence of this tradition in what is perhaps Eliot's most famous expression of fascination with death-in-lust: 'Whispers of Immortality' (1969: 52–3).

> Webster was much possessed by death
> And saw the skull beneath the skin;
> And breastless creatures under ground
> Leaned backward with a lipless grin.
>
> Daffodil bulbs instead of balls
> Stared from the sockets of the eyes!
> He knew that thought clings round dead limbs
> Tightening its lusts and luxuries.
>
> Donne, I suppose, was such another
> Who found no substitute for sense,
> To seize and clutch and penetrate;
> Expert beyond experience,
>
> He knew the anguish of the marrow
> The ague of the skeleton;
> No contact possible to flesh
> Allayed the fever of the bone.
>
> * * * *
>
> Grishkin is nice: her Russian eye
> Is underlined for emphasis;
> Uncorseted, her friendly bust
> Gives promise of pneumatic bliss.

> The couched Brazilian jaguar
> Compels the scampering marmoset
> With subtle effluence of cat;
> Grishkin has a maisonnette;
>
> The sleek Brazilian jaguar
> Does not in its arboreal gloom
> Distil so rank a feline smell
> As Grishkin in a drawing-room.
>
> And even the Abstract Entities
> Circumambulate her charm;
> But our lot crawls between dry ribs
> To keep our metaphysics warm.

The first half of the poem depicts a macabre but authentic seventeenth-century intelligence situated within the desires and corruptibility of the body: the second presents an opposition, banal yet apparently insuperable, between the engulfing bosom and 'feline smell' of Grishkin and the modern mind's preoccupation with the 'Abstract Entities'. This juxtaposition has frequently been read as an almost programmatic celebration of the undissociated sensibility of Metaphysical poetry: an accomplished versification of a literary manifesto. But it is not the text of *The Duchess of Malfi* but John Webster who is said to be 'possessed by death': we are invited to contemplate not poems but individuals, and, specifically, the sexual 'experience' of our fellow-men. 'Death' has its inevitable Jacobean pun on climax, a moment of revelatory intensity in which we are most conscious of ourselves as bodies and therefore mortal. Only an immersion in 'sense' so total that it will exhaust the possibilities of the 'flesh' can release us from the bondage of its desires.

'To seize and clutch and penetrate', however, only preserves an existential glamour so long as it is done by us and not to us. The combined transitive force of these verbs demands an object: Eliot's sexually charged meditation on death both presupposes and suppresses reference to a woman's body. The very absence of breasts and lips confirms the 'creatures under ground' to be female: 'Leaned' implies both the stasis of rigor mortis and the seductive beckoning of a compliant response. This furtive concealment accentuates rather than diminishes their erotic attraction, and thus their power. To see 'the skull beneath the skin' is to see the female body as prefiguring death, enticing towards it, and therefore demanding a further violence of repudiation. The resultant 'lusts and luxuries', though qualified by the supposedly neutral 'its', are anything but suprapersonal. 'Thought' first 'clings' child-like, dependent for nurture, eager for security: then reasserts itself through 'Tightening', a verb of male sexual arousal, and the contracting grip of strangulation. The scene is left suspended in a participle of increasing menace: notice how the 'creatures' through this action are reduced to inert 'dead limbs'.

In the second half of the poem, the female has seized control: a triple repetition of 'Grishkin' suggests that this is the inevitable consequence of dignifying her with a name, an identity. 'Couched' simultaneously endows Grishkin with drawing-room languor and the alertness of a predator poised for the kill. The ascendent woman is immediately translated into Swinburnian terms, with a queue of suburban Severins eager to be disciplined: both 'Compels' and 'crawls' carry titillating intimations of the flagellating brothel. What the example of the Jacobeans shows is that desire heightened to sufficient intensity, ruthlessness, can reverse this submission. An insistent series of parallels suggest that Grishkin's covering of flesh is only camouflage. Behind the 'Russian eye' lie the 'sockets of the eyes'; the 'friendly bust' conceals one of the 'breastless creatures'; and the 'subtle effluence' blends into the stench of 'dead limbs'.

Donne, it should be stressed, is above all concerned with his own body: anatomised, satiated, vulnerable. Eliot draws on a characteristically nineteenth-century convention of the fertility of a woman's body implying its precise opposite. In Tennyson's 'Merlin and Vivien', we find 'How from the rosy lips of life and love,/ Flashed the bare grinning skeleton of death' (846–7); in Rossetti's 'Chimes', 'Beauty's bower in the dust o'er blown/With a bare white breast of bone' (v. 5–6); and in the line from Browning's 'A Toccata of Galuppi's' used for the epigraph to 'Burbank with a Baedeker': 'Dear dead women, with such hair, too' (44).

Grishkin's carnal mastery must be countered through commitment to the 'pneumatic bliss'; the soft inflatability of her body demands to be punctured by the phallic response of the compressed air drill. This is the modern equivalent of the knowledge of Webster and Donne, that 'anguish' can be inflicted as well as undergone; that the 'fever of the bone' is also a longing to reveal it; that the 'skeleton' must be embraced before it may be transcended.

At the moment of this stripping away, it is bluntly asserted: 'No contact possible'. This is the moment of triumph, of proclaimed immunity. The sexual act becomes frankly solipsistic: its sensuality so completely devoid of reciprocation that the woman is refused even the status of object. Instead she is treated as mere occasion for the intensification of desire, reflected back upon a blameless and heroically questing male, who will move beyond dependence on the body, her body, into a higher and ascetic spiritual realm: 'As the soul leaves the body torn and bruised,/As the mind deserts the body it has used' ('La Figlia che Piange' 11–12: 34).

But is the role of 'Brazilian jaguar' any more demeaning than that of the 'scampering marmoset'? It might be argued that it requires a wilful and humourless severity to pursue such a reading; that the lurid rhetoric of 'Whispers of Immortality' is always held in check by the urbane propositional voice ('Donne, I suppose'), and by the deftness of the ubiquitous Eliotic irony. As Eliot argued in *After Strange Gods*, 'the indecent that is funny may be the legitimate source of innocent merriment, while the absence of humour reveals it as purely disgusting' (1934: 55–6).

This would, I think, more or less hold good for *Prufrock and Other Observations*. The expansive, yet nervously taut, conversational rhythms of these poems immediately place us within a subjectivity, which, for all its idiosyncratic intensities, remains recognisably in the tradition of Jamesian personae. The sexual vacillations of this consciousness seem obscurely vindicated through the guarded, almost surreptitious, lyricism of which it is capable: because there are 'mermaids singing' (124: 16), it is all too easy to forget that Prufrock wishes for a pair of 'ragged claws' (73: 15) to deal with them. The reverie of 'Rhapsody on a Windy Night' pivots around the encounter with a soliciting whore: 'The street-lamp said, 'Regard that woman/Who hesitates toward you in the light of the door/Which opens on her like a grin' (16–18: 24–6). A moment of opportunity beckons and vanishes, 'the passage we did not take/ Towards the door we never opened' ('Burnt Norton' 12–13: 171), and the remainder of the poem meanders through a grotesque catalogue of eroticised debris, the only sustenance of the solipsistic mind: the 'twisted branch' and 'broken spring' (25, 30); the 'old crab' gripping the end of a poking stick (44); and the depiction of the moon as 'aged whore' (50–61). The narrator totters home to a final assignation with his own solitude: so wryly impotent that the phallic menace of the curt imperative to 'mount' to deliver the 'last twist of the knife' scarcely registers. The female presents a perpetual challenge to the autonomy of Eliot's subjective idealism – 'Beyond the circle of our ideas she stands' ('On a Portrait' 12: 599) – and his apprehension can be regarded as a form of indirect tribute to her power. The woman in 'Conversation Galante' is dubbed 'eternal enemy of the absolute': she remains 'indifferent and imperious' towards her companion's attempts to 'body forth' his 'own vacuity': 'She then: "Does this refer to me?"/"Oh no, it is I who am inane"' (9–12, 14–16: 33). 'Portrait of a Lady' closes with a moment of reversal in which 'self-possession gutters' (101: 20), and the authority of the analytic voice is revealed as precarious, even completely illusory. Marianne Moore commented that she 'cursed the poet . . . for his cruelty' until reaching 'that ending. It is hard to get over this ending with a few moments of thought: it wrenches a piece of life at the roots' (1918: 36–7). The intimations of emasculation are wholly appropriate. The self-scepticism, both erotic and epistemological, of the early verse develops into the exacting, even purgatorial, ideal of humility in the later poems: the 'cruelty' of Eliot's treatment of women cannot match that directed towards himself.

It's far more difficult to pursue such mitigating readings for *Poems 1920*, and, I think, misguided to attempt them. Such a response, I believe, diminishes the poetry by refusing to acknowledge where the 'network of tentacular roots' of Eliot's language probe, 'reaching down to the deepest terrors and desires' (1951: 155). As satire, the collection shows no fellow-feeling or generosity, and little cultural insight: the famed telescoping of mythic past and sordid present only reveals a pondered cynicism, a self-regarding elitism of mode, and a scholastic erudition incongruously disproportionate to the targets on which it is expended. I would argue for a simple reversal of priorities. Instead of treating these poems as a social critique into which a misogynistic language accidentally seeps, they should be read primarily as articulations of a psychology of sexual fear and desired retaliation.

The 'reconsidered passion' of 'Gerontion' should, I believe, be read in terms of the literal fact of impotence and the consequent problem of how to 'excite the membrane, when the sense has cooled' (42, 64: 37–9). The poem's vision of the imminent demise of Western culture is symptom rather than diagnosis, an eloquent if ultimately futile compensation for an absolute severance from desire. There are obvious parallels with Tennyson's aged narrators such as Tithonus, 'A white-haired shadow roaming like a dream'

(8), and Ulysses, 'this gray spirit yearning in desire' (30). In Eliot, the stoic poignancy is imbued with corporeal reference: 'I have lost my passion: why should I need to keep it/Since what is kept must be adulterated?' (58–9). The unsavoury metaphor of untreated meat in 'adulterated' is characteristic of the continuous sexual dimension to the rhetoric: the longing to be at the 'hot gates', wading 'knee deep in the salt marsh, heaving a cutlass' (3–5); the opposition between 'the tiger springs' and to 'stiffen in a rented house' (49, 51); and the final flurry of emblems of cuckoldry, 'gull', 'horn' and 'white feather', set against 'Belle Isle' and the 'Gulf' (70–4). Tennyson's Ulysses envisages a similar finale: 'It may be that the gulfs will wash us down:/It may be we shall touch the Happy Isles' (62–3). In Eliot, however, the terms of sententious repudiation themselves ooze with imagery of siring and ejaculation: 'Till the refusal propagates a fear'; 'Unnatural vices/Are fathered by our heroism'; 'These tears are shaken from the wrath-bearing tree' (44–8). I would insist that for all its sermonic inclusiveness, the intimacy and veracity of the poem lie in its embodiment of a language of male desire; paradoxically its exclusive concern with sexual failure enhances rather than diminishes its erotic power.

The obvious contrast between the sprawling syntax and clammy and porous diction of 'Gerontion' and the formal regularity of Eliot's quatrain poems should not blind us to their essential continuity. These supposedly provide a much-needed infusion of hard, dry Parnassianism into English verse; the rigour of a new classicism achieved through assiduous cultivation of the 'historical sense'. But what is the nature of the history to which the famous choral finale of 'Sweeney among the Nightingales' appeals?

> The host with someone indistinct
> Converses at the door apart,
> The nightingales are singing near
> The Convent of the Sacred Heart,
>
> And sang within the bloody wood
> When Agamemnon cried aloud
> And let their liquid siftings fall
> To stain the stiff dishonoured shroud.   (33–40: 58)

The power of these lines derives from the endless vistas of sexual hostility opened behind the protagonists of the poem. The continuous present of 'singing' suddenly focuses back into 'sang' and 'cried', the only past tenses of the poem. This temporal movement backward is fused with a prepositional thrust inward, from the 'door' that is 'apart' to the 'Sacred Heart' that is 'near', and then yet further 'within'. The lassitude of the preceding stanzas suddenly concentrates into a single climactic gasp: notice how 'aloud', set against 'within', seems to locate the 'bloody wood' inside the body, a woman's body. This, the 'liquid siftings' and the 'stain' are all images of female sexuality as discharge, triumphing over the rigidity of Agamemnon: 'stiff' suggests that his sexual arousal continues even in death, enveloped and overcome by this viscousness. (In 'Mr Eliot's Sunday Morning Service' (7–8: 54–5), what renders Origen 'enervate' is the 'mens(tr)ual turn of time': a repulsion exacerbated by the running conceit on the multiple impregnation of the ovary in such terms as 'polyphiloprogenitive' and 'superfetation' (1, 6).) The parallel with a mother's lullaby to her child further stresses female power and male helplessness at the 'bewildering moment'. 'Let . . . fall' moves the tense forward again; the 'siftings' merge into the narrative present of 'singing', simultaneous aspects of the same event; and 'To stain' reaches ominously out into the future. The sexual act will always repeat the same confrontation, always conclude in the same betrayal and desecration of the male. Agamemnon is not 'dishonoured' by the inglorious parallels the poem establishes between past and present: for example, between the besmirched 'shroud', the net in which Clytemnestra entraps, murders and finally parades him, and the 'table-cloth' earlier in the poem on which a 'coffee-cup' has been overturned. The poem gives us no choice but to side with Sweeney, who becomes, in terms of patriarchal politics, not a degenerate descendant, but a final and even noble embodiment (for links with King Sweeney of Irish legend, see Knust 1967). 'Sweeney *guards* the hornéd gate' (my emphasis), and at the very least is wiser than Agamemnon in so far as he 'declines the gambit', though this may not be enough to save him.

The critical consensus towards the figure of Sweeney is largely sympathetic. It is assumed that there is a lost vitality in his absence of inhibition which Eliot, as one of the 'masters of the subtle schools' ('Mr Eliot's Sunday Morning Service' (31: 58)) must regard with scarcely concealed envy. The attitude expressed over fifty years ago by F. O. Matthiessen, that 'the double feeling of repulsion from vulgarity, and yet his shy attraction to the coarse emotions of common life have found their complete symbol in

Sweeney' (1935: 58) can easily be paralleled in more recent criticism: Robert M. Degraaff claims that Sweeney 'possesses the dignity of uncorrupted innocence', and so 'seems sympathetically human in a setting in which all other humanity has been distorted' (1985: 233); and Kinley Roby even finds his 'vital force' and 'demonic attractiveness' acting 'according to the imperatives of a higher order . . . implicitly made available through Christ's sacrifice' (1985: 4–5, 13). And this seems borne out by Eliot's own later description: 'a man who in younger days was perhaps a pugilist, mildly successful; who then grew older and retired to keep a pub' (Coghill 1948: 86). Against this benign domestication, I would stress two things. First, the sentiment expressed in *Sweeney Agonistes*: 'I knew a man once did a girl in/Any man might do a girl in/Any man has to, needs to, wants to/Once in a lifetime, do a girl in' (113–18: 124). Second, the most obvious source for the name is the folk-hero of popular music-hall, Sweeney Todd, demon barber, razor murderer, and pie-maker extraordinaire. The running implication is that someone is going to get slashed, soon.

At this point, I need to give a detailed reading of the poem which I feel most fully reveals the visceral force of Eliot's sexual rhetoric: 'Sweeney Erect' (1969: 42–3). To pause on the title: the genus Sweeney, a zoological classification that endows the narrator with the forensic detachment and control of a taxonomist. 'Erect': *erectus*, standing upright in contrast to the stooping of anthropoids and primates, and thus distinctively human, and tumescent (a pun so blatant that it is seldom acknowledged), a sexual and therefore animal being. A challenge is immediately thrown down to the idealising view of man expounded in Emerson's essay 'Self-Reliance', from which the seventh stanza will later be adapted. 'He who knows that power is inborn, that he is weak because he has looked for good out of him and elsewhere, and so perceiving, throws himself unhesitatingly on his thought, instantly rights himself, stands in the erect position, commands his limbs, works miracles' (1979: vol. ii, 50)

Sweeney's spontaneous and unrestrained appetite fulfils Emerson's demand for complete self-trust: man 'cannot be happy and strong until he too lives with nature in the present, above time' (1979: vol. ii, 39). Thus on one level, the poem argues for original sin and the necessity of conformity and self-suppression against Emerson's doctrine of innate goodness (see Sigg 1989: 6–9, 83).

On my saying, What have I to do with the sacredness of traditions, if I live wholly from within? my friend suggested – But these impulses may be from below, not from above?' I replied, 'They do not seem to me to be such; but if I am the Devil's child, I will live then from the Devil'
(Emerson 1979: vol. ii, 30)

So Sweeney offers a grim alternative version of the 'aboriginal Self' (Emerson 1979: vol. ii, 37), with a salutary 'insistence upon the degraded and helpless state of man' (Eliot 1951: 414). This must, however, be taken in the context of claims made elsewhere 'that the sexual act as evil is more dignified, less boring, than as the natural, 'life-giving', cheery automatism of the modern world' (1951: 427–8).

The epigraph from Beaumont and Fletcher's *The Maid's Tragedy* provides a female counterpoint to this biological categorising of the male: 'And the trees about me,/Let them be dry and leafless; let the rocks/Groan with continual surges; and behind me/Make all a desolation. Look, look, wenches!' This is part of the cry of 'wrong'd Aspatia' ('Elegy' 1973: 117), deserted by her betrothed: the voice of the betrayed, the anguished, the violated. (And also, it should be noted, the anonymous: it is by no means immediately obvious that the speaker is a woman.) It is useful to restore the lines to a fuller context:

> Suppose I stand upon the sea breach now,
> Mine arms thus, and mine hair blown with the wind,
> Wild as that desert, and let all about me
> Tell that I am forsaken. Do my face
> (If thou hadst ever feeling of a sorrow)
> Thus, thus, Antiphila: strive to make me look,
> Like Sorrow's monument; and the trees about me,
> Let them be dry and leafless; let the rocks
> Groan with continual surges; and behind me
> Make all a desolation. Look, look, wenches,
> A miserable life of this poor picture!   (II.ii.68–78)

How is the passage altered by Eliot's contraction? Most obviously, the 'structural emotion' vanishes: it is no longer apparent that Aspatia is instructing her gentlewomen to use her as model for the tapestry of Ariadne that they are weaving. The self-dramatisation, the stasis, the indulgence of wishing to serve as 'Sorrow's monument', all go. The epigraph taken in isolation sets up an immediate sexual dichotomy between the trees and the waves. But not a balanced one: the 'continual surges' increase in power at the expense of the permanent sterility of the 'dry and leafless' trunks. Eliot has edited a lament down into a threat: the spell of destructive passion of the sorceress. This establishes the logic of the poem. The victim threatens 'desolation' and so justifies her desertion: the reality of the woman is only fully revealed through violation and betrayal, which she is therefore seen as inviting.

The disruptive voice of female grief is immediately appropriated and suppressed. 'Look, look, wenches' becomes a dare, a challenge, a taunt from the narrator, to be pondered later in the poem by the 'ladies of the corridor', and Aspatia's lament is both preserved within and mocked by the opening stanzas. (The insertion of Ophelia's parting words at the close of 'A Game of Chess' has a similar effect: 'Good night, ladies, good night, sweet ladies, good night, good night' (172: 66). The line both juxtaposes an idealised version of female suffering with an actuality of fatigue and abortion, and transforms its plangency into a bitterly sarcastic authorial address which refuses to acknowledge any distinction between them.)

> Paint me a cavernous waste shore
> Cast in the unstilled Cyclades,
> Paint me the bold anfractuous rocks
> Faced by the snarled and yelping seas.
>
> Display me Aeolus above
> Reviewing the insurgent gales
> Which tangle Ariadne's hair
> And swell with haste the perjured sails.   (1–8)

A backdrop of a 'cavernous waste shore' is provided, as requested, but there is no audience for the female voice. It merges into the 'snarled and yelping seas' as an animal cry of threat and pain, to which the 'bold anfractuous rocks' remain sturdily indifferent. 'Yelping' is the first of many participles in the poem which suspend action in a continuous present. These allow the authorial voice to disengage, adopt the calm and analytic perspective of 'Aeolus above/Reviewing'. Again, reference can be made to *The Maid's Tragedy*, where, in a masque in the first act, Aeolus receives instructions from Cynthia: 'Hie thee then,/And charge the Wind go from his rocky den,/Let loose his subjects; only Boreas/Too foul for our intentions as he was,/Still keep him fast chain'd' (I.ii.172–6). But Boreas is out, and throughout the rest of the play, the sea provides images of turbulent and destructive passion. And in Eliot's poem, Aeolus, for all his apparent composure, unleashes and condones the 'insurgent gales', which, as they 'tangle Ariadne's hair', assist the escape of her lover, Theseus. (She is identified with the seas that threaten him through 'snarled', a synonym for tangled in American usage, OED 2.) The passionate woman provokes and therefore deserves betrayal. There's a paradoxical arousal through the very act of abandonment: the tumescence of 'swell with haste' refers to flight rather than to consummation. But to where?

> Morning stirs the feet and hands
> (Nausicaa and Polypheme).
> Gesture of orang-outang
> Rises from the sheets in steam.   (9–12)

Morning still has something of the 'rosy-fingered dawn' about it rather than the more typically Eliotic 'comes to consciousness'. ('Preludes' (1969: 22)). The impulse of 'insurgent' and 'swell' is continued in 'stirs' and 'Rises': the 'perjured sails' become 'sheets', as if the fleeing Theseus has literally been blown in. The casual mingling of Homeric reference suggests little more than an incongruous coupling, although Nausicaa repeats the theme of desertion and a source connecting Polypheme with razors has been suggested in Ovid's *Metamorphoses* (see Arrowsmith 1981: 37–8). More important is the reassertion of detachment through this facetious interjection, at the point when the wind and spray of the open sea thicken into a dank tropical 'steam', and the poem becomes menacingly opaque.

'Gesture of orang-outang' reinforces the separation of poised narrator from what is recounted, by suggesting a language of the body, and hence of animal desire, yet also a controlled performance beckoning outwards to the reader, to observe, to ponder, and to imitate. The phrase also brings in a third relevant source for the poem, Edgar Allen Poe's 'The Murders in the Rue Morgue'. (The text was singled out for praise by Eliot, along with 'The Assignation' and 'Shadow' (1921: 8).) In the drafts to *The Waste Land*, 'Elegy' contains the lines 'Reveal (as in a tale by Poe)/The features of the injur'd bride!' (1971: 117); Grover Smith notes, but does not develop, the possible link (1974: 47; and 1990; see also

Arrowsmith 1981: 24–9). In Poe's tale, the mysterious killings, which displayed 'an agility astounding, a strength superhuman, a ferocity brutal, a butchery without motive, a *grotesquerie* in horror absolutely alien from humanity' (1852: 110), are revealed to have been performed by an orang-outang, brought back from Borneo by a visiting sailor to Paris.

> Returning home from some sailors' frolic on the night, or rather in the morning of the murder, he found the beast occupying his own bedroom, into which it had broken from a closet adjoining, where it had been, as was thought, securely confined. Razor in hand, and fully lathered, it was sitting before a looking-glass, attempting the operation of shaving, in which it had no doubt previously watched its master through the key-hole of the closet.
>
> (Poe 1852: 117)

The orang-outang, afraid of being punished by whipping, breaks out, and makes his way into the room of two women in the Rue Morgue:

> As the sailor looked in, the gigantic animal had seized Madame L'Espanaye by the hair, which was loose, as she had been combing it, and was flourishing the razor about her face, in imitation of the motions of a barber. The daughter lay prostrate and motionless; she had swooned. The screams and struggles of the old lady, during which the hair was torn from her head, had the effect of changing the probably pacific purposes of the ourang-outang into those of wrath.
>
> (Poe 1852: 119)

This provokes him to the slaughter so clinically described by Poe earlier in the story. There are several obvious points of reference with 'Sweeney Erect': the orang-outang itself; the act of shaving; the 'motions of a barber' subsequent to 'flourishing the razor'; and the 'screams and struggles' of the old lady and the swooning of her daughter. By far the most important, however, is the ape's transformation through gazing into his master's 'looking-glass'. Is he liberated or unleashed through seizing the mirror? Is he frustrated by his own animality, the impossibility of being other than a beast? Or, more alarmingly, must the orang-outang become human to become inhuman, act out his master's secret fantasies? Numerous textual points support the second reading. The ape is first encountered through passing 'into the interior on a voyage of pleasure'; it falls into the sailor's 'own exclusive possession'; despite its 'intractable ferocity', he manages to keep it 'carefully secluded' in his Paris residence, only concerned not to attract 'unpleasant curiosity' (Poe 1852: 117). The ape does not simply flee: it encourages pursuit by 'occasionally stopping to look back and gesticulate at its pursuer' (1852: 117). The sailor is initially 'rejoiced and perplexed' when it breaks into the women's room; he ascends a convenient (and extremely phallic) lightning-rod which allows 'a glimpse of the interior of the room', and an intimate witnessing of the subsequent events. And in Poe, it should be noted, the orang-outang gets off unpunished, or at least with nothing worse than recapture by its master and being sold to the Jardin des Plantes. The whole purpose of Dupin's, and by implication the reader's, search was to locate and define the animal, but not to reprimand or change it.

> As the strong man exults in his physical ability, delighting in such exercises as call his muscles into action, so glories the analyst in that moral activity which *disentangles* . . . He is fond of enigmas, of conundrums, of hieroglyphics; exhibiting in his solutions of each a degree of *acumen* which appears to the ordinary apprehension praeternatural.
>
> (Poe 1852: 80)

A similar dualism is, I think, present in 'Sweeney Erect'. The analytic pleasure is one of re-enactment and covert approval of the 'exercises' of the 'strong man': for Poe, the ape, for Eliot, Sweeney. But the potency of Eliot's depiction of 'physical ability' takes us far beyond even the carnage in the Rue Morgue.

> This withered root of knots of hair
>   Slitted below and gashed with eyes,
> This oval O cropped out with teeth:
>   The sickle motion from the thighs
>
> Jackknifes upward at the knees
>   Then straightens out from heel to hip
> Pushing the framework of the bed
>   And clawing at the pillow slip.   (13–20)

If only on grounds of syntactic peculiarity, this passage should have attracted considerable critical attention. But instead it's almost invariably passed over, hushed up (the one extended discussion is Arrowsmith 1981). It fully reflects what Hugh Kenner called 'Eliot's besetting vice, a never wholly penetrable ambiguity about what is supposed to be happening' (1960: 92). Who does what to whom? The customary reading, if one could be said to exist, is that this is a peculiarly tortuous description of Sweeney gazing in a mirror prior to shaving. I take the first three lines as referring to the woman, or rather the male perception of her: the next two to the masculine response; and the final three to the woman's movements, though I accept that any distinction can only be tentative. Face, hair, razor, mirror, and reflection are all elements of a language of male sexuality intense and violent and brutally explicit. The dominant trope of the passage, and indeed of the poem, is of the phallus as blade operating on a female body both already maimed and inviting further mutilation.

Ariadne's 'tangled hair' has become 'knots' of pubic hair; the 'withered root' a remarkably direct depiction of the clitoris as stunted penis; the 'oval O' of the vagina, 'slitted below', instantly develops protective 'teeth'. (Compare the vagina dentata image in 'Ash Wednesday': 'There were no more faces and the stair was dark,/ Damp, jagged, like an old man's mouth drivelling, beyond repair,/ Or the toothed gullet of an aged shark' (9–11: 99).) These are assimilated into a single face that gazes back in a terrifying mirroring, premonition. (Recalling the 'snarled and yelping seas' that earlier 'faced' the rocks.) Freud argues no man can look at female genitals without fear of castration: for Eliot, that fear is alleviated by inflicting a comparable wound. The past participles seem to displace violence into a primordial act – 'Slitted', 'gashed' and 'cropped' – but also prefigure the imminent 'sickle motion'. 'Cropped' is an action already completed yet about to be performed. The abrupt staccato 'jackknifes' continues the blade motif; almost slicing from 'heel to hip', straightening out in the body. (The colon makes no syntactic sense unless the preceding three lines are taken as a collective object.) The focus then returns to the woman's body, unnamed, a mere site for the transference of 'motion' into 'pushing' and 'clawing'. There are no gender pronouns, no defined subject or predicate: whereas the past heroines are awarded resonant names, Ariadne and Nausicaa, the present of the poem defines woman solely in terms of voracious genitals and anonymous recoil. A temporal movement from completed past to present action to tableauesque participles is again used to contain and suspend while the authorial focus pans out.

Sweeney addressed full length to shave
Broadbottomed, pink from nape to base,
Knows the female temperament
And wipes the suds around his face.

(The lengthened shadow of a man
Is history, said Emerson
Who had not seen the silhouette
Of Sweeney straddled in the sun.)   (21–8)

There is a sudden pause as the male figure is named as Sweeney, presumably erect and thus 'full length'. The syntax is again difficult, but I think 'pink from nape to base' must refer to the woman viewed from behind prior to penetration. First, because Sweeney has already been compared to a (presumably hairy) orangoutang; second, because that it is the mating position of apes; and third because Sweeney is subsequently described as 'straddled', mounted, towering over. Again the female is elided even as a pronoun, merely 'Broadbottomed', her 'temperament' humiliatingly equated with mere 'suds', whether epileptic foam, shaving cream or sexual juices. The absence of a comma after 'shave' means the transitive force of the verb carries over the line-ending, slicing into the adjective. What also should be stressed is the deliberation, the savouring of dominance: 'addressed', poised, attentive, aimed in 'un instant de *puissance* et de délire' ('Dans le Restaurant' (14: 51; my emphasis)). The moment 'between the desire/And the spasm' ('The Hollow Men' (84–5: 85)) is prolonged by another supercilious interpolation, this time a conflation of a sentence from Emerson's 'Self-Reliance': 'An institution is the lengthened shadow of one man; . . . and all history resolves itself very easily into the biography of a few stout and earnest persons' (1979: vol. ii, 35–6). Institution' is significantly absent: discipline, tradition, control. 'Lengthened' continues the previous sexual pun: the shadow cast, by a man and man only, one of couplings and sirings (emphasised by the son/sun rhyme). (See also the epigraph to Emerson's essay taken from the epilogue to Beaumont and Fletcher's *Honest Man's Fortune*: 'Our acts our angels are, or good or ill,/Our fatal shadows that walk by us still'.) The scene suddenly opens up out of a sweaty bedroom as Sweeney expands, swells: like Antony in Cleopatra's dream, 'His legs bestrid the oceans; his rear'd arm/Crested the world' (V.ii.82–3) – a hero at his moment of triumph. For all the narrator's erudition, it is Sweeney who possesses the truly effective knowledge.

> Tests the razor on his leg
> Waiting until the shriek subsides.
> The epileptic on the bed
> Curves backward, clutching at her sides. (29–32)

The deferral of 'Tests' and 'Waiting' accentuates the pleasure of mastery and enforced submission. I think we are obliged to read 'the razor on his leg' as a periphrasis for erection (why the 'shriek' if he's trying out the blade's sharpness on himself?) The woman is dubbed 'epileptic', and so presumably 'snarled and yelping': her spinal contortions suggest an almost literal disembowelment, a response to a slashing and a maiming. (Eliot uses the term, 'succuba eviscerate' in 'Ode', a mock epithalamium only published in *Ara Vos Prec* (13: 30): this can, according to Harold Mason, 'mean little more than "disembowelled prostitute"' (1990: 317).) Again, the scene is suspended on a present participle of violent action – 'clutching' – which permits a movement away from the body to a wider environment.

> The ladies of the corridor
> Find themselves involved, disgraced,
> Call witness to their principles
> And deprecate the lack of taste
>
> Observing that hysteria
> Might easily be misunderstood;
> Mrs Turner intimates
> It does the house no sort of good. (33–40)

It seems to me comparatively unimportant whether the poem is set in a cheap boarding-house, with Mrs Turner as landlady; or in a brothel, with her as madam. (To give a single example from many bawdy usages: 'Women are caught as you take tortoises,/She must be turn'd on her back' (John Webster, *The White Devil* IV.ii.151–2).) In both cases, there is an outward address to a specifically female audience. (The early sonnet, 'Nocturne', also portrays an obscure act of violence after which 'the lady sinks into a swoon' and 'female readers all in tears are drowned', a reaction described as 'The perfect climax all true lovers seek!' (8, 13–14: 601).)

'Witness', 'principles' and 'Observing' are all authorial terms, comparable to the earlier 'reviewing': the narrator seeks to abstain from involvement and also to forestall protest by displacing his moral language on to 'The ladies of the corridor'. It is a matter to be decided among themselves. But on their lips, these words serve as no more than a fund of euphemisms to diffuse the 'lack of taste' of the preceding scene. 'Involved' contains a pun on vulva, recalling 'involved in her laughter' in 'Hysteria' (1–2: 32); and the 'corridor' has an obvious sexual dimension comparable to the 'cunning passages, contrived corridors/And issues' of Gerontion's extended apostrophe to the whore of History (32–3: 38). The women are implicated by their very bodies: hence 'disgraced' by the enforced recognition of the poem. They are presented as actively complicit with the designation of their own sexuality as hysteria and epilepsy: the 'it' which can be 'intimated' but never voiced, 'easily misunderstood'.

> But Doris, towelled from the bath,
> Enters padding on broad feet,
> Bringing sal volatile
> And a glass of brandy neat.   (41–4)

The arrival of Doris has often been read as a positive intervention, but I feel sceptical. She is 'towelled from the bath', cleansed of the blood and suds, purged by a perhaps not dissimilar 'steam'. (Tennyson's *Oenone* apostrophises 'Idalian Aphrodite beautiful,/ Fresh as the foam, new-bathed in Paphian wells' (170–1); more ominously the narrator of 'The Love Song of St. Sebastian' also enters 'with a towel in my hand' (22)). As she 'enters', in bovine fashion, 'padding on broad feet', impassive and compliant and unsuspecting, she appears the complementary, functioning side of the convulsing 'epileptic on the bed'. Smelling salts versus the razor seems a mismatch: for all her good intentions and stolid pragmatic aid, there appears to be every possibility of a further violent incision.

There can be no comfortable detachment or 'objective' stance towards such a poetry: it raises the question of gendered readings in a particularly acute and irrevocable fashion. 'What about Sweeney's victim', exclaims Ayres (Arrowsmith 1981: 45), 'or don't you men care?'. I would imagine that it is impossible to read this text 'as a woman' in any naïve sense: to attempt an immediate identification with the 'epileptic on the bed' can surely only be a traumatically masochistic exercise. (As Pinkney remarks, 'she is effectively a patient upon a table, though at this point an unetherised one' (1984: 86).) But other options are available. 'Sweeney Erect' could be treated as yet another of Eliot's 'Debates between Body and Soul', the second of which, written in 1911, was entitled 'Bacchus and Ariadne' (see Mayer 1989: 52, 102, 135). One of the Latin meanings of 'sal' is wit, and the poem may be read as a black comedy showing once again that 'Flesh and blood is weak and frail,/ Susceptible to nervous shock' ('The Hippopotamus' (5–6: 49)). The spirit is most certainly phallic, and the weakness of the flesh correspondingly female. Yet if it is accepted that women feel a degree of hate and resentment against their own bodies (see Dinnerstein 1976: 91–197), then they too may participate in the spiritual pilgrimage enacted through this savage excoriation of the flesh, their flesh.

Alternatively, Eliot's presentation of women could be seen as yet another appeal to automatic outrage at any inversion of gender hierarchies. His evocation of their threatening power would simply indicate his eagerness to enlist in the 'army of unalterable law' that scowls down on even the most minor liberties of Miss Nancy Ellicot (12: 30). As such, it would at best provide further confirmation of the reactionary nature of classic modernism. Thus one could expect no more than an 'endless recurrence' of stereotype to result from Eliot's continued reliance on the 'veritable iconography of misogyny' that Bram Dijkstra discerns in nineteenth-century art (1986: viii). Two immediate objections may be lodged. While 'male mastery and female submission' may represent a 'basic dualistic simplicity' during the period (1986: 114), the outcome of the play between the opposed terms need not be treated so reductively. And Dijkstra's habitual recourse to such composite terms as 'oppressive male sentimentality', 'nineteenth century males', and 'a male fantasy of ultimate power' (1986: 9, 16, 21) neither differentiates within the tradition nor investigates the source of its continued power. Whatever else Eliot's poetry may be, it is surely more than a manifestation of 'the prevailing masculine psychosadistic insistence everywhere' (1986: 23).

'The angry denunciations of feminists everywhere' (Dijkstra 1986: 33) are somewhat loosely invoked, but recent criticism has been more flexible in its response. Gilbert and Gubar's thesis in *No Man's Land*, of modernism as a collective reaction against increased female emancipation from the mid-nineteenth century onwards, makes no attempt to deny that 'belligerent passion ... generates texts marked by compelling intensity' (1988a: xiii). Thus their analysis serves as a kind of paradoxical justification rather than condemnation of literary misogyny: 'as the richness of the (male) modernist tradition attests, for many writers Beerbohm's futile rage became fertile rage, fueling the innovations of the avant-garde in order to ward off the assaults of women' (1988a: 130). The 'iconography' of the period, far from being a demeaning imposition, is treated as a potentially enabling myth: Kate Chopin's achievement as 'an innovative feminist myth-maker', for example, is dependent on 'such crucial male precursors as Flaubert, Whitman, and Swinburne' (Gilbert and Gubar1988b: 111).

So the tradition can be reclaimed on the level of archetype. This does not involve the claim that woman are actually dark, mysterious, and enigmatic, only that the uses to which this imagery may be put should not be too readily circumscribed. Camille Paglia's *Sexual Personae* eulogises the icon of the *femme fatale* for expressing man's 'terrible sense of woman's power, her imperviousness, her archetypal confederacy with chthonian nature' (1992: 12). The charge of essentialism may be deflected easily enough by translating her argument on to the plane of competing representations. The demonic female serves as a salutary corrective to both the ideal of purity and maternity of the Victorian period and to what Paglia would regard as the equally prescriptive and censorious puritanism of contemporary feminism. The cultural thesis propounded, of the continuous conflict between Apollonian and Dionysiac forces, is undeniably schematic, monolithic, and overdeterministic. What is more significant is her emphasis on the mobility of role adoption. The female reader is equally beguiled by the 'mystic hieraticism of power' in sado-masochistic representations (1992: 171): both dominance and submission are available, and gratifying, positions for her to occupy.

An alternative defence is available from a deconstructive perspective. It is the failure of Eliot's language that is to be celebrated: woman remains perpetually elusive, outside, subverting the structures in which he seeks to incarcerate her. As Maud Ellman puts it, 'the misogyny is so ferocious ... that it begins to turn into a blasphemy against itself' (1987: 98). And certain of the stylistic features that I have detailed – the omission of gender pronouns, the use of transitive verbs without objects, and the suspension of participles in a virtual gerundive form as if their action will never be carried through – would support such an emphasis. This would stress the frustration and bafflement felt towards the 'epileptic': the possibility that the sensual grace of 'curves' and even the 'shriek' might be of genuine ecstasy; that the 'ladies of the corridor' know exactly what lies behind 'hysteria', but they are not letting on. At the moment when female sexuality seems most rigidly confined in imagery of madness and disease, it retains an imperviousness and self-sufficiency from which the male remains permanently excluded.

Thus the adoption of the persona of Tiresias in *The Waste Land* carries a double significance. First, in classical legend, he had lived for a period as a woman (hence Eliot's description of him as 'throbbing between two lives' (218: 69)). Called upon to arbitrate whether men or women enjoyed love-making more, he revealed the greater sexual pleasure of the female. He was subsequently blinded by Juno, for giving away the most precious of her secrets, and compensated by Jupiter with the gift of prophecy and long life. Eliot considers the story sufficiently important to quote Ovid's version in full in the notes to the poem. Second, the persona possesses an androgynous capacity to move between genders: 'all the women of the poem are one woman, and the two sexes meet in Tiresias'. The oppositions of 'Sweeney Erect' are, arguably, designed to bring about a systematic exclusion of woman into the realm of 'hysteria'. Yet Eliot himself may be seen as seeking to appropriate this voice in his own poetry: the assimilation of Aspatia's lament may be seen as indicative of a general procedure (see Christ 1991; Koestenbaum 1989). This is perhaps most strikingly exemplified in the figure of Fresca, the poetess of *The Waste Land* drafts. Like her, Eliot was 'born upon a soapy sea/Of Symonds – Walter Pater – Vernon Lee'; like her, during the composition of the poem underwent a 'hysteric fit'; and like her, produces a prototypically modernist text: 'From such chaotic misch-masch potpourri/What are we to expect but poetry? (1971: 27, 41).

But to return to my opening question, what does it mean to read *Poems 1920* 'as a man'? Any apotheosis of woman as unknowable, undefinable, infinitely fluid and metamorphosing, is surely eminently compatible with traditional forms of gender idealisation: I can think of nothing more predictable than being perpetually enigmatic. It is mistaken, I think, to read Eliot's poetry for what it tells us about women: instead we should concentrate on the more difficult kind of awareness that it promotes of our own masculinity. I am inclined to respect Eliot's proclamation of impersonality: although I appreciate the urge to pull Old Possum off his institutionally sanctioned pedestal, I feel that much of the recent psycho-biographical emphasis teeters on the prurient and voyeuristic (see Miller 1977; Gordon 1988, 1991). In its tendency to reduce the poetry to a symptom, it merely duplicates Eliot's own project of disengagement towards 'stuff that the writer could not drag to light, contemplate, or manipulate into art' (Eliot 1951: 144). I feel it is self-righteous, self-protective, even fundamentally dishonest, to seek to confine and isolate and diagnose Eliot as an external phenomenon, an 'eccentricity'. His poetry simply does not permit any such position of assured superiority or analytic authority to be adopted.

What I feel should be challenged is not the impersonality of the author, but of the reader. In so far as I understand these 'thousand sordid images', ('Preludes' (27: 22)), I am implicated in and indicted by them. They are, as Eliot reminds us, that out 'of which your soul was constituted'. But I think any useful response to feminism must involve acceptance of this double-bind: reading more forthrightly, in a sense more culpably. Emerson has a fine sentence at the opening of 'Self-Reliance': 'in every work of genius, we recognise our own rejected thoughts: they come back to us with a certain alienated majesty' (1979: vol. ii, 27). I still believe that there is 'majesty' in Eliot's early writing, in the courage necessary to give expression to such 'stuff'. But the point is not to savour a momentary *frisson* of recognition and promptly consign those thoughts into oblivion again. That is to abandon any hope of change. I would justify this poetry, in all its negativity and horror, for the effort of recognition which it invites. As men, we can't glibly denounce Eliot until we have honestly acknowledged the extent to which we participate in these 'feelings which are not in actual emotions at all'. Perhaps then we may, with Eliot himself, come to 'know what it means to want to escape these things'.

But after such knowledge, what forgiveness?

7

'GET OUT AS EARLY AS YOU CAN'

Larkin's sexual politics

One scarcely thinks of sex in relation to the work of Philip Larkin; or, to qualify a little, only in terms of jaundiced disparagement, a fertile source of negation. The erotic Larkin would appear to be pretty meagre fare, in his own phrase from 'Spring', an 'indigestible sterility' (8: 39). Such an emphasis would seem unlikely to displace the more familiar image of Larkin as wry commentator on the 'lowered sights and patiently diminished expectations' of contemporary Britain (Davie 1972: 62). But the fact that the major English poet of the post-war period (and even the recent spate of iconoclastic polemic implicitly concedes this centrality) appears to be an uncompromising advocate of male celibacy should at the very least give pause for thought. The greater availability of biographical material (Thwaite 1992; Motion 1993) has revealed personal entanglements of some complexity. Nevertheless this does not alter the cumulative impact of his literary self-presentation. His verse immediately conjures up an image of sour and wizened bachelorhood – 'One of those old-type *natural* fouled-up guys', as Jake Balokowsky puts it (18: 170) – and its anti-paternity motif has often been noted. Far from being a minor aberration, this stance is integral to the characteristic persona of his poetry: the excluded onlooker, slightly wistful, yet nevertheless resolute in his self-conserving detachment. This point of vantage is well exemplified in 'Reasons for Attendance', where the narrator is momentarily drawn 'to the lighted glass/To watch the dancers':

>   sensing the smoke and sweat,
>   The wonderful feel of girls. Why be out here?
>   But then, why be in there? Sex, yes, but what
>   Is sex?   (2–3, 5–8: 80)

The question seems to be implicitly answered by the rhyme, 'what/Is sex'/'sweat', but this cannot quite stifle the appreciative 'wonderful feel of girls'. (The phrase is typical of the unobtrusive yet explicit quality of Larkin's sexual vocabulary, with the lascivious suggestiveness of a 'full feel' followed by the further specificity of 'in there'.) The balance is tilted, however, by the 'individual sound' of the trumpet that 'insists I too am individual' (13–14):

> Therefore I stay outside,
> Believing this; and they maul to and fro,
> Believing that; and both are satisfied,
> If no one has misjudged himself. Or lied. (16–20)

The emphasis on the insight gained through 'staying outside' recurs throughout Larkin's verse (as, indeed, does the uncomfortably equivocal relation between 'satisfied' and 'lied'). This can be linked to what I would venture to call the epistemological Larkin, whose unsparing meditation on ageing, death, 'endless extinction' (1983: 55) aspires to a kind of agnostic sainthood, to 'importantly live/Part invalid, part baby, and part saint' ('Waiting for breakfast, while she brushed her hair' (23–4: 20)). One cannot fear a thing one cannot know, and his poetry of mortality seeks to produce tangible cognitive equivalents to fill this gap. It stages a continual drama in which awareness of continual erosion ('Life is slow dying' (6: 138)) is countered by strategies of self-withholding – a refusal to expend, a kind of sustenance through habit, routine, and confinement. 'I *don't* want to take a girl out and spend *circa* 5 pounds when I can toss off in five minutes, free, and have the rest of the evening to myself' (quoted in Motion 1993: 62).

This aloofness inevitably comes into conflict with the demands of sexuality for a breaking down of the monadic self through contact with another being: 'saying love, but meaning interference' 'He Hears that his Beloved has become Engaged' (13: 66; see also 'Marriages' and 'Love'). Even a wedding-day, however, can be enlisted as testimony to our fundamental solitude: 'Church Going' speaks of 'marriage', along with 'birth,/And death', as 'what since is found/Only in separation' (50–1: 98). Similarly, the disquieting effect of the famous phrase from 'Talking in Bed', the 'unique distance from isolation', comes from the utter lack of enthusiasm with which this intimacy is regarded: it is presented in terms of intrusion, unwanted obligation, a 'distance' from the necessary privacy and preferred autonomy of 'isolation' (9: 129). Larkin responds to this temptation (or threat) through offering a cool, almost laconic, critique of the adequacy of the representations presumed to be the correlative of desire. The characteristic movement of his poetry involves freezing an image, detaching it, contemplating it, in a way that reduces its circumstantial narrative to selective emblems. The erotic Larkin is obsessed not so much with loss as with discrepancy: 'the enormous disparity between his imagination and what actually happened' (1964: 170). Here the Yeatsian heritage is crucial. The standard by which the contingent manifestations of desire prove insufficient is that of the ideal, 'eternal requirings' that are checked and qualified but never wholly rebuffed ('The Dedicated' (16: 10). I think there is far less 'settling for' in Larkin than Donald Davie and others would have us believe: the vision of 'such order, such destiny' that Katherine Lind experiences at the close of *A Girl in Winter* is achieved only through the arduous purging of delusion – 'Against this knowledge, the heart, the will, and all that made for *protest* could at last sleep' (1975: 248; my emphasis).

So, to summarise. The sexual politics of Larkin's verse can be seen as one of principled and unillusioned abstention. This is most immediately apparent in his meditations on paternity, but perhaps its most interesting developments concern the socially sanctioned image. It is striking how many of his poems start with representations of women in posters, magazines, photographs, and how his own memories take on a similarly estranged quality, a succession of frames rather than a fluid continuum. Sexuality is never the source of personal authenticity in Larkin. His verse displays a sophisticated semiotic conception of passion as constituted by images that have already been consumed and sullied. This helps to explain how what may initially seem a morbid singularity comes to assume a culturally representative status. Whereas Eliot's subjective idealism sought to dissolve the world into a system of private significations, Larkin has no wish to protect some privileged private space away from the public realm: he retains a quasi-Augustan faith in the accessibility of common experience. The price of this social consolation, however, is the reduction of desire to no more than 'Sharp sensual truisms' ('The Dance' (83: 156)): in *Jill,* John Kemp experiences a 'horrible embarrassment' that 'shocked him deeply', when he realises 'that what he had imagined to be his most secret feeling was almost cynically common' (1975: 109; compare Larkin's '*scorching embarrassment*' at a failed seduction (1992: 105)). In 'Annus Mirabilis', 'Sexual intercourse began/In nineteen sixty-three' in the sense of being identified with a new libertarian and consumerist ethic, which the poem defines in relation to a best-selling paperback ('Chatterley') and record ('the Beatles' first LP'), both of which are seen as contributing to an oppressive homogenisation of desire – 'Everyone felt the same' (1–2, 3–4, 12: 167). As 'Money' puts it, 'I am all you never had of goods and sex./You could get them still by writing a few cheques' (3–4: 198). Dignity and freedom can only be found in simultaneous acknowledgement of the socially constructed nature of desire, and voluntary estrangement from the continued barter and recirculation of 'the exchange of love' ('Ambulances' (26: 132)).

This aspect, I think, tends to be overlooked because of the undue emphasis on those great sombre orations, 'The Old Fools', 'The Building', and 'Aubade', as the necessary destination of Larkin's verse. It is important to realise that the preoccupation with imminent death only becomes the dominant strain in his late verse, and that a tendency to relatively simplistic polarities is introduced along with it. In this essay, I shall first examine the treatment of paternity in his final collection, *High Windows*, and elsewhere; second, look at 'Dry Point' and 'Wild Oats', and relate them to Larkin's early debt to Yeats in *The North Ship*; and then finally go on to discuss his mature handling of the iconography of desire.

In Larkin's later verse, there is an absence of participation in the sexual problematic. There is a shift from the children that might have been sired to the unedifying spectacle of other people's offspring: instead of the lingering attraction of choosing to 'erect a crop', a raucous contempt for 'putrid/Infancy' ('I am washed upon a rock' (20: 23); 'On being Twenty-Six' (49–50: 25)). To give a few further comments from *Required Writings*: 'children are very horrible, aren't they? Selfish, noisy, cruel, vulgar little brutes'; 'it was that verse about becoming as a little child again that caused the first sharp waning of my Christian sympathies'; 'children themselves have been devalued: we know them for the little beasts they are' (1983: 48, 111, 191). This is well demonstrated in the absolute division between young and old set out in 'High Windows':

> When I see a couple of kids
> And guess he's fucking her and she's
> Taking pills or wearing a diaphragm,
> I know this is paradise

> Everyone old has dreamed of all their lives –
> Bonds and gestures pushed to one side
> Like an outdated combine harvester,
> And everyone young going down the long slide
>
> To happiness, endlessly... (1–9)

One of Larkin's most famous pieces, and usually taken as one of his most representative. To point out some typical felicities: the arresting obscenities, or what he called in Anthony Powell the 'vernacular *oratio recta*' (1983: 222); the briskly demotic tone that can simultaneously contain a poignant formal cadence (if the stress is put on 'kids', 'couple' is simply an off-handed way of saying one or two; if on 'couple' itself, the sense shifts to bonded or wedded pair); the metrical nicety, pointed out by Barbara Everett, of the rhythmic linking of 'fucking her', 'diaphragm', and 'paradise' (1980: 239); the sly rhyming (for example, 'she's' and 'paradise'); and the imagery, which can both be curiously abstract and elusive (the 'long slide' of moral decline, sexual penetration, and children's playground), and boldly particular (the forlorn and cumbersome 'combine harvester'). As with much of the later verse, this starts out looking like a poem about sex, and becomes a poem about religion. The 'paradise' without 'Bonds and gestures' takes on an explicitly eschatological dimension in the final epiphany of 'the thought of high windows':

> The sun-comprehending glass,
> And beyond it, the deep blue air, that shows
> Nothing, and is nowhere, and is endless. (18–20: 165)

To be 'sun-comprehending' is also to be uncomprehending in any recognisably human sense; and this state of blankness and absence is valorised as a kind of 'solving emptiness' ('Ambulances' (13: 132)). I think the poem is vulnerable to the charge that it uses a churlish and ungenerous presentation of 'everyone young' to support a regression into an ecstatic nullity. On a basic level the argument simply will not hold: even if the pursuit of happiness through sexuality is squalid and misguided, that doesn't render religious consolation any the less 'outdated'. And compared to 'Church Going', this is poor stuff, so much less humanised in its 'devaluing dichotomies' ('On Being Twenty-six' 54: 25).

So I would dissent from the tendency to regard the symbolist leanings of Larkin's final volume as necessarily a laudable enlargement of his work. The negative critique, however, holds good; and its impact is further developed in 'This be the Verse', which might be seen as the retort of the 'kids' to their elders:

> They fuck you up, your mum and dad.
> They may not mean to but they do.
> They fill you with the faults they had
> And add some extra, just for you.
>
> But they were fucked up in their turn
> By fools in old-style hats and coats,
> Who half the time were soppy-stern
> And half at one another's throats.
>
> Man hands on misery to man.
> It deepens like a coastal shelf.
> Get out as early as you can,
> And don't have any kids yourself.   (180)

This is a poem about origins – 'fucked up' takes on the sense of knocked up, fortuitously concocted, a view of conception as mechanical, quantitative, and essentially meaningless continued in 'fill' and 'add' – but also about revenge, about injuries inflicted and compulsively repeated. 'Mum and dad' are subsumed into an anonymous 'they', the family scene, the collective destiny: there's an additional obscenity of molestation implied in the phrasing 'they fuck you up your . . . they were fucked up in their. . .'. This psychoanalytic slant is taken up in the latent pun on 'faults' and 'thoughts', and the second stanza becomes a comic depiction of parental sexuality, 'soppy-stern' before the children yet in private 'at one another's throats', voraciously, erotically. There's a passing intimation of fully-clothed marital relations, and one should not forget that in *The Interpretation of Dreams*, Freud equates hat with the male genitals and putting on a coat with wearing a contraceptive (1953–74: vol. iv, 186; vol. v, 360–2).

'Man hands on misery to man': the final stanza becomes a specifically masculine homiletic on the nature of paternity, bequeathing, 'handing on'. What is the 'it' that 'deepens like a coastal shelf'? Most obviously 'misery', but the pronoun also seems in opposition to 'man . . . to man'; the 'deepening' suggests both a gradual aggregation and a steep downward plunge, out of sight, unknowable, somehow vulval. 'Get out as early as you can': out of what? Out of the womb, of the woman, of the whole cycle of procreation, with its profligate expenditure of self and semen. Behind all these lies the insistent presence of death. On one level this simply reiterates the old truism of the moment of siring being a moment of transference, of the emergence of another being that will, to adapt the lines from 'Afternoons', 'push you to the side of your own life' (23–4: 121). 'Don't have any kids yourself' because they represent an acknowledgement of loss, displacement, and mortality: 'Unsheath/The life you carry and die' ('At the chiming of light upon sleep' (24–5: 14)); and will undoubtedly direct the sentiments of the narrator towards you. But there's also a positive force to this iconoclasm, a breaking with the overriding impulse of biological determinism, the necessity to reproduce: Larkin introduces the possibility of a standing back, a 'stuff the species' attitude which repudiates the encroachment of 'coarsened fertility' upon the individual (11: 14). (Compare Hardy's 'I said to Love': 'Man's race shall perish, threatenest thou,/Without thy kindling coupling-vow? .../We fear not such a threat from thee;/We are too old in apathy!' (23–4, 27–8)). It may be the case that 'No one can tear your thread out of himself./ No one can tie you down or set you free' ('Oils' (15–16: 36)), but under scrutiny 'Like a fuse an impulse busily disintegrates/Right back to its roots' ('Sinking like sediment through the day' (7–8: 27)).

High Windows tends to present this disengagement as sustainable in absolute terms: Larkin's earlier verse, however, explores the paradoxes of involvement in desire more subtly and poignantly. *The Whitsun Weddings*, in particular, gives a vivid and somehow appalling evocation of socially constructed and responsible masculinity, perhaps best exemplified in 'Self's the Man':

> Oh, no one can deny
> That Arnold is less selfish than I.
> He married a woman to stop her getting away
> Now she's there all day,
>
> And the money he gets for wasting his life on work
> She takes as her perk
> To pay for the kiddies' clobber and the drier
> And the electric fire,

And when he finishes supper
Planning to have a read of the evening paper
It's *Put a screw in this wall* –
He has no time at all,

With the nippers to wheel round the houses
And the hall to paint in his old trousers
And that letter to her mother
Saying *Won't you come for the summer.* (1–16: 117)

Though the typical motifs of 'having no time' and 'wasting his life', are present, the chief recoil appears to be from the passive acceptance of culturally sanctioned duty encapsulated in 'The Life with a Hole in it' by 'that spectacled school teaching sod/(Six kids, and the wife in pod...' (14–15: 202). Larkin gives a dramatisation of unparalleled eloquence of hostility towards obligation from a masculine viewpoint: 'the quarrel between the necessity & beauty of being united with a woman one loves, & the necessity of not being entangled or bullied or victimised or patronised, or any of the other concomitants of love & marriage' (1992: 151). The Freudian insights into the necessary burden of civilisation, the renunciation of instinctual satisfaction, are acted out in an inglorious suburban context. He praises Ogden Nash's 'let-down rhymes and wait-for-it metrics' as

> perfect stylistic equivalents for the missing chairs and slow burns of which civilised masculine living is compounded: waiting for women, putting up with children, social boredom and humiliation, having to work, the agenbite of inwit . . . He is in fact in line with those humorists who make you laugh at things not because they are funny but because laughing at them makes them easier to bear.
> (Larkin 1983: 135)

While there's a complete absence of pity towards Arnold ('He was just out for his own ends'; 'If it was such a mistake/He still did it for his own sake' (25–6)), the voice of the narrator is tinny, bereft of the social identity imposed on Arnold by his mundane routine. ('To the Sea' at least acknowledges the possibility that 'It may be that through habit these do best' (33: 173).) The poem finely balances two equally unappealing options: a masculine self either wholly identified with the onerous chores of man-about-the-house, or preserved by a peevish astringency towards this collective gender identity.

There is a reversal of power: the pursuer becomes captive. The home, as usual in Larkin, is a female domain: one thinks of Mr Bleaney at those curious lodgings, 'the Bodies', one of a succession of interchangeable tenants at the beck and call of an anonymous and autocratic landlady (2: 102); or Jake Balokowsky, obliged to carry through the drudgery of his research because of the need to support Myra and the kids (8–9: 170). The state of being homeless is also partly the state of being loveless as the title 'Places, Loved Ones' (99) suggests, but home involves ownership, long-term obligation, an abandonment of all claims to the 'unfenced existence' so hauntingly evoked in 'Here' (31: 137). The relative merits of the two positions are examined in 'Dockery and Son' (the title recalls *Dombey and Son*, the family firm and practical realities of inheritance). Journeying back from his old Oxford college, the narrator experiences a dynastic epiphany through the vision of 'ranged/Joining and parting lines' presided over by a 'strong/ Unhindered moon':

>   To have no son, no wife,
> No house or land still seemed quite natural.
> Only a numbness registered the shock
> Of finding out how much had gone of life,
> How widely from the others. (23–5, 25–9: 152–3)

To be without a son is immediately equated with the absence of property; the narrator has 'registered' neither birth certificates or title deeds. There is a defiant appropriation of 'natural' to the state of being unsonned, unlanded. The 'shock' comes in realising the depletion of the quantity of 'life', a usage hovering between time-on-earth, life-span, and physical potency. This second sense is taken up in Dockery's ability to 'take stock' and 'be capable of' (30–1), and his conviction that

>   he should be added to!
> Why did he think adding meant increase?
> To me it was dilution. (33–5)

Larkin is drawing on a venerable tradition here, dating back to Aristotle, of semen expenditure as permanent loss or 'dilution'. One notices how patrilineal the poem is: the issue of reproduction is discussed in terms of father and son, with the role of wife and mother entirely elided. The poem begins in the wholly masculine environment of a single-sex Oxford college (and behind that, military service, and the landscape of heavy industry, 'fumes/And furnace-glares' (20–1)); the question why there is no woman in the narrator's life simply does not arise. Instead the final meditation centres on the origin not of sons but of 'innate assumptions':

> Suddenly they harden into all we've got
> And how we got it;   (40–1)

The use of 'got' recalls the earlier 'did he get this son/At nineteen, twenty'; a typical combination of the colloquial and the Biblical. There is also a double play on 'harden' as both tumescence (hence transient, and also embarrassing in its 'suddenness') and the setting of a mould, permanent and enclosing. These premises 'warp tight-shut, like doors' (38) (recalling the earlier 'locked' college-room (9)):

> looked back on, they rear
> Like sand-clouds, thick and close, embodying
> For Dockery a son, for me nothing,
> Nothing with all a son's harsh patronage.   (41–4)

The parental terms, 'rear' and 'embodying', are set against the atomistic 'sand-clouds'. The balance at first seems one-sided in Dockery's favour, 'nothing' versus 'son', but this is wrenched back by the 'harsh patronage', a form of subtraction. Yet to what extent does this equation justify the bold sententiousness of the final lines?

> Life is first boredom, then fear.
> Whether or not we use it, it goes,
> And leaves what something hidden from us chose,
> And age, and then the only end of age.   (45–8)

Is this offered as diagnostic insight or as the forlorn bluster of a disappointed narrator? How legitimate is the move to the impersonal when the 'we' who 'use' life refers to Dockery and the narrator, hence an exclusively masculine and partial perspective? And what status have propositions on 'age, and then the only end of age' when their coherence depends on 'what something hidden from us chose'?

'Ignorance', the poem immediately after 'Dockery and Son' in *The Whitsun Weddings* isolates and concentrates the paradoxes of an empiricist semantics of death (a subject which leaves, as the title of another poem puts it, 'Nothing to be Said'). And these in turn become statements about bodies, sexuality, origin.

> Strange to know nothing, never to be sure
> Of what is true or right or real,
> But forced to qualify *or so I feel,*
> Or, *Well it does seem so:*
> *Someone must know.*
>
> Strange to be ignorant of the way things work:
> Their skill at finding what they need,
> Their sense of shape, and punctual spread of seed,
> And willingness to change;
> Yes, it is strange,
>
> Even to wear such knowledge – for our flesh
> Surrounds us with its own decisions –
> And yet spend all our life on imprecisions,
> That when we start to die
> Have no idea why.   (107)

The tone is deceptively casual, hesitant, self-deprecating: the rhyme, 'decisions'/'imprecisions', suggests a Prufrockian lineage for the persona. But though the final 'idea why' is plaintively colloquial, it also specifically alludes to the positivist criteria of verification. The 'things' that 'work' include the body's decline and its reproduction, the 'punctual spread of seed' and the imperative of 'change'. The 'willingness' to enter this cycle is set against ignorance as to its ultimate purpose. There's a peculiar detached air to these statements: the first sentence has no governing verb; the second only a deferred 'it is'. (Even if one inserts a 'so' before the final 'that', the literal grammatical meaning is that 'imprecisions have no idea why'.) What does it mean to say that 'our flesh/Surrounds us' when flesh is always someone's flesh, his or hers or yours or mine? Its 'decisions' are to grow old, to wear out, to perpetuate itself: the seemingly prolix diction conceals a sex/death equation in 'spend all our life' and the mordant Jacobean pun on 'start to die'. (The motif is reworked in the title poem of the collection, 'The Whitsun Weddings', where the marriages are perceived by the women as a 'religious wounding' and a 'happy funeral' (53, 55: 115).)

We 'wear such knowledge' rather than possess it; and the awkwardness of this relation points to a more general problem of the status of statements about desire, the body. How can one resist the perennial temptation to lay claim to a linguistic finality, to achieve the proto-immortality of an axiom, that separates off the speaker from the condition referred to? Larkin resorts to disclaimers, statements about ignorance, handled with a scrupulous sense of paradox. The poem compares favourably, I think, with the slightly specious resonances of 'Dockery and Son'; but there nevertheless remains something dowdy about such verse. I now wish to look at two poems in which Larkin tries to offer a more intimate rendition of the processes of desire: first a brief glance at 'Dry-Point', then a more sustained examination of 'Wild Oats'.

'Dry-Point' is a good example of Larkin as symboliste, or perhaps it is more accurate to say abstractionist, at any rate operating in a mode which he is commonly assumed to abhor. Increasing critical emphasis has been laid on the romantic tonalities in Larkin's verse in an attempt to establish its range and flexibility; but this has tended to concentrate on his response to the natural world, the poignant beauty of transience, the occasional intimation of a kind of an agnostic faith. The difficult Larkin still meets with general disapproval. This, it must be admitted, is a comparatively minor strain, quite prominent in *The Less Deceived* ('If, my Darling', 'Whatever Happened'), seldom glimpsed in *The Whitsun Weddings*, but regaining strength in *High Windows* ('Sympathy in White Major', 'Solar', 'Livings II'). What I would stress is that this is in accordance with the empiricist leanings of the earlier volume, of being 'forced' to the 'real'. Telling it how it is, the facts of the case, demands a convoluted, opaque idiom when the poem situates itself on the terrain of desire: the 'incessant recital' that 'If, my Darling' tells us must be 'double-yolked with meaning and meaning's rebuttal' (19, 21: 41).

> Endlessly, time-honoured irritant,
> A bubble is restively forming at your tip.
> Burst it as fast as we can –
> It will grow again, until we begin dying.
>
> Silently it inflates, till we're enclosed
> And forced to start the struggle to get out;
> Bestial, intent, real.
> The wet spark comes, the bright blown walls collapse. . .
> (1–8: 36–7)

The poem was originally published as the second of 'Two Portraits of Sex': its companion-piece, 'Oils', is a rather uncomfortable

Laurentian mythicisation (or mystification) of the sexual act ('Sun. Tree. Beginning' (1)). The OED defines 'dry-point' as a 'sharp-pointed needle used for engraving without acid'; so the title indicates a concern with images, creativity, fertility. (Compare 'to observe a life/ Dissolving in the acid of their sex' ('Disintegration' 5–6: 266).) But 'dry' also implies arid, infertile (as in 'dry-bob', intercourse without emission): 'bubble', 'wet spark', and the later 'salted shrunken lakes', contrast with the 'many rains and many rivers' in 'Oils' (5–6); the 'new delighted lakes' and 'all-generous waters' of 'Wedding Wind' (23: 11); and 'the emblematic sound of water' in 'Negative Indicative' (17: 79). 'Point' is an obvious colloquialism for penis (compare 'tip'); but it is also an emphatic direction and lesson learnt.

What happens? A bubble is blown up, increases in size till it entraps its originator, then bursts: so, on a basic level, this is a narrative of illusion and disenchantment, conducted in a surreally extrapolated erotic imagery. (Compare Freud's analysis of the dream of the 'captive balloon' (1953–74: vol. v, 364–6).) This occurs within indeterminate or rather discrepant temporal denotations: the adverbial time of 'Endlessly' (as in *High Windows*, tediously, predictably) and the more specific regulation of 'fast', 'again', 'until'. These perspectives in turn are set against the biological context of 'grow again, until we begin dying', with verbs of origin, 'start', 'begin', and the abrupt demise of 'Burst'.

The noun 'irritant' itself works on two levels: both as an immediate stimulation (clearer in the French '*irriter*', to excite sexually), and a longer-term inducement, as grit in the pearl-oyster. 'Burst it as fast as we can' can be read as either curt imperative of immediate pleasure ('Burst it', recalling the climactic line of 'Deceptions', 'To burst into fulfilment's desolate attic' (17: 32)) or wistful subjunctive of a deterministic cycle (though we may 'burst it, it will grow again'). In both senses, it prefigures the later appeal for release, 'Get out as early as you can'. Male sexuality becomes a simultaneous expression of aggression and helplessness, summarised by Larkin with magnificent judgemental explicitness: 'Bestial, intent, real'. The 'collapse' of 'the bright blown walls' refers most obviously to the shimmery inflated bubble of the erection, but also has intimations of Jericho: the breakdown of the barrier between self and other becomes a kind of pitiful exposure. It should be noted that the poem ignores any interpersonal contact: it is concerned with a relation to desire that is predefined as uncontrollable and inherently disappointing. It treats the physical fact of the rise and fall of male arousal as the determinant of sexual relations *per se*; the oxymoron of 'wet spark' insists on the intrinsically self-defeating nature of the experience. (Larkin himself summarised the theme of the poem as 'how awful sex is and how we want to get away from it' (Haffenden 1981: 85; see Hartley 1987.)

One may well wish Larkin had written more poems in this idiom; but I think it should also serve to highlight the strength of his more characteristic verse, its firm commitment to the public domain. I have chosen 'Wild Oats' as representative of this vein. Like 'Dry-Point', it offers a narrative of disillusion, clinging to an unattainable ideal, with the recurrence of certain key images such as 'spark', 'ring', and 'magic'. Here the sexual relationship possesses a social dimension, but one conducted through the mediation of received images.

> About twenty years ago
> Two girls came in where I worked –
> A bosomy English rose
> And her friend in specs I could talk to.
> Faces in those days sparked
> the whole shooting-match off, and I doubt
> If ever one had like hers:
> But it was the friend I took out.
>
> And in seven years after that
> Wrote over four hundred letters,
> Gave a ten-guinea ring
> I got back in the end, and met
> At numerous cathedral cities
> Unknown to the clergy. I believe
> I met beautiful twice. She was trying
> Both times (so I thought) not to laugh.
>
> Parting, after about five
> Rehearsals, was an agreement
> That I was too selfish, withdrawn,
> And easily bored to love.
> Well, useful to get that learnt.
> In my wallet are still two snaps
> Of bosomy rose with fur gloves on.
> Unlucky charms, perhaps. (143)

This seems to be a poem that, in the phrase Ashbery used of Larkin, 'has a bottom to it' (1984: 8a). It contains the recollection of specific occurrences, people, times and places; a moral anecdote, wry, precise, and downbeat, aspiring to the proverbial status of the title ('useful to get that learnt'). The oats that are sown, however, could hardly be classified as 'wild'. The poem establishes a running counterpoint between this staple diet and the longed-for, untouchable 'beautiful', the ideal and the plausibly available, 'A bosomy English rose/And her friend in specs'. Both are unnamed, along with the vast majority of women in Larkin's poetry – most notably, perhaps, the victim of 'Deceptions' and the narrator of 'Wedding Wind'. The only exceptions are Myra in 'Posterity' and the haunting close to 'Dublinesque': 'A voice is heard singing/Of Kitty, or Katy/As if the name meant once/All love, all beauty' (21–4: 178). In 'Maiden Name', the disparate 'old lists, old programmes, a school prize or two,/Packets of letters' are seen as no longer bound together in a single identity: 'You cannot be/Semantically the same as that young beauty' (10–11, 5–6: 101).

Their faces are similarly non-individual, but still (or perhaps therefore) capable of sparking 'The whole shooting-match off'. (Notice 'spark' recurring as a term of desire, igniting the 'match' that in turn would lead to 'shooting' or ejaculation.)

The final line gives a characteristic shift from the contemplation of ideal beauty to 'real action' (the theme of *Jill* in short (1964: 158)), and the second stanza recounts the numerically exhausted possibilities of courtship conventions: seven years, four hundred letters, ten-guinea ring. The 'friend' is conspicuously absent as the recipient of these attentions: they exist in their own right, to perform these ceremonies is to enter into negotiation with oneself. This is particularly apparent in the virtually intransitive use of 'met'; and yet the subsequent line retains considerable poignancy. The 'cathedrals' represent the kind of grand setting inaccessible to this kind of courtship; the 'numerous ... cities' open up a prospect of breadth and magnitude; the extent of the itinerary suggests an admirable degree of enthusiasm and stamina from both participants; and finally, to be 'Unknown to the clergy' implies a fuller sexual 'knowing' of each other.

This formal eroticism is taken up at the beginning of the third stanza: 'Parting', disengaging, withdrawing. The gerund is suspended in relation to the final 'agreement' of contractual self-accusation: 'That I was too selfish, withdrawn,/And easily bored to love'. (Given the sheer quantity of romantic gestures recorded in the previous stanzas, the charge of being 'too easily bored' seems particularly unfair.) The poem ends by returning to a contemplation of 'beautiful', as indeed have the preceding two stanzas:

> I doubt
> If ever one had like hers:
> But it was the friend I took out.
>
> I believe
> I met beautiful twice. She was trying
> Both times (so I thought) not to laugh.
>
> In my wallet are still two snaps
> Of bosomy rose with fur gloves on.
> Unlucky charms, perhaps.

Does this loyalty to the ideal involve the foolish sacrifice of possible happiness? Or is this a case-study to prove that 'love must be earned and not idly pursued' (1983: 243)? The option of reading the narrator ironically is certainly supported by his cultivated air of diffidence; by the grudging switches between women; and the muted and rather pathetic triumph he feels in getting the ring back 'in the end'. The 'two snaps' in the 'wallet' (like dirty postcards) are certainly more than slightly seedy; 'bosomy rose with fur gloves on' (and maybe nothing else), and the 'charms' can equally well be read as photos or her breasts. But the status of these hoarded images is no more and no less artificial than that the memories of the actual courtship, a similar frozen succession of framed tableaux. I think it is wrong to dismiss this as merely parodic, the pathetic gesture of a dessicated and self-deluding persona. The concluding possession of these images as a resource (like currency, stashed away) represents a logical progression, a stripping away of accidents from the ideal. (It should be compared, perhaps, to the effort of the narrator of 'Broadcast' to hold on to the thought of 'your face among all those faces/Beautiful and devout' (6–7: 140).) I would stress the degree of defiance with which this stance of continued invocation is invested. This is centred, paradoxically enough, in the throwaway 'perhaps', which goes against the whole self-belittling tone of the previous recital. Perhaps, but perhaps not. The possibility arises that for Larkin this effort of idealisation is absolutely intrinsic to desire. This may be compared to Yeats's 'The Lamentation of the Old Pensioner':

> There's not a woman turns her face
> Upon a broken tree,
> And yet the beauties that I loved
> Are in my memory;
> I spit into the face of Time
> That has transfigured me.   (13–18)

Take away the sham bravado, and Larkin's poem becomes a restatement of Yeats's theme: the preservation of ideal beauty in the context of personal decay. I now wish to go back to *The North Ship*, and trace the relation between the two poets in greater detail.

On first reading, one could hardly be blamed for not detecting genius in *The North Ship*; in fact one could be forgiven for doubting the presence of talent. Larkin's 1966 preface freely acknowledges a 'predominance' of Yeats; and in a later interview he was prepared to dismiss the collection as 'painfully imitative' (1983: 29, 42). Critical accounts of his development have tended to follow this lead, and celebrate the displacement of the 'Celtic fever' by the drab, empirical, and prosaic. Enter the Movement. I believe that the continuities between the phases of his writing are greater than commonly acknowledged; and that his first volume establishes the preoccupation with monadic and unreciprocated desire that will dominate the work of his maturity.

Larkin describes himself at the time of composition as 'isolated in Shropshire with a complete Yeats stolen from a local girls' school'; and this juxtaposition gives, I think, the crucial modulation of his precursor's 'particularly potent music' into an education of furtive desire. (What *Jill* described as 'iridescent, tingling feelings that had not any obvious cause, shadowy wishes and more shadowy dreams of fulfilment' (1983: 100).) Larkin dissolves the terse clarity of the idiom and transforms it into a vehicle for tentative sexual self-definition: nowhere in Yeats would we get so delicately vulnerable a phrase as 'the deft/Heart grows impotent' ('If grief could burn out' (11–12: 298)). Its onanistic basis is freely acknowledged, but not, as in the early poems of Dylan Thomas, endorsed without reservation: 'Last night you came/Unbidden, in a dream' is deflated by the quaintly explicit 'we've not met/More times than I can number on one hand' ('Morning has spread again' (6–7, 15–16: 281)); a prayer to the 'snow-white unicorn' closes with the ingenuous request that it 'put into my hand its golden horn' ('I see a girl dragged by her wrists' (53, 56: 279)). The dream does not subsume the real, but remains a subordinate interlude:

> I dreamed of an out-thrust arm of land
> Where gulls blew over a wave
> That fell along miles of sand;
> And the wind climbed up the caves
> To tear at a dark-faced garden
> Where black flowers were dead,
> And broke round a house we slept in,
> A drawn blind and a bed.
>
> ('I dreamed of an out-thrust arm of land', 1–8: 267)

'I was sleeping, and you woke me' (9): the poem traverses its slightly precious erotic landscape to finish by locating itself in a bed, a conversation, a restrained grief. And in this movement there always lies the possibility of disengagement:

> To wake, and hear a cock
> Out of the distance crying,
> To pull the curtains back
> And see the clouds flying –
> How strange it is
> For the heart to be loveless, and as cold as these.
>
> ('Dawn', 284)

In a reversal of the aubade form, the 'heart' remains 'loveless' and cold': but the 'strange' is unevaluative, certainly not pejorative. Instead of reciprocation or concern, the solitary awakening becomes the condition of a new finality of forensic insight.

> Here, where no love is,
> All that was hopeless
> And kept me from sleeping
> Is frail and unsure;
> For never so brilliant,
> Neither so silent
> Nor so unearthly, has
> Earth grown before.
>
> ('The horns of morning', 9–16: 275)

It is the 'hopeless' that becomes 'frail and unsure', and there is a slightly peevish identification between love and being 'kept . . . from sleeping'. The absence of love is what permits the earth to 'grow', and this reversal is in line with other occurrences of fertility imagery:

> Then the whole heath whistles
> In the leaping wind,
> And shrivelled men stand
> Crowding like thistles
> To one fruitless place;
> Yet still the miracles
> Exhume in each face
> Strong silken seed,
> That to the static
> Gold winter sun throws back
> Endless and cloudless pride. ('Winter', 23–33: 286–7)

What is disconcerting is the triumphant commitment to the 'fruitless place': the sterile landscape of 'wind', 'thistles', and 'shrivelled men'. The 'Strong silken seed' will not reclaim this desert: instead it can only be 'exhumed' from faces. Sex remains in the head rather than in the body (though notice the tactile exactitude of 'silken' for semen); but far from causing frustration, this becomes the justification of an 'Endless and cloudless pride'. (Compare the narrator's boast in 'No Road', that his 'liberty' lies in watching 'a world where no such road will run/From you to me/ . . . come up like a cold sun' (13–16: 47).)

There are five poems of direct address to a presumed lover ('Within the dream you said', 'Love we must part now', 'Morning has spread again', 'Is it for now or for always', and 'So through that unripe day'), plus a more characteristic indeterminate 'you' in several more. But there is no sense of apostrophe, invocation, the Petrarchan heritage that Yeats glories in – indeed little sense of any specific object of desire.

The characteristic posture of early Yeats is supplication to a woman reduced to an image: an unending pursuit of the 'glimmering girl' created out of the 'fire . . . in my head' ('The Song of the Wandering Aengus' (13: 2)). She must always remain an adjunct of the masculine passion – 'For *my* dreams of your image that blossoms a rose in the deeps of *my* heart' ('The Lover tells of the Rose in his Heart' (8); my emphasis). Even poems like 'He wishes for the Cloths of Heaven' become an indirect technique of control: such an extravagant gesture of self-abasement as 'Tread softly because you tread on my dreams' (8) serves to ratify the authorial power of conferring an idealisation, of fixing and ranking and passing judgement. (And being elevated into the symbolic pantheon is not without its drawbacks: in 'Michael Robartes and the Dancer', for example, woman's status as muse is used to justify not educating her.) The defining feature of Yeats's early poetry is its emphasis on romantic love as a relation to an image rather than to a person. Maud Gonne emerges as an icon with a cluster of heroic attributes; and it is this that permits the elaboration of concentric symbolic patterns around her. Thus a lyric such as 'He wishes his Beloved to be Dead' becomes the logical consequence of this attitude: not as a wish to spare her the torment of inevitable decline, but as a recognition that the poet's triumph lies in celebrating a perfection that has been wholly ascribed, and so can exist independently of its object.

The relation to the image, which in Yeats is resonant, confident, and brazen, becomes interrogatory and self-undermining in Larkin:

> And I am sick for want of sleep;
> So sick, that I can half-believe
> The soundless river pouring from the cave
> Is neither strong nor deep;
> Only an image fancied in conceit.
> I lie and wait for morning, and the birds,
> The first steps going down the unswept street,
> Voices of girls with scarves around their heads.
> ('The bottle is drunk out by one', 9–16: 277)

This plaintive and excluded eroticism, more early Eliot than Yeats perhaps, does not preclude a declared scepticism towards any 'soundless river' of potent subconscious desire (though the narrator still 'half-believes'). There is an implied movement from morbid self-preoccupation to the life of the street; but the apparently tangible 'girls with scarves around their heads', it should be noted, are equally an 'image fancied in conceit', evoked from their voices rather than seen.

'So through that unripe day' prefigures Larkin's later verse in viewing this distance as a source of comfort and security:

> So through that unripe day you bore your head,
> And the day was plucked and tasted bitter,
> As if still cold among the leaves. Instead,
> It was your severed image that grew sweeter,
> That floated, wing-stiff, focused in the sun
> Among uncertainty and gales of shame
> Blown out before I slept. Now you are one

SORDID IMAGES

> I dare not think alive: only a name
> That chimes occasionally, as a belief
> Long since embedded in the static past.
>
> Summer broke and drained. Now we are safe.
> The days lose confidence, and can be faced
> Indoors. This is your last, meticulous hour,
> Cut, gummed; pastime of a provincial winter. (1–14: 283)

This may perhaps be read as an expansion of the 'two snaps' of 'Wild Oats': 'leaves' and 'Cut, gummed' suggest the 'pastime' of the photo-album. The poem is not addressed to a woman, but to an image, a 'you' that is 'focused', defined solely through reference to a perceiver/collector, and in common with the vast majority of female figures in Larkin's poetry, unnamed. She nevertheless produces 'uncertainty' in the narrator; and also, it seems fair to infer from 'shame' and 'Blown out' (compare the 'bright blown walls' of 'Dry-Point' (8)), physical arousal. All the possible sexual immediacy of 'embedded', however, is stifled: a more specific erotic reference is momentarily glimpsed, though in negative form, in 'broke and drained' (what? our relation? me? my physical potency?), only to be finally expelled with the sanctimonious pronouncement, 'we are safe'. But what was the threat that had to 'be faced'? I would stress how the edgy nostalgia acquires peculiar mythic reverberations through a discreet series of Medusa references: the 'head' that has been 'severed', now 'cold', floating 'wing-stiff' in mid-air, the retrospect implied by 'name', 'belief', and 'past', and the hint of monstrosity of 'you are one/I dare not think alive'. (Compare Rossetti's 'Aspecta Medusa': 'Let not thine eyes know/Any forbidden thing itself, although/It once should save as well as kill, but be/Its shadow upon life enough for thee' (7–10).) Here I think that Freud's 1922 article, 'Medusa's Head' (1953–74; vol. v 105–6), can be relevantly invoked. It may seem excessive to treat the poem as a 'representation of woman as a being who frightens and repels because she is castrated': but at the very least it must be acknowledged that this detached contemplation of the image serves to ward off an unspecified but powerful anxiety. (Simon Petch, for example, describes the poem as 'chillingly defensive' (1981: 24–5).) And this compensatory domination becomes in Larkin a fundamental structure of desire.

This leads rather neatly into the opening poem of *The Less*

Deceived, 'Lines on a Young Lady's Photograph Album':

> At last you yielded up the album, which
> Once open, sent me distracted. All your ages
> Matt and glossy on the thick black pages!
> Too much confectionery, too rich:
> I choke on such nutritious images.   (1–5: 71–2)

Initially this appears to be no more than a rather stilted whimsy. But the stanza, once stripped down, takes on a decidedly Baudelairean air (for more in this vein, see 'Femmes Damnées' (270); and also Motion 1982: 73–4).

> At last you yielded up the **** which,
> Once open, sent me distracted. All your
> **** glossy on the thick black ****
> Too much confectionery, too rich:
> I choke on such nutritious images.

There is obviously an implied seduction where 'At last' a yielding occurs that sends the narrator 'distracted': notice how 'once open' becomes an explicit image of sexual availability. But the poem directs its attention not towards the control and domination of a woman who is present, but towards a collection of 'severed images'. The terms that I have omitted are of framing and estrangement – 'album', 'ages', 'matt', 'pages': even 'nutritious' suggests a dietary regime rather than a headlong plunge into desire. The overt voyeurism continues:

> My swivel eye hungers from pose to pose . . .

To revel in a succession of tableaux, the 'static past'.

> In pig-tails, clutching a reluctant cat;
> Or furred yourself, a sweet girl-graduate;
> Or lifting a heavy-headed rose
> Beneath a trellis, or in a trilby hat.   (6, 7–10)

There's a crude pun on pussy floating around, particularly in the context of puberty, maidenhood and innocence: 'furred yourself' set against the traditional emblem of the rose.

> From every side you strike at my control . . . (12)

A 'control' which is also the camera focus, and so the means of further images, gratification, as well as an appeal to self-restraint:

> But o photography! as no art is,
> Faithful and disappointing . . .
>
>   what grace
> Your candour thus confers upon her face!
> How overwhelmingly persuades
> That this is a real girl in a real place,
>
> In every sense empirically true!   (16–17, 22–6)

The apostrophe is significantly lower-case, the absence of art and elevation: yet the 'real girl in a real place' is none the less fictive, invoked, an effort of 'persuasion'. And is to be 'empirically true' the same as being emotionally faithful, or its utter antithesis, because acknowledging the distance between past and present?

>   you
> Contract my heart by looking out of date.
>
> Yes true; but in the end, surely, we cry
> Not only at exclusion, but because
> It leaves us free to cry.   (29–2)

To 'Contract' is both to reduce and engage; and 'looking out of' seems to suggest the gaze being returned from the past. There's a complex sense of freedom in detachment, 'exclusion' as a privilege: despite the preceding reference to 'misty parks and motors', 'to cry' comes across as a gesture of self-assertion rather than of defeat, and the subsequent 'grief' still contains a possible exuberance, predatoriness, even relief:

>   So I am left
> To mourn (without a chance of consequence)
> You; balanced on a bike against a fence;
> To wonder if you'd spot the theft
> Of this one of you bathing; to condense,
>
> In short, a past that no one now can share,
> No matter whose your future; calm and dry,
> It holds you like a heaven, and you lie
> Unvariably lovely there,
> Smaller and clearer as the years go by.   (36–45)

There is a peculiar disjunction between the apparently intransitive 'mourn' and its deferred object 'You' (the first occurrence of the pronoun since the opening line, introducing four rapid usages). This in turn has no unchanging essence but instead becomes equated with a 'past' that we are obliged to interpret and 'condense', and an unspecified future (note the humility in the lack of any prediction, the unfettered choice granted as a kind of benediction). There is no attempt to pass the sequence of images off as a human identity; but conversely there is no attempt to pretend that any individual can be known other than through the mediation of such images. To 'yowl across/The gap from eye to page' (35–6) becomes the paradigm of interpersonal knowledge: there is always the text of the other to be transcribed in a kind of 'theft'.

So this is a poem about the truth of images, perhaps in all human relations, but here particularly associated with knowledge of the 'young lady'. It offers an ocular but unbodily desire (only one passing reference to 'faintly disturbing'); one unwilling to forgo the 'control' and prepared to pay the cost of 'exclusion' in return for being 'free to cry'. The poem succeeds in establishing the relation of the 'swivel eye' to 'nutritious images' as central to the process of desire; 'If, my Darling' conjectures what would happen if the woman 'were once to decide/Not to stop at my eyes,/But to jump, like Alice, with floating skirt into my head' (1–3: 41). This is presented not as an unassailable urge, but as subject to sceptical analysis, the choice of abstention. ('I find it easier to abstain from women than sustain the trouble of them and the creakings of my own monastic character' (cited Motion 1993: 186).) But one can only choose not to desire, not to desire differently, purely.

The photographic motif is continued in 'Whatever Happened?':

> At once whatever happened starts receding.
> Panting and back on board, we line the rail
> With trousers ripped, light wallets, and lips bleeding.
>
> Yes gone, thank God! Remembering each detail
> We toss for half the night, but find next day
> All's kodak-distant. Easily, then (though pale),
>
> 'Perspective brings significance, 'we say,
> Unhooding our photometers, and, snap!
> What can't be printed can be thrown away.

> Later it's just a latitude: the map
> Points out unavoidable it was:
> 'Such coastal bedding always meant mishap.'
>
> Curses? The dark? Struggling? Where's the source
> Of all these yarns now (except in nightmares of course)?
>
> (1–14: 74)

Here we rejoin the 'Dry-Point' idiom, tortuous, opaque, yet here curiously jaunty. The title of the poem itself seems to shift from a direct question to a euphemism ('What can't be printed'). An inquiry into desire can only be answered in words, which are inevitably secondary, self-deluding. Where should we locate ourselves in order to achieve the 'Perspective' that will 'bring significance' to sexual pleasure ('bedding'), an experience that 'At once . . . starts receding', ludicrous and perhaps degrading to recall? A dive into oceanic emotions is here imaged as a comic routine of clambering back 'on board', 'With trousers ripped, light wallets, and lips bleeding', the final image unexpectedly disquieting (whose blood?). The sequence of sea-voyage imagery is continued in 'latitude' (or permissiveness), 'map', 'coastal' and 'yarns'. In this context, 'kodak-distant' most obviously evokes a tourist souvenir, but it should also be read as a mechanism constitutive of desire, preserving and making safe. 'Remembering each detail/We toss for half the night', another of Larkin's audacious obscenities; and more comically 'Unhooding our photometers, and snap!'. The camera is an erotic device; the stability of its images hold at bay the 'nightmares' of carnal fantasy: 'Curses? The dark? Struggling? Where's the source . . .'.

Here, and elsewhere in *The Less Deceived*, the relation of camera to image, desire to its object, tends towards the solipsistic: its equivocations are something to be worked out privately as aspects of a wholly personal identity. (Though 'Wants' offers an appealing image of the connection between political and patriarchal authority: 'However the family is photographed under the flagstaff' (4: 42).) In *The Whitsun Weddings*, it becomes a form of cultural analysis of consumer longings. The volume begins with 'residents from raw estates' who

> Push through plate-glass swing doors to their desires –
> Cheap suits, red kitchen-ware, sharp shoes, iced lollies,
> Electric mixers, toasters, washers, driers –
>
> (12, 14–16: 136)

and this conjunction of 'driers' and 'desires' reaches a crescendo in the final poems. The billboards of 'Essential Beauty', with their 'sharply-pictured groves/Of how life should be' (5–6: 144) are followed by 'the trite untransferable/Truss-advertisement, truth' in 'Send no Money' (23–4: 146); and this concern continues in 'the albums lettered/*Our Wedding*, lying/Near the television' in 'Afternoons' (12–14: 121), and the climactic icon of matrimonial love in 'An Arundel Tomb' (110). 'The Large Cool Store' is perhaps the finest example of the radical edge to Larkin's political verse (as opposed to the occasional flourishes of romantic patriotism):

> The large cool store selling cheap clothes
> Set out in simple sizes plainly
> (Knitwear, Summer Casuals, Hose,
> In browns and greys, maroon and navy)
> Conjures the weekday world of those
>
> Who leave at dawn low terraced houses
> Timed for factory, yard and site.
> But past the heaps of shirts and trousers
> Spread the stands of Modes for Night:
> Machine-embroidered, thin as blouses,
>
> Lemon, sapphire, moss-green, rose
> Bri-Nylon Baby-Dolls and Shorties
> Flounce in clusters. To suppose
> They share that world, to think their sort is
> Matched by something in it, shows
>
> How separate and unearthly love is,
> Or women are, or what they do,
> Or in our young unreal wishes
> Seem to be: synthetic, new,
> And natureless in ecstasies.   (1–20: 135)

This is a poem of desire and commodity, or rather, desire as commodity. The first point I would make is the acuity of the verb 'conjures'. The 'large cool store . . . Conjures the weekday world'. In one sense it evokes the whole environment of 'those/Who leave at dawn low terraced houses', and their precisely 'Timed' routine. Are these the 'store's' employees or its customers? Is there any distinction to be made? And this leads on to the second sense: that the store 'conjures', magics up through spells, a world of illusion for them all to inhabit, a sorcerer, benign or otherwise. But it's not drab realism versus pathetic fantasy; both worlds are equally constructs, products of incantations, 'Machine-embroidered'. There's a peculiar cartoonic sense of the independent lives of clothes; 'those' are certainly less specified or animated than the 'heaps of shirts and trousers' before whom the 'Modes for Night' are 'spread' enticingly. (Their sexual gender is acquired, determined solely by what they have bought.) The descriptive tone is still dominated by the initial 'plainly'; to be 'thin as blouses' implies meagreness rather than slimness, a sense taken up in the later 'Shorties', anaemic, undernourished. The use of 'rose' as both adjective and verb is a characteristic Yeatsian device (compare 'rose/Bri-Nylon Baby-Dolls', Aphrodite-like from the 'stands' with 'The Sorrow of Love' (Yeats 1950: 45)), and 'Shorties/ Flounce' can similarly be read as a compound noun, or a subject/ verb, with homonyms on pounce and flaunt. Who governs 'To suppose', does 'that world' belong to readers, customers, or garments, or is 'their sort' (fate, kind, social grouping) indistinguishable? To be 'Matched' is to have compatible garments, or sexual partners; both, however, are a nebulous 'something'. Here we have a move from commodity fetishism to a quasi-Platonic realm; or rather the whole process is judged against the standard of a 'separate and unearthly love' (see Booth 1992: 125). The 'young unreal wishes', handled almost tenderly here, contain longing both for the ideal and also for the actual 'Baby-dolls' that are none the less fabricated, and so equally 'unreal'. (Compare 'The Whitsun Weddings': 'the perms,/The nylon gloves and jewellery-substitutes,/The lemons, mauves, and olive-ochres that/ Marked off the girls unreally from the rest' (38–41: 114).) Desire is viewed as 'synthetic' from its very outset: it has no definite object – in the case of women, 'are', 'do' and 'Seem to be' are interchangeable, there is no distinction between reality and appearance. There's a vivid eroticism in 'natureless in ecstasies': free from nature, without essence, but therefore assembled, marketed along with other commodities.

'Sunny Prestatyn' continues this opposition between purchased fantasy and actual world:

LARKIN'S SEXUAL POLITICS

> *Come to Sunny Prestatyn*
> Laughed the girl on the poster,
> Kneeling up on the sand
> In tautened white satin.
> Behind her, a hunk of coast, a
> Hotel with palms
> Seemed to expand from her thighs and
> Spread breast-lifting arms.   (1–8: 149)

'The girl on the poster': yet another of Larkin's precise observations on mass-produced ideals, giving a compliant come-on which involves the expenditure of hard cash, in this case beckoning towards what is presumably an illicit amorous weekend. So she laughs: at her clients, at what she is offering, out of general exuberance perhaps. 'Kneeling up' involves a more definite act of submission; 'In tautened white satin', both her swimsuit and her skin, that has become another glossy commodity. 'Tautened'; skimpy, pulled tight over, but also perhaps a term of arousal in the male spectator (subsequently supported by 'expand'). This leads into the positioning 'Behind her' of a 'hunk of coast', a 'hunk' being the slang term for an attractive man as well as an outcrop, and by extension, a sexual reference. The 'palms' can be seen as themselves phallic but the more subtle reference comes with the pun on hands, which seem to come from between her thighs in order to 'Spread breast-lifting arms': to borrow a term from 'Maiden Name', she is by no means 'unfingermarked' (18: 101). This erotic dimension becomes clearer if the localising references are removed: poster, sand, coast, hotels:

> the girl
> Kneeling up
> In tautened white satin.
> Behind her, a hunk . . .
>   palms
>   expand from her thighs and
> Spread breast-lifting arms.

A real girl in a real place, the place of fantasy and potential violence.

> She was slapped up one day in March.
> A couple of weeks, and her face
> Was snaggle-toothed and boss-eyed;

SORDID IMAGES

> Huge tits and a fissured crotch
> Were scored well in, and the space
> Between her legs held scrawls
> That set her fairly astride
> A tuberous cock and balls   (9–16)

She ceases to exist in an inviolate realm of images, 'slapped up', casually plastered on, given a beating. A tone of shrugging inevitability ('A couple of weeks, and . . .'), with an undertow of approval particularly in the use of 'well in', and also with 'fairly', appropriately, justly. The point is, I think, that this is not degraded reality replacing unavailable ideal (the 'unfocused she' of 'Essential Beauty' (29: 144)) but the translation of one image of desire into another. 'The space/Between her legs held scrawls': an absence, lack, inviting inscription, here by the 'cock and balls'. (The banter of college high-table in 'Livings III' (7: 188) displays the same impulse to impose 'Names for *pudendum mulieris*' (rhyming with 'fairest').)

> Autographed *Titch Thomas*, while
> Someone had used a knife
> Or something to stab right through
> The moustached lips of her smile.
> She was too good for this life.
> Very soon a great transverse tear
> Left only a hand and some blue.
> Now *Fight Cancer* is there.   (17–24)

There is an allusion to the colloquialism for penis, John Thomas; Titch may be compensatory or triumphant. Who performs this act, a 'someone'? A child, a youth? Or every man in every penetration, a form of hatred, an assertion of ownership, a desecration of a false ideal? The 'tuberous cock', clumsy, vegetable, comparatively innocent, becomes 'a knife/Or something to stab'; and 'right through' has a similar sense of validation as the previous 'well'. 'She was too good for this life': the glimpse of beauty, paradise, escape, or a pretentious mockery of 'this life', our life, and therefore deserving of assault. (Note that 'this life' bound by rhyme to 'knife', has becomes synonymous with the blade, the 'cock and balls', the violation.) The 'great transverse tear' recalls the continental dimensions of 'fissured' (and the 'coastal shelf' of 'This be the Verse' (10: 180)), but also gives the fleeting possibility of weeping. The 'hand' could be imploring; or the masturbatory clutch of the onlooker, taking satisfaction in 'some blue', sexually explicit material. The poem can be turned inside out: '*Fight Cancer*' can refer to the disease of sexual violence, its hopeless and irreversible encroachment; or it can be yet another irrelevant slogan, vacuous inducement. What is the appropriate response for the male reader? To feel liberated by the violation of the image (distinct from violence against actual women); satisfied by the desecration as prefiguring violence against them; or appalled by this depiction of his own 'tuberous' sexuality? (This may be compared to the 'corpse-faced undergraduate' whose pin-up collection 'Baited his unused sex like tsetse flies/Till maddened it charged out without disguise/And made the headlines' in 'Under a splendid chestnut tree' (15, 22–4: 43); and the magnificent close to 'Love again: wanking at half past three', 'Something to do with violence/A long way back and wrong rewards,/And arrogant eternity' (16–18: 215)).

It's interesting to look at responses to the poem in gender terms: male critics almost invariably stress the falsity of the ideal rather than the savagery of the treatment meted out to it. To take a couple of examples from usually illuminating commentators. Simon Petch claims 'the violence of the human response expresses an enraged insistence that the image on the poster accords with no reality whatever' and that 'the natural impulse reacts angrily against the imposition of an illusion' (1981: 77). Terry Whalen comments that 'it is, of course, the "less deceived" mentality of the rebellious graffiti which captures Larkin's praise', to the point of the poem being a 'celebration of the act' which is 'relished' for its 'healthy rebellion' and its 'ironic vengeance' (1986: 44). The opposing view is put forward by Janice Rossen (wondering 'how much complicity the poet shares in the act' (1989: 74)) and Matt Simpson (arguing that 'the poet, in the act of recording, discovers himself to be too intently voyeuristic, an accomplice' (1989: 178)). Neither party is prepared to acknowledge that the relation of viewer to poster might represent a more general underlying structure, the possibility that all desire might be subject to this falsity to some extent. And neither can bring themselves to condemn the exhibition of male sexual violence that retaliation against this 'imposition' might involve.

Where Larkin outmanoeuvres his critics is in his awareness of the constructedness of both sides of the equation: the ideal and its violation. 'But I thought wanting unfair:/It and finding out clash', as 'Send no Money' puts it (7–8: 146), and the strength of his erotic poetry lies not only in its awareness of exclusion from the 'fair', the just and the beautiful, but also in its direct and unsparing address of the comparable inauthenticity of masculine desire. Its emblems undoubtedly verge on cliché but are occasionally no less ferocious for that: the narrator of 'A Study of Reading Habits' fondly recalls

> ripping times in the dark.
> I clubbed women with sex,
> Broke them up like meringues. (10–12: 131)

'Meringues' serves as an oddly disconcerting mot juste: white and brittle on the outside, creamy inside, yielding to the uninhibited pressure of teeth, 'broken up' with a kind of brutal analytic impulse. But to 'club women with sex' has no intrinsic neanderthal authenticity: it remains as culturally derived as the 'girl on the poster': this time from popular Gothic fiction rather than the jargon of holidays in the sun. For Larkin, 'finding out' involves a refusal of illusion so fundamental that it repudiates the whole biological imperative of what 'Wants' calls 'the printed directions of sex' (3: 42) (genetically imprinted, photographically reproduced, listed in a popular erotic manual); and challenges outright any lingering assumption that sex must necessarily be good for us, where we must find our happiness or not at all.

I do not accept that this resolute espousal of 'the patience to expose/Untrue desire' ('Many famous feet have trod' (17–18: 18)) lays Larkin open to the charge of being irredeemably negative, anti-life, displaying at best 'intelligent rancour,/An integrity of self-hatred' ('Marriages' (28–9, 64)). An immediate defence might be offered by stressing the Laurentian elements of his work, such as the evocations of the 'vast flowering' of the natural world in 'Long roots moor summer' (13: 96); the sacramental reverence for the rite of consummation in 'Wedding Wind'; and the lyrical evocation of sexual release at the climax of 'The Whitsun Weddings'. (The influence is repeatedly confirmed in the correspondence (1992: 12, 19, 21, 56, 140; Rossen (1989: 67) suggests its negative impact on Larkin's actual relations with women.) The terse and understated idealism of poems such as 'When first we faced' is itself a rare and precious quality:

> Admitted: and the pain is real.
> But when did love not try to change
> The world back to itself – no cost,

> No past, no people else at all –
> Only what meeting made us feel,
> So new, and gentle sharp, and strange? (13–18: 205)

I would prefer, however, to stress the seriousness with which Larkin addresses the whole question of sexual identity. John Bayley (Hartley 1987: 200) stressed Larkin's awareness that 'femininity was invented in words by men'; and this insight is neatly brought out in 'Breadfruit':

> So absolute
> Maturity falls, when old men sit and dream
> Of naked native girls who bring breadfruit,
> Whatever they are. (15–18: 141)

The point being that the final clause applies as much to the 'girls' themselves as to the exotic fruit, 'Whatever they are': both are equally only known through the medium of 'uncorrected visions' (9). There is an acceptance of a gap between representation and woman ('such a jumble of forms & ideas about them in one's head' (1992: 151)), with a pessimism about knowing beyond the image, and a fierce resentment as to how it has been inculcated. There are poems of sexual fear: 'Next, Please' reverts to an opposition between the life-giving 'figurehead with golden tits' which 'never anchors' and the 'black/-sailed unfamiliar' in whose wake 'No waters breed or break' (21–4: 52); and 'Myxomatosis' transforms the sufferings of a wounded rabbit into the common predicament of the male:

> *What trap is this? Where were its teeth concealed?*
> You seem to ask.
> I make a sharp reply.
> Then clean my stick. I'm glad I can't explain
> Just in what jaws you were to suppurate: (3–8: 100)

The 'jaws' are simultaneously of the trap, of death, and of the *vagina dentata*; and 'suppurate' identifies the dying animal with a diseased wound or organ. (One may perhaps recall Rossiter's description of the male as a 'thinking rabbit'.) What should surprise us is not that some element of this imagery is present, but that it should assume so little prominence: there is no possibility of compiling 'daily quotations for a misogynist's calendar' from his verse (1983: 261). And where it appears, it will tend to be explicitly ascribed to a masculine perspective: in 'The North Ship', for example, the warning that 'A woman has ten claws' is followed by 'Sang the drunken boatswain' ('Above 80 degrees north' (1-2: 305)). As Janice Rossen notes, Larkin 'capitalizes on the energy which derives from seeing sexual politics solely from the man's point of view' (1989: 70). This holds true for Larkin's use of abstract language: it is acknowledged as interested, for example, in the pronoun shift at the end of 'Reasons for Attendance', 'If no-one has deceived *him*self' (20; my emphasis). The most emphatic example comes in 'Deceptions'. The poem opens with an epigraph from Mayhew describing the abduction and rape of a young girl: the subsequent evocation of the sensations of her awakening mind is abruptly retracted in the second stanza:

> Slums, years, have buried you. I would not dare
> Console you if I could. What can be said,
> Except that suffering is exact, but where
> Desire takes charge, readings will grow erratic?
> For you would hardly care
> That you were less deceived, out on that bed,
> Than he was, stumbling up the breathless stair
> To burst into fulfilment's desolate attic.   (10-17: 32)

Larkin has often been criticised for equating the suffering of the victim with the self-delusion of her assailant (Holderness 1989; Rossen 1989: 88-90; Booth 1992: 111, 127). 'Slums, years' have buried him with equal thoroughness, but something in his action is seen as inviting and enticing continued empathy. Here we see the transferred epithets of 'breathless' (because doped) and 'desolate' (because ravished) ascribed to the male perception. Yet to make no claim to speak for the woman other than to state 'suffering is exact' is perhaps a question of moral tact; the specific issue of gender allegiance emerges in the decision not to claim distance from her violator. The lines, 'I would not dare/Console you *if I could*' (my emphasis) are surely a declaration that 'where/Desire takes charge', the masculine perspective is the only one the poet can truly share, however 'erratic' the subsequent 'readings'. To be 'less deceived' involves a refusal of pious disavowal, an open acknowledgement of shameful complicity.

I would like to close by stressing the regenerative aspects of this refusal of illusion, this opting out of the coercive force of contemporary sexual ideology. Larkin's uniquely acute sense of the intrusive and demeaning nature of desire brings about a corresponding upgrading of alternative human bonds. We should not underestimate how often and how movingly, in particular in *The Whitsun Weddings*, he offers direct propositions about human love:

> The glare of that much-mentioned brilliance, love,
>   Broke out, to show
> Its bright incipience sailing above,
> Still promising to solve, and satisfy,
>   And set unchangeably in order.
>   ('Love Songs in Age', 17-21: 113)

> In everyone there sleeps
> A sense of life lived according to love.
> To some it means the difference they could make
> By loving others, but across most it sweeps
> As all they might have done had they been loved.
>   ('Faith Healing', 22-6: 126)

> On me your voice falls as they say love should,
> Like an enormous yes.
> ('For Sidney Bechet', 13-14: 83)

Is 'love' here opposed to desire or subsuming it or in some other more elusive relation? Is its assent, order, permanence, unavailable, or at least unenduring in the context of mortality? 'Love Songs in Age' ends with 'lamely admitting how/It had not done so then, and could not now' (23-4: 113): 'Faith Healing' closes with the assertion that 'all time has disproved' (30: 126); and 'For Sidney Bechet' can only sustain its 'appropriate falsehood' for the duration of a single 'note' (1: 83). There's no cancellation of the aspiration, however, but rather a poignant impasse, and this is most fully explored in the closing poem of *The Whitsun Weddings*, the justly celebrated 'An Arundel Tomb'.

> Side by side, their faces blurred,
> The earl and countess lie in stone,
> Their proper habits vaguely shown
> As jointed armour, stiffened pleat,
> And that faint hint of the absurd –
> The little dogs under their feet.

> Such plainness of the pre-baroque
> Hardly involves the eye, until
> It meets his left-hand gauntlet, still
> Clasped empty in the other; and
> One sees, with a sharp tender shock,
> His hand withdrawn, holding her hand.   (1–12: 110)

It is important to stress the position of the poem as the culmination of the sequence dwelling on emblems of desire (note the quasi-photographic 'blurred' and 'vaguely shown'). Whatever affirmation is here forthcoming must be made in full awareness of the preceding sceptical analysis and the difficulty of finding what 'Talking in Bed' famously described as 'words' that were 'not untrue and not unkind' (13–14: 129).

The narrator begins by contemplating the 'faithfulness in effigy' of the tomb-carvings of an unnamed medieval couple. Their individual 'identity' (31) has been eroded: they no longer possess feudal or dynastic claims. The 'endless altered people' (30) treat them merely as a source of casual spectacle. All that distinguishes them is their gesture of clasped hands. In a complex and paradoxical development, it is this unconcerned anonymity, their reduction to a single 'attitude' that allows them to be 'transfigured' into a 'final blazon' (36, 37, 40). The poem celebrates the perfect icon of desire, one sufficiently deracinated to be cast forward in time, to be shared without self-deception or appropriation. The generous, indeed rhapsodic, finale, can only exist in conjunction with an unceasing undertow of scepticism: the truth-claim involved in an 'almost-instinct' that is 'almost true' fluctuates on every reading (41).

But more is offered than the emotional agnosticism of the freely acknowledged 'untruth' (38). There is also a fundamental renunciation of the privileged masculine gaze on the representation of the female. The refusal to exempt the 'earl' from a similar arrestedness in 'stone fidelity' (38) places the masculine simultaneously inside and outside the frame. The inevitable condescension of the detached observer ('One sees') experiences a 'sharp tender shock' not only at the embrace but also the empty gauntlet that reaches out to meet the eye. There is both a present intentionality about 'holding her hand' and a kind of voluntary self-exposure: the omission of 'he' as governing subject seems to parallel the removal of the armour. 'What will survive of us is love' (42), and the 'us' reaches out to include narrator (and reader) in its plea for a relinquishing of mastery and possession in a humility of ardour.

There are those who remain resolutely unconvinced even by the finale to 'The Arundel Tomb'. Andrew Motion, for example, argues that 'behind the tender triumphalism of its ending lies an assumption that no living couple could ever be truly happy and remain permanently in love' (1993: 275); and the recent publication of Larkin's letters has provided plentiful ammunition for denunciations of his 'easy misogynism' (Jardine 1992). Even here, the disparaging asides to his male friends ('as far as I can see, all women are stupid beings' (1992: 63; see also 104, 119, 150, 165) must be set against the warmth and intimacy of his correspondence with Judy Egerton, Barbara Pym, and Winifred Bradshaw. And it is naïve to assume that the letters somehow represent the truth behind the poetry rather than the assumption of a different set of (equally ironised) epistolary conventions. Statements such as 'my relations with women are governed by a shrinking sensitivity, a morbid sense of sin, a furtive lechery & a deplorable flirtatiousness' clearly possess a strong element of comic, if self-defensive, hyperbole (1992: 157). His predilection for pornography ('WATCHING SCHOOLGIRLS SUCK EACH OTHER OFF WHILE YOU WHIP THEM' (1992: 596)) is perhaps more difficult to accept, although one might argue that his acute sense of the intrusiveness of erotic representations was derived from his familiarity with this area. The letters may, as Lisa Jardine claims, serve to 'alert us to a cultural frame within which Larkin writes, one which takes racism and sexism for granted as crucially a part of the British national heritage'. This might, however, not be the least of their value, in so far as his work continues to elicit the hermeneutic quality which she elsewhere defines as 'strenuous denial' (Jardine 1983: 4).

It is undeniably tempting simply to endorse Martin Amis's description of 'the reaction against Larkin' as 'unprecedently hypocritical, tendentious, and smug' (1993: 6). Nevertheless, Jardine's argument raises a crucial question which may be applied not only to Larkin but to all the other writers in this volume. To varying degrees, they may be seen as participating in and perpetuating a history of injustice. If this is the case, why continue to study their texts?

Larkin's collection of pornography may well take its place alongside Shakespeare's second-best bed, Pope's escapade at a brothel, and Eliot's traumatic first marriage-night, as part of a larger cultural narrative which is itself intrinsically misogynist. It would be foolish to deny that these figures bring with them cultural prestige and a cumulative momentum of imposition. But the formalist question of the capacity of the text to generate meanings remains to be answered. Why do these poems retain their power to compel attention?

Sexist language requires an intention: to remain dominant if not to insult, whether this is placed at the level of individual agency or cultural formation. So if linguistics has concentrated on individual terms, the sentences in which they function, and the positions from which they are delivered, how do texts differ? Through the simple fact of temporal deracination, they cannot work in the same way. They are better thought of as something made rather than spoken: the hermeneutic relation is between reader and text, the language having undergone a process of distanciation. A text cannot be sexist in the way a direct enunciation can: certain institutional usages may be made of it, but in itself it escapes the specificity of context in which the authority of masculine speech resides. Either this is externally acquired or internally produced. The difference between the sexist statement and the misogynist text is one of formal coherence and disengagement from empirical rationale.

Misogynist texts are commonly regarded by feminist criticism as a particularly blatant and brutal form of support for a repressive hierarchy. It seems to me premature and unsatisfactory to treat them simply as instruments of consolation, reassurance, or cultural reinforcement. One can perhaps endorse stereotypes, feel familiarity, recognition, and approval towards them. But this is not necessarily to value them. They are boring for male readers too. These poems seem more designed to promote rather than alleviate anxiety, to disrupt and disorientate rather than to naturalise and justify. Their attraction lies not in the way they assert control but in the way they threaten it. The complexity of the mechanisms of ascription and reattribution in these texts should not be underestimated. Put crudely, power in these texts lies at least as much with what is denounced as with who denounces.

The question that still remains is whether threat, disruption, subversion merely results in an ever-firmer reinscription. And it remains to be shown why the repetition of crisis should not be as tedious as the repetition of stereotype.

In one tradition of feminist reading, what is disturbing is not the representation but the structure which it exemplifies. The question of value is oddly inverted. Pragmatically speaking, the worst images are the best because exemplifying the violence of the underlying structures most clearly (as sadistic pornography is frequently held to exemplify the field as a whole).

Yet even the pornographic imagination remains an imagination; and the effectiveness of any given hermeneutic stance must be assessed in terms of its productivity. Here I would insist on the priority of close textual analyses over the totalising ambitions of all too many theoretical models. The actual practice of interpretation reveals a precarious, intermittent and paradoxical authority in these texts, at least as much concerned to disown and disavow as to impose and dominate.

It is difficult to find a vocabulary that does not resort to a euphemistic aestheticism: vividness, force, impact. This is a non-cathartic aesthetic. It arouses rather than purges, and the emotions with which it deals may themselves rightly provoke suspicion. Yet if feminist criticism does not seek fairness, balance, progressiveness, but instead seizes upon that which it would deny, male criticism must also have a legitimate interest in these texts.

There is no comfortable position to adopt with regard to them. The misogynist text is something which one undergoes, resists, protests against. It makes demands.

On a simple empirical level, its language is dense, provocative, opaque. It is not subject to abrupt demystification because the act of scepticism itself bears testimony to the paradoxical productivity of these texts. They must be acknowledged to possess the meaning-generating and world-disclosing capacity traditionally ascribed to the poetic. They can perhaps no longer be 'believed in as the most reliable', but they are not simply 'therefore the fittest for renunciation' (Eliot, 'Dry Salvages' (59–60: 185)). In renouncing, we create. Doubt, scepticism, and repudiation need not be regarded as antithetical to the male reading, but may be incorporated within it as a necessary stimulus. It is in this interplay of power and loss, complicity and disengagement, that the fascination of these texts lies. It is in this sense that I would justify Larkin's verse, along with all the other 'sordid images' that I have studied in the course of writing this book. If, in the wake of feminism, literary texts must be acknowledged to be misogynistic, the converse, I would contend, is also the case: misogynistic texts must be respected as literary: the great tradition.

BIBLIOGRAPHY

Abdoo, Sherlyn (1984) 'Woman as Grail in T. S. Eliot's *The Waste Land*', *The Centennial Review* 28: (1): 48–60.
Abel, Elizabeth (ed.) (1982) *Writing and Sexual Difference*, Chicago: University of Chicago Press.
Ackland, Michael (1983) "The Embattled Sexes": Blake's Debt to Wollstonecraft in *The Four Zoas*', *Blake: an Illustrated Quarterly* 16 (3): 172–93.
—— (1989) 'Ingrained Ideology: Blake, Rousseau, Voltaire, and the Cult of Reason', 7–18 in Bevan, David (ed.), *Literature and Revolution*, Amsterdam: Rodopi.
Ackroyd, Peter (1984) *T. S. Eliot*, London: Abacus.
Aers, David (1981) 'Blake: Sex, Society and Ideology', 27–44, in Aers, David, Cook, Jonathan and Punter, David (eds) *Romanticism and Ideology: Studies in English Writing 1765–1830*, London: Routledge & Kegan Paul.
Ames, Richard (1691) *The Folly of Love: A Satyr*, reprinted Nussbaum (1977).
Amis, Martin (1993) 'A Poetic Injustice', *Guardian Weekend* August 21, 6–9.
Anderson, Mark (1984) 'Oothon, Failed Prophet', *RP&P* 8 (2): 1–21.
Anon. (1742) *Sawney and Colley, a Poetical Dialogue: Occasion'd by A Late Letter from the Laureat of St. James's, To the Homer of Twickenham*, London: for J. H. in Sword and Buckler Court, Ludgate Hill.
Arnold, Matthew (1880) Introduction i, xvii–xlvii, in *The English Poets* (5 vols), Ward, T. H. (ed.) London: Macmillan; reprinted as 'The Study of Poetry', in *Essays in Criticism*, Second Series (1888).
—— (1965; 1969) *The Complete Poems*, Allott, Kenneth (ed.); Miriam Allott (2nd edition ed.), London: Longman.
Arrowsmith, William (1981) 'The Poem as Palimpsest: A Dialogue on Eliot's "Sweeney Erect"', *The Southern Review* 17 (1): 17–68.
Ashbery, John (1984) 'Profile', *The Times*, Aug. 23, 8a.
Atkins, G. Douglas (1986) *Quests of Difference: Reading Pope's Poems*, Lexington: University of Kentucky Press.
Auden, Wystan Hugh [1935] (1977) 'Psychology and Art To-day', 332–42, in *The English Auden*, Mendelson, Edward (ed.), London: Faber.
Auerbach, Nina (1985) *Woman and the Demon: The life of a Victorian Myth*, Cambridge: Harvard UP.
Ault, Donald (1987): see Bracher and Ault.

BIBLIOGRAPHY

Ayre, William (1745) *Memoirs of the Life and Writings of Alexander Pope, Esq.*, London: Booksellers of London and Westminster.
Baghee, Shyamal (1990) *T. S. Eliot: A Voice Descanting: Centenary Essays*, London: Macmillan.
Baker-Smith, Dominic (1990) 'Original Sin: T. S. Eliot and T. E. Hulme', 271–82 in Barfoot and D'haen.
Barbach, Lonnie (ed.) (1986) *Pleasures: Women Write Erotica*, London: Futura.
Barber, C. L. (1959) *Shakespeare's Festive Comedy: A Study of Dramatic Form and its Relation to Social Custom*, Princeton: Princeton UP.
Barfoot, C. C. and D'haen, Theo (eds) (1990) *Centennial Hauntings: Pope, Byron and Eliot in the Year 88*, Atlanta: Rodopi.
Barker, Jonathan (1985) '"Wanna Go Home Baby?": Sweeney Agonistes', *Agenda* 23 (1–2): 103–10.
Barnard, John (ed.) (1973) *Pope: The Critical Heritage*, London: Routledge and Kegan Paul.
Barnes, Barnabe [1593] *Parthenophil and Parthenope: Sonnets, Madrigals, Elegies and Odes*, in Lee (1904), vol. i, 165–316.
Barnfield, Richard ([1594] 1936) *Poems*, Summers, M. (ed.), London: Fortune Press.
Barreca, Regina (ed.) (1990) *Sex and Death in Victorian Literature*, London: Macmillan.
Barry, Jackson G. (1981) '"Had, Having and in Quest to Have, Extreme": Shakespeare's Rhetoric of Time in Sonnet 129', *Language and Style* 14 (1): 1–12.
Bataille, Georges ([1957] 1987) *Eroticism*, Dalwood, Mary (trans.), London: Boyars.
Bayley, John (1984) 'Larkin and the Romantic Tradition', *Critical Quarterly* 26 (1–2): 61–6.
—— (1987) 'Too Good for this World', 198–212 in Hartley.
Beer, Gillian (1982) '"Our Unnatural No-Voice": The Heroic Epistle, Pope and Women's Gothic', in *Heroes and the Heroic*, Hunter, G. K. and Rawson, C. J. (eds) *The Yearbook of English Studies* 12: 125–51.
Benjamin, Jessica (1988) *The Bonds of Love: Psychology, Feminism and the Problem of Domination*, New York: Panther.
Bentley, G. E. (ed.) (1975) *William Blake: The Critical Heritage*, London: Routledge and Kegan Paul.
—— (1989) 'Marie Wollstonecraft, Godwin, and William Blake in France: The First Foreign Engravings after Blake's Designs', *Australian Journal of French Studies* 26 (2): 125–47.
Bentley, Thomas (1735) *A Letter to Mr. Pope, Occasion'd by Sober Advice from Horace, &c.*, London: T. Cooper.
Benzon, William L. (1981) 'Lust in Action: An Abstraction', *Language and Style* 14 (4): 251–69.
Berglund, Lisa (1990) 'The Language of the Libertines: Subversive Morality in *The Man of Mode*', *SEL* 30 (3): 369–86.
Bergonzi, Bernard (1978) *T. S. Eliot*, London and New York: Macmillan.
Betjeman, John and Taylor, Geoffrey (eds) (1957) *English Love Poems*, London: Faber.

BIBLIOGRAPHY

Blake, William (1965; rev. 1982) *The Poetry and Prose of William Blake*, Erdman, David V. (ed.), Bloom, Harold (commentary), Berkeley and Los Angeles: University of California Press.
—— (1973) Erdman, David V. and Moore, Donald (eds) *The Notebook of William Blake: A Photographic and Typographic Facsimile*, Oxford: OUP.
—— (1975) *The Illuminated Blake*, Erdman, D. V. (ed. and commentary), New York: Anchor Press/Doubleday.
—— (1971; 1989) *Blake: The Complete Poems*, Stevenson, W. H. (ed.), London: Longman.
Blamires, Alcuin (1992) *Woman Defamed and Woman Defended: An Anthology of Medieval Texts*, Oxford: Clarendon.
Bloch, Jean H. (1989) 'Rousseau and Education in Revolutionary Discourse', *Studies in Voltaire and the Eighteenth Century* 264: 729–32.
Bloch, R. Howard (1991) *Medieval Misogyny and the Invention of Western Romantic Love*, Chicago: Chicago UP.
—— and Ferguson, Frances (eds) (1989) *Misogyny, Misandry, and Misanthropy*, Berkeley: California UP.
Bly, Robert (1990) *Iron John: A Book about Men*, Shaftesbury, Dorset: Element Books.
Bold, Alan (ed.) (1978) *Making Love: The Picador Book of Erotic Verse*, London: Pan.
Boone, Joseph A. and Cadden, Michael (eds) (1990) *Engendering Men: The Question of Male Feminist Criticism*, London: Routledge.
Booth, James (1992) *Philip Larkin: Writer*, Hemel Hempstead: Harvester.
Booth, Stephen (1969) *An Essay on Shakespeare's Sonnets*, New Haven: Yale UP.
—— (ed.) (1977) *Shakespeare's Sonnets*, New Haven: Yale UP.
Bracher, Mark (1984) 'The Metaphysical Grounds of Oppression in Blake's *Visions of the Daughters of Albion*, *Colby Library Quarterly* 20 (3): 164–76.
—— and Ault, Donald (eds) (1987) *Critical Paths: Blake and the Argument of Method*, Durham and London: Duke University Press.
Bradford, Richard (1987) 'Richard Lovelace and Eliot's "Whispers of Immortality"', *Trivium* 22: 103–12.
Bray, Alan (1980) *Homosexuality in Renaissance England*, London: Gay Men's Press.
—— (1990) 'Homosexuality and the Signs of Male Friendship in Elizabethan England', *History Workshop Journal* 29: 1–19.
Bright, Susie (ed.) (1990) *Herotica I*, Down There Press: San Francisco.
—— (1992) *Herotica II*, Plume Books: San Francisco.
Brinton, Laurel J. (1985) 'The Iconic Role of Aspect in Shakespeare's Sonnet 129', *Poetics Today* 6 (3): 447–59.
Brod, Harry (1990) *The Making of Masculinities: The New Men's Studies*, Boston: Allen & Unwin.
Bronfen, Elisabeth (1992) *Over her Dead Body: Death, Femininity, and the Aesthetic*, Manchester: Manchester UP.
Brooks, Cleanth (1947; 1968) 'The Case of Miss Arabella Fermor', 74–93 in *The Well-Wrought Urn*, London: Dennis Dobson.
Brown, Laura, (1985) *Alexander Pope*, Oxford: Blackwell.
Browning, Robert (1981) *Robert Browning: The Poems* (2 vols), Pettigrew, John and Collins, Thomas J. (eds) Harmondsworth: Penguin.

BIBLIOGRAPHY

Buchbinder, David (1989) 'Some Engendered Meaning: Reading Shakespeare's Sonnets', *Works and Days* 7 (2): 7–28.

Burford, E. J. (ed.) (1982) *Bawdy Verse*, Harmondsworth: Penguin.

Burnett, Gilbert (1680) *Some Passages of the Life and Death of the Right Honourable John Earl of Rochester who died the 26th of July, 1680*, London: R. Chiswell.

Burnham, Michelle (1990) '"Dark Lady and Fair Man": The Love Triangle in Shakespeare's *Sonnets* and *Ulysses*', *Studies in the Novel* 22 (1): 43–56.

Bush, Ronald (ed.) (1991) *T. S. Eliot: the Modernist in History*, Cambridge: CUP.

Butler, Melissa A. (1988) 'Wollstonecraft versus Rousseau: Natural Religion and the Sex of Virtue and Reason', 65–73 in Mell, Donald C. (ed. and pref.) *et al., Man, God, and Nature in the Enlightenment*, East Lansing, Mich.: Colleagues.

Byron, George Gordon Baron (1977) *Byron's Letters and Journals*, (12 vols, 1973–82) Marchand, Leslie A. (ed.), *Between Two Worlds* (1820: vol. 7), London: William Clowes & Son.

Cameron, Deborah (1985; 1992) *Feminism and Linguistic Theory*, Basingstoke: Macmillan.

—— (1990) *The Feminist Critique of Language: A Reader*, London: Routledge.

Carew, Thomas (1949) *The Poems of Thomas Carew*, Dunlop, Rhodes (ed.), Oxford: Clarendon.

Carter, Angela (1979) *The Sadeian Woman: An Exercise in Cultural History*, London: Virago.

Charney, Maurice (1981) *Sexual Fiction*, London: Methuen.

Chaucer, Geoffrey (1986) *Troilus & Criseyde: A New Edition of 'The Book of Troilus'*, Windeatt, B. A. (ed.), Longman: London.

Chester, Laura (ed.) (1988) *Deep Down: The New Sensual Writing by Women*, London: Faber.

Christ, Carol (1977) 'Victorian Masculinity and the Angel in the House', 146–62 in Vicinus, Martha (ed.), *A Widening Sphere: Changing Roles of Victorian Women*, Bloomington: Indiana UP.

—— (1984) 'Self-Concealment and Self-Expression in Eliot's and Pound's Dramatic Monologues', *Victorian Poetry* 22 (2): 217–26.

—— (1991) 'Gender, Voice and Figuration in Eliot's Early Poetry', 23–37 in Bush.

Churchill, Charles (1956) *The Collected Poems of Charles Churchill*, Grant, Douglas (ed.), Oxford: Clarendon.

Cibber, Colley (1742) *A Letter from Mr. Cibber to Mr. Pope, Inquiring into the Motives that might Induce Him in his Satyrical Works, to be so Frequently Fond of Mr. Cibber's Name*, London: W. Lewis.

Cixous, Helene (1980) 'The Laugh of the Medusa', 245–64 in Marks, Elaine and Courtivron, Isabelle de (eds), *New French Feminisms*, Amherst: Univ of Mass. Press.

—— (1981) 'Castration or Decapitation?', Kuhn, Annette (trans.) *Signs* 7: (1): 41–55.

Claridge, Laura (1988) 'Pope's Rape of Excess', 129–43 in Day, Gary and Bloom, Clive (eds) *Perspectives on Pornography: Sexuality in Film and Literature* (eds), New York: St. Martins.

BIBLIOGRAPHY

Coates, J. (1986) *Women, Men and Language: A Sociolinguistic Account of Differences in Language*, London: Longman.

Coghill, Nevil (1948) "Sweeney Agonistes": An Anecdote or Two', in *The Style of the Master: T. S. Eliot*, Tambimittu, Thurairajah and March, Richard (eds), London: Poetry Editions.

Colman, E. A. M. (1974) *The Dramatic Use of Bawdy in Shakespeare*, London: Longman.

Conger, Syndy McMillen (1987) 'The Sentimental Logic of Wollstonecraft's Prose', *Prose Studies* 10 (2): 143–58.

Coote, Stephen (1983) *The Penguin Book of Homosexual Verse*, Harmondsworth: Penguin.

Cornillon, Susan K. (ed.) (1973) *Images of Women in Fiction: Feminist Perspectives*, Bowling Green: Ohio.

Corse, Taylor (1987) 'Force and Fraud in *The Rape of the Lock*', *Philological Quarterly* 66 (3): 355–65.

—— (1987) '"Heaven's Last Best Work": Pope's *Epistle to a Lady*', *SEL* 27 (3): 413–25.

Cowley, Abraham (1905) *The Poems of Abraham Cowley* (2 vols), Walton A. R. (ed.), Cambridge: CUP.

Crawford, Robert (1987) *The Savage and the City in the Work of T. S. Eliot*, Cambridge: CUP.

Crosman, Robert (1990) 'Making Love out of Nothing at All: The Issue of Story in Shakespeare's Procreation Sonnets', *Shakespeare Quarterly* 41 (4): 470–88.

Culler, Jonathan (1983) 'Reading like a Woman', 43–63 in *On Deconstruction: Theory and Criticism after Structuralism*, London: Routledge.

Cunningham, Allan (1975) 'William Blake' [1830], reprinted *William Blake: The Critical Heritage*, Bentley, G.E. (ed.), London and Boston: Routledge & Kegan Paul.

Damrosch, Leopold Jr (1980) *Symbol and Truth in Blake's Myth*, Princeton: Princeton UP.

—— (1987) *The Imaginative World of Alexander Pope*, Berkeley: California UP.

Davie, Donald (1955; 1976) *Articulate Energy: An Inquiry into the Syntax of English Poetry*, London: Routledge & Kegan Paul.

—— (1972) *Thomas Hardy and English Poetry*, London: Routledge & Kegan Paul.

Dawson, Jill (ed.) (1992) *The Virago Book of Wicked Women*, London: Virago.

de Beauvoir, Simone ([1949] 1972) *The Second Sex*, Parshley, H. M. (ed.), Harmondsworth: Penguin.

—— ([1951–2] 1989) 'Must We Burn Sade?', Introduction to Marquis de Sade, 3–64, *One Hundred and Twenty Days of Sodom*, Michelson, Annette (trans.), London: Arrow.

[Defoe, Daniel] [1722 for 1721] *The Works of Sir Charles Sedley*, in Farley-Hills 1972.

Degraaff, Robert M. (1985) 'The Evolution of Sweeney in the Poetry of T. S. Eliot', 220–6 in Roby.

de Kretser, Michelle (1988) 'Larkin(g) Around: Beyond the Pleasure Principle?', *Poetics* 17 (1–2): 69–80.

BIBLIOGRAPHY

Dennis, John (1939–43) *The Critical Works of John Dennis* (2 vols), Hooker, Edward N. (ed.), Baltimore: Johns Hopkins.
Dijkstra, Bram (1986) *Idols of Perversity: fantasies of feminine evil in fin-de-siècle culture*, Oxford: OUP.
Dilworth, W. H. (1759) *The Life of Alexander Pope*, London: J. Wright.
Dinnerstein, Dorothy (1976) *The Mermaid and the Minotaur: Sexual Arrangements and Human Nurture*, New York: Harper & Row.
Dollimore, Jonathan (1991) *Sexual Dissidence: Augustine to Wilde, Freud to Foucault*, Oxford: Clarendon.
Donne, John (1965) *The Elegies and the Songs and Sonnets*, Gardner, Helen (ed.), Oxford: Clarendon Press.
Drayton, Michael (1594–1619; 1904) 'Idea', in Lee (1904), vol. ii, 179–212.
Druce, Robert (1990) 'The Mask of Agamemnon: Reflexions upon Eliot's "Sweeney among the Nightingales"', 283–301 in Barfoot and D'haen.
Dryden, John (1958) *The Poems of John Dryden* (4 vols), Kinsley, James (ed.) Oxford: OUP.
—— ([1678] 1973) *All for Love*, Vieth, David M. (ed.), London: Edward Arnold.
Dubrow, Heather (1987) *Captive Victors: Shakespeare's narrative poems and sonnets*, Ithaca: Cornell UP.
Duffy, Edward (1979) *Rousseau in England: The Context for Shelley's Critique of the Enlightenment*, Berkeley: Univ. of California Press.
Duncan-Jones, Katherine (1991) *Sir Philip Sidney: Courtier-poet*, London: Hamish Hamilton.
Dworkin, Andrea (1981) *Pornography: Men Possessing Women*, London: The Women's Press.
Eagleton, Terry (1982) *The Rape of Clarissa: Writing, Sexuality and Class Struggle in Samuel Richardson*, Oxford: Blackwell.
Eliot, T. S. ([1917] 1992) *Eeldrop and Appleplex*, Langton Green: Foundling Press.
—— (1920) 'Ode', *Ara Vos Prec*, London: Ovid Press.
—— (1921) 'Prose and Verse', *Chapbook* 22: 3–10.
—— (1934) *After Strange Gods: a Primer of Modern Heresy*, London: Faber.
—— (1951) *Selected Essays* third edition enlarged, London: Faber.
—— (1969) *The Complete Poems and Plays of T. S. Eliot*, London: Faber.
—— (1971) *The Waste Land: a facsimile and transcript of the Original Drafts including the Annotations of Ezra Pound*, Eliot, Valerie (ed.), London: Faber.
—— (1988) *The Letters of T. S. Eliot* (vol. 1 1898–1922), Eliot, Valerie (ed.) London: Faber.
Ellison, Julie (1990) 'Redoubled Feeling: Politics, Sentiment and the Sublime in Williams and Wollstonecraft', *Studies in Eighteenth Century Culture* 20: 197–215.
Ellmann, Maud (1987) *The Poetics of Impersonality: T. S. Eliot and Ezra Pound*, Hassocks: Harvester.
—— (1990) 'Eliot's Abjection', 178–200 in Fletcher, John and Benjamin, Andrew (eds) *Abjection, Melancholia and Love: The Work of Julia Kristeva*, London: Routledge.
Emerson, Ralph Waldo (1979) *The Collected Works of Ralph Waldo Emerson* (2 vols), Slater, Joseph, Ferguson, Alfred R. and Carr, Jean F. (ed.),

Cambridge, Mass. and London: Harvard UP.
Epstein, Julia and Straub, Kristina (eds) (1991) *Body Guards: The Cultural Politics of Gender Ambiguity*, London: Routledge.
Erdman, David V. and Moore, Donald (eds) (1973) See 'Blake, William'.
Essick, Robert N. (1986) 'How Blake's Body Means', 197–217 in Hilton and Vogler.
—— (1991) 'William Blake's "Female Will" and its Biographical Context', *SEL* 314: 615–30.
Everett, Barbara (1980) 'Philip Larkin: After Symbolism', *Essays in Criticism* 30(3): 227–42.
—— (1982) 'The Sense of Nothing', 1–41 in Treglown.
—— 'Larkin's Edens', *English* 31: 41–53.
—— (1984) 'The New Style in "Sweeney Agonistes"', 243–63, in Rawson and Kernan.
—— (1989) 'Art and Larkin', 129–39 in Salwak.
Everest, K. D. (1987) 'Thel's Dilemma', *Essays in Criticism* 37 (3): 193–208.
Fabricant, Carole (1974) 'Rochester's World of Imperfect Enjoyment', *Journal of English and German Philology* 73 (3): 338–50.
Fairer, David (1984) *Pope's Imagination*, Manchester: Manchester UP.
—— (ed.) (1990) *Pope: New Contexts*, London: Harvester Wheatsheaf.
Farley-Hills, David (ed.) (1972) *Rochester: The Critical Heritage*, London: Routledge.
—— (1978) *Rochester's Poetry*, London: Bell & Hyman.
Feinberg, Nora (1987) 'Erasing the Dark Lady: Sonnet 138 in the Sequence', *Essays* 4: 97–108.
Felperin, Howard (1988) 'The Dark Lady Identified; or, What Deconstruction Can Do for Shakespeare's Sonnets', in Atkins, G. Douglas and Bergeron, David M. (eds), *Shakespeare and Deconstruction*, New York: Peter Lang.
Ferguson, Frances (1989) 'Wollstonecraft our Contemporary', 51–62 in Kaufman.
Ferguson, Rebecca (1986) *The Unbalanced Mind: Pope and the Rule of Passion*, Brighton: Harvester.
—— (1992) '"Quick as her Eyes, and as Unfix'd as Those": objectification and seeing in Pope's *Rape of the Lock*', *Critical Survey* 4 (2): 140–6.
Fineman, Joel (1981) 'The Structure of Allegorical Desire', 26–60 in Greenblatt, Stephen J. (ed.), *Allegory and Representation*, Baltimore: Johns Hopkins Press.
—— (1986) *Shakespeare's Perjured Eye: The Invention of Poetic Subjectivity in the Sonnets*, Berkeley: California UP.
—— (1989) 'Shakespeare's Ear', *Representations* 28: 6–13.
Finke, Laurie A. (1987) '"A Philosophic Wanton": Language and Authority in Wollstonecraft's *A Vindication of the Rights of Woman*', 155–76 in Ginsberg, Robert (ed.), *The Philosopher as Writer: The Eighteenth Century* London: Associated UPs.
Fitz, Reginald (1971) 'The Meaning of Impotence in Hemingway and Eliot', *Connecticut Review* 4: 16–22.
Foucault, Michel (1981–) *The History of Sexuality*, Hurley, Robert (trans.): (1981) vol. 1 *An Introduction*, Harmondsworth: Penguin; (1987) vol. 2

The Use of Pleasure, London: Penguin; (1990) vol. 3 *Care of the Self*, London: Penguin.
Fowler, Alastair (1988) 'The Paradoxical Machinery of *The Rape of the Lock*', 151–70 in *Alexander Pope: Essays for the Tercentenary*, Nicholson, Colin (ed.) Aberdeen: Aberdeen UP.
Fox, Susan [1976–7] (1986) 'The Female as Metaphor in William Blake's Poetry', *Critical Inquiry* 3: 507–19; reprinted 75–90 in *Essential Articles for the Study of William Blake*, Hilton, Nelson (ed.), Hamden, Conn: Archon Press.
Freud, Sigmund (1953–74; 1981–6) *The Standard Edition of the Complete Psychological Works of Sigmund Freud* (24 vols) Strachey, James (trans.), London: Hogarth Press and the Institute of Psychoanalysis.
Friday, Nancy (1975) *My Secret Garden* London: Virago.
—— (1991) *Women on Top: How Real Life has Changed Women's Sexual Fantasies*, London: Hutchinson.
Frosch, Thomas A. (1974) *The Awakening of Albion: The Renovation of the Body in the Poetry of William Blake*, Ithaca: Cornell UP).
Froula, Christine (1989) 'Eliot's Grail Quest: or, the Lover, the Police, and *The Waste Land*', *The Yale Review* 78: (2): 235–53.
Frye, Northrop (1947) *Fearful Symmetry: A Study of William Blake*, Princeton: Princeton UP.
Fuller, John (ed.) (1990) *The Chatto Book of Love Poetry*, London: Chatto.
Fuss, Diana (ed.) (1991) *Inside/out: Lesbian Theories, Gay Theories*, London: Routledge.
Gallop, Jane (1992) *Around 1981: Academic Feminist Literary Theory*, London: Routledge.
Gardner, Helen (1949) *The Art of T. S. Eliot*, London: Cresset Press.
George, Diana Hume (1980) *Blake and Freud*, Ithaca: Cornell UP.
Gilbert, Sandra M. (1980–1) 'Costumes of the Mind', *Critical Inquiry* 7: 391–417; reprinted as 193–220 in Abel 1982.
—— and Susan Gubar (1979) *The Madwoman in the Attic: The Woman Writer and the Nineteenth Century literary imagination* New Haven: Yale UP.
—— (eds) (1985) *Norton Anthology of Literature by Women: The Tradition in English*, New York: Norton.
—— (1988a) *No Man's Land: The Place of the Woman Writer in the Twentieth Century* vol. 1, *The War of the Words*, New Haven: Yale UP.
—— (1988b) *No Man's Land...* vol. 2, *Sexchanges*, New Haven: Yale UP.
Gilbert, Thomas (1747) *Poems on Several Occasions*, London: J. Bathurst.
Gilfillan, George (1856) 'Satire and Satirists', 15–28 in *Scottish Review*, January 1856, Glasgow: Scottish Temperance League.
Gordon, Lyndall (1977) *Eliot's Early Years*, Oxford: OUP.
—— (1988) *Eliot's New Life*, Oxford: OUP.
—— (1991) 'Eliot and Women', 9–22 in Bush.
Goslee, Nancy Moore (1990) 'Slavery and Sexual Character: Questioning the Master Trope in Blake's *Visions of the Daughters of Albion*', *ELH* 57 (1): 101–28.
Gould, Robert (1682) *Love Given O're: Or, a Satyr against the Pride, Lust, and Inconstancy &c, of Woman*, in Nussbaum (1977).

BIBLIOGRAPHY

Graddol, David and Swain, Joan (eds) (1989) *Gender Voices*, Oxford: Blackwell.

Graves, Robert and Riding, Laura (1929) *A Survey of Modern Poetry*, London: Heinemann.

Greenblatt, Stephen (1988) *Shakespearean Negotiations: The Circulation of Social Energy in Renaissance England*, Oxford: Clarendon.

Greene, Thomas M. (1982) 'Anti-Hermeneutics: The Case of Shakespeare's Sonnet 129', 143–61 in Mack, Maynard and Lord, George deForest (eds) *Poetic Traditions of the English Renaissance*, New Haven: Yale UP.

—— (1985) 'Pitiful Thrivers: Failed Husbandry in the Sonnets', 230–44 in Parker, Patricia and Hartman, Geoffrey (eds), *Shakespeare and the Question of Theory*, New York: Methuen.

Greville, Fulke (1939) *Poems and Drama of Fulke Greville, First Lord Brooke Caelica* (2 vols), in Bullough, Geoffrey (ed.) Edinburgh and London: Oliver & Boyd.

Griffin, Dustin (1978) *Alexander Pope: The Poet in his Poems*, Princeton: Princeton UP.

—— (1988) 'Rochester and the "Holiday Writers"', 33–66 in *Rochester and Court Poetry*, Roper, Alan (ed.), Los Angeles: William Andrews Clark Mem. Lib., University of California.

Griffin, Susan (1981) *Pornography and Silence: Culture's Revenge Against Nature*, London: Women's Press.

Grigson, Geoffrey (ed.) (1973) *The Faber Book of Love Poetry*, London: Faber.

Grimsley, Ronald (1982) 'Rousseau and his Reader: The Technique of Persuasion in *Emile*', 225–38 in Leigh R. A. (ed.), *Rousseau after Two Hundred Years*, Cambridge: CUP.

Gubar, Susan (1977) 'The Female Monster in Augustan Satire', *Signs* 3 (2): 380–94.

Gunner, Jeanne (1985) *T. S. Eliot's Romantic Dilemma: tradition's anti-traditional elements*, New York: Garland Press.

Hadfield, John (1980) *The Everyman Book of Love Poetry*, London: Dent.

Haffenden, John (1981) *Viewpoints: Poets in Conversation with John Haffenden*, London: Faber.

Hagstrum, Jean (1980) *Sex and Sensibility: Ideal and Erotic Love from Milton to Mozart*, Chicago and London: Chicago UP.

—— (1985) '"Arrows of Desire" and "Chariots of Fire"', 109–45 in *The Romantic Body. Love and Sexuality in Keats, Wordsworth, and Blake*, Knoxville: the University of Tennessee Press.

Haigwood, Laura Ellen (1985) 'Blake's *Visions of the Daughters of Albion*: Revising an Interpretive Tradition', *San Jose Studies* 11 (2): 77–94.

Hammond, Brean S. (1986) *Pope*, Brighton: Harvester.

Hardin, Richard F. (1982) 'Marston's Kinsayder: The Dog's Voice', *Notes and Queries* 29(227: 2): 134–5.

Hardy, Thomas (1982) *The Complete Poetical Works of Thomas Hardy* (3 vols), Hynes, Samuel (ed.), Oxford: Clarendon.

Hargrove, Nancy D. (1985) 'The Symbolism of Sweeney in the Works of T. S. Eliot', 147–69 in Roby.

Harrison, James (1989) 'Shakespeare's Sonnet 129', *Explicator* 47 (4): 6–7.

BIBLIOGRAPHY

Harsnett, Samuel (1604) *A Declaration of Egregious Popish Impostures . . . Under the Pretence of Casting out Devils*, London: J. Roberts.
Hartley, George (ed.) (1987) *Philip Larkin 1922-1985: a tribute*, London: The Marvell Press.
Hazlitt, William (1930-4) *The Complete Works of William Hazlitt*, Howe, P. P. (ed.), London: J. M. Dent.
Heath, Stephen (1978) 'Difference', *Screen* 19: 51-112.
—— (1987) 'Male Feminism', 1-32 in Jardine and Smith.
Heffernan, James A. W. (1991) 'Blake's Oothon: The Dilemmas of Marginality', *Studies in Romanticism* 30: 3-18.
Hill, Geoffrey (1986) *Collected Poems*, London: Deutsch.
Hilton, Nelson (1982-3) 'Some Sexual Connotations', *Blake: An Illustrated Quarterly* 16: (3): 166-71.
—— (1986) 'An Original Story', 69-104 in Hilton and Vogler.
—— Vogler, Thomas A. (eds) (1986) *Unnam'd Forms: Blake and Textuality*, Berkeley: University of California Press.
Hobbes, Thomas ([1651] 1991) *Leviathan*, Tuck, Richard (ed.), Cambridge: CUP.
Hoeveler, Diane Long (1979) 'The Erotic Apocalypse: The Androgynous Ideal in Blake's "Jerusalem"', *Essays in Literature* 6: 29-42.
Holderness, Graham (1989) 'Reading "Deceptions" – A Dramatic Conversation', *Critical Survey* 1 (2): 122-9.
Holton, Robert (1991) 'Sexuality and Social Hierarchy in Sidney and Rochester', *Mosaic* 24 (1): 47-65.
Horne, R. C. (1986) 'Voices of Alienation: The Moral Significance of Marston's Satiric Strategy', *The Modern Language Review* 81 (1): 18-33.
Hubler, Edward (ed.) (1962) *The Riddle of Shakespeare's Sonnets*, London: Routledge & Kegan Paul.
Hughes, John (ed.) (1713) *Letters of Abelard and Heloise*, (3rd edition), London: J. Watts.
Hunt, Leigh (1832) *Poetical Works*, London: Edward Moxon.
—— (1846) *Wit and Humour, Selected from the English Poets*, London: Smith, Elder & Co.
Hunter, G. K. (1953) 'The Dramatic Technique of Shakespeare's Sonnets', *Essays in Criticism* 3: 152-62.
Ingrassia, Catherine (1990) 'Women Writing/Writing Women: Pope, Dulness, and "Feminisation" in *The Dunciad*', *Eighteenth Century Life* 14 (3): 40-58.
Irigaray, Luce (1985) *Speculum of the Other Woman*, Gill, Gillian C. (ed.), Ithaca: Cornell UP.
Jacobus, Mary (1986) *Reading Woman: Essays in Feminist Criticism*, London: Methuen.
—— (1989) *Romanticism and Sexual Difference: Essays on 'The Prelude'* Oxford, Clarendon.
Jakobson, Roman and Jones, Lawrence G. (1987) *Shakespeare's Verbal Art in th' Expence of Spirit*, 198-215 in Pomorska, Krystyna and Rudy, Stephen (eds) *Language in Literature: Roman Jakobson*, Cambridge, Mass.: Harvard UP.
Jardine, Alice A. (1985) *Gynesis: Configuration of Woman and Modernity*, Ithaca: Cornell UP.

BIBLIOGRAPHY

—— and Smith, Paul (eds) (1987) *Men in Feminism*, London: Methuen.
Jardine, Lisa (1983) *Still Harping on Daughters*, Hassocks: Harvester.
—— (1992) 'Saxon Violence', *The Guardian*, Dec. 8, section 2: 4–5.
Jarrell, Randall ([1948] 1968) 'T. S. Eliot as International Hero', 44–5 in A Collection of Critical Essays on 'The Waste Land', Martin Jay (ed.), Eaglewood Cliffs: Prentice-Hall.
Jay, Gregory (1983) *T. S. Eliot and the Poetics of Literary History*, Baton Rouge: Louisiana UP.
Johnson, J. W. (1987) 'Did Lord Rochester write *Sodom?*', *Papers of the Bibliographical Society of America* 81 (2): 119–53.
Johnson, Maurice (1969) 'T. S. Eliot on Satire, Swift, and Disgust', *Papers on Literature and Language* 5: 310–15.
Johnson, Samuel (1905) *Lives of the Most Eminent English Poets*, (3 vols) Hill, G. Birkbeck (ed.) Oxford: Clarendon.
Jones, G. P. (1981) 'You, Thou, He or She? The Master-Mistress in Shakespearean and Elizabethan Sonnet Sequences', *Cahiers Elizabethains* 19: 73–84.
Jonson, Ben (1975) *The Complete Poems*, Donaldson, Ian (ed.) Oxford: OUP.
Joyce, James, (1984) *Ulysses* (3 vols), Gabler, Hans W. (ed.), New York: Garland Press.
Kaplan, Cora (1985) 'Pandora's Box: Subjectivity, Class and Sexuality in Socialist Feminist Criticism', 146–76 in Greene, Gayle and Kahn, Coppelia (eds) *Making a Difference: Feminist Literary Criticism*, London: Methuen.
—— (1986) 'Wild Nights: Pleasure/Sexuality/Feminism', 31–56 in *Sea Changes: Culture and Feminism*, London: Verso.
Kappeler, Susanne (1986) *Pornography and Representation*, Cambridge: Polity.
Kaufman, Linda (ed.) (1989) *Gender and Theory: Dialogues on Feminist Criticism*, Oxford: Basil Blackwell.
Keats, John (1970) *The Poetical Works of John Keats*, Garrod, H. W. (ed.), Oxford: OUP.
—— (1958) *The Letters of John Keats 1814–21* (2 vols), Rollins H. E. (ed.), Cambridge Mass.: Harvard UP.
Kenner, Hugh (1960) *T. S. Eliot: The Invisible Poet*, London: W. H. Allen.
Kerrigan, John (ed.) (1986) *The Sonnets and A Lover's Complaint*, Harmondsworth: Penguin.
—— (ed.) (1991) *Motives of Woe: Shakespeare and 'female complaint': A Critical Anthology*, Oxford: Clarendon.
Kesler, R. L. (1990) 'The Idealisation of Women: Morphology and Change in Three Renaissance Texts', *Mosaic* 23 (2): 107–26.
Kidd, W. (1975) 'A Study of Images Produced Through use of a Male Pronoun as the Generic', *Movements: Contemporary Rhetoric and Communication* 1: 25–30.
Knight, G. Wilson (1961) *The Mutual Flame: An Interpretation of Shakespeare's Sonnets*, London: Methuen.
Knust, Herbert (1967) 'Sweeney among the Birds and Beasts', *Arcadia* 2: 204–17.
Koestenbaum, Wayne (1989) '*The Waste Land*: T. S. Eliot's and Ezra Pound's Collaboration on Hysteria', 112–39 in *Double Talk: The Erotics of Male Literary Collaboration*, London: Routledge.

BIBLIOGRAPHY

Kraft, Elizabeth (1988) '"A Great Humour which is Serious": Caricature and the Development of T. S. Eliot's Poetic Vision', *Essays in Literature* 15 (2): 221–35.

Krieger, Murray (1961) 'The "Frail China Jar" and the Rude Hand of Chaos', *Centennial Review of Arts and Sciences* (5): 176–94.

Kristeva, Julia (1982) *Powers of Horror: An Essay on Abjection*, Roudiez, Leon S. (trans.), New York: Columbia UP.

—— (1984) *Revolution in Poetic Language*, Roudiez, Leon S. (trans.), New York: Columbia UP.

—— (1987) *Tales of Love*, Roudiez, Leon S. (trans.), New York: Columbia UP.

Lacan, Jacques (1977) *The Four Fundamental Concepts of Psycho-Analysis*, Jacques-Allain Millais (ed.), Harmondsworth: Penguin.

—— (1982) *Feminine Sexuality: Jacques Lacan and the Ecole Freudienne*, Mitchell, Juliet (ed. and trans.), Rose, Jacqueline (ed.), London: Macmillan.

Lakoff, Robin (1975) *Language and Women's Place*, New York: Harper & Row.

Langland, Elizabeth (1987) 'Blake's Feminist Revision of Literary Tradition in the SICK ROSE', 235–43 in Bracher and Ault.

Lanham, Richard (1972) '"Astrophil and Stella": Pure and Impure Persuasion' *ELR* 2: 100–15.

Laqueur, Thomas (1990) *Making Sex: Body and Gender From the Greeks to Freud*, Cambridge: Harvard UP.

Larkin, Philip (1946; 1964) *Jill*, London: Faber.

—— (1947; 1975) *A Girl in Winter*, London: Faber.

—— (1983) *Required Writings: Miscellaneous Pieces 1955–82*, London: Faber.

—— (1988) *Philip Larkin: Collected Poems*, Thwaite, Anthony (ed.), London: Faber.

—— (1992) *Selected Letters of Philip Larkin, 1940–1985* Thwaite, Anthony (ed.), London: Faber.

Lawrence, D. H. (1956) *Selected Literary Criticism*, Beal, Anthony (ed.), London: Heinemann.

Lee, Judith (1983) 'Ways of their Own: The Emanations of Blake's Vala, or, The Four Zoas', *ELH* 50 (1): 131–53.

Lee, Sidney (ed.) (1904) *Elizabethan Sonnets Newly Arranged and Indexed* (2 vols), Westminster: Archibald Constable & Co.

Leishman, J. B. (1961; 1967) *Themes and Variations in Shakespeare's Sonnets*, London: Hutchinson.

Levin, Richard (1965) 'Sonnet CXXIX as a "Dramatic" Poem', *Shakespeare Quarterly* 16: 175–81.

Lewis, C. S. ([1936] 1977) *The Allegory of Love: A Study in Medieval Tradition*, Oxford: Clarendon.

Linkin, Harriet Kramer (1990) 'Revisioning Blake's Oothon', *Blake: an Illustrated Quarterly* 23: (4): 184–94.

Lipking, Lawrence (1988) *Abandoned Women and Poetic Tradition*, Chicago: Chicago UP.

Lodge, Thomas (1593; 1904) *Phillis Honoured with Pastorall: Sonnets, Elegies and Amorous Delights*, in Lee (1904), vol. ii, 1–22.

BIBLIOGRAPHY

Longenbach, James (1985) 'Guarding the Horned Gates: History and Interpretation in the Early Poetry of T. S. Eliot', *ELH* 52: (2): 503-27.

Longino, Victoria (1989) '"Smaller and Clearer as the Years go by": Women and Girls in the Works of Philip Larkin', *DAI* 50 (5): 1312A-13A.

McClenahan, Catherine L., (1990) '"No Face like the Human Divine?": Women and Gender in Blake's *Pickering Manuscript*', 189-207 in Rosso, G. A. and Watkins, Daniel P. (eds), *Spirits of Fire: English Romantic Writers and Contemporary Historical Methods*, Rutherford, N.J.: Fairleigh Dickinson UP.

McClintock, Anne (1992) 'Gonad and the Barbarian and the Venus Flytrap: Portraying the Female and the Male Orgasm', 111-31 in Segal, Lynne and McIntosh, Mary (eds) *Sex Exposed: Sexuality in the Pornography Debate* London: Virago.

Mack, Maynard (1982) 'The Least Thing Like a Man in England', 372-92 in *'Collected in Himself'; Essays Critical, Biographical, and Bibliographical on Pope and Some of his Contemporaries*, Newark: Delaware UP.

—— (1985) *Alexander Pope: a life*, New Haven: Yale UP.

Mahood, M. M. (1957) *Shakespeare's Wordplay*, London: Methuen.

Marston, John (1961) *The Poems of John Marston*, Davenport, Arnold (ed.), Liverpool: Liverpool UP.

Martin, J. R. (1985) *Reclaiming a Conversation: The Ideal of the Educated Woman*, New Haven, Yale UP.

Martin, Mildred (1972) *A Half-Century of Eliot Criticism*, Lewisburg: Bucknell UP.

Marvell, Andrew (1927; 1961) *The Poems and Letters of Andrew Marvell* (2 vols), Margoliouth, H. M. (ed.) Oxford: Clarendon.

Mason, H. A. (1990) 'Eliot's "Ode" – A Neglected Poem?', *The Cambridge Quarterly* 19 (4): 303-35.

Matthews, Susan (1990) '"Matter too soft": Pope and the Women's Novel', 103-20, in Fairer.

Matthiessen, F. O. (1935) *The Achievement of T. S. Eliot: An Essay on the Nature of Poetry*, London: OUP.

Mayer, John T. (1989) *T. S. Eliot's Silent Voices*, New York: OUP.

Means, James A. (1983) 'Pope and Rochester', *Notes and Queries* 30(228) (1) (Feb.), p. 34.

Medcalf, Stephen (1988) 'T. S. Eliot's "Metamorphoses": Ovid and *The Waste Land*', 223-46 in Martindale, Charles (ed.), *Ovid Renewed: Ovidian Influences on Literature and Art from the Middle Ages to the Twentieth Century*, Cambridge: CUP.

Melchiori, Giorgio (1976) *Shakespeare's Dramatic Meditations: An Experiment in Criticism*, Oxford: Clarendon.

Mellor, Anne K. (1982-3) 'Blake's Portrayal of Women', *Blake: an Illustrated Quarterly* 16: 148-55.

—— (1988) 'Blake's *Songs of Innocence and Songs of Experience*: A Feminist Perspective', *Nineteenth Century Studies* 2: 1-17.

Middleton, Peter (1986) 'The Academic Development of *The Waste Land*', 153-80 in Weber, Samuel (ed.), *Demarcating the Disciplines: Philosophy, Literature, Art*, Minneapolis: Minneapolis UP.

BIBLIOGRAPHY

—— (1992) *The Inward Gaze: Masculinity and Subjectivity in Modern Culture*, London: Routledge.
Miles, Josephine (1957) *Eras & Modes in English Poetry*, Berkeley and Los Angeles: California UP.
—— (1973) 'Blake's Frame of Language', 86–95 in Paley and Phillips.
Miller, James E., Jr. (1977) *T. S. Eliot's Personal Wasteland: Exorcism of the Demons*, University Park and London: Pennsylvania State UP.
Miller, Christopher (1983) 'The Egotistical Banal, or, Against Larkitudinising', *Agenda* 21 (3): 69–103
Millett, Kate (1969; 1977) *Sexual Politics*, London: Virago.
Milroy, J. and Milroy L. (1986) *Language and Authority*, Oxford: Blackwell.
Milton, John (1966) *The Complete Poems of John Milton*, Bush, Douglas (ed.) London: OUP.
Mitchell, Orm (1984) 'Blake's Subversive Illustrations to Wollstonecraft's *Stories*', *Mosaic* 17 (4): 17–34
Montagu, Lady Mary Wortley ([1733] 1977) 'Verses address'd to the Imitator of the First Satire of the Second Book of Horace. By a Lady', in *Essays and Poems, and Simplicity a Comedy*, Halsband, Robert and Grundy, Isobel (eds) Oxford: Clarendon.
Moore, Marianne (1918) 'A Note on T. S. Eliot's Book', *Poetry* xii: 36–7.
Morgan, Fidelis (ed.) (1989) *A Misogynist's Source-Book*, London: Cape.
Morse, Jonathan (1985) 'Sweeney, the Sties of the Irish, and *The Waste Land*' 135–46 in Roby.
Motion, Andrew (1982) *Philip Larkin*, London: Methuen.
—— (1993) *Philip Larkin: A Writer's Life*, London: Faber.
Mulford: Wendy (ed.) (1990) *The Virago Book of Women's Love Poetry*, London: Virago.
Murphy, Karleen Middleton (1982) '"All the lovely sex": Blake and the Woman Question', in Bogan, James and Goss Fred (eds) *Sparks of Fire: Blake in a New Age*, Richmond, Calif.: North Atlantic.
Newman, Jenny (ed.) (1988) *The Faber Book of Seductions*, London: Faber.
Nicholson, Marjorie Hope and Rousseau G. S. (1968) *'This Long Disease, My Life': Alexander Pope and the Sciences*, Princeton: Princeton UP.
Nokes, David (1987) 'Wielding the Gendered Shears', *TLS*, 20 Feb., 4377: 182.
Nussbaum, Felicity A. (1977) (ed.) *Satires on Women*, Augustan Reprint Society no. 180, Los Angeles: University of California.
—— (1984) *The Brink of All We Hate: English Satires upon Women, 1660–1750*, Lexington: University of Kentucky Press.
—— (1990) *The Autobiographical Subject: Gender and Ideology in Eighteenth Century England*, Baltimore and London: Johns Hopkins.
—— and Brown, Laura (eds) (1987) *The New Eighteenth Century: Theory, Politics, Literature*, London: Methuen.
Ober, William B. (1979) *Boswell's Clap and Other Essays: Medical Analyses of Literary Men's Afflictions*, Carbondale: Southern Illinois UP.
Oldham, John (1987) *The Poems of John Oldham*, Brooks, Harold F. and Selden, Raman (eds) Oxford: Clarendon.
Osborn, James M. (1966) *Observations, Anecdotes and Characters of Books and Men* (2 vols), Oxford: OUP.

BIBLIOGRAPHY

Osbourne, Charles (1988) *Favourite Love Poems*, London: O'Mara.
Ostriker, Alicia [1982-3] (1986) '"Desire Gratified and Ungratified": William Blake and Sexuality', *Blake: An Illustrated Quarterly* 16: 156-65; reprinted as 211-36 in *Essential Articles for the Study of William Blake*, Hilton, Nelson (ed.), Hamden Conn.: Archon Press.
Paglia, Camille (1990) *Sexual Personae: Art and Decadence From Nefertiti to Emily Dickinson*, London: Yale UP.
Paley, Morton (1973) 'The Figure in the Garment in "The Four Zoas", "Milton" and "Jerusalem"', 119-40 in *Blake's Sublime Allegory: Essays on 'The Four Zoas', 'Milton' and 'Jerusalem'*, Curran, Stuart and Wittreich, Joseph A. (eds) Madison: Wisconsin UP.
—— and Phillips, Michael (eds) (1973) *William Blake: Essays in Honour of Sir Geoffrey Keynes*, Oxford: Clarendon.
Parker, Derek (ed.) (1980) *A Collection of Erotic Poetry*, London: Constable.
—— (1981) *A Collection of Erotic Prose*, London: Constable.
Parker, Patricia (1987) 'Coming Second: Women's Place', 178-233, in *Literary Fat Ladies: Rhetoric, Gender, Property*, London: Methuen.
Partridge, Eric (1947) *Shakespeare's Bawdy*, London: Routledge.
Patmore, Coventry (1949) *The Poems of Coventry Patmore*, Page, Frederick (ed.), Oxford: OUP.
Paulson, Ronald (1978) 'Rochester: The Body Political and the Body Private', 103-21 in *The Author in his Work: Essays on a Problem in Criticism*, Martz, Louis L. and Williams, Aubrey (eds), New Haven and London: Yale UP; reprinted in Vieth 1988, 45-67.
Payne, Deborah C. (1991) 'Pope and the War against Coquettes; or, Feminism and *The Rape of the Lock* yet again', *The Eighteenth Century: Theory and Interpretation* 32 (1): 3-24.
Pequigney, Joseph (1985) *'Such is my Love': A Study of Shakespeare's Sonnets*, Chicago: Chicago UP.
Petch, Simon (1981) *The Art of Philip Larkin*, Sydney: Sydney UP.
Peterson, Douglas L. (1965) 'A Probable Source for Shakespeare's Sonnet CXXIX', *Shakespeare Quarterly* v: 381-4.
Petrarch, Francesco (1976) *Petrarch's Lyric Poems*, Durling, Robert M. (trans. and ed.), Cambridge: Mass.: Harvard UP.
Pickles, Sheila (1988) *Love: Penhaligon's Scented Treasury of Love and Prose*, London: Pavilion.
Pinkney, Tony (1984) *Women in the Poetry of T.S. Eliot: A Psychoanalytic Approach*, London: Macmillan.
Pinsker, Sanford (1989) 'T. S. Eliot as Culture Hero', *The Gettysburg Review* 2(2): 242-9.
Piper, David (1982) *The Image of the Poet: British Poets and their Portraits*, Oxford: Clarendon.
Pitt-Kethley, Fiona (ed.) (1992) *The Literary Companion to Sex*, London: Bloomsbury.
Poe, Edgar Allan (1852) 'The Murders in the Rue Morgue', 80-121 in *Tales of Mystery, Imagination, and Humour; and Poems*, London: Clarke, Beeton & Co.
—— ([1846] 1965) 'The Philosophy of Literary Composition', 20-32 in *Literary Criticism of Edgar Allan Poe*, Hough, R. L. (ed.), Lincoln: University of Nebraska.

BIBLIOGRAPHY

Pohli, Carol Virginia (1985–6) '"The Point where Sense and Dulness Meet": What Pope Knows about Knowing and about Women', *Eighteenth Century Studies* 19: (2): 206–34.

Pollak, Ellen (1985) *The Poetics of Sexual Myth: Gender and Ideology in the Verse of Swift and Pope*' Chicago: Chicago UP.

Polwhele, Richard ([1798] 1810) 'The Unsex'd Females; a Poem Address'd to the Author of the Pursuits of Literature', 35–44 in vol. ii of *Poems*, (5 vols), London: J. Mitchell.

Poovey, Mary (1984) *The Proper Lady and the Woman Writer: Ideology as Style in the Works of Mary Wollstonecraft, Mary Shelley and Jane Austen*, Chicago: Chicago UP.

Pope, Alexander (1939–69) *The Twickenham Edition of The Poems of Alexander Pope*, Butt, John, *et al.* (eds), New Haven and London: Yale UP.

—— ([1713] 1982) 'The Club of Little Men', *The Guardian* 92, Stephens, J. C. (ed.) Lexington: Kentucky UP.

Porter, David (ed.) (1992) *Between Men and Feminism*, London: Routledge.

Porter, Peter (1982) 'The Professional Amateur', 58–71 in Treglown.

Praz, Mario (1933; 1951) *The Romantic Agony*, Oxford: OUP.

Prior, Roger (1982) 'Some Shakespearian Puns and their Implications', *Cahiers Elizabethian* 22: 15–24.

Punter, David (1984) 'Blake, Trauma, and the Female', *New Literary History* 15: 475–90.

Quincey, Thomas de (1889–90) *The Collected Writings of Thomas De Quincey* (14 vols), Masson, David (ed.) Edinburgh: Adam & Charles Black.

Ralegh, Sir Walter (1984) *Selected Writings*, Heard, Gerald (ed.), Manchester: Carcanet.

Ransom, John Crowe (1938) 'Shakespeare at Sonnets', *The World's Body*, London and New York: Scribner's.

Rawson, Claude (1985) 'System of Excess', *TLS*, 29 March: 335–6.

—— (1991) 'Larkin's Desolate Attics', *Raritan* 11 (2): 25–47.

—— (ed. and intro.) and Kernan, Alvin (intro.) (1984) *English Satire and the Satiric Tradition*, Oxford: Blackwell.

Reichard, Hugo M. (1954) 'The Love Affair in Pope's *The Rape of the Lock*', *PMLA* 69: 887–902.

Reiss, Timothy J. (1989) 'Wollstonecraft, Women and Reason', 11–50 in Kaufman.

Reyes, Alina (1992) *The Butcher*, London: Minerva.

Richards, I. A. (1926), 'On Mr Eliot's Poetry', Appendix B to *Principles of Literary Criticism* (second edition), pp. 289–95, London: Kegan Paul, Treach, Trubner & Co.

—— (1970) 'Jakobson's Shakespeare: The Subliminal Structures of a Sonnet', *TLS*, 28 May: 589–90.

Richardson, Samuel ([1747–8] 1985) *Clarissa or The History of a Young Lady*, Ross, Angus (ed.), Harmondsworth: Penguin.

Richmond, Hugh (1986) 'The Dark Lady as Reformation Mistress', *The Kenyon Review* 8: (2): 91–105.

Ricks, Beatrice (1980) *T. S. Eliot: A Bibliography of Secondary Works*, New Jersey: Metachen.

Ricks, Christopher (1988a) *T. S. Eliot and Prejudice*, London: Faber.

—— (1988b) 'Donne after Love', 33–69 in *Literature and the Body*, Scary, Elaine (ed.), Baltimore: Johns Hopkins.
Riede, David G. (1981) 'The Symbolism of the Loins in Blake's *Jerusalem*', *SEL* 21 (4): 547–63.
—— (1987) 'Blake's Milton: on membership in the Church Paul', 255–77 in Nyquist, Mary and Ferguson, Margaret W. (eds) *Re-Membering Milton: Essays on the Texts and Traditions*, New York: Methuen.
Righter [later Barton], Anne (1967) 'John Wilmot, Earl of Rochester', *Proceedings of the British Academy* 53; reprinted in Vieth 1988, 1–16.
Roberson, Susan L. (1986) 'T. S. Eliot's Symbolical Woman: from Temptress to Priestess', *Midwest Quarterly* 27: (4): 486.
Robinson, Ken (1984) 'The Art of Violence in Rochester's Satire', 93–108 in Rawson and Kernan.
Roby, Kinley E. (1985) *Critical Essays on T. S. Eliot: The Sweeney Motif*, Boston: G. K. Hall.
Roche, Thomas Jr. (1987) '"Astrophil and Stella": A Radical Reading', 185–226 in *Sir Philip Sidney: An Anthology of Modern Criticism*, Kay, Dennis (ed.), Oxford: Clarendon.
Rochester, John Wilmot, Earl of, ([1680] 1970) *Poems on Several Occasions*, Antwerp [London] fac: Scolar Press, Menton.
—— (1685) *Valentinian: A Tragedy: as 'tis Altered by the Late Earl of Rochester*, London: Timothy Goodwin.
—— (1904 [1905]) *Rochester's Sodom*, von Romer, L. S. A. M. (ed.), Paris [Amsterdam]: H. Welter.
—— (1980) *The Letters of John Wilmot, Earl of Rochester*, Treglown, Jeremy (ed.), Oxford: Blackwell.
—— (1984) *The Poems of John Wilmot, Earl of Rochester*, Walker, Keith (ed.), Oxford: Basil Blackwell.
Rogers, Katherine M. (1966) *The Troublesome Helpmate: A History of Misogyny in Literature*, Seattle: Washington UP.
Rogers, Pat (1975) *An Introduction to Pope*, London: Methuen.
Ronan, Clifford J. (1986) 'Eliot's Polypheman Pastorals', *Yeats Eliot Review* 8: (1–2): 109–18.
Rose, Jacqueline (1986) *Sexuality in the Field of Vision*, London: Verso.
Rosmarin, Adena (1985) 'Hermeneutics versus Erotics: Shakespeare's Sonnets and Interpretive History', *PMLA* 100 (1): 20–37.
Ross, Andrew (1984) '*The Waste Land* and the Fantasy of Interpretation', *Representations* 8: 134–58.
Rossen, Janice (1989) *Philip Larkin: His Life's Work*, Iowa City: University of Iowa Press.
Rossetti, Dante Gabriel (1913; 1968) *Poems and Translations*, Milford: Humphrey (ed.), Oxford: OUP.
Rossiter, A. P. (1961; 1989) *Angel with Horns: Fifteen Lectures on Shakespeare*, London: Longman.
Rosslyn, Felicity (1988) '"Dipt in the Rainbow": Pope on Women', 51–62 in Rousseau and Rogers.
Rousseau G. S. and Rogers, Pat (eds) (1988) *The Enduring Legacy: Alexander Pope Tercentenary Essays*, Cambridge: CUP.
Rousseau, Jean Jacques (1761) *An Inquiry into the Nature of the Social Contract*

BIBLIOGRAPHY

or Principles of Political Right, London: G. G. J. & J. Robinson.
—— (1762) *Emile, ou de l'éducation* (4 vols), Amsterdam [Paris]: J. Neaulme.
—— (1763) *Emilius, or, a Treatise on Education*, Nugent, Thomas (trans.), Edinburgh: A. Donaldson.
—— (1767) *Emilius and Sophia, or, a New System of Education* (second edition) (4 vols), Kenrick, William (trans.), London: T. Becket and P. A. de Hondt.
—— (1974) *Emile*, Foxley, B. (trans.), London: J. M. Dent.
Rubinstein, Frankie Rada (1984; 1989) *A Dictionary of Shakespeare's Sexual Puns and their Significance*, London: Macmillan.
Rudat, Wolfgang E. H. (1974) 'Belinda's "Painted Vessel": Allusive Technique in *The Rape of the Lock*', *Tennessee Studies in Literature*, 19: 49–55.
Rude, Donald W. (1990) 'Mr Eliot looks into Chapman's Homer: A Possible Source for "Sweeney Erect"', *Classical and Modern Literature* 11 (1): 55–8.
Ruffhead, Owen (1769) *The Life of Alexander Pope*, London: C. Bathurst *et al.*
Rumbold, Valerie (1989) *Woman's Place in Pope's World*, Cambridge: CUP.
Sackville, Charles, Sixth Earl of Dorset, (1979) *The Poems of Charles Sackville Sixth Earl of Dorset*, Harris, Brice (ed.), New York & London: Garland.
Saintsbury, George (1908) *A History of English Prosody* (3 vols), London: Macmillan.
Salwak, Dale (1989) *Philip Larkin: The Man and his Work*, Iowa City: Iowa UP.
Sampley, Arthur M. (1968) 'The Woman Who Wasn't There: Lacunae in T. S. Eliot', *South Atlantic Quarterly* 67 (4): 603–10.
Schoelder, Amy and Silverberg, Ira (eds) (1991) *High Risk: An Anthology of forbidden writings*, London: Serpent's Tail.
Schwartz, Joel (1984) *The Sexual Politics of Jean-Jacques Rousseau*, Chicago, Chicago UP.
Schwarz, Delmore ([1945] 1970), 'T. S. Eliot as the Internaitonal Hero', 120–8 in Dike, D. A. and Zucker, D. H. (eds) 'Selected Essays of Delmore Schwartz', Chicago and London: University of Chicago Press.
Schweickart, Patrocinio P. (1989) 'Reading Ourselves: Towards a Feminist Theory of Reading', 17–44 in Showalter, E. (ed.), *Speaking of Gender*, London: Routledge.
Schwenger, Peter (1984) *Phallic Critiques: Masculinities and Twentieth-century Literature*, London: Routledge.
Sedgwick, Eve Kosofsky (1985) *Between Men: English Literature and Male Homosocial Desire*, New York: Columbia UP.
—— (1989) 'Critical Response 1: Tide and Trust', *Critical Inquiry* 15 (4): 745–57.
—— (1991) *Epistemology of the Closet*, Hemel Hempstead: Harvester Wheatsheaf.
Seidler, Victor J. (1989) *Rediscovering Masculinity: Reason, Language, and Sexuality*, London: Routledge.
—— (ed.) (1991) *Achilles Heel Reader: Men, Sexual Politics and Socialism*, London: Routledge.
Selden, Raman (1991) 'Rochester and Oldham: "High Rants in Profaneness"', *The Seventeenth Century* 6 (1): 89–103.

BIBLIOGRAPHY

Severin, Laura Ruth (1990) *The Significance of Gender: Male Patterns of Understanding in T. S. Eliot's work, DAI* 50 (12): 3955a–6a.

Shakespeare, William (1951) *William Shakespeare: The Complete Works*, Alexander, Peter (ed.), London: Collins.

—— (1986) *The Sonnets and A Lover's Complaint*, Kerrigan, John (ed.), Harmondsworth: Penguin.

Shelburne, Steven R. (1989) 'Principled Satire: Decorum in John Marston's "The Metamorphosis of Pigmalion's Image" and "Certaine Satyres"', *Studies in Philology* 86 (2): 198–218.

Showalter, Elaine (1983) 'Critical Cross-Dressing: Male Feminists and The Woman of the Year', *Raritan* 3: 130–49.

—— (ed.) (1986) *The New Feminist Criticism: Essays on Women, Literature and Theory*, London: Virago.

—— (ed.) (1989) *Speaking of Gender*, London: Routledge.

Sicker, Philip (1984) 'The Belladonna: Eliot's Female Archetype in *The Waste Land*', *Twentieth Century Literature* 30 (4): 420–31.

Sidney, Philip (1962) *The Poems of Sir Philip Sidney*, Ringler, William A., Jr (ed.), Oxford: Clarendon.

Sigg, Eric (1989) *The American T. S. Eliot: A Study of the Early Writings*, Cambridge: CUP.

Simpson, Matt (1989) '"Never Such Innocence" – a reading of Larkin's "Sunny Prestatyn"', *Critical Survey* 1: (2): 176–81.

Smith, Amy Elizabeth (1992) 'Roles for Readers in Mary Wollstonecraft's *A Vindication of the Rights of Women*', *Studies in English Literature* 32 (3): 555–70.

Smith, Grover, Jr (1956; 1974) *T. S. Eliot's Poems and Plays: A Study in Sources and Meaning*, Chicago: Chicago UP.

—— (1990) 'Eliot and the Ghost of Poe', 149–63 in Baghee.

Smith, Joan (1989) *Misogynies*, London: Faber.

Smith, P. M. (1986) *Language, the Sexes and Society*, Oxford: Blackwell.

Sonntag, Susan (1969) 'The Pornographic Imagination', 35–73 in *Styles of Radical Will*, London: Secker & Warburg.

Spacks, Patricia Meyer (1984) '"Imaginations warm and tender": Pope and Lady Mary', *South Atlantic Quarterly* 83: 207–15.

—— (1990) 'Fictions of Passion: The Case of Pope', *Studies in Eighteenth Century Culture* 20: 43–53.

Spence, Joseph (1966) *Observations, Anecdotes and Characters of Books and Men* (2 vols), Osborn, James M. (ed.), Oxford: OUP.

Spender, Dale (1980; 1985) *Man-made Language*, London: Routledge.

Spenser, Edmund (1932; 1958) *The Works of Edmund Spenser*, vol. 5, *The Minor Poems*, Greenham, Edwin, Osgood, Charles Grosvenor and Padelford, Frederick Morgan (eds) Baltimore: Johns Hopkins UP.

Stallworthy, Jon (ed.) (1973) *The Penguin Book of Love Verse*, Harmondsworth: Penguin.

Stephen, Leslie (1880) *Alexander Pope*, London: Macmillan.

Stephenson, Raymond (1991) 'The Love Song of Young Alexander Pope: Allusion and Sexual Displacement in the Pastorals', *English Studies in Canada* 17 (1): 21–35.

Stevenson, W.H. (1971; 1989) See 'Blake, William'.

BIBLIOGRAPHY

Still, Judith (1991) 'From the Philosophy of Man to the Fiction of Woman: Rousseau's *Emile*', *Romance Studies* 18: 75–87.
Storch, Margaret (1981) 'Blake and Women: "Nature's Cruel Holiness"', *American Imago* 38 (2): 221–46.
Straub, Kristina (1991) 'Men from Boys: Cibber, Pope, and the Schoolboy', *The Eighteenth Century: Theory and Interpretation* 32 (3): 219–39.
Suckling, Sir John (1971) *The Works of Sir John Suckling: The Non-dramatic Works*, Clayton, Thomas (ed.), Oxford: Clarendon.
Suleiman, Susan Rubin (ed.) (1986) *The Female Body in Western Culture*, Cambridge: Harvard UP.
Swift, Jonathan (1984) *The Complete Poems*, Rogers, Pat (ed.), New Haven: Yale UP.
Swinburne, Algernon (1926) *The Complete Works of Algernon Swinburne*, Bonchurch edition (2 vols), Gosse, Sir Edmund and Wise, Thomas James (eds), London: Heinemann.
Tate, Alison (1988) 'The Master-Narrative of Modernism: Discourses of Class and Gender in *The Waste Land*', *Literature and History* 14 (2): 160–71.
Tate, Allen (1977) *Collected Poems 1919–1976* New York: Farrar Strauss Giroux.
Tennyson, Lord Alfred (1969; 1987) *The Poems of Tennyson* (3 vols), Ricks, Christopher (ed.) London: Longman.
Terrasse, Jean (1989) 'Les manipulations du lecteur dans *Emile*', *Studies on Voltaire and the Eighteenth Century* 264: 735–7.
Thackeray, William M. (1853) 'Prior, Gay, and Pope', 138–86 in *The English Humorists of the Eighteenth Century*, New York: Harper & Brother.
Theweleit, Klaus (1987) *Male Fantasies* vol. 1, *Women, Floods, Bodies, History*, Minneapolis: Minneapolis UP.
—— (1989) *Male Fantasies*, vol. 2, *Psychoanalysing the White Terror*, Minneapolis: Minneapolis UP.
Thompson, Francis (1910) 'Pope', 191–200, in *A Renegade Poet and Other Essays*, Boston: G. K. Hall.
Thomson, James (1895) *The Poetical Works of James Thomson* (2 vols), Dobrell, Bertram (ed.) London: Reeves & Turner & Dobrell.
Thormahlen, Marianne (1988) 'Rochester and the Fall: The Roots of Discontent', *English Studies* 69 (5): 396–409.
—— (1993) *Rochester: The Poems in Context*, Cambridge: CUP.
Thwaite, Anthony (ed.) (1982) *Larkin at Sixty*, London: Faber.
—— (1992) See 'Larkin, Philip'.
Tobin, David Ned (1977) *The Presence of the Past: T. S. Eliot's Victorian Inheritance*, Michigan: Michigan UP.
Traub, Valerie, (1992) *Desire and Anxiety: Circulations of Sexuality in Shakespearean Drama*, London: Routledge.
Treglown, Jeremy (ed.) (1982) *Spirit of Wit: Reconsiderations of Rochester*, Oxford: Blackwell.
Trengrove, Graham (1988) 'What Happens in "Whatever Happened"', 317–26 in Peer, Willie van (ed.), *The Taming of the Text: Explorations in Language, Literature, and Culture*, London: Routledge.
Turner, James Grantham (1988) 'Pope's Libertine Self-Fashioning', *The*

BIBLIOGRAPHY

Eighteenth Century: Theory and Interpretation 29 (3): 123–44.
Untermeyer, Louis (1957) *A Treasury of Ribaldry*, London: Elek.
van Leer, David (1989a) '"The Beast in the Closet": Homosociality and the Pathology of Manhood', *Critical Inquiry* 15 (3): 587–605.
—— (1989b) 'Critical Response II: Trust and Trade', *Critical Inquiry* 15 (4): 758–63.
Vanpee, Janie (1990) 'Rousseau's *Emile ou de l'éducation*: A resistance to reading', *Yale French Studies* 77: 156–76.
Vendler, Helen (1973) 'Jakobson, Richards and Shakespeare's Sonnet CXXIX', in Brewer, Reuben, Vendler, Helen and Hollander, John (eds) *I. A. Richards: Essays in his Honour*, New York: OUP.
Vickers, Nancy (1985) '"The blazon of sweet beauties best": Shakespeare's *Lucrece*', 95–115 in Parker, Patricia and Hartman, Geoffrey (eds) *Shakespeare and the Question of Theory*, London: Methuen.
Vieth, David M. (ed.) (1968) *The Complete Poems of John Wilmot, Earl of Rochester*, New Haven: Yale UP.
—— (1988) *John Wilmot: Earl of Rochester: Critical Essays*, New York: Garland.
Vlasopolos, Anna (1980) 'Mary Wollstonecraft's Mask of Reason in *A Vindication of the Rights of Women*', *Dalhousie Review* 60 (3): 462–71.
Wang, Orrin N. C. (1991) 'The Other Reasons: Female Alterity and Enlightenment Discourse in Mary Wollstonecraft's *A Vindication of the Rights of Women*', *The Yale Journal of Criticism* 5 (1): 129–49.
Ward, Edward (1729) *Apollo's Maggot in his Cups*, London: Booksellers of London and Westminster.
Wasserman, Earl (1966) 'The Limits of Allusion in Pope's *Rape of the Lock*', *JEGP* LXV: 425–44.
Webber, Andrew Lloyd (1981) *Cats: The Book of the Musical*, London: Faber & Faber and The Really Useful Company.
Weber, Harold (1992) '"Drudging in fair Aurelia's Womb": Constructing Homosexual Economies in Rochester's Poetry', *The Eighteenth Century* 33: (2): 99–117.
Webster, Brenda S. (1983) *Blake's Prophetic Psychology*, Athens, Ga.: University of Georgia Press.
—— (1987) 'Blake, Women and Sexuality', 205–24 in Bracher and Ault.
Weeks, Jeffrey (1985) *Sexuality and its Discontents: Meanings, Myths, and Modern Sexualities*, London: Routledge.
Weinberg, Kerry (1984) 'The Women of Eliot and Baudelaire: The Boredom, the Horror and the Glory', *Modern Language Studies* 14 (3): 31–42.
Weinbrot, Howard D. (1982) *Alexander Pope and the Traditions of Formal Verse Satire*, Princeton: Princeton UP.
Whalen, Terry (1986; rev. 1990) *Philip Larkin and English Poetry*, London: Macmillan.
Whitworth, John (ed.) (1990) *The Faber Book of Blue Verse*, London: Faber.
Wilcoxon, Reba (1979) 'Rochester's Sexual Politics', *Studies in Eighteenth-Century Culture* 8: 137–49; reprinted in Vieth (1988) 113–26.
Winn, James A. (1979) 'Pope Plays the Rake: His Letters to Ladies and the Making of the *Eloisa*', 89–118 in *The Art of Alexander Pope*, Erskine-Hill, H. and Smith, Anne (ed) New York: Harper & Row.

BIBLIOGRAPHY

Wilkie, Brian (1990) *Blake's Thel and Oothon*, Victoria, British Columbia: Univ. of Victoria.

Williams, Linda (1990) *Hard Core: Power, Pleasure, and the 'Frenzy of the Visible'* London: Pandora.

Wilson, Anna (1989) 'Mary Wollstonecraft and the Search for the Radical Woman', *Genders* 6: 88–101.

Wilson, Edmund (1931) *Axel's Castle: A study in the Imaginative Literature of 1870–1930*, New York and London: Scribner's.

Wilson, Penelope (1986) 'Feminism and the Augustans: Some Readings and Problems', *Critical Quarterly* 28 (1–2): 80–92.

—— (1988) 'Engendering the Reader: "Wit and Poetry and Pope" once more', 63–76 in Rousseau and Rogers.

Wilson, Thomas (1553) *The Arte of Rhetorique, For the Use of All Suche as are Studious of Eloquence*, London: R. Graftonus.

Wintle, Sarah (1982) 'Libertinism and Sexual Politics', 133–65 in Treglown.

Wollstonecraft, Mary [1790] (1989) *A Vindication of the Rights of Men in a Letter to the Rt. Hon. Edmund Burke: Occasioned by his Reflections on the Revolution in France* and [1792] *A Vindication of the Rights of Woman, with Strictures on Political and Moral Subjects*, in vol. 5, Todd, Janet Butler, Marilyn and Rees-Mogg, Emma (eds) *The Works of Mary Wollstonecraft* (7 vols), London: Pickering.

Wolseley, Robert (1685) Preface, 1–23 in *Valentinian: A Tragedy: as 'tis Altered by the Late Earl of Rochester*, London: Timothy Goodwin.

Woods, Gregory (1987) *Articulate Flesh: Male Homo-eroticism and Modern Poetry*, New Haven: Yale UP.

Woolf, Virginia ([1929] 1992) *A Room of One's Own* and *Three Guineas*, Schiach, Morag (ed.) Oxford: OUP.

Wordsworth, William (1940–9) *The Poetical Works of William Wordsworth* (4 vols), Selincourt, E. de (ed.), London: Clarendon.

Yeats, William Butler (1950) *Collected Poems*, London: Macmillan.

Young, Edward (1728) *Love of Fame, the Universal Passion. In Seven Characteristical Satires*, London: J. Tonson.

—— (1759) *Conjectures on Original Composition, in a Letter to the Author of Sir Charles Grandison*, London: A. Millar.

INDEX

Abdoo, Sherlyn 189
abstractionism 231–3
Ackland, Michael 140, 152
'Advice, The' (Rochester) 93, 103, 105–6
Aers, David 168
After Strange Gods (Eliot) 202
'Afternoons' (Larkin) 226, 245
'Against Constancy' (Rochester) 102
'Against Marriage' (Rochester) 90
Alexander Pope (Brown) 108–9
All's Well that Ends Well (Shakespeare) 48
All for Love (Dryden) 98
Allegory of Love (Lewis) 11
'Allusion to Harold, An' (Rochester) 78–9, 84, 97, 98
'Ambulances' (Larkin) 223, 224
Ames, Richard 125, 134–5, 137
Amis, Martin 255
Amoretti (Spenser) 54, 61
'Annus Mirabilis' (Larkin) 222–3
anthologies of love poems 3–7
anti-feminism 1; Pope 125–8, 131–3; Rochester 77–82, 90, 96
'Antiquated Coquette, The' (Dorset) 102
Antony and Cleopatra (Shakespeare) 62
aphorism/aphoristic mode 174, 179
Apollo's Maggot in his Cups (Ward) 114
apostrophic model 11, 19, 24, 52–66, 166
Ara Vos Prec (Eliot) 214
Ardener, Edwin 26
Arnold, Matthew 110, 193
arousal, desire and 14–18
Arrowsmith, William 209–10, 212, 215
Arte of Thetorique (Wilson) 67
'Arundel Tomb, An' (Larkin) 245, 253–5
Ashberry, John 234
'Aspecta Medusa' (Rossetti) 240
'Astrophil and Stella' (Sidney) 40–2, 46, 63–4
'Aubade' (Larkin) 223
Auden, W.H. 156
auto-eroticism 17–18, 79, 89–90, 171–2, 248–9
Ayre, William 113

Balokowsky, Jake 220
Barbach, Lonnie 5, 13
Barber, C.L. 35
'Bard, The' (Gray) 77
Barnes, Barnabe 40
Barnfield, Richard 50
'Barren Spring' (Rossetti) 195
Barry, Elizabeth 88
Baudelaire, Charles Pierre 1, 32
bawdy poety (explicitness) 7–14
Bawdy Verse (ed. Burford) 4
Bayley, John 251
Beaumont and Fletcher 207–9, 213
beauty, death and 192–4
Behn, Aphra 76

INDEX

Bentley, Thomas 130
Bergonzi, Bernard 190
Betjeman, John 4, 15
Between Men (Sedgwick) 38
biological determinism 226
bisexuality 51–2, 143–4
Blake, William 1, 2, 30, 79; desire–reason relation (in *Jerusalem*) 172–87; feminist studies 138–40; proclamation of joy 163–72; Rousseau and 140–54, 158, 163–4, 168–9, 176, 183–4, 187; sexual differentiation in early works 153–63
Blamires, Alcuin 6
'Blessed Damozel, The' (Rossetti) 195
Bloch, R.H. 32
Blount sisters (Pope correspondence) 108–9, 118, 120, 134, 137
body: experiences 28–9; failure 101–7; female 12, 13, 22–3, 80–1, 91–2, 101–7; male 22, 101–7, 109–20
Bold, Alan 4, 7, 10–12, 13, 17–18, 19, 22–5
Book of Athania (Blake) 172
Book of Urizen, The (Blake) 138
Booth, James 246, 252
Booth, Stephen 37, 53, 60, 76
'Breadfruit' (Larkin) 251
Bright, Susie 5
Brink of All We Hate, The (Nussbaum) 108
'Broadcast' (Larking) 235
Bronfen, Elisabeth 193
Brooks, Cleanth 112, 125
Brown, Laura 108–9, 133–4
Browning, Robert 1, 23, 36, 194, 201
'Building, The' (Larkin) 223
Burford, E.J. 4, 6, 7–8, 11, 13, 15, 25
'Buried Life, The' (Arnold) 193
Burnett, Gilbert 79
Butcher, The (Reyes) 82
Byron, Goerge Gordon, Lord 1, 89

Caelica (Greville) 41, 43, 47, 55, 66
Campbell, Thomas 22
Carew, Thomas 30
Carter, Angela 99
castration 28, 29–30, 212, 240
cathetic model 178
Cats (Webber musical) 193
celibacy 220
'Change' (Donne) 84
Charles II 103–4, 136
Charney, Maurice 5
Chatto Book of Love Poetry, The (ed. Fuller) 4
Chaucer, Geoffrey 40
Chester, Laura 5, 14
Chopin, Kate 217
Christ, Carol 218
'Church Going' (Larkin) 221, 224
Churchill, Charles 22
Cibber, Colley 114–15
Cixous, Hélène 28
Coghill, Nevil 206
Collection of Erotic Poetry, A (ed. Parker) 4
Colman, E.A. 35
'Colon' (Rochester) 75
commodity fetishism 245–6
condemnation, desire in form of 61–74
Confessions (Rousseau) 140, 142
contract notion 88, 89
Coote, Stephen 20–2
Cornillon, Susan K. 5
courtship 9–10, 14, 17, 20, 40–1, 62, 148, 234
Cowley, Abraham 82, 83, 86
creation myths 138, 139, 140
Cunningham, Allan 155
'cycle of generation' 180
'Cyril Tourneur' (Eliot) 191–2

Damrosch, Leopold Jr. 112, 164, 177
'Dance, The' (Larkin) 222
'Dante at Verona' (Rossetti) 197
Davie, Donald 156, 220, 222
Dawson, Jill 5
de Beauvoir, Simone 99
De Quincey, Thomas 110

INDEX

death, feminity and 192–4
death-in-lust 199–203
'Deceptions' (Larkin) 232, 234, 252
deconstructive model 31, 42, 217–18
decontextualisation 43
'Dedicated, The' (Larkin) 222
Deep Down: The New Sensual Writing by Women (ed. Chester) 5, 14
Defoe, Daniel 75–6
Degraaf, Robert M. 206
Dennis, John 115, 122, 124
desire 10, 33–4; arousal and 14–18; as commodity 245–6; female 119–20, 147–50; gratified (Pope's reinstated vocabulary) 128–37; Larkin's iconography 240–57; male 1–7, 22–3, 25–6, 29, 145–6, 148–9, 232–3, 249–50; Pope's exorcism of 108–37; –reason relations 146, 148, 172–87; repression 61–74, 148–9; seduction 13, 14, 19, 25, 241; sexual differentiation 153–63; in Shakespeare's sonnets 52–3, 57, 59, 61–74; *see also* lust; sexuality
Devil in Miss Jones, the 92
'Dialogue' (Rochester) 83, 84, 87, 90, 93, 95
didacticism 19, 22–4, 28, 33
Dijkstra, Bram 193, 199, 216
Dilworth, W.H. 109, 117–18
Dinnerstein, Dorothy 216
'Disabled Debauchee, the' (Rochester) 79, 83, 85
'Discovery, The' (Rochester) 88
disillusion (in 'Wild Oats') 233–6
'Dockery and Son' (Larkin) 228–9, 231
Donne, John 1, 11, 18, 36, 43, 46, 48, 62, 84, 89, 97, 201
Dorset, C.A. 102
Drayton, Michael 52
dreams 17
'Dry Point' (Larkin) 223, 231–3, 240
'Dry Salvages' (Eliot) 257

Dryden, John 98, 110, 111, 128, 132–3
Duffy, Edward 142
Duncan-Jones, Katherine 63
Dunciad, The (Pope) 108, 111, 117
Durfey, Tom 85
Dworkin, Angela 25

'Eeldrop and Applepex' (Eliot) 193
Egerton, Judy 255
egocentrism 40
Elegy to the Memory of an Unfortunate Lady (Pope) 115, 117, 119
Eliot, T.S. 2, 70, 103, 110, 154; critical responses 188–90; debt to other poets 192–8; emotion in 191–2; escapes from personal 190–1; female power in 199–203; perversity in 188, 203–19; Rossetti and (textual links) 195–8
Eliot, Valerie 193
Ellman, Maud 217
Eloisa to Abelard (Pope) 115, 117–20
Emerson, Ralph Waldo 206–7, 213, 219
Emile (Rousseau) 140–53 *passim*
emotion/structural emotion 191–2, 207
Endymion (Keats) 17, 90
Enlgish Love Poems (eds Betjeman and Taylor) 4, 15
epideictic tradition 39–40, 42, 52, 158
'Epilogue' (Rochester) 79, 90
Epistle to Cobham (Pope) 121, 133
Epistle to Dr Arbuthnot (Pope) 112, 114, 116, 118
Epistle to a Lady (Pope) 103, 108–9, 114–16, 118, 120, 123, 126, 129, 133–7
Erdman, David 160, 161
erotic poetry: desire and arousal 14–18; explicitness 7–14; sexual gossip and 23
Essay on Criticism (Pope) 129

INDEX

Essay on Man, An (Pope) 113, 121, 127
'Essential Beauty' (Larkin) 245, 248
essentialism 26, 42, 217
Everett, Barbara 75, 76, 92, 95, 98–9, 101, 224
Everyman Book of Love Poetry, The (ed. Hadfield) 4
exhortatory modes 23
explicitness 7–14

Faber Book of Blue Verse, The (ed. Whitworth) 4
Faber Book of Love Poetry, The (ed. Grigson) 4, 14
Faber Book of Seductions, The (ed. Newman) 5
Fabricant, Carole 75, 101
'Fair Chloris' (Rochester) 17, 79, 87, 88
Fairer, David 125, 135
'Faith Healing' (Larkin) 253
'Fall, The' (Rochester) 77, 87, 130
Family Reunion, The (Eliot) 193
fantasy 13, 16, 21, 23, 33, 79, 247–8
'Farewell to London, A' (Pope) 130
Farley-Hills, David 76, 85
Favourite Love Poems (Osbourne) 4
Fearful Symmetry (Frye) 176
fecundity principle 90–1
Felperin, Howard 60
female: body 12, 13, 22–3, 80–1, 91–2, 101–7; character (Pope on) 134–7; desire 119–20, 147–50; grief (voice of) 208; insatiability 22–3; maternal dominance 28–30, 180–5; mind (Pope's depiction) 120–8; power 85–7, 199–203; reading of misogynist texts 24–5; reason (Blake) 138–87; writing 27–34; *see also* heterosexuality; lesbianism
feminism 25–7, 32, 33, 256–7; and anti-feminist text 1–2, 5
feminist criticism 24, 27–8, 34, 149; of Blake 138–40, 172–3; Eliot 216–17; Rochester 75

'Femmes Damnées' (Larkin) 241
Ferguson, Rebecca 116, 121
fetishism 13, 245–6
Fineman, Joel 38–9, 40, 42–3, 50, 52
Fitz, Reginald 189
Fletcher, John 207
Folly of Love, The (Ames) 125–6, 134–5
'For "Ruggerio and Angelica" by Ingres' (Rossetti) 195–8
'For Sidney Becket' (Larkin) 253
Four Zoas, The (Blake) 139, 150, 153, 158, 161–2, 167, 168
Fowler, Alastair 123–4, 125
Fox, Susan 139, 168
'Fragment of a Satire on Men' (Rousseau) 140
Freud, Sigmund 30, 31, 52, 143–4, 156, 212, 225, 232, 240
Friday, Nancy 5
Frosch, Thomas A. 180
Frye, Northrop 139, 176
Fuller, John 4, 6, 1–12, 14–15, 17, 18, 23
Fuseli, Henry 151

Gallop, Jane 5
'Garden of Love, The' (Blake) 161–2
gender: differentiation 153–63; identity 3; imbalances (in love poetry) 5–7; Pope's treatment of 120–8; sexism 6, 255–6; *see also* female; male
generic inversion of lyric 82–7
generosity ethic 90
'genital allegory' 50
George, Diana Hume 176
Gilbert, Sandra M. 5, 138, 194, 216–17
Gilbert, Thomas 110
Gilfillan, George 78, 110
Girl in Winter, A (Larkin) 222
'Good Morrow, The' (Donne) 97
Gordon, Lyndall 189, 193, 198, 219
Gould, Robert 75, 125–6, 137
Graddol, David 29
Greek Anthology 8

INDEX

Greenblatt, Stephen 37, 38, 48
Greville, Fulke 41, 43, 47, 55, 66
Griffin, Dustin 75, 101, 119
Griffin, Susan 25, 138
Grigson, Geoffrey 4, 6, 14
Gubar, Susan 5, 135, 138, 194, 216–17

Hadfield, John 4
Haffenden, Jean 233
Hagstrum, Jean 173, 177, 181
Half-Century of Eliot Criticism, A (Martin) 189
Hamlet (Shakespeare) 60, 64, 66
Hammond, Brean S. 112, 119
'Happy Minute' (Rochester) 83
Harsnett, Samuel 45
Hartley, George 233, 251
hate, love and 52–3, 58
Hazlitt, William 80, 112, 116
Hegel, G.W.F. 157
Herotica I and II (ed. Bright) 5
heterosexuality 19, 21, 35, 38, 43, 45, 52
High Risk (eds Schoelder and Silverberg) 15–16
High Windows (Larkin) 223–32 *passim*
Hill, Geoffrey 56
Hilton, Nelson 164, 171, 172, 173
Hobbes, Thomas 87, 88
Holderness, Graham 252
Homer 110
homosexuality 20–1, 22, 31, 38, 43, 49–52
homosocial bonding 21; Blake on 173; Rochester 96–100; in Shakespeare sonnets 43–50, 52–60
Honest Man's Fortune (Beaumont and Fletcher) 213
Hunt, Leigh 110
Hunter, G.K. 37

iconography of desire (Larkin) 240–57
idealisation 11–12, 23, 26, 29, 30, 144, 235–6
'Ignorance' (Larkin) 229–30

Iliad (Pope's translation) 113
illusion, refusal of (Larkin) 249–57
images (in photographic motif) 241–4
Images of Women in Fiction (Cornillon) 5
Imitations of Horace (Pope) 98
'Imperfect Enjoyment, The' (Rochester) 76, 81, 90, 105
'In Proemium' (Marston) 78
'Insulting Beautiful' (Rochester) 88
Interpretation of Dreams, The (Freud) 225
invocations 11 *bis*, 13, 17; repression of desire 61–74
Irigaray, Luce 30, 144

Jacobus, Mary 144
Jakobson, Roman 37, 67–70, 71–4
Jardine, Lisa 27, 255
Jarrell, Randall 188
Jenny (Rossetti) 137
Jerusalem (Blake) 138, 140, 142, 149–50, 153, 154, 156–7, 163, 172–87
Jill (Larkin) 222, 234, 236
Johnson, Maurice 189
Johnson, Samuel 110, 111, 117–19, 121, 123, 125, 126, 129, 133, 165
Jones, Lawrence G. 37, 66, 69–74 *passim*
Jonson, Ben 9
joy (Blake's proclamation) 163–72
Joyce, James 29, 106
Juvenal 21, 22, 132

Kaplan, Cora 151
Keats, John 1, 17, 37, 89–90
Kenner, Hugh 212
Kenrick, William 145, 147–8
Kerrigan, John 6, 17, 29, 33, 38, 67
Knight, George Wilson 37
Knust, Herbert 205
Koestenbaum, Wayne 190, 218
Krieger, Murray 125

Lacan, Jacques 28, 158

INDEX

'Lamentation of the Old Pensioner, The' (Yeats) 235–6
Langland, Elizabeth 1, 160
language-vision relationship 42
Lanham, Richard 63
Laqueur, Thomas 48
'Large Cool Store, The' (Larkin) 245–6
Larkin, Philip 2, 33; debt to Yeats 235–40, 246; disillusion 233–6; iconography of desire 240–57; paternity (treatment of) 222–31; sexual politics 220–2; symboliste/abstractionist 231–3
Lavater (annotations to) 155, 157
Lawrence, D.H. 1, 154
Lear (Shakespeare) 22, 45, 48, 55, 69
Lee, Judith 152
lesbianism 21, 22, 38
Less Deceived, The (Larkin) 231, 240–4
'Letter from Artemiza, A' (Rochester) 83–4, 86, 87, 88, 89, 90, 100
Leviathan (Hobbes) 88
Levin, Richard 68
Lewis, C.S. 11
libertine ethics of natural polygamy 12
libertinism (of Rochester) 77, 87–96
'Life with a Hole in it, The' (Larkin) 227
'Lines on a Young Lady's Photograph Album' (Larkin) 241–3
Literary Companion to Sex, The (ed. Pitt-Kethley) 4
'Livings II' (Larkin) 231, 248
Locke, John 157
'Long roots moor summer' (Larkin) 250
love, hate and 52–3, 58
Love: Penhaligon's Scented Treasury of Love and Prose (Pickles) 4
'Love a woman!' (Rochester) 90, 101
'Love and Life' (Rochester) 83–4

Love Given O're (Gould) 125–6
love poetry: contemporary construction 3–7; desire and arousal 14–18; misogyny (new perspectives) 24–34; origins 10–11; private realm 18–24; sexual explicitness 7–14
'Love Song of St Sebastian, The' (Eliot) 193, 194, 215
'Love Songs in Age' (Larkin) 253
Love's Labour Lost (Shakespeare) 64
lust: death-in (Eliot) 199–203; in Shakespeare's sonnets 35–74; *see also* desire; promiscuity; seduction
lustful joy 167–72

McClintock, Anne 92
Mack, Maynard 110, 112, 120, 130
Madwoman in the Attic, The (Gilbert and Gubar) 138
Mahood, M.M. 37
Maid's Tragedy, The (Beaumont and Fletcher) 207, 208–9
'Maiden Name' (Larkin) 234, 247
Making Love: The Picador Book of Erotic Verse (ed. Bold) 4
male: body 22, 101–7, 109–20; desire 1–7, 22–3, 25–6, 29, 145–6, 148–9, 232–3, 249–50; misogyny *see* misogynist texts; paternity 222, 223–31; writing 5–7, 11, 12, 19–20, 22–3, 29–31; *see also* heterosexuality; homosexuality; homosocial bonding; patriarchy
Mallarmé, Stéphane 154
Marriage of Heaven and Hell, The (Blake) 159–60, 162, 165, 174, 175
'Marriages' (Larkin) 250
Marston, John, 1, 77, 78
Martin, J.R. 142
Martin, Mildred 189
Marvell, Andrew 1, 40, 98
masculine desire *see* male
Mason, Harold A. 214
masturbation 17–18, 79, 89–90, 171–2, 248–9

INDEX

maternal dominance 28–30, 180–5
Matthews, Susan 150
Matthiessen, F.O. 205
Mayer, John T. 193, 198, 216
Means, James A. 130
'Medusa's Head' (Freud) 240
Mellor, Anne 139
Mental Traveller, The (Blake) 161, 180
'Merlin and Vivien' (Tennyson) 201
Metamorphoses (Ovid) 209
Miles, Josephine 154
Miller, James E. Jr. 189, 219
Milton (Blake) 138–40, 153, 162, 176
Milton, John 1, 11, 79, 138, 143, 171, 176, 184
misogynist texts 1–3, 5–6, 22–3; Blake 139; Eliot 189, 217–18; Larkin 255–7; new perspectives 24–34; Pope 108, 125–8, 131–7; Rochester 75–82, 107; Rousseau 149–50; Shakespeare 35, 43
Misogynist's Source-Book, A (Morgan) 5
'Mr Eliot's Sunday Morning Service' 195, 205
'Mistress, The' (Rochester) 83, 85, 97
Mitchell, Orm 152
modernism 29, 216–17
Montagu, Lady Mary Wortly 113–14, 120
Moore, Donald 160, 161
Moore, Marianne 203
Morgan, Fidelis 5
Motion, Andrew 220–1, 241, 243, 255
Motives of Woe: Shakespeare and 'female complaint' (Kerrigan) 6
Much Ado About Nothing (Shakespeare) 57
Mulford, Wendy 5, 11
'Murders in the Rue Morgue, The' (Poe) 209–11
My Secret Garden (Friday) 5
'Myzomatosis' (Larkin) 251

Nash, Ogden 227
'Negative Indicate' (Larkin) 232
New Criticism 188
New Feminist Criticism, The (ed. Showalter) 26
Newman, Jenny 5, 8, 13, 14, 25
'Next, Please' (Larkin) 251
Nicholson, Marjorie Hope 112
No Man's Land (Gilbert and Gubar) 216–17
'Nocturne' (Eliot) 193, 214
North Ship, The (Larkin) 223, 236–40, 252
Norton Anthology of Literature by Women (eds Gilbert and Gubar) 5
Notebook Poems (Blake) 150–1, 155, 160–1
Novelle Heloise, La (Rousseau) 140, 152
Nowottny, Winifred 255
Nugent, Thomas 145–6, 147–8
'Nuptial Sleep' (Rossetti) 197–8
Nussbaum, Felicity 75, 79, 96, 101, 108, 109, 133

Ober, William B. 96
Oenone (Tennyson) 215
'Oils' (Larkin) 231–2
'Old Fools, The' (Larkin) 223
Oldham, John 1, 30, 75, 76–7, 80, 125
'On his Mistris' (Donne) 84
'On Mistress Willis' (Rochester) 81, 85, 89
'On Poet Ninny' (Rochester) 99
onanism 16–17, 236
Osborn, James M. 86
Osbourne, Charles 4, 6
Ostriker, Alicia 139, 161, 177, 183
Othello (Shakespeare) 56–7
Ovid 19, 209

Paglia, Camille 186–7, 217
pain, pleasure and 84–5
Paley, Morton 181
Paradise Lost (Milton) 11, 143, 171, 176, 184

INDEX

Parker, Derek 4, 6, 9–10, 12, 15–20, 22–4
Parker, Patricia 144
Parthenophil and parthenope (Barnes) 40
Partridge, Eric 35, 38
'Pastoral Dialogue' (Rochester) 85–6, 88, 100–6
paternity (Larkin's treatment of) 222, 223–31
Patmore, Coventry 193
patriarchy 25–6, 109, 138, 172, 174, 244
Paulson, Ronald 98
Penguin Book of Homosexual Verse, The (Coote) 20–2
Penguin Book of Love Verse, The (ed. Stallworthy) 4
Pequigney, Joseph 38, 43, 50–2
Petch, Simon 240, 249
Peterson, Douglas L. 67
Petrarch, Francesco 39, 40
Petronius 67
Philosophy of Composition, The (Poe) 192
Phoenix and the Turtle, The (Shakespeare) 35
photographic motif 241–4
Pickles, Sheila 4
Pinkney, Tony 193, 194, 198, 215–16
Piper, David 115
Pitt-Kethley, Fiona 4, 6, 17, 32
Plato 12, 30, 156, 158
pleasure, pain and 84–5
Pleasures: Women write erotica (ed. Barbach) 5
Poe, Edgar Allan 154, 192, 209–11
Poems 1920 (Eliot) 188, 203–19
Poems on Several Occasions (Rochester) 130
poet–appreciator relation 19–20
Poetics of Sexual Myth, The (Pollak) 108–9
Pollak, Ellen 108–9, 128, 135
Polwhele, Richard 172
Poovey, Mary 151
Pope, Alexander 2, 23, 30, 86, 98–9, 103; approach (responses to) 108–9; critical reception 109–15; treatment of gender 120–8; vocabulary of desire 128–37; writings (his body in) 115–20
pornography 13, 15, 16–17, 32, 33, 138, 255, 257
Pornography and Silence (Griffin) 138
Porter, Peter 75, 77
'Portrait, The' (Rossetti) 197
'Portrait of a Lady' (Eliot) 103
post-sexual poetry 14
'Posterity' (Larkin) 234
Powell, Anthony 224
praise 39, 40–2, 60
Praz, Mario 193
'Preludes' (Eliot) 1, 219
Preludium to America (Blake) 157, 161–3
Prior, Roger 1, 54
private realm (articulation of) 18–24
'progressivism' of Rochester's libertinism 87–96
promiscuity 53–4, 58
Prufrock and Other Observations (Eliot) 202–3
psychoanalytic theory 28–32, 178
Pym, Barbara 255

Ralegh, Sir Walter 62
'Ramble in Saint James's Park, A' (Rochester) 80–1, 83, 86–9, 92–6, 99, 100
Ransom, John C. 37
Rape of Lucrece, The (Shakespeare) 36
Rape of the Lock, The (Pope) 99, 108–9, 111–13, 116, 118, 120–8
ratiocination 109
rationalist ideology 174–6, 178
Rawson, Claude 90
reality 13
reason 72; –desire relation 172–87; female (Blake on) 138–87
'Reasons for Attendance' (Larkin) 220–1, 252

Reichard, Hugo M. 125
repression-displacement mechanisms 178
Required Writing (Larkin) 223
Revenger's Tragedy, The, Eliot on 191–2
Reveries of the Solitary Walker (Rousseau) 140, 143
Reyes, Alina 82
Richards, I.A. 68, 71, 188
Richardson, Samuel 119
Ricks, Beatrice 89, 189
Ricks, Christopher 190
Riede, David G. 176, 184
Righter, Anne 83
Rime Sparse (Petrarch) 40
Robinson, K. 82, 105
Roby, Kinley E. 206
Roche, Thomas, Jr. 63
Rochester, John Wilmot, Earl of 2, 7, 13, 17–18; anti-feminist satire 77–82, 90, 96; dramatisation of bodily failure 101–7; explicitness 75–7; generic inversion of lyric 82–7; homosocial bonding 96–100; plaintiveness and vulnerability 100–1; Pope (comparison) 129–32; 'progressivism' of his libertinism 87–96
Rochester's Sodom 84, 90, 95, 122
Rogers, Pat 125
Ronsard, Pierre de 39
Room of One's Own, A (Woolf) 34
Rossen, Janice 249, 250, 252
Rossetti, Dante Gabriel 1, 30, 137, 201, 240; Eliot and (textual links) 195–8
Rossiter, A.P. 35, 251
Rosslyn, Felicity 124
Rousseau, G.S. 112
Rousseau, Jean Jacques 168–9, 176, 183, 187; Blake and 140–54 *passim*, 158, 163–4, 168–9, 176, 183–4, 187
Rubenstein, F.R. 35, 38
Ruffhead, Owen 113, 114
Rumbold, Valerie 112

Sade, Marquis de 99
sado-masochistic writings 15–16, 217
Saintsbury, George 110, 111
'salacious poems' 23
Sampley, Arthur M. 189
Samson Agonistes (Milton) 176, 184
satire 1, 2, 15, 20–4; anti-feminist 77–82, 90, 96; Eliot 203–19; Pope 114–19, 125–6, 131–4, 136–7
'Satire on Charles II' (Rochester) 103–4
'Satyr against Reason, A' (Rochester) 84–5, 87, 90, 95, 97, 99, 104, 131
Satyr upon a Woman, A (Oldham) 80, 125
Sawney and Colley (Anon.) 114, 129
Schoelder, Amy 15–16
Schwartz, Joel 143
Schweickart, Patrocinio 27
scopophilic models 13
sea-voyage imagery 243–4
Second Discourse, The (Rousseau) 140, 142
'Second Prologue' (Rochester) 87, 90
Sedgwick, Eve 37, 38, 43–5, 49–50, 53
seduction 13, 14 19, 25, 241; *see also* desire; lust
self-articulation 40
'Self-Reliance' (Emerson) 206, 213, 219
'Self's the Man' (Larkin) 226–7
'Send no Money' (Larkin) 245, 249–50
sentimentalism 177–8
sexiam 6, 255–6; *see also* misogynist texts
sexual autonomy 13
sexual differentiation 153–63
sexual explicitness 7–14
Sexual Fiction (Charney) 5
'sexual gossip' 23
Sexual Personae (Paglia) 217
sexual politics 13; of Larkin 220–57

INDEX

sexual psychology of *Jerusalem* 172–87
sexual representation 13, 25
sexuality: arousal 14–18; bisexuality 51–2, 143–4; heterosexuality 19, 21, 35, 38, 43, 45, 51–2; homosexuality 20–2, 31, 38, 43, 49–52; lesbianism 21, 22, 38; promiscuity 53–4, 58; *see also* desire; lust; seduction
Shakespeare, William 2, 22, 98, 157; homosocial bonding 43–50; lust in sonnets 35–70; Pequigney and 50–2; precedents 60–4, 69; responses to 35–8; sonnet tradition 39–43; Sonnet 129 66–74; sonnets 13, 21, 52–61
Shakespeare's Perjured Eye (Fineman) 38
Shaw, G.B. 27
Showalter, Elaine 26–7
'Sick Rose, The' (Blake) 160–1
Sicker, Philip 189
Sidney, Philip 15, 39–41, 45, 48, 52–3, 60, 61, 63–4, 68, 198
Sigg, Eric 206
'Signior Dildo' (Rochester) 77, 90, 104
'Silent Silent Night' (Blake) 161
Silverberg, Ira 15–16
Simpson, Matt 249
Sixth Satire (Juvenal) 132
Smith, Gover, Jr. 209
Sober Advice from Horace (Pope) 118, 123, 130, 131–2
social class 7–9
Social Contract, The (Rousseau) 140, 142, 154
social reality 33
'Solar' (Larkin) 231
somatic theory of writing 28
'Song' (Rochester) 82, 84, 86–9, 91, 95, 97
Songs of Experience (Blake) 160
Songs of Liberty (Blake) 159
sonnets (lust in Shakespeare's) 35–74

'Sorrow of Love, The' (Yeats) 246
Spacks, Patricia M. 120, 130
'specularisation' 30
Spence, Joseph 129, 130
Spenser, Edmund 1, 37, 39, 54, 61–3, 73–4
'Spring' (Larkin) 220
Stallworthy, Jon 3, 4, 10, 11, 12, 14, 17, 25
Stephen, Leslie 110
stereotypes 5, 6, 25, 109, 111, 139, 216, 256
Stevenson, W.H. 152, 185
Straub, Kristina 115
structural emotion 191–2, 207
Studies in Classic American Literature (Lawrence) 154
'Study of Reading Habits, A' (Larkin) 250
'Submission, The' (Rochester) 95
Such is my love (Pequigney) 38
'Sunny Prestatyn' (Larkin) 246–8
'Surpeme Surrender' (Rossetti) 195
Swain, Joan 29
'Sweeney Erect' (Eliot) 198, 204–7, 210, 211–14, 215–16, 218
Swift, Jonathan 23, 126
Swinburne, Algernon Charles 1, 85, 113
symbolism (of Larkin) 224–5, 231–3
'Symapathy in White Major' (Larkin) 231
Symposium (Plato) 158

T.S. Eliot: Bibliography of Secondary Works (Ricks) 189
'Talking in Bed' (Larkin) 221–2, 254
Tate, Allen 115
Taylor, Geoffrey 4, 15
Tennyson, Alfred 30, 193, 201, 203–4, 215
Thackeray, W.M. 114
Theweleit, Klaus 33
'This be the Verse' (Larkin) 225, 248
Thomas, Dylan 1–2, 236

INDEX

Thompson, Francis 111
Thomson, James 193
Thwaite, Anthony 220
Tillotson, Geoffrey 123
'Timon' (Rochester) 76, 91, 97, 99–101, 102, 105
'To the Sea' (Larkin) 227
Tradition and the Individual Talent (Eliot) 188
Traub, Valerie 35
Troilus and Cressida (Shakespeare) 37, 157
Troilus and Criseyde (Chaucer) 40
'Tunbridge Wells' (Rochester) 86, 101, 130
Turner, James G. 130
'Turtle Dove, The' (Hill) 56
Twelfth Night (Shakespeare) 85
'Two Portraits of Sex' (Larkin) 231

Ulysses (Joyce) 106
Untermeyer, Louis 7, 15, 18
'Upon His Drinking a Bowl' (Rochester) 101
'Upon his leaving his Mistress' (Rochester) 91
'Upon Nothing' (Rochester) 83

Valentinian (Rochester) 87
van Leer, David 49
Vendler, Helen 68, 69, 71, 73
Venus and Adonis (Shakespeare) 36
Vindication of the Rights of Men, A (Wollstonecraft) 153
Vindication of the Rights of Women, A (Wollstonecraft) 148–53, 163, 184
violence 82, 123, 145, 164–5, 183–4, 186–7, 212, 214–16, 247–52; sadomasochist writings 15–16, 217
Virago Book of Wicked Women, The (ed. Dawson) 5
Virago Book of Women's Love Poetry, The (ed. Mulford) 5
vision–language relationship 42
Vision of the Last Judgement (Blake) 138, 156

Visions of the Daughters of Albion (Blake) 140, 147, 150, 152–3, 163–72
Voltaire 140, 142
voyeurism 13, 21, 79, 123, 180, 241, 249

Ward, Edward 114, 118
Wasserman, Earl 122
Waste Lan, The (Eliot) 32, 189–90, 193–5, 209, 218
Webber, Andrew Lloyd 193
Weber, Harold 96, 104–5
Webster, John 214
'Wedding Wind' (Larkin) 232, 234, 250
Weinbrot, Howard 117
Whalen, Terry 249
'Whatever Happened?' (Larkin) 243–4
'Whispers of Immortality' (Eliot) 199–202
White Devil, The (Webster) 214
Whitsun Weddings, The (Larkin) 226–31, 244–5, 246, 250, 253–4
Whitworth, John 4, 6
Wilcoxon, Reba 75
'Wild Oats' (Larkin) 223, 233–6, 240
Will sonnets 13, 47–8
Williams, Linda 13, 82
Wilson, A. 122, 123
Wilson, Edmund 189
Wilson, Thomas 67
Windsor-Forest (Pope) 116, 124
Winn, James A. 120, 130
Winter's Tale, The (Shakespeare) 37
Wintle, Sarah 75, 87–8, 89
Wollstonecraft, Mary 184–5, 187; Blake and 163, 165–6, 168–9, 171; response to *Emile* 140, 142–3, 146–53
Wolseley, Robert 76
Woman Defamed and Woman Defended (Blamires) 6
'Woman's Honor' (Rochester) 85, 90
women: power of 85–7, 199–203; readers of misogynist texts

INDEX

24–5; writers 27–34; *see also* female; feminism
'Women about Town, The' (Rochester) 103
Women on Top (ed. Friday) 5
'Women's Superstituion' (Rochester) 86

Woolf, Virginia 34
Wordsworth, William 36

Yeats, W.B. 223, 235–40, 246
Young, Edward 110, 112

For Product Safety Concerns and Information please contact our EU representative GPSR@taylorandfrancis.com
Taylor & Francis Verlag GmbH, Kaufingerstraße 24, 80331 München, Germany

www.ingramcontent.com/pod-product-compliance
Lightning Source LLC
Chambersburg PA
CBHW071158300426
44113CB00009B/1246